"[An] entertaining recollection."
—*People* (critic's choice)

"Fast-paced and never dull . . . *Confessions of a Master Jewel Thief* delivers what it promises."
—Cleveland *Plain Dealer*

"A compelling story."
—*The Atlanta Journal-Constitution*

"Fascinating book . . . This absorbing memoir will catapult [Mason] to prominence as he revives in mesmerizing detail his extraordinary criminal exploits that were headline news. . . . Has "movie" written all over it. Too bad the most glamorous cat burglar of them all, Cary Grant, isn't available to play the lead."
—*The Miami Herald*

"*Confessions of a Master Jewel Thief* is the kind of book that drives crime-fiction writers like me up a wall: No one would ever believe these amazing, compelling stories of theft and deception if they weren't sitting on the nonfiction rack. Mason tells his life story with such flair and confidence that I felt like I was dangling from a twenty-story ledge right along with him. *Confessions of a Master Jewel Thief* is the ultimate kind of guilty pleasure, because even though you know it's so wrong, it feels so right."
—ERIC GARCIA, author of *Matchstick Men*

"[A] cool-witted and frequently jaw-dropping memoir . . . Reads like a night's worth of the greatest barstool tales ever told, as Mason spins his own legend without the need for embellishment. Offering an irresistible taste of the derring-do to come, the book opens with a prologue worth of a Jules Dassin heist picture. . . . It's hard, as a reader, not to root for his success."
—*The Onion*

"There must be a touch of larceny in most of us, otherwise how to explain the kick we get from reading about the exploits of cat burglars. . . . In this vastly entertaining book, Mason tells of his various heists, most of which he carried out for the thrill and the challenge rather than the monetary reward. . . . His exploits were so amazing the media dubbed him 'ghost' and 'phantom.' Using a combination of skill, daring, good preparation and caution, Mason led the good life until, inevitably, he got caught. Read, enjoy, and get some tips on how to avoid becoming a mark."
—*Toronto Sun*

"Fans of classic caper films . . . will be fascinated by the true-life adventures of jewel thief Mason, who had a long and successful career. . . . His crimes, recollected in engrossing detail, involved careful planning and research, but he never fails to credit luck and simple human carelessness."
—*Publishers Weekly*

"Engaging, extravagant account of life on the wrong side of the law."
—*Kirkus Reviews*

"Entertaining."
—*Library Journal*

Confessions of a Master Jewel Thief

Bill Mason

with Lee Gruenfeld

VILLARD / NEW YORK

2005 Villard Books trade paperback edition

This work was originally published in hardcover by Villard Books, an imprint of The Random House Publishing Group, a division of Random House, Inc., in 2003.

Library of Congress Cataloging-in-Publication Data

Mason, Bill.
Confessions of a master jewel thief / Bill Mason with Lee Gruenfeld.
p. cm.
ISBN 0-375-76071-7
1. Mason, Bill. 2. Jewel thieves—United States—Biography. 3. Celebrities—Crimes against—United States. I. Gruenfeld, Lee. II. Title.

HV6653.M3A3 2004
364.15'52—dc21
[B]   2003053758

Villard Books website address: www.villard.com

Design by Meryl Sussman Levavi/Digitext

Printed in the United States of America

246897531

For those who loved me anyway

Contents

PART II

PART III

PART IV

Prologue

PRETTY MUCH anybody who was anybody in southern Florida lived close to the ocean between Miami and Palm Beach, and anytime a lot of well-off people are squeezed into one area, the natural human instinct to compete sets in. When you don't have a job and you don't do anything athletic and you're filthy rich, the way you compete is by trying to convince everybody else that you're richer than they are. South Florida's high-net-worth ladies did this by wearing their money on their bodies in the form of jewelry and then trying to get photographed. Maybe they thought only other high-net-worth ladies read the society pages, but, to a thief, all those photos and stories read like advertising brochures.

I didn't have much of a problem getting dressed up and crashing charity balls and other posh events. I didn't like to do it, because I didn't want my face to become familiar, and it was also tough to explain to my wife why I was heading out on a Saturday evening dressed to the nines and not taking her with me. I did it only when the circumstances called for it, and I usually got into the party by attaching myself to a large group of people on their way in and then acting like I belonged there.

I made it a point to start conversations but then let the other person do all the talking—not much of a trick, believe me—and became fairly adept at spotting who was just trying to impress others and who really had the goods. I also learned where people lived and a good deal about the habits of the idle rich. For example, I learned that if a woman was planning to attend a big bash of some kind, she'd spend the afternoon at the beauty shop, but only after laying out her clothes and baubles first. That meant an empty apartment with exposed jewelry, and, if there was a safe, an open one. The same people who wouldn't think of leaving a safe unlocked when they were home with it at night thought nothing of leaving it wide open if they were out for the day. One of the perceived cardinal rules of robbery is that you never do it during daylight. But the real rule is just a variation of baseball player Willie Keeler's famous comment on his batting strategy, "Hit 'em where they ain't."

I first became aware of Mrs. Armand Hammer at some high-society ball. I didn't know who she was at first; all I saw was a very beautiful woman wearing some very serious stones. It didn't surprise me to learn that she was the wife of one of the richest men in the country.

Dr. Armand Hammer insisted on being identified as "Dr." even though he'd gotten his medical degree over fifty years before and had never practiced. He was the chairman of Occidental Petroleum, one of the biggest oil companies in the country. He'd bought it when it was near bankruptcy and spent years building it into the giant conglomerate it had become by the mid-seventies. Hammer was a major philanthropist as well, donating massive sums of money and significant works of art to a variety of prestigious institutions. Maybe it was about time he donated a little something to me.

The city directory told me where the Hammers lived, which was in a high-class condo right on the beach in Fort Lauderdale. Their apartment was on the fifteenth floor, which was terrific news for me; they probably assumed they were invulnerable. But the building had doormen, so I'd have to do some careful watching to see how to get into it. Not exactly tough duty. I could sit on a beach lounge chair and watch not just the building but gorgeous women in skimpy bathing suits gliding by.

The building was shaped like a series of staggered square columns, with four apartments to a floor. Each room was set at right angles to the ones on either side of it, effectively making every room a new corner. Two of the apartments faced the ocean to the east, and the other two faced the Intracoastal Waterway on the west side of the building. A narrow ledge, barely noticeable from street level, zigzagged its way completely around the building on every floor, but it looked more like an architectural flourish than a feature of any real use. There was an open stairwell running from the second story all the way to the roof. Anybody in that stairwell would have access to the entire building. Iron bars encircled the second-floor landing, but above that, all the landings were open-air. I guess the working assumption was that no intruder could get above that barred second story, so why spoil the appearance of the building by encasing the whole stairway?

Eventually I'd seen all I was going to see from the ground, so it was time for a little up-close testing. Late one evening I threw a grappling hook up to the second-story ledge between two apartments, climbed up, then rehooked to the third-floor stairway landing above the iron bars. I climbed the stairs another twelve stories and found myself standing right in front of Mrs. Hammer's door. It had a big, bright ADT warning sticker on it and two pretty formidable-looking locks in addition to the standard one just above the doorknob. No way to tell if the place was really alarmed, or if the sticker was only for show, or if they habitually armed the thing. I swear, it was getting harder and harder to make a decent living. Why couldn't they have lived in the unit next door, which had only the standard lock that came with the place originally? This was not looking good.

A shame, too, because I was starting to get a handle on Mrs. Hammer's habits, and I was sure there was a load of treasure inside. I was able to follow her easily as she went in and out of the building. I kept my car about a hundred yards up A1A, the road that parallels the waterway, and watched for her car from the beach using binoculars. She was a slow driver and it was a simple matter to catch up with her once I'd established her direction. She liked to do her own food shopping, and I once followed her around inside a grocery store just to see what kind of stuff she was wearing. Nothing, as it turned out, which meant all of it was still upstairs in the apartment.

Mr. and Mrs. Hammer would almost always go out for dinner, usually returning by around ten o'clock. I started watching the place at night. Two of the other units were almost always lit up, and I never saw a single time when they were both dark. But the fourth one, the one with the cheap lock, was always dark. I'd already checked and knew it wasn't for sale, so I went back to the city directory and discovered that it was listed as a guest apartment for some corporation. I grappled my way back up the building one night and saw that if I could get into the guest unit, I should be able to get out on that skinny ledge and work my way over to the Hammer place.

The guest unit was on the side of the building opposite the Hammer apartment. The thought of walking all the way across the front of the building (including five right-angle turns to get past all those corners) on an eighteen-inch-wide ledge and with no rope to hold on to was not particularly appealing. Not with a fifteen-story fall as a reward for a slipup.

The challenge of planning a caper is to anticipate as much as possible and prepare accordingly. In addition to things like escape routes and contingencies in case you trip an alarm, you have to decide what kinds of tools you're likely to need and what backup items make the most sense to drag along as well. I had a pretty good feel for what I was likely to be up against in the Hammer apartment, but I was also starting to come to grips with the fact that there was no choice but to navigate that sliver of a ledge and go in through a window. The door was just too risky. But with my back literally to the wall and the tips of my shoes sticking out over the edge, there wouldn't be any way to carry a whole load of tools with me. And if I ended up tripping an alarm before I even reached the unit, it would be tough enough moving quickly along that ledge without being further encumbered by a lot of weighty gear strapped to my body and not easily undone and dropped.

The answer, when it came to me, was so simple I kicked myself for not having thought of it sooner: I could carry all the tools I wanted up to the guest apartment and stash them there before I went out on the ledge. Once I was inside the Hammer place, all I had to do was go out their door and across the hall to the guest unit, pick up all my stuff and carry it right back.

All I really needed to have with me out on the ledge were some glass-cutting tools. If the Hammer patio door was locked and I suspected it was armed, I could cut a hole in it big enough to crawl through and then disable the alarm system from inside. This was in the days before ultrasonic motion detectors, so once I was in, there'd be nothing further to trip.

Best of all, I wouldn't have to get back out on that hairy ledge to leave once I was done. I could just go down the stairs, same way I got up.

This was looking better and better. It further occurred to me that if I found I was missing a tool, I could simply leave the building altogether— using the stairs and the grappling hook—go get what I needed and come back. Again, no second outing on the ledge.

My escape route in case I somehow tripped a silent alarm in the guest apartment was looking good, too. I'd have such a good view from that ledge I'd be able to see flashing lights from miles away, with plenty of time to get inside and hide in almost any unoccupied unit with a cheap lock.

By the time I was ready to do the job, I'd identified three such apartments and knew how to open the doors on all of them. As long as I didn't have to cut through the glass in the patio door, there would be no trace of my having been in the building at all, and it would be treated as a false alarm. I could then come back after things had settled down and try a different tack.

The ideal time for a job like this would normally have been when the Hammers were planning to go to some fancy do, which I'd be able to know in advance from the society pages. But that would probably be on a Friday or Saturday evening, and the beach area those afternoons would be teeming with people who could spot me easily. If I hit the place when they weren't in the process of getting ready for some event, though, there might not be anything worth stealing. It was certainly possible that they kept the baubles in a safety-deposit box and took out what Mrs. Hammer needed only when she needed it. So one time when I knew they were scheduled to attend a particularly fancy gala, I followed the Mrs. around for two days to see if she went to the bank, and she didn't. That told me they had a safe up there, and I included on my list of tools the stuff I'd need to get into that.

More important, though, all that surveillance and analysis led me to a truly unpleasant conclusion: As if that ledge wouldn't be dangerous enough, I decided that this job needed to get done on a stormy night, when the beach would be deserted and there'd be the sound of thunder and rain to drown out any noise I might make. It also had to be on a night when the Hammers weren't going to be at a posh soirée, because I didn't want to go into that apartment on a night when Mrs. Hammer's best stuff was around her neck instead of in her safe.

Windy, wet and dark . . .

Over the next few days I started looking at the wisp of a ledge in a whole new light.

~

About two weeks later a perfectly timed storm roared in from the south. It began in the late afternoon of a weekday, and by the time I'd grappled my way up to the stairs, stashed the hook and rope in a fire-extinguisher case and walked up to the fifteenth floor, it was coming down like a monsoon. I got into the guest unit without incident and did a quick look around to make sure I was really alone. I stayed busy and fast and wasted no movement, because I didn't want to dwell on what it would be like out on that ledge. I had planned this down to the tiniest detail, had even thought of carrying a washcloth to wipe the bottoms of my shoes so no-body could tell afterward how I'd gotten in, and so now all that was left was to execute the plan, not give it any more thought. Front door closed but unlocked, bag of tools just inside of it, nothing sticking out of my jacket or pants to impede travel. That was the extent of my mental check-list, so I opened a window and put one leg through it, setting my foot down onto the ledge and sliding it around to test the traction.

It wasn't good. I'd assumed the surface was of rough concrete and would have decent grip, but it was smoother than I'd anticipated and the water from the rainstorm only made it worse. I'd have to make sure to set each foot straight down with every step so as to rely as little as possible on friction to stop my forward motion, which is not the normal way of walk-ing. I got my other leg through and then I was standing up on the outside of the building, still holding on to the bottom of the open window. I leaned back to slide it shut, in order to keep the rain out of the room, leav-ing a small gap to make sure I could get my fingers in to open it again. Not that it would have locked, but with no real purchase on that tiny ledge, I didn't want to be shoving upward on the glass itself trying to get it open. Finally, I let go completely and stood up again, then started moving.

I'd envisioned the whole trip with my back to the wall, but after about ten feet of futilely wiping rain from my eyes and imagining my feet slid-ing out from under me in a heel-to-toe direction, I turned around and hugged the wall instead. I wiggled my feet slightly with each step, feeling for any changes in traction, and the way my shoes were sliding on that slick surface started up a sickening feeling in my belly. I wondered what the police would make of a body squashed on the concrete far below if I slipped. A suicide, perhaps?

It was a truly horrific goddamned trip. I'd already done some high-wire heists, like at the ultra-ritzy Fountainhead, but that was a cakewalk compared to this. That had been a vertical climb, and I'd had a nice com-fortable rope to hang on to with both hands, could even wrap my legs around it if I needed a rest, and at worst would have had a forty-foot drop to some sand and a broken leg or two if it all went to shit.

But *this* . . . this was insane. One sneeze and I could be over the edge. I hadn't fully appreciated before this how reassuring it was to have some-thing—anything—to grab on to. All I had here were my hands flat along the wall, and every gust of wind that whipped at my back was like a malevolent force trying to tear me off the building and fling me into the void.

Maybe you were expecting some bullshit about how I stared imminent death in the face and forced it to keep its distance. Well, forget it. I was scared shitless. I was *always* afraid on scores. Not to be would have been lunacy, and this was the most lunatic situation I'd ever launched myself into. On top of all the inherent physical danger was the fact that I was engaged in a criminal activity, so at the same time that I was trying not to die, I was also trying not to be seen. The trick was not to be afraid of being afraid, because fear was a healthy thing in this game, and what you were really after was balance: Be afraid enough to keep you on your toes but not so much that it compromises the execution of the plan. If you're going to let fear get in the way, this is the wrong business to be in.

Stepping onto the Hammer balcony was such a relief, I just sat there and gulped air for a minute, gripping the railing so hard I wasn't sure I'd ever be able to uncurl my fingers from it. When I finally did, I found that the patio door was unlocked and there were no sensors anywhere to be seen. That bit of good fortune should have had a calming effect on me, but my mind was racing nevertheless. This was going almost too smoothly, notwithstanding the nightmare trip along the ledge. I started to wonder if I'd really thought of everything, but I drove that out of my head immediately. It wasn't too likely I was going to think of anything useful while in the thick of things that I hadn't already considered during weeks of careful planning.

I stepped into the apartment and just listened for a while, then did a thorough search to make sure I was absolutely alone. It was dark, but I didn't want to turn on any lights, so I used my penlight. Last stop was the bedroom, and what do you know: There was a large jewelry box right on top of the dresser. The lid was flipped open and the top section was nearly overflowing with fabulous stuff. Santa Claus never had it this good, and he was only after cookies.

This moment, right here, was why I was a jewel thief. It was like a narcotic, being someplace that everyone assumed no one could possibly get into. People spent fortunes, even altered their lifestyles, trying to protect valuables like these from people like me, and here I was, all alone, inches from the treasure. As I liked to do, I'd leave the premises looking exactly like they had before my arrival. To the astonished occupants, it would seem as if the jewels had simply evaporated. This wasn't some mind game I was playing, though, not thumbing my nose or demonstrating any superiority or trying to make a point. It was simply how I avoided getting caught. No changes meant no clues. By keeping my ego in check and my

The Hammer condo was third from the top on the far right, just above the shuttered windows. I got out onto the ledge from the leftmost unit on the same floor.

methods obscure, everything the police came up with concerning how I might have done the job was the purest speculation, and the more they had to guess, the safer I was.

I wasn't going to need any of the tools I'd brought, so there was no sense making a trip next door and back. I grabbed a pillow off the bed, stripped it, then emptied the jewelry box into the pillowcase. At that point I'd been there just five minutes but was already anxious to get the hell out, so I didn't bother looking around for additional goodies. Incredibly, not only was the front-door alarm unarmed, but neither of the additional locks had been engaged. Had there been any way for me to know that in advance, I could have avoided that walk along the ledge.

I went across the hall and got my unused tools from the guest unit, closed the window I'd left partially open and wiped down the sill. After locking the door behind me, I walked down to the third floor and retrieved the grappling hook from the fire-extinguisher case. The pillowcase full of jewels tucked under my shirt, I lowered myself down to the ground, shook the hook loose, then headed across the street and straight to the water's edge, where I walked two blocks to my car. Once safely away from the building I started going over everything in my mind. Had I left anything at all up there that could be traced? I thought I'd been careful, but I wasn't above second-guessing myself.

I drove to my office and allowed myself a quick look at the loot before stashing it. There were a large number of diamond pieces, mostly bracelets, earrings and pins, and some beautifully worked gold items, including an exquisite gold filigree bracelet. The most outstanding item was a custom-made pin in the shape of a rose. It had diamond-encrusted gold petals that folded open to reveal a three-carat diamond mounted inside. It was absolutely stunning. What a shame it would have to be broken down and sold in pieces so nobody could recognize it and tie me to the heist.

The police never did find out who'd done the robbery, nor did they figure out how the "thieves" (they assumed there was more than one) had gotten in. It was a major embarrassment to everybody concerned: the building's managers, who had assured their tenants of world-class security; the police, who weren't able to figure out how the job was done and had no clues or leads; and the Hammers themselves, who would rather the outside world didn't know they'd left a fortune in jewels lying around their condo and hadn't set the alarms. It seemed to be in everybody's interest to keep the whole incident quiet, so no mention of it appeared in any of the local media.

Four years later, when the police still hadn't identified a single suspect, I would confess to having been the thief.

Part
I

1

~

Beginnings

My name is Bill Mason. If that name is not familiar to you, then I've done a good job of keeping things to myself, which was my way of keeping myself out of jail, at least most of the time.

In a "career" spanning nearly three decades I've stolen many millions of dollars' worth of jewelry, gotten shot and almost died, wrecked a good marriage and raised three great kids despite their father's odd (pre)occupation. Although law enforcement authorities were aware of many of my scores, I've never been convicted of stealing jewels.

I've taken rare gems and jewelry from the likes of Robert Goulet, Johnny Weissmuller, Truman Capote and Phyllis Diller (twice), and even cracked a safe belonging to the underboss of a major Mafia family. I've also had some scores that didn't work out, including attempts to rob Marvin Davis, Elizabeth Taylor, Margaux Hemingway and the McGuire Sisters.

I've been chased all over the country by local cops, state cops and the FBI, some of whom I've even developed odd sorts of relationships with. And on the subject of odd friendships, I was the key figure in a major scandal involving a prominent heiress that shocked Cleveland high society.

I didn't have very good reasons to steal; I was by no means poor and my upbringing was perfectly normal, so when you get right down to it, the reason I stole was because I felt like it. Call it a personality defect—many have thought so, including me—but I didn't really need the money.

This book is by no means a justification of how I chose to live my life. I was a criminal and there is no justification for that unless you're starving or living under a system where the laws themselves are unjust or you're forced to break them for some higher purpose. None of those motives was applicable in my case, and I wasn't some kind of Robin Hood stealing from the rich to give to the poor, so you're not going to find any excuses in these pages.

Rather, this book is simply a description of what I did, how I came to do it, how I felt about it and how it affected those close to me. The reason I can tell the story now is that I'm no longer "in the life" and the statute of limitations has run out on the last of my scores.

Everything you'll read is true, with the exception of an occasional hazy date, imperfectly recalled conversation or altered name. In some cases, people who were robbed of precious gems, jewelry or cash are going to learn for the first time who it was that stole them. A good many of my targets, including the Mob, were convinced all along that they were hit by a gang and will be surprised to find out it was just me, acting alone.

I don't expect any more forgiveness from friends and family for the pain I caused them; what I've already received from them is well beyond what I had any right to expect. I just want them to understand a bit more than I was ever willing—or able—to explain while the events in this book were taking place. This is their story as much as mine.

~

I think the most extraordinary thing about my life is how ordinary it was—at least if you don't count my little hobby of stealing jewels.

When I decided to write this book, I thought one of the more interesting aspects of the effort would be to reflect on my childhood days and try to identify those experiences that pushed me in such a questionable direction. I'd read some biographies of unusual people and there always seemed to be large forces prodding them inexorably toward their destiny. The way those books were written, you'd think it was impossible for them to have turned out any other way than they did.

But biographers, and that includes autobiographers, tend to focus on those things that support the impressions they're trying to establish. The way they write makes it seem that absolutely nothing else was going on in their subjects' lives other than the handful of specific events and experiences that turned them into musicians or politicians or scientists.

Fact is, children are bombarded with all kinds of influences, and it's nearly impossible to tell which ones had which effect. Just because it makes a good story doesn't make it true. My guess is that Newton would have figured out gravity whether that apple had hit him on the head or not, if it ever really hit him in the first place.

I think what's actually going on is that childhood is like an allergy test for talent. If you've ever been tested for allergies, you know that the doctor rubs your skin with hundreds of different substances until one of them raises a welt. In the same way, a kid comes across hundreds of opportunities to uncover some latent talent until one of them hits, and then his course in life starts to take on some direction. Sometimes it's obvious, like when a seventh-grader is six feet tall and can dribble a basketball blindfolded with either hand, or a grade-schooler builds a radio out of old washing-machine parts.

Sometimes it's not so obvious, as in my case. I could climb trees like a monkey and take apart all kinds of machines and put them back together; there was little that frightened me and I could keep my mouth shut while listening. But so what? How did those thing add up to a career?

It wasn't until I went out and tried to steal something that I realized what my odd collection of skills might be good for.

~

As I said, nearly everything about my life was ordinary, including my early childhood.

I was born in 1940 in a small West Virginia burg called Hundred. It was in Monongalia County, which was known as the mother county of northern West Virginia because eighteen other counties, some in Pennsylvania, had been carved out of it since its creation in 1776. Hundred was about three miles and fifty years from the Pennsylvania border, rural and mostly dirt-poor.

Many of my earliest memories were wrapped around the things people generally did in those years to support the war effort and not go broke. It was a time of great thrift, and, like other families, we saved everything: foil from cigarette packs, cooking fat, string, paper . . . anything that might conceivably be turned to a further purpose rather than discarded. We didn't know at the time to give it a fancy name like "recycling."

There were nightly blackouts, even in the heartland, where the likelihood of an attack was pretty remote, unlike in the coastal communities 350 miles to the east. I can still easily summon up the fear I felt as a four-year-old—depending on the darkness to keep us safe, hoping that the Germans couldn't see our small town and drop a bomb on us.

It's an easy leap, I suppose, to the conclusion that my strong need for financial security and the comfort I feel in darkness were shaped at that time, but thousands of kids scrimped pennies and sought refuge from the enemy behind blackout curtains without turning into criminals, so who knows?

Don't get me wrong, though, because aside from the occasional stresses of wartime, it was a great time and place to be a kid. I was the adored only child of educated parents. I had acres of open land on which to roam and explore, farm animals to play with and the kind of delicious freedom available only to children in wide-open rural areas.

Best of all were the trees. As far as I was concerned, they were put on earth for me to climb, and I was good at it. By the time I was five, I was able to climb without using my legs, just my arms. When horizontal branches were too high to reach from the ground, I was often able to shinny right up the trunk, like a koala bear.

Things changed when I was six. Both my parents were teachers—Ella, my mother, taught third grade in the local elementary school, and Ora, my father, was a gym teacher and coach at Waynesboro High School in Pennsylvania—but the region was in dire straits. Monongalia County, an apparent spelling error on early documents, was named after the Monongahela River. It meant "river of crumbling banks," and that pretty much described what was happening to the local economy. My father found a better-paying job but had to go to Detroit for it. He was gone for long stretches at first, but that became too much, and he eventually decided to move us all to Detroit, where we lived with my aunt Nell. She had two children, and they became like my brother and sister. Still, I missed West Virginia and kept alive the hope that we'd move back there someday.

But about two years after that move my father was offered another job, and as much as he didn't want to relocate us again, this was too good to turn down. My uncle, who owned two apartment buildings in Cleveland, hired Dad to manage them, and we moved to Shaker Heights. Taking up residence in that more affluent neighborhood was quite an occasion for my parents but devastating to me.

Shaker Heights had high-rise apartment buildings, paved streets and sidewalks, and hand-planted trees with wire fences around them to keep kids off. It had neighbors who were ten feet away instead of a ten-minute walk, and many of them were the well-off kind who liked children polite and quiet and clean. One quick glance around the concrete-and-asphalt prison of Shaker Square Apartments and I knew that my days of running in fields, milking cows and climbing trees were behind me for good. I doubt either of my parents truly understood how miserable that move made me. I was lonely and despondent, and used to daydream about running away from home and going back to West Virginia. Eight years old and convinced my life was already ruined.

I hated apartment buildings from the very moment I first laid eyes on one. If adults chose to live in oversized chicken coops, that was their business, but what's the point of condemning a kid, and a country-raised one at that, to that kind of stifling confinement? Nevertheless, kids adapt; stuck for anything else to do, I started climbing buildings instead of trees. I discovered roofs and basements and they became my playgrounds. As a result I became friendly with a lot of maintenance men and building superintendents, and thereby got a first-class education in matters that Boulevard Elementary School didn't seem to feel were important.

People who take care of apartment buildings are underappreciated masters of many arts. They do the work of electricians, plumbers, carpenters, masons, painters, locksmiths, glaziers and machinists, often all in the same day. Something I noticed early on was that their orientation was 100 percent practical; they weren't interested in the purity of craft, they just needed to get stuff *working,* and quickly, in order to avoid bringing down the wrath of demanding tenants.

Imagine having all those skills and nobody to show them off to. Then imagine that a curious kid shows up; he's interested in everything and he doesn't start yawning every time you try to share your wisdom. He's good with his hands, too, and helps out whenever he can.

I learned a lot from those guys, not because I had any life plan or was consciously preparing for anything, but just because I found it interesting and fun. Always handy with things mechanical, I badgered maintenance men into letting me try to fix washing machines and refrigerators that they'd given up on as hopeless or not worth the effort. There was little downside if I couldn't fix them, as they were slated for the junk heap anyway, but after I managed to get some things working again, I was allowed to tackle tougher jobs. A couple of guys also began taking time to teach me a few things.

Locks were particularly fascinating. Precision mechanisms full of tiny springs and bits of metal machined to close tolerances, they got slammed and banged around all day yet hardly ever failed. About the only reason to take them apart was to change over to a new key, or if someone broke a key while fumbling to get a door open when he was drunk or in a hurry and left a piece inside the mechanism. When that happened, the quickest fix was to just replace the lock, but a couple of the handier maintenance men were able to dismantle the mechanism right down to individual components, put it all back together and avoid the cost of a new lock. I watched them do that for hours on end, began helping out and gradually got to the point where I could do it by myself. There's no better way to learn how something mechanical works than by taking it completely apart.

I was more comfortable around working adults than I was with my fellow elementary school students. Around kids and teachers I was very quiet, less interested in the kinds of questions they wanted me to ask than in those I really wanted answers to. The practical aspects of how things worked in the real world were of more immediate concern than whether you used "I" or "me" in a sentence. I remained a kind of introvert through high school, which somehow must have increased interest in me among the female student body. I wasn't aggressive about pursuing girls but was never short of dates.

~

As I got older, I began helping my father in the buildings he managed. I enjoyed the work, but the best part was that I got to read all the magazines the tenants discarded. *The New Yorker* and *The Saturday Evening Post* were among my favorites. I managed to earn some change running errands for tenants, and when I was old enough, I got a newspaper route. Here was one great advantage of apartments over widely spaced houses: I could deliver nearly five hundred papers on a Sunday morning, and the money I earned looked like a small fortune to me.

Once I got into the upper grades, I started enjoying school more, too. I played a lot of football and was on a championship dodgeball team, and I even liked some classes, especially science and history. And even though I was getting up at five every morning to deliver papers, I still had enough stamina to go to a lot of parties and after-school events.

I got along well with my father and felt a little bad for him at the same time because I thought he was getting the short end of the stick from my mother's family. That was on account of Uncle Rudy, my mother's brother, better known as Dr. Richard Renner. My mother's family had struggled through some very difficult times to put him through medical school, and after he'd become a doctor, he became the family's pride and joy. He founded a prestigious hospital in Cleveland and was one of the city's more visible and esteemed VIPs. Next to Uncle Rudy, it was impossible for Dad to measure up, and although he kept well hidden any resentment he might have felt, I had trouble doing the same. It wasn't until much later in my life that it occurred to me to wonder whether my father's constant struggle with severe ulcers might have had something to do with the stress of living in Uncle Rudy's shadow.

Dad and I saw each other a good deal because we were working together, and we also went to a lot of ball games. Which is not to say we were a pair of good old buddies on an equal level. He kept a pretty firm grip on me, and he didn't kid around. One wild weekend I got a tattoo of a snake on my right arm, and managed to keep it hidden from him for nearly a year. When he found out about it, he threw a serious fit. You know the conventional wisdom that says you can't remove a tattoo? Bullshit, even in the days before lasers. Dad dragged me to a doctor on 105th Street who froze my arm with dry ice and then took a high-speed rotating wire brush to my skin. That night as I was hurting and bleeding, all I could think about was that I'd have to go through it again after the first treatment healed. It ended up taking three scrapings altogether, removing every trace of not only that tattoo but also any desire I might ever have to get one again. I had to pay the doctor out of my own pocket, too. I generally behaved myself because of Dad and didn't start fucking up in earnest until high school.

One thing that was new in high school was that differences in social status began to take on increasing importance. Most of the kids in the lower grades weren't really aware of the family backgrounds of other students and tended to form groups based on shared interests like sports. But as we got older, we became more aware of who came from what kind of background. We were a mixed lot, and once those differences began to surface, there was a clear realignment of friendships.

Shaker Heights is on land originally owned by the Shaker sect and sold to a pair of land developers in 1905. Their idea was to create one of the first "garden city" suburbs in the United States, and part of the plan for attracting a high caliber of resident was to emphasize superior education. Shaker Heights High was one of the top schools in the country, and about 90 percent of its students were the children of wealthy parents, some of them old money and some genuine rags-to-riches American success stories. Those students dressed in expensive clothes, traveled a good deal and got exposed to a lot of culture.

Like Beverly Hills High, though, Shaker Heights High was public and had to accept anyone within its designated geographical boundary. The other 10 percent of the student body, of which I was a part, were from the other side of the tracks—some literally—but entitled to attend by virtue of their addresses inside the school district. Tough guys who wore leather jackets and Elvis Presley haircuts, we were called "rackies" for reasons that now escape me. There was no celebration of diversity, no multicultural festivals of mutual understanding, nothing like that. The more these two groups kept to themselves, the more the differences between them seemed to grow. There was no way my side could keep up with the swells in terms of cars, clothes and other material things, so our choice was either to withdraw and feel inferior or to strut what we had and try to be proud of it. All we had, though, was attitude, and we made sure there was plenty of it. I was among the more belligerent of the rackies, forever getting into fights and other trouble, proud of my bad-boy image the same way the rich kids were proud of their snooty upper-class airs.

My particular situation was compounded by the fact that most of my teachers liked me. The dreaded phrase—"He's not living up to his potential"—attached itself to me like a persistent rash. If they'd thought I was beyond hope, I could have sailed through high school unmolested, but it seemed that every other week some goody-ass teacher was calling up my parents to complain about how I wasn't living up to my potential, how I was wasting my time and talent getting into scrapes, cutting classes and Lord only knew what else. My parents' reaction was to get mad and ground me, which only increased my resentment of those meddling teachers even more, making me surlier and even harder to deal with.

Paradoxically, although I was clearly identified with the rackies, I had a lot of friends among other groups of students, including the wealthier kids and those in the grades above me. People today recall me as having gotten along pretty well with everybody, and that's my memory, too, even though I got into fights on a fairly regular basis. I played on the school football team, so maybe that was some kind of a sign that I wasn't a total outsider.

Getting into trouble in that unenlightened era was a self-perpetuating situation. Administrators who meted out punishment didn't do so with uplifting thoughts of straightening us out and being helpful: They were just pissed off, didn't know us very well and had already decided we were incorrigible and not worth their effort. They seemed to enjoy making our lives miserable, more in the way of retribution than rehabilitation, or so it seemed to us. This, of course, only made us angrier and more determined to cause trouble, and so around and around it went. We couldn't wait to get out of school, and they couldn't wait to get rid of us. The only thing that came between me and expulsion was the strong presence of my father. With him in my life there was a line I wasn't willing to cross.

Through it all, though, I managed to get halfway decent grades without ever really trying. Maybe that's why my teachers thought I was worth saving. I graduated in the spring of 1958 and was entitled to attend Ohio University. I don't think anybody in that high school ever seriously considered that I'd actually go to college, least of all me, but by that time I had a pretty strong incentive. Not to go to just any college, but to Ohio in particular.

~

One afternoon when I was in the tenth grade, I was pitching quarters against a wall with a few friends. One of them was Bobby Luria, a smallish kid with a slight lisp. I don't remember how it came about, but it seemed I'd become his protector. (He's a lawyer now and we're still friends.)

Bobby pitched a "leaner," a quarter that stood up against the wall and was an automatic winner. He jumped forward to collect his winnings, but just as he reached down, a hand came around the corner and scooped up the money.

"Hey!" Bobby yelped as he drew back in surprise.

It took me a second to realize what had happened. I ran around the corner and saw some guy running away, the back of his open leather jacket flapping noisily. I took off after him, closing a lot of ground before he figured out someone was after him. By the time he kicked up to a higher gear, my momentum had carried me right to him. I grabbed a loose fold of his jacket, spun him around and pressed him up against the wall of the building.

"Let's have it!" I snarled at him as his hands wrapped around my wrists.

"What are you—?"

I didn't give him a chance to finish the question, but pushed harder, lifting him onto his toes. "Givitta me, or I beat the shit out of you and get it anyway!"

My intensity was out of all proportion to his crime, and maybe that scared him a little. He let go of my wrists and nodded. I let him down and stepped back, but kept a fist cocked inches from his face. I recognized him as Bob Benz, an eleventh-grader and a certified troublemaker, like me, but he was a real hoodlum type, and it was probably just as well I'd been too pissed off to take much time to consider who his friends might be.

"Don't hafta get crazy," he said as he handed over the coins.

"Kid's half your size!" I shot back at him.

"Din't know whose it was, asshole. Was four guys pitchin' quarters."

"So what'd you think . . . out of four guys not one was going to come after you?"

It was like he'd never even thought of that, just had an impulse and went for it. He looked at me quizzically, then scratched his head. "Fuck," he muttered. It was that kind of thought process of Bob's that would get me into a lot of trouble later.

I can't recall exactly how it happened, but Bob and I became friends. His father, who owned a bar in Beachwood, was hardly ever around, but I liked his mother a lot, and she liked me as well. I was always welcome in their big old house on Warrensville Center Road. I don't know if his parents realized at the time how much trouble Bob and I got into together. I lost count of how many times we'd been caught sitting in his car right near the school, smoking cigarettes instead of attending class. As dangerously impulsive as Bob could be, he still had my admiration for his brashness and his guts.

I also came to admire his sister.

Although nearly a year younger than her brother, Barbara Benz was also in the eleventh grade, which put her a year ahead of me. (Bob had missed a year of school when he was younger because of an operation on his leg.) She was beautiful—five feet six, slim, dark-haired and dark-eyed—and smart, too. Though shy, she was self-possessed in a way not typical of a high school junior. One of the "good" girls in the school, Barb was often embarrassed by the very visible shenanigans of her brother the hood, and at first looked askance on the new friend he started bringing home. Soon, though, a mutual attraction began to set in, but we danced around it for quite a while, even as we began to spend time together.

Barb knew I was a rackie, as were most of the guys who came from the Woodland Avenue area in the western part of Shaker Heights, but she also knew I was very much my own person and friendly with kids from a lot of different groups. I was even dating the homecoming queen, despite the fact that she was sixteen and I fifteen. Barb hung with a bunch of nice girls, all seniors. I got along with them and we enjoyed one another's company, so it was natural for all of us to do things together. Eventually, though, the sparks flying between Barb and me were too bright to ignore, and we began to date on a more "official" basis. We always doubled, though, usually with another guy from Woodland and his girl, because I didn't have a driver's license yet.

I got one when I turned sixteen, in my junior year, and with the money I'd saved from paper routes and helping maintenance men in apartment buildings, I bought a 1949 Ford convertible. It had no heat and so many rattles you could hear me coming three blocks away, but at least I was mobile now. I began driving clear across Shaker Heights to pick Barb up for school and going over to her house nearly every night after dinner. Dating was so much simpler then, and you rarely needed more than five bucks. A movie for fifty or seventy-five cents, popcorn for a quarter, a burger afterward and you still had change from the fin. A few minutes of frantic necking in the driveway topped off a perfect evening.

By summer we were an item, and there are few better times and places to be in love than in small-town America in the summer. The days were long and lazy and hot, and Barb and I would drive thirty miles to Mentor to swim at the mile-long natural-sand beach at Headlands Beach State Park. Not surprisingly, one night I got a traffic ticket for something or other, and in those days they didn't fine minors—they suspended their licenses. It was a fate worse than prison (or so I foolishly thought at the time).

By coincidence, my parents were heading out of town the very next weekend. Unable to drive, I had the perfect excuse to have Barb over to the empty house, not realizing that I didn't really need an excuse. It was an unforgettable weekend of amorous exploration, two people who deeply cared about each other expressing it in as many ways as two novices could come up with on their own.

Neither of us wanted to break the magic of that glorious summer by bringing up the fact that she'd just graduated and was going to start college soon, but there was no getting around it. "It's Ohio University," she reminded me often. "It's not like I'm going to Outer Mongolia. We'll be able to see each other."

"But not every day," I'd respond morosely. I'd gotten used to being with her all the time, and I didn't know what it was going to be like when that was no longer possible.

As it happened, I missed her terribly, even though she was only a four-hour drive away and we did manage to see quite a bit of each other.

My grades up until that point had not been all that awful, but suddenly I had some real motivation to do well academically: I wanted to go to Ohio the following year. I had nothing better to do anyway, because I was without Barb most of the time and didn't feel like dating any other girls, so I knuckled down—or at least what passed for knuckling down relative to what I had been doing—and had a pretty good year. I graduated and was accepted into the university.

Barb and I had another terrific summer together. There was no holding back on how we felt about each other, and we were excited that we'd be going to the same college in the fall. Skittish talk about marriage came up occasionally, but mostly in a far-off, what-if kind of way, and my life was looking up.

That August, though, just days before I was to join Barb at the university, it all started to fall apart.

2

~~~

Circumstance

It was a Tuesday night, I think, although with no school it was tough to keep the days of the week straight.

I had been out with Barbara and came home about midnight to find my father lying on the living room sofa, a hand clutching his belly, his face grimacing in pain. My mother was visiting Aunt Nell in Detroit, so he'd been by himself all evening.

"The usual," he grunted when I asked him what was wrong. "Goddamn ulcer."

But I could see that this was much worse than usual. "I think we maybe oughta get you to the hospital," I suggested.

"You too?" He waved it away and tried to sit up. "Already got an appointment with Uncle Rudy," he said with some effort. "It'll wait till then." Then he groaned and sank back onto the cushions.

"What do you mean, 'You too'?" I asked.

Turned out he'd actually spoken with Uncle Rudy, who'd not only suggested he get to the hospital but had already made arrangements to admit him. "Except he's not there tonight," he added, which was probably why he didn't want to go.

I made it clear we were through negotiating, got him into the car and drove him to Doctors Hospital atop Cedar Road in Cleveland Heights. Uncle Rudy, who had founded the facility, would examine Dad the next day.

I had no interaction with any of the doctors there. I hung around after they whisked Dad off to a room, but it was clear nobody was going to tell me anything. Just before dawn, dog-tired and mentally exhausted, I got into my father's Chevy and headed home.

All I can figure is that I fell asleep at the wheel, because the next thing I remember was coming to in a hospital room, covered in bulky bandages and in more pain than I ever thought possible. I had trouble speaking. Couldn't move my mouth for some reason.

Seemed I'd run right into a tree on Fairhill Road at high speed. Slowly, so as not to shock me, the nurses eventually ran down the inventory of my injuries: tongue torn half off, most of my upper teeth knocked out, jaw broken, leg broken, a handful of internal injuries and so many stitches in my face and leg they'd lost count after the first hundred. They also described some internal injuries, but I didn't really understand most of those.

They also told me I was in Saint Luke's. It hurt just to turn my head, but before I lost consciousness again I managed to let them know I wanted to be moved to Doctors so I could be with my father. When I woke up again, my mother had arrived. I found out later that when the hospital had called her, they'd told her I might not make it. She explained to me that my jaw had been wired shut, which was why I couldn't speak clearly. With some effort I told her that I wanted to be moved to Doctors Hospital. It took some doing, but that afternoon I ended up in the same room as Dad, who'd been operated on the day before.

Two days after that we were both doing much better. I was hazy from pain medication but not so out of it so as not to notice when I was moved to another room.

"What's going on?" I asked a nurse who'd come in to check my blood pressure. I was getting better at making myself understood while my teeth were still clamped together. "Where's my father?"

She smiled vacantly and said, "Everything's fine."

As she headed for the door, I called her back, as best I could with my immobile jaw. "I didn't ask you that; I asked where my father was. Why was I moved?"

"You get some rest," she breezed back, then left.

Angry at the curt dismissal and worried about my father, I reached for the call button and hit it, then hit it again, then again and again until another nurse appeared, a scowl on her face.

"Where's my father?" I demanded.

She stared at me stonily. "He's fine. Now, why don't you put down that—"

"Why was I moved if he's fine!" It was agony to speak but angry adrenaline overcame the pain.

"Would you please lower your voice!" she insisted.

But I wouldn't, and shortly thereafter they told me my father had a blood clot in his leg. I insisted they take me to his room, and after a lot of arguing they finally did, although they weren't too gentle with my wheelchair.

My father's eyes were closed and there were tubes coming out of his mouth and nose. Sinister-looking machines whirred and clicked, and there were a lot of blinking lights.

There were also a lot of nurses and two doctors. They peered intently at the machines, took notes, felt his pulse and took his temperature and consulted one another in low voices and frowned. . . .

But nobody was actually *doing* anything for him.

"What's going on?" I managed to mumble.

"Blood clot," someone answered.

"So what are you doing for it?"

"We're monitoring him," a doctor said.

"I meant, about the blood clot."

"Your father's physician isn't here," a nurse finally said. "We've put in a call. Don't worry, everything will be fine."

"But who's doing something until he gets here?"

"Dr. Renner is in charge of his care," a different nurse informed me archly.

"But he's not here!" I could feel panic creeping into my garbled voice. "Shouldn't somebody do something?"

There was a lot of shuffling and averted eyes. Was the staff so intimidated by Uncle Rudy that they were afraid to lay a hand on one of his patients? My father was unconscious and deathly pale. I pleaded with them to do whatever needed doing. They ordered me not to get myself agitated. The doctors kept looking at instruments, while the nurses plumped my father's pillows and shuffled in and out of the room with great purpose but no effect. I grew more and more tired, having been weak to begin with and worn out even further from the frustration of futile negotiation on behalf of my father. Eventually I sank into sleep in the wheelchair.

When I awoke, I was back in the other room. My mother stood in the doorway, nodding dumbly as the same doctors who'd been with my father, cowed and submissive then but supercharged with confidence now, explained things to her in officious tones, told her why it couldn't be helped, how they'd done everything possible for him. They patted her arm comfortingly, which was a good deal more than they'd done for my father, who I now understood was dead.

My mother looked over to see me crying and assumed it was in grief. That was only partially true. While I struggled beneath an overwhelming sadness, I also felt a helpless, burning anger. I wanted to kill those doctors and nurses, I wanted to kill Uncle Rudy, just like they killed my father. His whole adult life, all my father ever heard about in the family was Rudy this and Rudy that, what a great and prominent man he was, how he healed the sick and got rich in the process. Now the sonofabitch hadn't even shown up the one time my father needed him.

I wasn't just angry at him and the hospital staff, I was mad at the whole goddamned world, including myself. I was less than ten feet away from my father and there wasn't a damned thing I could do for him, couldn't even persuade the people who might have been able to help him to do so.

I was released that night so I could be with my mother at home. Someone drove us, but I don't remember who. I was so broken up over losing my father, and over how he had died, that I couldn't think straight.

My wired jaw hurt like hell. The rage I couldn't get rid of didn't help, as I kept tensing the muscles in my face. I sat in stony silence through the funeral, and when I got home, I grabbed a pair of cutting pliers, hobbled over to a mirror, and started to snip the wires holding my jaw together.

A friend grabbed my arm. "You crazy, Mason?"

I shoved his hand away. "I don't give a shit." I cut all the wires and never went back to see the doctors.

I've thought about this a good deal in later years, and I'm willing to believe that I've blown it up in my mind and that my recollections may be harsher than the reality warranted. After all, it's hard to believe that a bunch of doctors and nurses would stand around and let a patient die just because they were afraid to infringe on a superior's territory.

But that's the way I remember it.

~

A few weeks later I left to join Barbara at Ohio University, but whatever academic goal I had arrived with was quickly short-circuited. I was in a bad frame of mind and didn't even make a serious attempt to get into college life. My mother wasn't doing well on her own and needed me, and I felt guilty about not being with her. I hung in until Barbara sat me down one evening.

"You don't belong here," she said, point-blank.

That threw me. She was the primary reason I had come there in the first place. "Why would you say that?"

"Doesn't matter. You know it's true. You can drag it out a little longer if you want to, but eventually . . ." She shrugged and left the rest unspoken.

She was right. I didn't belong there, but didn't want to admit it to myself. And I didn't want to leave her. Aside from the fact that I didn't like it when we were apart, I wasn't about to take the chance of losing her. I think she sensed the cause of my hesitancy.

"It won't change anything between us," she assured me. "Stay here, and you're only going to get more miserable, and that's the worst thing that could happen to us."

She was right again—I was to learn, much too late, that she was almost always right—so after one semester I dropped out and returned home, bitter and resentful.

I got a job at a General Electric factory making flashbulbs. It was a union job, paying about seven or eight bucks an hour, which was good money, but even after all the years that have passed since then it remains the worst job I ever had, at least outside of prison. Boring beyond words. All I did was watch four machines, and when something got stuck I unstuck it. I had too much time to think, to dwell on how pissed off I was. I lasted three months and then quit, knowing I never wanted to step foot inside a factory again unless I owned the place. I started doing maintenance work in apartment buildings.

My new situation and my state of mind were a volatile mix. Full of rage over how my father died, I now had no father to keep a tight rein on how I vented that rage. With time I might have gotten over it, calmed down, maybe even gone back to college. Who knows? All I do know is that my recklessness and vulnerability to influence collided with circumstance, and the direction of my life veered off on a severe tangent.

Barbara stayed at the university and I started spending more time with Bob, her older brother. Whether that was because of his outlaw reputation or because it was a way to stay close to Barb's family, I can't really say. Bob was a good guy, but by then he'd had a few run-ins with the law—he was actually on probation—and he was exactly the wrong person for me to have resumed a friendship with.

Just before Thanksgiving of the following year, he and I were drinking one night and bullshitting, as moderately inebriated men will. "What we oughta do?" Bob said. "We oughta knock over that Sunoco station down on SOM Center and Miles."

"Yeah." I laughed. "Good idea. Maybe a bank on the way home."

Bob didn't laugh back. "I know a guy used to work there. Said the boss always leaves money overnight." When I stopped laughing, he said, "No safe. Just a file cabinet."

I took a sip of my scotch, whether to buy time to think or just to steady myself, I'm not sure. "You got a plan?"

Now he did laugh. "A plan? Yeah, I got a plan. We go in the back window, grab the cash and get the fuck out."

He must have seen my face fall or something, because he frowned and shook his head. "It ain't a big deal. You're in and out so fast, it don't matter if the alarms go off."

He was serious. I asked a few questions; he winged a few answers. We had a few more drinks.

It was a badly conceived, badly planned and amateurish job that sounded a lot better talking about it when we were drunk than it did actually doing it when we were sober. I parked my car about five hundred feet from the gas station. We walked up and broke the rear window, cleared the glass away and climbed through.

Looking around in the gloomy interior, we couldn't see a file cabinet right off and began rooting around for it. There were piles of tires and discarded parts everywhere, along with scattered tools and other gear.

Suddenly Bob grabbed my arm, and as he did so I noticed a light climbing along the far wall. It was coming from a car outside. I stepped into a shadow and looked out into the front counter area and through the large plate glass window. A police car was cruising slowly by. I saw its brake lights come on as it slowed but didn't quite stop, as if the driver was trying to make a decision.

"You think he knows something?" I asked.

Bob shrugged. "Doubt it. Probably just—"

The brake lights went off and the squad car turned in to the gas station. It was still moving very slowly. I didn't see how the cop could have known there were people inside, but *something* had made him turn in.

I headed for the rear window and climbed out, slowly and with no noise. I wanted to get away, just in case, but there was no sense announcing ourselves if the cop was just checking things out as part of his routine. I dropped to the ground and sprinted away, Bob close behind.

Instinctively, I ran away from my car. If the cop caught on to us, we were much better off on foot, for a lot of reasons. Whether or not we could outrace him in the car was irrelevant, because he'd make the vehicle and track us down eventually. Aside from that, though, it's much easier for a person to lose himself than to lose himself plus a vehicle.

All this was so obvious to me that I lost a second or two while my mind tried to process the fact that Bob was heading straight for my car. Not only was that a dumb idea, but he had to cross a lighted street to do it. When I could no longer see him, I dove into some shrubbery and scrabbled my way through it, reached a lightly wooded area just beyond and kept running.

About ten minutes later I sank down against a tree to catch my breath and gather my thoughts.

Now that I was safe, I began to worry about Bob. I got up, found a pay phone and called Barbara's younger brother, Augie, to see if he'd heard from him. He hadn't, and I told him what had happened.

"What do we do?" he asked.

Good question. It was probably not a good idea to phone the police station and ask if they had a Robert Benz in custody. "Maybe we'd better look for him," I suggested.

Augie picked me up and we drove around trying to find Bob. Keeping safely within the speed limit, we headed down to the corner of SOM Center and Miles. "That's where my car was parked," I said to Augie, pointing to an empty spot.

"You think maybe he took it and got away?"

There was no way to know, so we decided to keep driving around. About two blocks later blinking red lights suddenly appeared behind us, lighting up the whole inside of the car.

"License and registration," the policeman said to Augie after we'd pulled over and he'd walked up next to the window. As Augie handed them over, the cop leaned down, looked at me and said, "You, too."

He glanced only briefly at my license before waving to his partner, who came out and walked up to the passenger side. He opened my door and said, "Out."

Less than a minute later Augie and I were in the rear seat of the squad car, handcuffed.

⌣

The cop at the gas station had driven around back and seen the broken glass. He'd nailed Bob before Bob had even gotten to my car. There were other cars parked on the street, but somehow the cop pegged mine. I don't know if he had guessed which car Bob was aiming for or if Bob had talked, but it only took a quick call into the station house with the plate numbers and he had my name, which had then been broadcast to every squad car in the area. (Bob never told me whether he'd given me up, and I never asked.)

They let Augie go after a few hours, but I spent the night in jail. Bob and I were charged with burglary the next morning, and both of us pleaded innocent at the arraignment. My mother came down and bailed me out (she was furious, and made me pay her back later), but there was no bail set for Bob. Because of the trouble he'd been in before, they kept him locked up.

I hired a private lawyer, and for two months we met and planned how we were going to handle the case at trial. He thought I was in good shape, that the evidence was skimpy and circumstantial, and that I had little to worry about. He even speculated that the state would drop the matter prior to the trial, as the weakness of the case against me would only make the assistant district attorney look like an idiot in front of the judge.

Bob was kept locked up the entire time. Because he'd been on parole at the time we hit the gas station, he was already under a prison sentence, and the state had the right to put him back in custody pretty much whenever it felt like it. I visited him often and assured him he'd be out a day or two after the trial started.

Sure enough, the day before the trial I got a call from my lawyer. "Assistant D.A. wants to meet with us." He practically snickered.

I was elated and hurried down to the court. The lawyer, the ADA and I sat down in a small meeting room, and the ADA wasted no time getting right to the point.

"If you plead guilty," he said to me, "you do thirty days, two years' probation, and we'll drop the charges against your buddy Benz. Guy's done two months already. . . . That's enough."

In light of my expectations it was a body blow, and I found myself unable to respond right away. My lawyer, who was well used to this stuff, said, "What kind of deal is that? You got no case here. You can't win at trial and you know it. Hell, the judge'll probably throw it out on day one."

The ADA replied, "You're right. Your client will probably walk." Then he turned to me. "Thing is, if you take this to trial, win or lose, we're going to violate your buddy's parole. That means he goes back up the river." He actually said that: "up the river."

"Hey, wait a minute!" my lawyer exclaimed angrily.

The ADA stood up and headed for the door. "That's the deal. Once the trial starts, it's off the table."

My lawyer was outraged, of course. Here were men charged with the public trust who were unmercifully preying upon a suspect, making him personally responsible for the incarceration or freedom of his friend, knowing full well that, innocent or guilty, someone with any conscience at all wouldn't make a decision to save his own ass by getting his friend thrown into prison. Where was the justice here? What did that shitty deal have to do with my guilt or innocence? Why didn't they just go pick up one of Bob Benz's friends at random and offer him the same deal!

After my lawyer finished fuming, I told him to take the offer. I wasn't happy about it, but the fact was, I did try to knock over a gas station. I knew it, the cops knew it, and even though the way they handled it might have violated a half-dozen basic civil liberties precepts, we could hardly make the argument that justice wasn't served. Besides, there was no way I was going to be responsible for Bob's going back to prison.

I did the thirty days, in an old Cuyahoga County shit hole that I'm glad I didn't know about before I'd made the decision. It was dirty, scary and despicable, a terrible place in which to be kept apart from friends and family for the first time in my life, and I hated it. The thought of ever repeating that experience—and it was only thirty days—would keep me cautious for the rest of my life.

Afterward, I was so well behaved for the first year of probation that they formally waived the second half, proclaiming me a law-abiding citizen who'd just made a silly mistake, who'd learned his lesson and who was ready to take up his rightful and productive place in society once more.

I'd learned my lesson, all right: Never use a partner.

3

~~~~~

First Score

ASTONISHINGLY, BARBARA stuck with me after that harrowing and acutely embarrassing experience, and I don't think it had anything to do with my standing up for her brother.

We hated being away from each other and spent more and more time together. We'd ride around affluent neighborhoods searching out "For Sale" signs and then pretend we were newlyweds as we checked the places out, making sure there were enough bedrooms for all the kids we were going to have. Pretty soon the joking around about being married shifted subtly, until we were no longer sure of the difference between fantasy and planning. It kept getting harder to say good-bye so often, and somehow we both started to get the notion that everything would be easier and less wrenching if we were really married. Soon our conversations turned to when and how.

We didn't want to make a big deal about it or even tell too many people. With her staying in college and me at home, it would have been awkward. We finally did the deed at a small church halfway between Cleveland and Akron, with only our mothers in attendance, Barb's father having passed away the year before. Our honeymoon consisted of two nights in a motel, then she went back to college and I went back home.

Helluva two nights, though: Barely a month later Barb found out she was pregnant. She dropped out of school and we rented a small apartment in Cleveland. This was a year after I got out of jail.

As much of a fuckup as I'd been in high school, it's hard to believe how responsible I got in such a short time. One of the benefits of caring for a family, I suppose. The next year I'm twenty-two years old, living in a small but comfortable apartment with my wife and Suzanne, our daughter, and spending three nights a week earning my real estate license at Case Western Reserve, a short drive away. I've got a good job managing an apartment complex, earning a hundred dollars a week, which isn't too bad for 1962 but a far cry from where I hoped to be in the next few years.

I had a lot of ideas about where that was but not too many about how to actually get there. The old saw about it taking money to make money was nowhere as true as in the real estate business, where you needed some minimum threshold amount of ready cash to even think about getting into the game. I didn't know exactly what that amount was, but I knew for damned sure it was more than I had, and more than I was likely to get anytime soon with just my salary and a new family to support. I put some thought into how much we'd have to set aside on a regular basis to get into some small investments, and how long it was likely for them to take to mature to the point where we could roll the cash into some larger ones so we could do it all over again and again. In my mind's eye I saw my future as a very long, very slow road with a goal so distant, I could barely make it out.

Then I suddenly developed a passion for miniature golf.

⌣

One night after classes I was having a drink with a buddy, Sam Schneerman. I knew him in high school as this goody-two-shoes kid who never got into a lick of trouble, but I liked him anyway. He was starting his third drink before I'd finished my first, and looked as though he'd been up against it all day.

"What the hell, Sam," I kidded him, "too much pressure at work?"

He took a deep drag off his cigarette and nodded morosely. "You wouldn't believe it."

I felt my smile devolving into a gape. Was he kidding me back? "You work at a miniature golf course, for chrissakes!"

"Yeah. You try it for a day. Screaming kids, screaming parents . . ." He tried to wave the memory of his day away. "Some living. At least it's got a driving range. I take out my frustration on helpless golf balls."

"So why do you do it?"

"Pay's good." He signaled for another drink, even though he hadn't yet finished the one in front of him.

I laughed at that. "Yeah, right. Kiddie golf."

"I'm not kidding. The boss rakes it in hand over fist; he owns the building and has practically no expenses except me and the electricity. Regular gold mine."

I could see his point. "And all cash, too."

Sam nodded. "IRS thinks he's barely breaking even, and meanwhile he's stuffing money in his safe."

"A safe?" I felt something tickle the base of my spine. "What, you mean a real one, right there?"

"Yeah. Behind the counter in the concession stand. Keeps the weekend receipts there until the banks open Monday morning."

I flicked my hand dismissively and picked up my drink. "How much money could it possibly be, a place like that?" I asked as casually as I could.

There was something playful in Sam's voice as he said, "Few thousand, more or less." He pulled out a fresh cigarette and stuck it between his lips.

It was an effort to keep my hands steady as I lit a match and held it to the tip as he inhaled. "That much?"

"Easy." He pulled back and exhaled a cloud of thick blue smoke. Watching me.

"Huh." I shook the match out. "Imagine that."

I then steered the conversation elsewhere while a piece of my brain thought about what I could do with an extra few thousand in cash. It was all just wishful thinking, of course, but the next morning I was still thinking about it, and the day after that as well.

⌣

"This is a joke, right?"

Barb was half smiling out of the side of her mouth, as though waiting for a punch line. She had a dishrag in one hand and a pot or something in the other.

"No joke," I assured her. "Come on, it'll be fun."

"Fun. Right. Since when is your idea of fun to—"

"You finish up here," I said as I walked out of the kitchen. "I'll go get Suzi."

Helluva game, miniature golf. Couldn't seem to get enough of it. I dragged Barbara and little Suzi over there every weekend, which turned out to be fine with Barbara. I think she was glad to see me relaxing, even if miniature golf was a strange pastime for a former rackie tough guy.

I didn't have any real intention of doing anything about the safe. I just thought it would be kind of interesting, a harmless diversion, to check out the premises and play a few mental what-if games. Truth was, I was having a hard time keeping my mind on my job because it kept wandering back to that damned golf course. I figured that once I actually saw the place, I'd quickly identify a dozen obstacles that would make any kind of actual attempt infeasible. Then I could finally stop thinking about it all the time, except for the laughs I'd have about it with Sam over another round of drinks.

I didn't bother with the driving range; it was too far from the concession building to be useful. Miniature golf was my game, and I tried to take in as many details as I could about the layout while Barb concentrated over her putter and little Suzi gurgled happily at the windmill, storybook castle and other brightly painted props around the course.

The parking lot was wide open to view from the street and was empty every night. Any car left there after hours would be noticed immediately by the cops, who patrolled the area frequently. The closest place to leave a car was about a quarter mile north, at a motel where cars came and went at all hours and there was plenty of parking. I noticed a ravine that ran parallel to the road, right past the motel parking lot. There was a trickle of water at the bottom, and I guessed that the depth probably varied with each rainfall or dry period. I got an idea about how that ravine might be useful in a pinch.

The safe was right where Sam said it would be, behind the counter. After having thought about it so much, actually seeing it there in real life filled me with feelings I hadn't been at all prepared for. One of them was an odd but powerful attraction—so strong I had trouble tearing my eyes away. Another was dread, almost a foreboding, that if I didn't cut this off right now, I might find myself sliding out of control down a steep, slippery hill. It was like staring at a high diving board and being simultaneously drawn to it and terrified of it, all of that layered over a core of inevitability that became harder and harder to ignore with every passing minute.

I didn't know anything about safes, but this one looked like a real piece of junk, massive and squat, about three feet on each side, with a round door, its fading green-enamel paint chipped in dozens of places. How hard could it be to smash open an antique like that?

The alarm "system" was so rudimentary, I didn't pay it much attention. It wasn't even monitored but was just a bell to scare away casual vandals. I'd seen similar cheap setups in dozens of apartments in the building I managed, and the only trick here would be to find out how it was powered, where the triggers were and if there was a second bell.

So, okay, there were plenty of obstacles, just as I'd thought. But with each subsequent visit I thought of ways around them. I tried my damnedest to think of every possible problem, but no matter what I came up with, I had a solution as well. At the same time, my mind-set had shifted out of hypothetical mode. I found myself spending hours visualizing every step of an actual robbery, right down to what my hands would be doing, how things would look at various distances from the streetlights, even what the temperature would be and how I should dress. I began writing down the kinds of equipment that would be required and how it should be packed, and I made adjustments as I thought of potential problems. Eventually, about three weeks after our first round of miniature golf, I couldn't think of anything else.

It was good timing, because Barbara was starting to wonder about these little trips. I spent nearly all our time there looking around at everything other than her and Suzi and the idiotic windmill on the fifteenth hole, and it wouldn't be long before it became obvious I had something other than a career on the pro tour in mind.

That I was actually going to do it was by then a given. I didn't recognize this trait of mine at the time, but I would later. Once I began thinking about how to pull off a dangerous and difficult heist, I wasn't much different from a research scientist or an inventor: Hell or high water, I would find a way to solve the puzzle and then I'd do it.

~

The Sunday night after our last visit I parked my car in the motel lot and slipped into the ravine. "Slipped" is the right word, too, because I was loaded down with nearly a hundred pounds of gear and could barely keep my footing. I had no idea how to crack a safe, so I brought along everything I could think of to smash my way into it: sledgehammer, chisels, assorted power tools, you name it. I also had a flatbed dolly tucked under my arm. If I couldn't get into the safe on-site, I'd just haul the whole damned thing away and work on it elsewhere.

The bottom of the ravine was mucky, so I had to walk along the side. My load was heavy and uneven and I was panting by the time I came abeam the concession building and finally climbed out. Getting inside was as easy as I thought it would be. One snip with bolt cutters and the large padlock on the door fell off with a loud clatter.

I went around the counter and stopped to consider the safe, which, now that the moment had come, looked twice as heavy and solid as it had before, as if defying me to breach its walls.

It was a good call on the safe's part.

At about three A.M. I sank back against the wall, thoroughly exhausted and bathed in sweat. I'd spent well over two hours working on the safe. After smashing it repeatedly with the sledgehammer, jamming chisels into every available crack, destroying three rotary-saw blades, and bending two unbendable iron pry bars, I finally got the top layer of steel off, only to find concrete jacketing underneath. More banging, chiseling, drilling and sawing, and I came to more steel under that. Two solid hours and I'd gotten maybe two inches into what was probably eight inches thick altogether. I decided to try another tack and smashed the combination dial off. The handle held as firmly as ever, and now that the dial was gone, there was no way to get at the mechanism that moved the interior steel bars holding the door shut.

It was frustrating as hell because by now the door had loosened a little, with about an eighth of an inch or so of play between it and the body of the safe. But I knew that was only because a hinge was slightly out of alignment; it didn't mean the door would be any easier to open, and I knew that further attempts would be futile. I needed some serious tools, not the kind that could be hauled around in a gunnysack.

I wasn't ready to give up. Although I'd brought a dolly, I hadn't contemplated using it to haul the safe away, but now I had no choice. I managed to upend the safe and get it onto the dolly, then gathered up my tools, set them on top of the safe and shoved it toward the door.

Everything was fine as I pushed the thing along the paved path past the mini golf course, but as soon as I rolled it off the asphalt and onto the grass near the creek bed, the dolly wheels sank deep into the soft ground. And that ground was much firmer than the creek bed.

I leaned on top of the safe, not knowing whether to laugh or cry. I had a vision of the owner returning on Monday morning to see his safe sitting out on the grass atop a hopelessly mired dolly, laughing his ass off over what kind of dumb schmuck had tried to rob him. It gave me strength.

I upended the safe, flipping it off the dolly and onto the grass. Then I flipped it again, grunting and wheezing with the effort, then stopped, looked around and listened. Once again, two flips, stop and listen, but not as long as I should have. I felt very exposed and wanted to get to that creek quickly. I wasn't quite sure how I was going to lower the safe down when I got there, but that decision was made for me when it let go before I was ready and tumbled over the edge, crashing through the underbrush and slamming into the muddy bottom with a sound like . . . well, like a three-hundred-pound safe falling ten feet onto mud: a squish, splat and splash all rolled into one. I threw the dolly and my tools down after it and then climbed down myself.

It took some doing to flip the safe out of the muck that seemed determined to suck it back, only to have it plop right down again, albeit now three feet closer to the motel. I did it again, four more times, then went back to pick up the tools and dolly. In the dim light of a quarter moon, the creek looked like it stretched into the darkness forever. As I caught my breath, I tried to tell myself that it wasn't important what it looked like, only how far it really was. I started to do a quick mental calculation: A quarter mile to go, that was about thirteen hundred feet, with three feet of progress every time I flipped that green monstrosity on its side, that was how many times I'd have to do this? I decided I didn't want to know and bent to the task once again. At least I wasn't exposed anymore.

The mud was killing me. I tried to move slightly up the side of the creek bed to firmer ground, but the resultant awkward angle of the safe—think of skiing across the fall line—meant I could never let go and take a break, so that didn't work. I tried opening the tool sack and laying it down in front of the safe. That was slightly better, but then there was nothing left to put in front for the next flip, because the bag was now underneath the safe. I decided it wasn't worth the effort, and now I also had a soaking wet, muddy sack of tools to contend with, which only made the whole enterprise even more obnoxious.

One glance at my watch told me I'd better stop feeling sorry for myself and get on with it. All I needed was for the sun to come up while I was still in the gully. At least the moon had already gone down.

Eventually, somehow, I made it. Thoroughly wrung out after some six difficult hours of nonstop work, I can't even conjure up how I managed to roll the safe up the side of the creek bed, but I did. I could see the first faint hints of sunlight to the east and hurried to bring my car around to where I'd left the safe. When I drove up, headlights off, I could just make it out in the starlight, a squat, ugly, malevolent thing. In my weakened, suggestive state I could feel it mocking me.

I backed the car to within a foot of the safe, got out and opened the trunk. Heaving, struggling, straining, I simply could not get the thing up and over the lip of the trunk. It was too damned heavy and the lip too high. But I couldn't give up, not after the insane ordeal of getting it this far. There had to be a way.

The car was an old two-door Comet with very wide openings into the front. Feeling I no longer had many options (but plenty of tools), I unbolted the bench-type seat and put it in the trunk, then got the safe up and over the doorsill and into the car where the seat used to be. I covered it with a towel and got in. There wasn't enough room to push it completely away from the driver's side to the passenger's, so the only way I'd be able to drive was to sit on top of the thing. I had to bend forward with the back of my head wedged against the roof and my toes barely touching the pedals. I drove away like that, not even daring to think what I would say to any cop who pulled me over.

I drove to the building I managed, changed cars and drove home. That was even harder than stealing the safe in the first place, because despite being tired, wet, scared, relieved and half a dozen other things I couldn't sort out, I was so thoroughly exhilarated, I could hardly sit still to drive.

Trying to sleep was even worse, but I think I managed an hour or two.

~

Before dawn on Monday I muscled the safe down into the basement workroom using a heavy-duty hand truck and went to work with an oxyacetylene cutting torch. It wasn't very difficult to get the door off with that tool; I'd thought about it the night before and realized that all I had to get through were the hinges. I had it done by midmorning.

Inside, it was a mess. Sure, there was plenty of cash, but muddy water had gotten in through the loosened door while I was rolling it along the creek, and I was looking at one giant, filthy, soggy mass of green and brown. Unable to tell a bill from a rotted leaf, I loaded the whole cruddy pile into two plastic garbage bags and threw them in the backseat of the car. I got the safe into the trunk using the hand truck and two boards propped up to form ramps, then headed far out of town, dumped the safe into a lake and drove home.

After emptying the bags into the bathtub, I ran the shower and was able to separate out the cash and the leaves as the water rinsed the dirt away. After I loaded the junky stuff back into the plastic bags, I grabbed some bills and stuck them to the tiled walls to dry. By the time those walls were completely covered, I'd barely made a dent in the pile, and so proceeded out to the hall, then the bedroom, then the kitchen.

I'd hoped to get this all done and put away before Barbara came home, but that part of the plan didn't work out. When she walked in that afternoon, just about every square inch of the downstairs rooms and half the upstairs was covered with ones, fives, tens and twenties. Not just the walls, either. There was money on the floors, tables, chairs, lamps, television set, cabinets . . . everywhere. As Barbara stood and stared, openmouthed and speechless, a dried bill came loose and fluttered to the floor. Her eyes followed it, and when it landed, it seemed to snap her out of whatever shock she was in.

"What the hell is this!" she demanded, her eyes flashing menacingly as she waved a hand around the room.

"It's money." I didn't mean it to sound sarcastic, but I guess it did.

"I know it's money," she hissed through clenched teeth. "Whose is it and what's it doing on our walls!"

"It's mine. Ours. It got wet and I needed to dry it out."

To say that she was angry doesn't quite do justice to her reaction, but despite how she was feeling, she stopped talking at that point and literally bit her lip. She knew I'd done something illegal and also knew that if I wanted to tell her, I would, so there was no sense in her badgering me, and even less sense in my toying with her. She also knew that whatever explanation I came up with was going to be pure bullshit, and I knew that she'd know. "I broke into a safe."

Her eyes started to roll back into her head, but she recovered quickly. "What safe? Where?"

"The miniature golf course."

I could see her instantly realizing all the implications, and, as it happened, the worst ones occurred to me at the same time. I hadn't put them together fully until that very moment.

"All that time we were there together," she said, her voice on the edge of cracking, "it wasn't for us? You were planning a robbery?"

I was pretty well prepared to take some serious abuse for having committed a crime, but what I wasn't ready for was Barb's intense feeling of having been betrayed. To her, the worst part of the episode was that I'd deceived her. She'd gone along with what seemed to her an oddball passion for miniature golf, and the whole time it was going on, I'd really been lying to her. She seemed to be having trouble deciding whether to be crushed or angry, but anger was easier for her to deal with, so she went with that.

That anger had other sources as well, the most obvious being that I'd put her and our daughter in jeopardy in addition to myself. Despite Barb's absolute innocence in the matter, a gung-ho prosecutor could make the case that she'd helped me scope out the job. And if both of us went away for it, where would that leave little Suzanne?

Barb had already seen firsthand the kind of grief that lawless behavior could bring down on a family. She'd been through it with her brother, then again with him and me when we'd hit that gas station. She married me anyway, believing or hoping I'd had all the larceny knocked out of me after my monthlong stint in the Cuyahoga County cooler, then she walks into the apartment one day and sees money plastered all over the place. She knew instantly that trouble was about to come her way again.

Luckily, Barb's way of being righteously pissed off was to clam up and refuse to talk to me. She didn't even help peel the bills off the walls and furniture before storming out of the house. Later, when we did talk about it, I assured her in no uncertain terms that it was a snap opportunity that was so easy, I couldn't turn it down, a one-shot deal to get our bank account jump-started, the last sowing of my wild oats, what kind of father and husband would I be if I ever pulled something like that again, and on and on until she was finally convinced it would never happen again and didn't every family need at least one great big secret that fifty years from now would seem funny and romantic?

Truth was, I was deceiving her again, because I couldn't say for sure that it was really just a single opportunity seized, to be repeated no more and therefore pointless to dwell on. I hadn't taken any time at all to think about the larger implications and honestly didn't know what any of it meant.

There was over five thousand dollars in that safe, which may not seem like a lot of money now, but in 1962, to a new family man working as a building manager, it was nearly a year's salary. Nevertheless, about a week later I offered half of it to Sam. After all, he'd tipped me off to the opportunity. To my great surprise, he wouldn't take a penny, no matter how hard I tried to convince him he had it coming.

I finally gave up, but I had to ask: "Why me? What made you think I'd do it?"

He shot me a cockeyed, knowing grin. "Had a strong feeling you maybe had, I don't know"—he waved a hand in the air as he searched for the right words—"kind of a knack."

That took me back a bit. I hadn't even known I had a knack. What had Sam seen in me I hadn't known was there? "But if you didn't want any part of it, why put someone up to it in the first place?"

The grin started to fade. "Owner's a real sonofabitch. It was right, somebody ripped him off."

And he figured—somehow—that I was the guy. Interesting. It wasn't like Sam, as straight as they come, had special insight into the criminal personality. He's been a friend of mine for over forty years and I don't believe he's ever had so much as a parking ticket.

Kind of a knack. Even while I was rolling that safe along the creek bed, I'd been struck by how many things I'd failed to anticipate that, in retrospect, seemed so obvious. I'd never cracked a safe before, so I shouldn't have assumed I could do it right on the spot. Maybe I should have scoped out someplace closer to move it to, so I could come back with the car to pick it up. Should I have rented a truck or borrowed one?

Despite that self-criticism, I had a great sense of accomplishment at having been able to pull it off anyway, to think on my feet when problems arose, without having panicked or given up and without any help. It wasn't lost on me how great a role luck had played in my eventual success, but I also credited myself with the ability to take advantage of that luck.

I decided that Sam was right: I had a knack.

~

A lot of things started clicking after that experience. As scary as it was to have been doing something that foolish and risky, there was an eerie feeling of familiarity about it. It wasn't one of those past-lives kinds of things, or déjà vu, exactly, but something else, like putting on a pair of shoes that look weird as hell but fit perfectly right out of the box, as though they'd been made with you in mind. Strangely enough, the fact that I now had a nice pile of cash—ostensibly the reason for having done the job in the first place—seemed of almost secondary importance.

I'd always been fascinated by crime, the outlaw aspect combined with the extraordinary creativity of the more celebrated criminals in both real life and fiction. I was certainly not unique in that fascination. Newsstands in the fifties overflowed with magazines about crime fighters and criminals, writers like Mickey Spillane regularly topped the bestseller lists, and *On the Waterfront, Twelve Angry Men, Witness for the Prosecution* and *Anatomy of a Murder* were all Oscar-nominated movies when I was a teenager. Crime as mass entertainment is a staple of American culture, and the bad guys are portrayed sympathetically at least as often as the good guys. (If you don't believe me, who were you rooting for in *The Godfather*?)

I remember when thieves broke a hole through the roof of the Franklin Simon department store on Shaker Square. The papers described how they ripped the layers off the safe and cleaned it out. The whole town was talking about it, but very few people were shaking their heads and clucking their tongues over how awful it was; instead, their faces were lit up with excitement and wonder as they endlessly recounted every detail. Little kids were clambering around rooftops pretending to be the robbers, and I don't remember any of them pretending to be the police or detectives.

As I mentioned earlier, without realizing it I was getting schooled in the fine art of thievery from several quarters, starting with those apartment-building maintenance guys I spent a lot of time with. But all that was just technical stuff; what remained was for me to be around people for whom the criminal life wasn't the distant, unimaginable world "normal" citizens thought it was. I'd bought my '49 Ford convertible from a man named Tony Tarrascavage, who owned an auto body shop on the next block. I hung around that shop a lot and was pretty handy and quick to learn, so Tony taught me how to use an oxyacetylene cutting torch just to give me something to do and keep me from getting underfoot. His shop was a hangout for a lot of shady guys, many of whom are now prematurely dead or serving long prison sentences. Once they got used to me, they no longer clammed up when I was around. They talked about crime constantly—and knowledgeably—and it was fascinating to listen to their conversations. At first it threw me pretty good, because these characters weren't just turning over garbage cans or throwing eggs at cars, but it's said you can get used to damned near anything, and after a while I got used to the idea that there were a lot of people in the world who didn't live like my parents. The first time you hear about a bank robbery from an actual participant it blows your mind, but after the tenth or twentieth time it loses its power to shock, and after that it starts to sound almost normal. When you spend a lot of time inside this strange and unfamiliar world and begin to see that career criminals aren't necessarily a bunch of snarling, wild-eyed dogs, what they do starts to seem less and less alien and forbidding. I imagine that professional assassins, whether employed by governments or gangsters, go through the same kind of psychological adaptation until they're like Clemenza in *The Godfather* telling one of his men not to forget the cannoli after they just whacked another wiseguy.

People with something to hide tended to open up to me. It might have had to do with the fact that I was a patient and interested listener, or maybe that's just flattering myself and there was something about me that told career criminals I was a fellow traveler at heart. I honestly don't know, but throughout my life people were always telling me things they probably wouldn't even tell their shrinks. And in the environments I was hanging out in, a lot of hardened crooks told me a lot of interesting things.

Still, at that point I didn't see myself as a career criminal, just an ordinary guy dedicated to his family and his business. Our son, Mark, was born about a year after I hit the golf course, and I didn't pull another robbery until another six months had gone by, and that was a purely opportunistic and unproductive situation: A lady was out at the opera for an evening; I broke into her apartment and got very little (although I did get my first nickname in the papers: the "Opera Burglar"). Like an unwitting gambling junkie, I really believed that all I needed was one great score, and that would be it for me, and I was cocky enough to think I was ready to pull off something significant before calling it quits. I had no idea that I was about to uncover an irresistible appetite that had nothing at all to do with money.

4

Luck

A MAJOR score is an intricate puzzle that needs to get solved, but all the detailed planning and meticulous preparation in the world don't mean a thing if the gods aren't on your side. Luck is a critical factor, and it would seem to be the only one you can't do anything about, although, as golfer Ben Hogan once put it: "The more I practice, the luckier I get."

On the other hand, Hogan never pushed his luck by trying to rob a safe owned by the Mob.

In the months following John F. Kennedy's assassination there was a sadness in the air, the feeling that something had changed forever, but nobody was quite sure what. No one seemed to know how to behave or what was to be done next, as if we were all in some kind of strange limbo, waiting for a sign that it was appropriate to move on. That pervasive uncertainty weighed on me; I got restless and itchy and decided I needed to go out and steal something big. I can't say I'd been particularly vigilant for opportunities after the miniature golf course and "opera" job, but now I concentrated, trying to push the process a little instead of just waiting for something to fall into my lap.

Which is not to say that I was now a full-fledged thief—after all, I'd done only two jobs in as many years. But I'd done them well and thought that if I could pull off one more great big one, I'd be set forever and would never have to do it again. A truly original thought, that one.

There was a very exclusive private club I'd been going to one or two afternoons a week, an obvious source, but I hadn't really worked it. I decided to become more aggressive, not just listening in on random snatches of conversation but poking here and there, drawing people out with some innocent-sounding questions.

This club was the kind where all of the members had their own keys to the front door. It was located in a Cleveland landmark known as the Highlander, a complex that included a good-sized hotel and a number of upscale shops and restaurants. It was a place where the upper crust could let loose and feel secure, because the Highlander was owned by a man named "Big Ange" Lonardo and his cousin "Little Ange." Big Ange was underboss of the Cleveland Mafia, and if there was one thing the Mob was particularly good at, it was protecting their business interests. They were not about to let anybody hassle the clientele, nor would the Lonardos themselves ever try to take a customer down, because rich people with money to burn constituted a renewable but fickle revenue source. Let those paying patrons get the slightest suspicion that the Highlander was less than a safe haven and they'd move on to another watering hole in a New York second.

The most visible part of the complex was a large and very swank supper club that offered nightly entertainment. Along with the old-money crowd from neighborhoods such as Shaker Heights, it hosted a lot of heavy-hitting politicos, businessmen and hoods. It was *the* spot in town at the time for those who wanted to be seen rubbing shoulders with others who wanted to be seen, and its exclusivity derived primarily from its high prices.

The key club, on the other hand, was truly exclusive, populated by the real elite whose concern was privacy, not visibility, and who wanted the company of others similarly inclined. It was expensively fitted out, the food and drinks were first-rate, and the waitresses, all clad in Playboy Bunny–style attire, were beautiful.

I didn't have my own key to the club. That's because I wasn't actually a member. I just picked the lock whenever I wanted to get in. It had only two pins, and I'd done it so often I could let myself in as fast as someone with a legitimate key, so I no longer had to wait until nobody else was around. (Later in life, friends would joke that I picked locks when I was in a hurry because using a key was too slow.) Once inside I simply acted as if I belonged, and no one ever questioned my presence. They all thought I was a big shot in real estate, a business I knew something about and could discuss knowledgeably if I had to.

The clientele was composed mostly of business executives, unwinding after a stressful day—or sometimes in the middle of one. The club generally opened at around eleven in the morning, and by noon there were a surprisingly large number of people already drinking.

I was accepted in the club as a regular by virtue of my frequent presence and air of belonging. The waitresses pretty much knew what I was up to, although not why. They just thought I was a well-dressed, not-painful-to-look-at gate crasher who enjoyed the club and its denizens. They all liked me, especially after they thought I'd started up a thing with Rose Marie, who handled the bar and padded my drinks onto other people's expense-account-subsidized bar bills so I never had to pay.

Since my function was to listen and learn, I didn't say much, mostly just grunted and nodded encouragingly at others who felt compelled to tell a complete stranger intimate details of their lives. Assuming I was a kindred spirit in the brotherhood of loose capitalist ethics, they casually revealed tales of indictable business practices as though they were recounting the weekend's golf scores. Had I been a blackmailer or an extortionist, I would have been in hog heaven, but I was a budding thief and none of this was doing me much good.

A week or two after I'd decided to turn up the juice a notch, I was in the Highlander restaurant, drinking coffee and watching the sun come up. The restaurant was closed, and only employees and their friends like me were in there. I don't know if it was because I'd been looking a bit bored of late or restless or what, but Rose Marie poured herself a cup of coffee and said, "Did you know there was another club? A private one?"

Something about the way she said it put me on alert, as though she were letting slip a secret she'd debated with herself about telling me. I forced myself into feigned indifference and looked at her. "That so?"

She nodded. "But not in the hotel. Couple miles away, I'm not sure where."

"Whose owns it?"

"The Lonardos."

Now I couldn't hide my surprise. These were the same guys who owned the key club. "Why a second club?"

She shrugged. "Beats me. But I think there's gambling there." She took another sip, then set the cup down and started for the door. "What I hear, it's high rollers only."

I thought I caught a petulant look on her face, which I didn't understand at first. Was she afraid I was getting bored with the key club—and, by implication, with her company—and looking to move on? By the time that realization dawned on me, it was too late for me to say anything to assuage her worry.

"I think Vinny's a member, if you really want to find out," she called back over her shoulder before heading out through the hotel lobby.

To a thief, one tidbit of inside information can be worth more than a truckload of fancy tools.

~

"Vinny" was Vinny Ovino, a regular at the key club. He was a drunk and a heavy gambler, the kind who would place a bet on which of two sugar cubes a fly would land on first, which explained where his money went but not where it came from. I knew him because he lived in one of the luxury buildings I managed at Shaker Square.

Ovino was a real character, always swaggering around and bragging, but he seemed harmless enough and people tolerated him because he was colorful. He'd pay the bar girls one or two at a time to sit in his car and watch him play with himself, which was pretty easy money once they got used to it, and he paid well.

More than anything, Ovino liked to talk, especially about himself, and it didn't take long to get him to tell me about the other club, which was only open on weekends. The main attraction, as Rose Marie had surmised, was gambling. There was heavy book in horse racing, football and baseball, as well as high-stakes poker games, backgammon and craps.

Everything about it screamed money at me. Serious money, too, because if someone like me had never even heard of it, this was an operation that didn't need to advertise.

Ovino looked at me slyly, then leaned in so close I could have gotten drunk off his breath. "Y'wanna see it?" he said with a wink.

I pretended to think about it for a second, then said, "Nah . . . sounds a little rich for my blood."

He straightened back up and frowned. "Tell ya the truth, Bill," he said, with what looked like an effort-filled reining in of his braggadocio, "it's a little rich for mine." He took a small swig of his Manhattan. "But the pussy is top-shelf!"

I breathed a sigh of relief that I'd gotten off the hook so easily. There were two reasons I didn't want to go there. First, I didn't have the kind of scratch to participate in the gaming. I'm sure it looked like a warm, friendly place with a lot of old-world backslapping and glad-handing, but I had little doubt that watchful eyes knew exactly what everyone in the place was doing at all times, and it wouldn't take long for somebody to figure out that I was taking up space and soaking up booze and not laying down any bets.

Second, and more to the point, there was no way I wanted to be seen anywhere near that place. A little more digging and it might prove to be worth pulling off a job there, and until I had a fully formulated plan, I didn't want to risk contaminating the waters if that plan called for my being a complete nonpresence. If it should prove to be of benefit to me to be seen there, I could always take care of that at some point, but there was no way to reverse things should the opposite be true.

I began checking it out surreptitiously to see if it might indeed be a fertile hunting ground.

~

The first thing I noticed was that the patrons of this club were several cuts above what I had thought, up to that point, was the highest layer of Cleveland upper crust that would be seen in a Mob gambling den. From my car half a block away I recognized at least a quarter of the people going in and out, and recognized the clothes worn by another quarter as the kind of stuff you didn't get in the local department store. To my eye they might as well have had their bank balances tattooed on their foreheads.

It sure looked like the mother lode, but I entertained no illusions about what I'd be up against. Every one of these people had to know who was running the club, and it wasn't the police they were looking to for protection. Were I to be caught, there'd be nothing as safe and comfortable as a jail cell at the other end.

I had no idea what I was going to do at that point, but a familiar feeling told me that, as Sherlock Holmes might have put it, the game was afoot. I settled into a strangely calm kind of patience and committed to at least the first stage of any complex operation: watching and learning. I observed the place for several weeks and learned a good deal.

The club closed just before three A.M. on Saturdays. Little Ange handled day-to-day operations. Through my binoculars I could see him come out a few minutes after the doors closed, carrying a black bag. He'd then get in his Cadillac and drive off in the direction of the Highlander.

One night I followed him there, with a pretty good idea of exactly where he was heading.

I knew they maintained a windowless office on a secure second-story floor of the hotel that required a key for access. There were about fifty hotel rooms on the floor in addition to the office, and a stairwell at either end of the long corridor.

I had my own key, and when Little Ange entered at one end, I went in the other, and up the stairwell. I wanted to take off my shoes to keep the sound down but would have had a tough time explaining my bare feet if someone came upon me at that late hour. I counted on the length of the corridor to prevent any sounds from reaching Little Ange.

Knowing he was likely heading for that office, I'd brought along a small periscope I'd made out of an empty paper-towel tube, two mirrors and some Scotch tape. I got down on the top steps and set it on the floor, so I could see around the corner without being spotted. If anybody came upon me, I'd roll over on top of the 'scope, act drunk and say I tripped.

I watched as Ange appeared at the other end of the corridor, opened the office door and went in. He stayed for about five minutes, then came out, turned to set some kind of an alarm and left.

Without the black bag.

~

The Highlander's imposing front building, containing the main office and supper club, was located on a very busy street in a suburb just outside of Cleveland. Behind it was the hotel, which was made up of a pair of two-story high-roofed wings separated by a large swimming pool and patio. Private balconies faced the pool on the second story of each wing.

Behind the hotel were eight apartment buildings three stories high, each containing about a hundred units. Rose Marie lived there, as did many of the restaurant employees and the girls who worked in the key club.

The Highlander was a large and bustling place, with a lot of activity going on all the time. It was easy to move around without attracting attention, especially for someone like me, a familiar sight around the complex. I'd even taken Barbara there on a number of occasions, not only to the restaurant but to the pool. All of this made it easy for me to continue my observations unnoticed.

The Mob office was the second door in on the secure floor. The first door opened into the chambermaids' supply room, which had an alarm and was locked at night with a heavy dead bolt and a separate padlock. All the rest were ordinary hotel rooms. The supply room generally remained open during the day so the maids could easily get at their carts, vacuums and linens. A security guard came by frequently while it was open, but by chatting up a couple of maids it was no trick for me to get a look at the alarm sensor on the door, which was a simple magnetic trip.

I was never able to see into the office, though. The door was never left open, and trying to be present at the exact moment that someone went in or out was much too risky.

The laundry room down on the first floor was underneath the maids' supply room and the office. I'd have guessed that it would be operated at night, but it never was, which made sense. If it were, the hotel would've needed two complete sets of bed linens and towels. By running the laundry during the day while the chambermaids worked, they wouldn't require nearly as much stock.

That was fine with me, because an empty laundry room below would help to muffle any noise I might end up making.

I had to make a lot of assumptions. One of them was about the type of alarm on the office, but the way Little Ange set it told me a lot. He didn't enter any combinations or press multiple buttons; it looked like he just flipped a switch and shut the door, which made it likely that it was the same kind of simple trip as the one on the maids' room, a reasonable construction decision that bolstered my conviction somewhat.

The next assumption was about where the alarm actually rang if tripped, and that almost certainly had to be the front desk. That it might be connected to the local police station wouldn't make any sense, because the front desk was manned twenty-four hours a day and could outrespond the police hands down. Couple that with the absurd proposition that the owners of the Highlander would ever call on the police for help with a security problem, and it was a dead certainty that the alarm signal never left the complex. It was even likely that the office alarm shared a wire down to the front desk with the maids'-room alarm.

It was significant that I'd never heard an alarm go off when Ange opened the door. In those days, before such sophistication as digital delay circuits and motion detectors, most setups would trigger the alarm when the door was opened, and the ringing would stop as soon as a switch in a hidden location was flipped. Walk down any street in a retail section at opening time and you'd hear dozens of alarms going off for three or four seconds at a time.

But since there was no such sound when Little Ange opened that office door, it confirmed that it must have sounded at the front desk. The clerk would know when the office was usually entered, and would expect a few seconds of the alarm and ignore it. Anything else, and I had little doubt that a few highly motivated thugs would quickly be summoned to dispense a bit of instant justice to an intruder, who would have no warning whatsoever that he'd even set off an alarm.

Dealing with that alarm was the first challenge.

The second was the roving guard, and that was mostly a question of learning his habits and hoping that they were very regular. If he made his rounds like clockwork, I'd know just how much time I had to work with and could plan accordingly. If his walks around the complex were random and too closely spaced, I might have to call it off altogether.

The third challenge, and the biggest one, was how to get into a safe I'd never seen. Rose Marie had been in the office once and I'd heard her tell some people at the bar about "this gigundo safe" in there. She'd put her hand, palm flat, way above her head for emphasis, so I knew it had to be a monster. Even though my skill with safes had improved since the mini golf course score, I still couldn't crack one like you see in the movies, so it would have to be a brute-force entry. That would take time and made the matter of the guard even more important.

Finally, there had to be enough money in the safe to make the whole enterprise worth it. It was now early June, and the next time there would be a high likelihood of a good haul would be the Fourth of July. I'd already learned that a number of private parties were planned for that weekend, so that was my target, Monday night specifically, when the coffers would be fullest and not emptied until the banks reopened on Tuesday.

I had a month to plan. Or to call it off.

I don't know the exact moment when I'd made the decision to go through with this job, and to hit the Lonardos directly instead of taking off one of their glamorous customers, but by this time there was no question about it in my mind: If I could solve all the puzzles, I'd go for it.

~

The initial shock of the Kennedy assassination hadn't even died down before the Warren Commission investigation was in full swing. It seemed that the more witnesses they interviewed and the more evidence they uncovered, the murkier the whole story became. At the time I was planning the job, the final report was still three months away from being issued, but already the accusations of a cover-up were loud and strident.

A good part of the focus was on Jack Ruby, who'd shot and killed Lee Harvey Oswald in the basement of the Dallas Police Department two days after Oswald allegedly assassinated Kennedy. Understandably, speculation had immediately arisen that Ruby had acted on behalf of members of a conspiracy that had planned the killing of Kennedy and wanted to silence Oswald.

What made all of this relevant to my situation were the stories that Ruby had been closely tied in with the criminal underworld. He'd grown up in Chicago, in a tough neighborhood where he'd been friends with local criminals, and those kinds of associations had flowered when he became a nightclub operator. He was a known gambler, he had visited Cuba as the guest of professional gambler Lewis McWillie, and his partner in his Vegas club had a criminal record.

All of this brought an extraordinary amount of unwanted attention to the Mob. I'm talking about the *real* players now, not the swaggering wiseguys who populated the lower ranks of foot soldiers, but the head men who, with one or two especially visible exceptions, kept a deliberately low profile because they had no need to strut in public. People who counted knew who they were, and that was all that mattered.

But with the Warren Commission delving into Jack Ruby's background, and every Pulitzer-seeking investigative reporter pounding the pavement and pressuring sources in an attempt to one-up the commission, the Mob was as skittish, tense and twitchy as they had been back when the Kefauver investigation and Knapp Commission hearings were under way.

And Angelo Lonardo was the last person you wanted to be around when he was twitchy.

Big Ange's father, Joe Lonardo, had emigrated from Licata, Sicily, in 1905, along with his three brothers and another set of brothers, the Porellos. He'd become wealthy dealing in corn sugar, which was the main ingredient in bootleg liquor during Prohibition. "Big Joe" was the original Cleveland *padrino,* or godfather, and the eldest Porello was one of his corporals.

Porello left Lonardo in 1926 to form his own corn sugar business with his six brothers, and they became Big Joe's primary competitors. When Big Joe went back to Sicily to visit his mother and left his brother John in charge, he returned to discover that the Porellos had taken advantage of John's lack of business sense and pretty much cornered the local market.

Seeking to avoid bloodshed, Big Joe offered to negotiate. The Porellos agreed, then had the two Lonardo brothers shot to death in a barbershop, after which Porello the Elder appointed himself the new *capo* of the Cleveland Mafia. As Porello's power and influence grew, so did the rage and thirst for revenge among the family and associates of the murdered Lonardo brothers. One day in 1929, Big Joe Lonardo's son Angelo, all of eighteen years old, drove his mother to the Porello headquarters and sent in a message saying that she wanted to speak to "Black Sam" Todaro, one of the Porello gunmen who'd killed the Lonardo brothers. As Todaro approached the car, Angelo pulled out a gun and emptied it into him.

Angelo was arrested for the murder and sentenced to life in prison, but he won a new trial and was released after serving only eighteen months. He later came to be known as "Big Ange" Lonardo.

This was the guy I was planning to rob.

~

The next weekend I followed Little Ange as usual, except that this time I peeled off toward the registration desk when he headed for the office. Feigning some mild drunkenness, I made small talk with the clerk at the counter. Sure enough, a moderate dinging sounded from somewhere beneath the desk at just about the time Ange should have been opening the office door. The sound stopped a few seconds later.

I'd guessed right, and all I had to do was disable that alarm sometime after Ange made his cash drop on the Fourth. I couldn't do it in advance of that because the clerk would be expecting to hear it a little after three A.M. That meant that disconnecting the ringer right in the front office was not an option. What pretense could I possibly cook up to get under the counter in the wee hours of the morning that wouldn't get me cemented into a steel drum and dropped into the middle of Lake Erie?

Two days later I dressed in rough work clothes and began walking around the complex with a worn clipboard and a set of tools strapped to my belt. I asked a lot of questions—it's amazing what people will tell you if you look like you have the right to know—and easily located the electrical junction box. The next step was to identify the alarm wire, which I could cut after Little Ange made his drop. I felt a thrill as I picked the cheap lock and opened the box.

An incomprehensible profusion of wires confronted me. There were more than two hundred rooms in the hotel, and lines from every one of them fed through this box. Wires were jammed so tightly, they looked like a single solid mass, and I sweated as I pulled and twisted, trying not to break any as I looked for the one or two that would appear different from the others and tell me they were for the alarm.

I never found them. Half an hour of separating every individual wire in the mass only confirmed that the alarm wasn't wired through the main box. Dejected, I nevertheless took the time to get everything back in place so as not to arouse suspicion.

This was not getting off to a good start.

˜

The problem of the alarm system was obsessing me, so I decided to work on some other aspects of the plan, confident that an answer would present itself to me along the way if I got in a less desperate frame of mind.

"How about a weekend out on the town? Just the two of us."

My wife looked up from the paper, eyebrows raised in surprise. "What's the catch?"

"We have to set new records for drinking and screwing."

She pretended to think about it for a few seconds, then nodded. "I can handle that. Where?"

"The Highlander."

Her mouth twisted sidewise into a sneer at the mention of a local place rather than some exotic foreign setting, and she went back to the paper. "Very funny."

"I'm not kidding." I sat down across from her and pushed her paper aside. "It'll be fun, like another honeymoon. My mother's already volunteered to baby-sit."

She began to realize I was serious, so I pressed ahead. "No kids, no laundry, no cooking . . . We won't tell anyone where we are and no phone calls, either. We can do whatever we want. What do you say?"

As I ticked off the list of things she wouldn't have to worry about for three days, I could see her eyes soften and knew I had her.

It really was a fun weekend, and more like a hot courtship than a second honeymoon. We drank well, ate well and made love like teenagers, which only partially distracted Barbara from the fact that I kept looking out the window. Any less partying and she would have asked me about it a hundred times instead of the merely fifty or so she brought it up.

It wasn't lost on me how much I was risking with respect to my marriage. Barbara had been devastated by what she perceived as emotional betrayal when she found out that I'd really been casing the miniature golf course for a robbery. My deceitful behavior had bothered her much more than the fact that I'd committed a Class A felony, and it took me a long time to persuade her that it was strictly a onetime aberration, and that I'd felt as bad about it as she had. The reason I was able to convince her was because I truly—*truly*—believed it.

And now here I was in a nice hotel, wining, dining and loving her, except that I was really casing the place for a robbery. I felt bad about it, but I was helpless; once the notion of knocking off that safe got planted firmly in my brain, it took over as surely as if it had been baked into my very DNA. This time, though, the outcome would be different. There would be no wet money plastered all over the house, and Barbara would never even know it happened.

At least it would if it worked and I didn't get caught.

I learned a good deal over that weekend, and it buoyed my spirits more than I'd anticipated. The guard was lazy, probably a minimum-wager who wasn't about to put himself in harm's way for a few bucks an hour. That didn't mean he wouldn't raise an alarm, of course, but he made rounds just six times a night and spent the rest of it napping in vacant rooms. He must have known it was a Mob operation and assumed, logically, that no one in his right mind would make trouble there. The only reason I'd seen him check the maids' supply room so often in the past was that it had been during the day, when the people who paid his salary were around to watch him work.

On the other hand, maybe the guard was a light sleeper and would waken instantly at the first sound of some kind of disturbance. After all, the walls were so thin I could hear the guy in the next room brushing his teeth.

The second day of our stay, in the wee hours of the morning, I walked up to the room the guard was napping in and could hear him snoring through the cheap door. I coughed lightly. Nothing. A little louder this time. Still nothing. I went into a combination asthma attack and full-scale smoker's cough that started lights turning on and shining from under the doors of half a dozen other rooms, but the rhythm of the guard's snoring didn't change in the slightest.

Satisfied that this obstacle was safely out of the way, I started back for my room, when it hit me: I'd been so focused on the office door and its simple but exasperating alarm that I'd failed to try thinking outside the box: Why attack the toughest part of the chain rather than its weakest link?

If the walls in the rooms were that thin, how hard could it be to cut through one of them right into the office, bypassing the door and alarm altogether? I wouldn't be able to do it through the supply room, obviously, because it was alarmed as well, but the office also adjoined an ordinary hotel room. Perfect!

Elated at the idea that I could cut my own door right where I needed one, it didn't occur to me until later that day that I'd somehow have to make sure that the room next door to the office was vacant on the night of the job. So I'd merely traded one problem for another, but I was a lot happier with this one and put it aside for the time being to give the safe some more thought instead.

~

Although my safecracking skills might not have been very sophisticated, I was good with tools and mechanical things in general. Not knowing exactly what I'd be facing but certain the safe would be built like an armored tank, I gathered an array of equipment that would have made a professional salvage diver proud. I had a high-speed electric drill with carbaloid bits, two sledgehammers, chisels, hacksaws and a pair of crowbars, one of them extra long and with an angled tip to get more leverage.

My pride and joy, though, was a Porta Power hydraulic jack, which I'd bought especially for this job. The jack exerted ten tons of pressure through a rod coming out one end. I was planning on drilling into the outside of the safe, peeling back a small area of the metal using the Porta Power, chiseling the concrete on the interior between the layers, then drilling into the second layer of metal. Nothing except the chiseling would cause much noise. The Porta Power exerted a tremendous amount of pressure, but the only thing you would hear would be the metal shell of the safe ripping apart. I was hoping to cover that with the bedding and blankets in the hotel room. I also prepared a handful of rags and a bottle of alcohol for rubbing away my fingerprints in case any of the gear had to be left behind.

I also had a portable oxyacetylene cutting torch, asbestos gloves, a leather apron, a flip-down face mask and two extra tanks of fuel. I'd gotten a lot of experience with cutting-type torches at Tony Tarrascavage's auto body shop, and I was pretty sure that, if all else failed, I could cut my way into the safe. The downside was that it would take a lot more time and throw off a good deal of smelly smoke. I would use it if I had to but left it in the car for the time being because there was almost too much to carry as it was. I had everything packed in a long canvas duffel bag that probably weighed 150 pounds. One of the crowbars was too long to fit inside, so it was strapped between the handles. This made the huge bag even more awkward, but not knowing in advance exactly what I'd need, I had to have it all with me to minimize trips back and forth.

I never did solve the problem of making sure the room adjoining the office would be vacant. I'd even briefly considered checking in to it my-self, maybe wearing a disguise, but dismissed that as too dicey. I could have had a friend from another town check in for me and then disappear, but there were plenty of good reasons why I wanted to work alone and I'd sooner abandon the job than change that policy in the heat of the mo-ment. I'd just have to chance that the room would be empty.

~

It wasn't. More bad luck. An elderly couple checked in on Sunday, the day before I was planning to do the job.

I work well under pressure, and by the time they'd gotten their lug-gage in from their car I'd already come up with an idea. But it required them to leave the room, and there were no signs of life over the next few hours, not even a trip for a bucket of ice. Worse still, I couldn't observe their door directly because someone would notice me hanging around on a secure floor for no reason, so I had to stake out the stairwell doors at ei-ther end of the ground-floor corridor instead.

My eyes were so fixated on those doors for the rest of the afternoon that I started to get dizzy, but finally, at around six, one of them opened and the couple emerged. It looked like they were dressed to go out to dinner.

I waited until they got into their car and drove off, then grabbed a few hand tools I'd prepared and went up to their room. I stuck a strip of cel-luloid between the door and the jamb, pushed the lock bolt back and went in, heading directly for the bathroom. Kneeling beneath the sink, I loosened the nut connecting the cold-water supply line until it began leaking, then bent the edge of the fitting so it couldn't easily be retight-ened. It took less than a minute and then I was back at the door, when something occurred to me: As accessible and obvious as that fitting was, it wouldn't take a plumber much time to replace it. Even if the couple moved to another room, a maintenance guy would have all of Monday to work on it, and someone else could then check in.

So I went back and loosened the nut all the way, until water came pouring out and began soaking the carpet. A few minutes later I tightened it back down to a trickle. I wasn't looking for a major emergency here, just something that would get these people into another room and make sure this one didn't get handed to anyone else the next day.

I didn't stick around to watch the old folks raise a ruckus on their re-turn, but when I came back in the middle of the night to make sure Little Ange made his usual cash drop, I checked the location of their car. Sure enough, it was now on the other side of the complex.

As far as I was concerned, I'd passed what pilots call the "go–no go" point and, barring any last-minute snafus, was fully committed. Everything was in place and there was nothing left to do but wait out the next twenty-four hours.

～

I went on a picnic with my family on Monday. It was a wonderful day but a mistake: Nothing can make you more apprehensive and fearful about losing your freedom than spending the day with people you love just before risking it all on a frankly self-indulgent adventure.

My plan that night was to sleep until midnight, but I should have realized how impossible that would be and planned for it. Instead, I tossed all over the place, which turned out to give me just the excuse I needed to get out of bed, because by that time Barbara was so relieved to see me get up I didn't even have to make up a story.

I checked everything for the thousandth time, then drove to the Highlander. Little Ange showed up right on time, and within minutes of his departure I had opened the door to the flooded hotel room and left it ajar so I could get in quickly after I'd hauled my gear upstairs.

When I returned, I heaved the bag up onto the bed to keep it dry. The place smelled musty because of the wet carpet, and there was a squishing sound as I walked across it to the far wall with my drywall knife out and ready.

Getting through the wall was even easier than I'd expected, and there was plenty of room between the sixteen-inch studs to squeeze myself through. The safe was the first thing I saw and, as advertised, it was a monster, over six feet high, with double doors. I could feel my heart beating and, despite the limited time available in which to work, forced myself to stop, get calm and listen for any noises that might signal I'd caused a disturbance of some kind.

I took advantage of the lull to assess the situation. In the dim light of my pencil flashlight I could see that the combination dial on the safe was about six inches in diameter, just left of the dully shining handle. I looked at my watch. It was 3:40, and I figured I had about three hours before anybody was likely to come by.

The office was windowless, so I turned on the light, then reached back through the wall to get my tools and equipment, which I arrayed within easy reach of the front of the safe, along with a bottle of water to keep myself from getting dehydrated during what was sure to be a long stretch of hard work. I rolled an office chair over so I could get comfortable, did a quick examination of the safe's hinges, took a deep breath and rolled up my sleeves. I'd start with the drill set on its highest speed and take it from there.

I leaned back to grab the drill and felt the chair start to tip, so to balance myself better I reached for the handle on the safe.

Which promptly snapped downward with a loud click.

So startled I nearly tipped over completely, I put down the drill and sat up straight, staring at my fingers wrapped around the handle, which now faced downward instead of sideways. Stunned, and hoping against hope, I blinked a few times and then pulled. The huge door swung open easily.

Now *that's* what I call luck.

In addition to the money in Ange's black bag, the safe was filled with cash stacked in neat five-thousand-dollar bundles. There were some nice pieces of jewelry, too, and I grabbed those first, then stuffed as many bundles of cash as I could fit into my carryall and threw it through the wall along with Ange's bag. I gathered up all that unused equipment and pushed it back through as well. Once I'd gotten myself through, I repacked my gear and strapped the carryalls onto my back, then began to drag everything back down the hallway as quietly as I could. I left such a trail of sweat behind me, it was a good thing that DNA tests weren't used in those days.

Less than an hour after first pushing back the lock on the vacant room, I quietly pressed the trunk lid of my car closed. I stopped by one of my buildings to stash the loot and equipment in an unused locker, and was back home and in bed before five A.M. Barbara never even realized I'd been away.

That was lucky, too.

⌣

I could no more sleep after the job than I could before. Even two large glasses of vodka did nothing to calm a nervous system still oozing adrenaline. It was all I could do to just lie there fighting the urge to get up every five minutes and look at the haul, to convince myself I'd really pulled it off.

Wednesday afternoon I headed back to the key club, as usual. There's an old adage about a criminal always returning to the scene of the crime. I don't know if that's true or not, but what I did know was that the worst thing you could do to draw attention to yourself when you were under the gun was to change your habits, so I wasn't about to change mine.

I'd barely gotten my first drink in hand before I was regaled with the story. "Buncha guys hit the Anges for a bundle!" one besotted middle manager gushed, trying to sound more like a gangster than someone in charge of an accounts-receivable department.

Somebody else chimed in with a dollar figure. "And some jewels, too," he added. A third guy said the amount was even higher. It went on like that the whole time I was there. I guess the amount rising with each successive telling of the tale was somehow supposed to make the story, and therefore the storyteller, more important. The real amount was a little over a hundred thousand dollars, but these guys were already up to five times that.

When I shook my head and took a deep swig of my drink, it might have looked like sympathy for the Lonardos, or resignation at what this world was coming to, but it wasn't that at all. It was amusement over the fact that everyone assumed a whole gang had pulled off the job. I took it as a compliment, and it was fairly evident that, even at this early stage, I was pretty good at this stuff and, with practice, could get a good deal better. Was it any wonder that my thoughts were already turning to the next score?

There was one other thing I thought about, much later, and that was what was likely to occur when the Lonardos realized there'd been no damage whatsoever to the safe. Little Ange wasn't going to remember that

Angelo "Big Ange" Lonardo,
underboss of the Cleveland Mafia,
shown during his 1977 arrest for
the murder of another mobster.

he'd forgotten to lock it—or admit it if he did—which meant they'd assume that either some extraordinarily skilled safecracker had opened it or someone who knew the combination had. I didn't even want to think about the future prospects of anyone on that short list of possibilities.

~

A little historical postscript: About twelve years after I pulled this job, a power struggle erupted that eventually led to a Mob war in Ohio and an unusually intense investigation by federal, state and local officials. (Its repercussions were still being felt as late as 2002, when James Traficant of Ohio became only the second person since the Civil War to get kicked out of Congress.) One of the more shocking developments occurred when Angelo Lonardo, at the age of seventy-two, turned government informant after being tried and sentenced to life plus 103 years for drug and racketeering offenses. At the time, he was the highest-ranking mobster ever to testify for the government, and his courtroom appearance helped put away Mob bosses from the Genovese, Lucchese and Colombo Mafia families. Afterward, Big Ange went into the federal government's Witness Protection Program and engineered his own disappearing act.

Little Ange died of natural causes in 1998, but as far as I know, Big Ange is still living somewhere in northeastern Ohio, with no idea who hit his safe those many years ago.

Until now. I sure hope he's the forgiving type . . . or too old to care anymore.

5

Glitz

SOMEONE ONCE said of flying that it is hours of utter boredom punctuated by moments of sheer terror. The life of a big-ticket thief is something like that, although I'd substitute "normalcy" and "exhilaration" for boredom and terror.

Discounting for the moment the occasional score, my life in the mid-sixties really was quite uneventful, and happy as well. I had a wife and kids I adored, although I didn't spend nearly enough time with them, for the usual and perfectly ordinary reason: I was working too hard at my perfectly ordinary job.

I wasn't exactly "in real estate," as I'd mentioned to the patrons of the key club when someone occasioned to ask. What I did on a daily basis was manage about five hundred luxury apartments in the Shaker Heights area on behalf of the landlords who actually owned them, nearly all of whom were my cousins. I was up in the morning and off to work, just like the accountants and store owners and carpenters and salespeople in the neighborhood. I collected rent from late payers, prodded vendors to make deliveries on time and kept an eye out for lazy maintenance men who painted around flowerpots. Very exciting stuff.

But income property fascinated me, and the hands-on experience I got in that job was invaluable. The more I did it and the more I learned, the more I wanted to be on the other side of the table, with the owners rather than the tenants and staff.

After finishing up at Case Western, I got my real estate broker's license and managed to sell a few houses fairly quickly. I hadn't put out a shingle or anything formal like that, but some elderly people who wanted to sell their large houses and move into one of the buildings I managed gave me the listings. Although showing open houses on a Sunday afternoon was not my idea of a good time, I had little trouble establishing rapport with prospective purchasers and did a good job for my elderly clients who would soon become my tenants.

All of this further stoked my interest in income property. I read every real estate investing book I could get my hands on, including ridiculous ones that promised to turn pennies into millions overnight. Even those had occasional pearls of wisdom, and I wanted to know it all.

Soon it was time to do something productive with all that cash I'd stolen from the Lonardos, and I began scouting around for some income property that might suit my inclinations and skills. In addition to the money, I had about thirty employees in mind who I was pretty sure would come to work for me. These were people I'd worked closely with, who appreciated my expertise and the respectful way I managed them, and whom I could trust to keep whatever I bought in top-notch condition. World-class maintenance was something I'd determined would be a hallmark of whatever I ended up owning.

Once I'd put the word out, it wasn't long before I learned that a building with which I was already familiar was coming on the market. It was a stunning eighteen-unit Tudor that had won awards for its beautiful architecture. Every apartment was completely different, some with sunken living rooms and twenty-five-foot ceilings, others with spiral staircases leading up to cavernous master suites, and all with working fireplaces. I got dizzy at the thought that I might actually own it.

Not only was the Mafia money enough for a down payment, it was also enough to impress the local bank with my financial stature and apparent business acumen. They gave me a mortgage, and at the tender age of twenty-five I was landlord of one of the most prestigious buildings in the area.

But the pattern of secrecy I'd already established, and which would afford me so much protection throughout my life, extended as well to my legitimate endeavors. I never announced to the existing or prospective tenants that I was the owner of the building. I just let everybody think it was yet another acquisition by the management company I was working for. As for Barbara and my mother, they thought I'd borrowed a good deal more of the total amount than I actually had.

This harmless deception was reinforced by my hands-on approach to keeping the building up. I loved to do manual work and spent a good deal of time getting down and dirty with plumbers, electricians and carpenters (not to mention locksmiths) as we worked to improve the property. I was too busy to give much thought to my other little "hobby" and found it easy to keep my darker inclinations in check.

At least during the first year, when I thought I was on my way to becoming the Donald Trump of Cleveland. Savvy people in local real estate circles had noticed what I was doing and began sounding me out on other investment opportunities. I did some scouting around on their behalf as well as my own, quickly expanding the scope of the search far outside of Cleveland and Ohio, which was when I discovered Florida.

Miami and Fort Lauderdale were growing explosively as the seventies rolled around. Together with Palm Beach, they were the hottest winter-resort destinations in the country, attracting the rich and famous along with hundreds of thousands of lesser mortals with money to burn. These "snowbirds" were little affected by the growing hippie-led backlash against conspicuous consumption that was taking hold throughout the rest of the country, and took unselfconscious delight in parading their fancy cars, expensive jewelry and lavish lifestyles at every opportunity.

The temptation for an energetic young man of few scruples, few talents and a growing family—Laura had just been born, Suzi was eight and Mark was six—was almost overwhelming. But . . . I still lived in Cleveland with my wife and three kids, bound to business responsibilities entirely of my own volition and making, and into which every bit of cash I owned was sunk. So for financial reasons alone, a move to South Florida was a distant, albeit persistent, dream.

To all outward appearances I was just another average hardworking American with big ambitions.

~

Summertime in Ohio was beautiful, and one of the season's biggest attractions was MusiCarnival, a tented theater-in-the-round on the grounds of the Thistledown Race Track. It seated fifteen hundred and was originally intended to host summer theater, but it also drew some of the biggest names in entertainment. Duke Ellington performed there regularly, as did Steve Lawrence and Eydie Gorme, Robert Goulet . . . and a stand-up comedienne named Phyllis Diller.

I'd seen Diller, an Ohio native, some months before on *The Mike Douglas Show*, which was a morning program on Cleveland television at the time. The only thing I remember was the crazy amount of large jewelry she was wearing, and wondering if it was real. I didn't give it much thought beyond that until I found out she was going to be appearing at MusiCarnival.

I bought a ticket for opening night but had waited too long and could only get a seat toward the back. Even from there, though, all the bangles and baubles she was dripping glittered brightly, and I got the strong impression that they were all the real deal.

Hardly aware of having consciously gone through any kind of decision process, I found myself planning a new score.

Diller was slated for a weeklong run, so I returned the next night and waited for the show to end, then followed as she left the theater in a limousine. It wasn't hard to keep track of her, given how few limos there were in the suburbs of Cleveland. I was also very familiar with the roads and could guess where the next turn would be without needing to get too close.

As it happened, the more we drove, the more familiar the roads became, because Diller was heading for a restaurant that was just down the street from the Highlander, on Northfield Road. It was called the Blue Grass Motel and Lounge and had the same kind of clientele as the hotel.

I went to the bar as Diller headed for the dining room, and was able to observe her without being noticed. She was with two men, beefy types who I assumed served as security.

After they finished dinner and got up to leave, I stayed put and went to the front door only when I was sure they wouldn't notice me. As I got there, I saw them getting into the limo and also noted which way they headed down the street.

They drove slowly, and a thought suddenly occurred to me: Was it possible . . . ?

It was. From a quarter mile away I could see them pulling into, of all places, the Highlander.

~

I guess it shouldn't have surprised me, since the Highlander was the toniest place in town. But to think Diller would be staying in a place with which I was already intimately familiar was too much to hope for. Just another example of the role luck plays in this kind of work.

The next night I waited at the Highlander and watched as one of the bodyguards walked her into the lobby and then returned to the limo. She proceeded alone from there, which surprised me a little until I learned that her entourage had taken up an entire floor of the hotel, an arrangement that probably made her feel pretty secure. I also noticed that she hadn't bothered to check any of the trinkets she was wearing in to the hotel's safe. What I didn't know was whether she was wearing everything she'd taken with her on the road or if more goodies were left in the room when she was out. And was there anybody else in the room, maybe her faceless husband, "Fang," the butt of so many of her onstage jokes?

What I needed to know was which room she was staying in, how I could get in and out and what security was like when she wasn't on the property. I already knew when she'd be gone because of her show schedule at MusiCarnival.

The next morning I fell back on my most sophisticated and reliable reconnaissance equipment, old work clothes and a clipboard. Because I knew people at the Highlander, I also wore sunglasses and a cap pulled down low on my forehead. Armed with a retractable tape measure, I walked the floor she and her entourage were staying on, measuring everything in sight and making careful notes of absolutely nothing, but I sure looked like I knew what I was doing.

She had to be in a suite, but there were three of those on the floor and I couldn't find a way to tell which was hers. A few people wandered by and paid no attention to me, but at some point I'd start to be noticeable to anybody who passed by me more than once.

Just as I was running out of things to measure, a bellman appeared with a breakfast tray. Paying even less attention to me than the guests had (one of the few joys to be found in a menial job is snubbing someone else who you think is even lower on the food chain than you are), he walked to one of the three suites and knocked. I watched as the door was answered by a sleepy woman with short hair, no makeup, tired slits for eyes and wearing an old bathrobe. Seeing her without the huge wigs, flashy bangles and trademark cigarette holder, it took me a few seconds to realize that it was Diller herself.

Now that I knew the right room, I exited the floor, frowning at my clipboard and scratching my head in deep concentration, a simple workman contemplating the complexities of a job and not amenable to light conversation from passersby.

Trying to get into her suite through the corridor was out of the question; there was too much traffic on that floor and I knew that most of the entourage did not attend the show every night. There were only two possible ways in. One was to go through a wall. I already knew from the Mob hit that the walls were very thin and could easily be breached, but there were a couple of problems, chief among them being that I would need an adjoining room to be vacant, and the floor was full.

The only other option was her private balcony, but to avoid detection I'd have to come in from above, and the balcony was twenty feet below the high-peaked roof. It was my only choice, though, and the good news was that getting through a sliding glass patio door is not much of a trick.

~

The next night I dressed in black from head to toe, including black crepe-soled shoes and dark gloves. Carrying a rope and some tools in an ordinary overnight bag, I went up to the roof of the wing Diller was staying in. It was secured with a heavy-duty combination lock, which I opened, and then I jammed the standard doorknob lock with a toothpick. I stashed the rope behind a vent pipe on the roof, then went back into the building and pulled the door shut behind me.

I went down to ground level and crossed over to the opposite wing, then went up to that roof. The door there had a combination lock equally as formidable as the other one, and again I—

A word of warning here: If you like to think that hotshot burglars open locks using secret methods that would make Houdini green with envy, you might want to skip this next bit.

I didn't use paper clips to crack those locks, or a set of lock picks in a classy leather pouch or some super-hi-tech electronic gadget with glowing numbers. The only place thieves pick industrial-strength locks in three seconds is in the movies, which you already know if you've ever gotten locked out of your apartment and called in a locksmith. They show up with a belt full of exotic-looking tools, fiddle with your lock for half an hour, and 90 percent of the time end up just smashing it in. And these are guys who spend forty hours a week working on locks.

Three weeks before, I'd visited both doors and jotted down the serial numbers of the two locks. Using stationery from the building management company I worked for, I wrote to the Master Lock Company with the numbers and told them I had two of their locks hanging uselessly from opened doors in a building I'd just taken over, and hated like hell to use bolt cutters on them because they were such great locks and I'd like to be able to use them, so couldn't they help me out? A few days later a cheerfully worded letter ("We're only too delighted to be of service, Mr. Smith") came back with both combinations. Letterhead stationery is one of the most useful tools for both business and burglary. Later on I even got them to send me master keys for the entire Ramada Inn and a bunch of other hotels.

Once on the roof and sure that I was in deep shadow, I trained a pair of binoculars on Diller's balcony. The lights in the suite were on and the curtains were parted slightly. There was no movement that I could see, but I forced myself to watch for a full hour to make sure no one was inside.

Time passes with excruciating slowness when you're in a risky situation and doing absolutely nothing, and there's an almost overwhelming temptation to jump the gun because you're sure it's been long enough. The best way to stop yourself from doing that is to plan ahead as much as possible and avoid making on-the-spot judgments. My plan that night called for me to watch the room for an hour, and I did it by the watch.

Convinced now the room was empty, I went back down to the bottom level and crossed over to her wing and up to the roof again. I swung open the door I'd jimmied earlier and retrieved the rope, then walked over to a vent stack closer to the edge and tied the rope around it. Once it was secure, I pulled on it as hard as I could, but the vent didn't budge.

Playing the rope down the slanted part of the roof and then out over the edge—slowly, to make sure it didn't flop around and attract attention—I lined it up with the edge of the balcony rather than the middle. That would make it even harder to spot, for someone either down below or in the room. I waited ten minutes, strictly by the watch again, then backed myself down the slanted part, stepped over the edge and began lowering myself down.

I heard music coming from somewhere, but I couldn't locate it. Music, like any "natural" noise, could be both a help and a hindrance. It helped because it could mask suspicious sounds I might make, but it was also a problem because it could mask sounds I needed to hear, like someone pushing a chair back because I'd somehow alerted them to my presence, or someone opening a door to come into a room I happened to be occupying illegally at the moment.

The music grew louder as I got lower, and as I came within a few feet of the balcony, I realized why: It was coming from inside Diller's room.

This was not good. Who could possibly be listening to music in there, and doing it without moving around at all? I'd watched the place for a solid hour and hadn't seen a single sign that anybody was in there. Was it possible they'd come in while I was making my way to the other roof?

Not likely. I could see Diller maybe leaving someone behind in there when she left, but if anyone came in afterward, they'd need a key to the room, which was a different story. What was much more likely was that Diller had left music playing either by accident or to ward off an opportunistic thief who might be wandering by. She'd spent thousands of nights in hotels like this and, like many experienced travelers, probably knew a bunch of little tricks to give herself a slight edge against casual troublemakers. (Leaving the radio or television on, as well as the lights, is a pretty good one. Another is to *never* use one of those "Service Please" door tags that tell chambermaids they can come in and make the beds but also tell the whole world the room is empty. Let the desk know on your way out instead, or phone up housekeeping just before you leave.)

I set down on the balcony as softly as I could and waited again, hands wrapped around the rope in case I needed to get back up quickly, but there was no sound other than the music, and still no movement. It was time to go to work on the sliding glass doors, which was when I noticed the inside curtain fluttering slightly, as if in a breeze. Sure enough, the doors were not quite touching and obviously not latched together.

Heart pounding almost painfully, I slid one open quietly. I pushed the curtains apart very slowly and looked around, but there was no one there, and I stepped inside. I would have loved to turn down the music, but I didn't want to take a chance that someone in an adjacent room might know Diller was gone and wonder who lowered the volume.

Clothes were scattered everywhere, as were used plates and silverware. Bureau drawers were half open, closet doors were ajar, carelessly thrown towels were visible through the bathroom door . . . the suite looked like someone had tossed a hand grenade into it. I remember wondering, given the condition of the room, how long it would take someone to notice that a robbery had even occurred.

The first place I looked was the top bureau drawer, and it was the only place I needed. A box inside was filled nearly to overflowing with a huge amount of jewelry. It was hard to figure out if my pulse was racing because of the danger I was in or because of the sight of those glittering gems and shining precious metals. I emptied all of it into my black canvas carryall, relishing the weight of it, then slung it over my shoulder and headed back to the sliding doors.

With the treasure in hand, I forced myself to slow carefulness, fighting the urge to scramble away as fast as I possibly could. I knew that leaving could be even more dangerous than entering: By now, anybody who had seen me at any point thus far would have had plenty of time to summon a security guard or the cops. If they didn't know exactly where I was, they'd be waiting and watching for someone to make sudden, furtive movements.

Worse still, I was now holding. If I'd been nabbed on the way in, all they'd have on me were suspicious clothes and some tools, and I'd have plenty of reasonable doubt on my side. Now, though, I'd be hard-pressed to explain away a bag of jewels. Even if I managed to fling them away from me, someone might see me do it and be willing to testify to it.

As carefully as I moved, I was still back on the balcony and up to the roof less than five minutes later. I pulled the rope up behind me, untied it from the vent pipe and put it in the bag with the jewels. On the way out I took the toothpick out of the lock and shut the door behind me, then resecured the combination lock. Every trace of how I got into the room was now gone. They might figure it out eventually, but there was no sense helping them. First suspicion would fall to anybody on the hotel staff who had a master key, which was probably dozens of people. The resulting confusion would work to my benefit, and once that avenue was exhausted, there'd be no place else for the police to go.

I'd considered the possibility that the lock company might have had the letter from "Mr. Smith" on file, but there was nothing to suggest that the robbery had been done from the roof. Even so, I couldn't imagine the police ever making the leap to the fact that someone might have contacted the lock company to get the roof lock combinations.

The sweet heat of triumphant elation was beginning to radiate in my chest, but on the way back to my car, sauntering between the middle buildings as casually as possible, I noticed a guy who seemed to be watching me. The heat turned into a hard knot at the pit of my stomach: How could this guy possibly have any idea what I'd just done?

I tried to chalk it off to paranoia, but as I passed, he stood up and turned in my direction, and I almost went dizzy as blood rushed out of my face. He didn't seem at all shy about staring directly at me. I tried even harder to look casual, which never works and only made me feel like I had a neon sign on my back. I was suddenly conscious of my black outfit and hoped the bag over my shoulder looked like the kind any hotel guest might be carrying.

My mind raced through a whole menu of alternatives, but all I did was veer away from the parking lot. I didn't want him to see me getting into my car. Even if he wasn't on to me, he might be a compulsive type who would note the make and model and even write down the license plate number. After the theft was discovered and reported in the news, he might put it together with his sighting of me and tell the police.

Trying not to change my posture or gait, I went out onto the street before circling back out of his sight. The parking lot was huge and I'd left my car at the far end. There was no way he could see me as I got in and drove off, but I took it slow and quiet anyway, and kept the headlights off until I was halfway down the street.

Once I'd ascertained that I wasn't being followed, I didn't exactly relax, but the worst of the anxiety began to dissipate and I started critiquing myself. What had I done wrong? What evidence might I have left behind? How could I have played it better? Should I have driven away with the headlights off like I did? If the guy watching me had been teetering on the brink of suspicion, that would have been a giveaway that I was dirty. On the other hand, the objective was for him not to know where I was in the first place once I'd circled away on foot.

I could speculate about it forever, but the only certainty was that I'd gotten away at least for the moment, so it was fruitless to second-guess myself at that point.

Never wanting to bring anything home, or even to a building I owned myself, I took the clothes and the goods to my locker at one of the buildings I managed, then headed home for what was becoming a traditional two-shots-of-vodka-and-no-sleep-at-all night. I was actually looking forward to the typical postscore letdown; at least I'd be able to get some sleep.

~~~

The next day at work I got down to the business of examining the haul with a jeweler's loupe.

In the aftermath of so much adrenaline and tension, my memory overlaid the score with a surreal, almost dreamlike quality. As I opened the bag now, though, the hard evidence of what I'd done stared right up at me. The rings, bracelets and pins were big and gaudy and all the stones were real.

The most interesting piece was a Cartier watch with an inscription reading "Love to Phyllis from Bob Hope." Sometime later I bought a new back and melted down the old one along with gold from some other pieces. I hated like hell doing that and regret it still, but I was first and foremost a professional and didn't want anything that identifiable in my possession.

The theft was a page-1 banner-headline story in the next day's afternoon papers. I almost choked at Diller's report to the police—and, undoubtedly, her insurance company—that the stuff was worth over a quarter of a million dollars, which probably meant it was really worth maybe half that. Truth was, I'd admired the pieces but hadn't done even a preliminary appraisal and had no idea it was that high. My shock was further compounded later when I went through the pieces in detail and discovered that Diller had made an accurate report and hadn't fudged the value at all. It would prove to be one of the few times in my entire career that somebody I'd robbed had filed an honest report. Let's face it: The ones *really* getting robbed—by both my victims and me—were the insurance companies.

Of much more immediate concern to me, though, was that cops were crawling all over the Highlander. They'd thoroughly canvassed the area and I had little doubt they'd found the guy who'd been watching me from the lobby. Over the next few days I pored through every edition of every paper, convinced that before too long I'd be reading a detailed description of myself. It didn't happen, but the story stayed alive for a long time anyway, much longer than it would have in a major city. Nothing much happened in Cleveland, so this was big news.

As the media finished milking it for all it was worth and the stories began petering out, so did my anxieties. I even managed a smile at what was starting to become a trademark of press coverage of my scores: Everybody assumed it had been done by a "gang," and every reference was to the "thieves" that pulled it off.

I also questioned Diller's wisdom in leaving so many valuables lying around in a hotel room. She's a very smart lady, so it occurred to me that she might have felt protected knowing that the place was owned by the Mob, and was probably unaware that someone (yours truly) had already robbed a safe there right under their noses. Of course, that score wasn't something too many people knew about outside the Highlander. Big Ange wasn't likely to let the police know, and it wasn't something he'd want publicized.

Anyway, I now had a financial security blanket and felt that I was one step closer to moving to South Florida.

~

That feeling of security was a bit premature. Even though the press soon forgot about the theft, the cops didn't. They were dead determined to solve this one, and one of the things they were sure to be doing, in addition to hoping an informant showed up, was keeping tabs on the local fences in case any of the stolen items turned up.

I wasn't worried about informants, since I worked alone and no one else knew I'd been involved. The fences were another story, though, and I decided I wasn't going to worry about that because none of this stuff was going to turn up. I was still employed and had regular rental money coming in, so I was in no hurry to convert the loot. Determined not to make amateur mistakes—Diller had undoubtedly described each piece in detail to the police, who would have notified every pawnbroker and jeweler in the entire region—I forced myself to be patient and sit on the haul.

Nearly ten years would pass before I finally decided to see what could be done with the goods. I took some of the pieces to a jewelry store on Madison Avenue in New York, prepared with a creatively elaborate story of how they'd come into my possession, but nobody asked a single background question. After leaving the goods on consignment, I had a momentary jolt of panic when I saw them displayed prominently in the window the next day, and breathed a sigh of relief when they were sold to a private European buyer two weeks later.

That experience emboldened me somewhat. Later, when I was a fugitive, I got dressed to the nines one day and strolled into Christie's, one of the world's most prestigious auction houses. Believing it would be entirely too coincidental for Diller to show up at a sale, I adopted the moniker "John Welling" and presented some pieces to be auctioned off. Nobody seemed to care about the origin of the jewels. Even when they asked if I wanted to have pictures of them printed alongside the catalog text and I blurted out "Absolutely not!" in too loud a voice (Diller might not attend the sale but who knew if, like many others, she liked to browse the catalog?), nobody blinked an eye. They were much too eager to get the pieces and the commissions to question why I'd reacted so strongly.

And speaking of John Welling . . .

Until now, nobody knew that I had been the one to rob Diller, although some people had their suspicions. On Friday nights a group of guys from my school days hung around a neighborhood bar in Shaker Heights called The Place. John Welling—the real one—and I worked as a team on the one pool table, taking on all comers at eight ball for a buck a game and a beer each. He and I had been good friends since we were in Shaker Heights High together. Many years later when I became a fugitive, he would help me craft a duplicate identity of himself—including a driver's license, a passport and credit cards—I could use to evade the authorities and that I would also use to auction jewelry at Christie's and Sotheby's. John was of medium build, like me, but his Perry Como face was far softer, almost babylike, and he looked anything but threatening when offering bets around the pool table.

One night about eighteen months after the score, John and I had a large winning streak going for us at The Place and quite a few beers already laid to rest. In the resultant happy glow, he pulled me aside, threw an arm across my shoulder and said, "I gotta ask, man: Were you the guy who pulled the Diller job?"

I prayed that he was too loaded to sense the shock that raced through me. Strictly a solo practitioner, I made a point of keeping my little hobby to myself. It wasn't that I took pride in that level of discretion, it was simply the surest way I knew to protect myself. For this grinning, reeling guy to hit me with a question like that right out of the blue, and eighteen months after the fact, was like a body blow, and I needed a few seconds to make sure I was composed before answering.

I was sorely tempted to tell him. He was a good buddy and it was clear there was some admiration behind the question. But even as brain-fuzzy as I was, my carefully thought out, ongoing survival plan kicked in, as if on autopilot. "You gotta be kidding!" I said with a laugh, shaking off his arm and heading back to the table for the next game. "I'da done that job, you think I'd be in here shooting pool with a lowlife bum like you?"

He laughed back, but I had a nagging feeling he didn't believe me and I felt bad about trying to convince him that he'd guessed wrong.

I was also troubled about why he'd seen fit to ask me about the Diller score in the first place. He knew that I hung around the Highlander a lot. Had I given him some inadvertent hints in casual conversation that I was knowledgeable or curious about fields of endeavor far removed from real estate?

It wasn't until sometime later that I found out his brother, Bill, was a bank robber, and then it became clearer. When you're close to that life, you become ultra-sensitive to bits of inside jargon, behavioral cues to a special kind of carefulness or watchfulness—a whole host of largely subliminal signals that someone has a lot to hide. I hated lying to him, but I got away with it, and why not? I'd deceived my own wife so many times, it was becoming second nature.

John eventually found out the truth, and a lot more besides, as the years passed and his brother became one of the very few people I trusted with my life.

Like I said, nobody knew "the gang" had been me, a gang of one. Unfortunately, years later I robbed Diller a second time, and that job didn't turn out nearly as well. In fact, it pretty much ended my career.

But that was still way off in the future. Here and now, the Diller score had given me some valuable lessons about the lifestyles of the highly visible and the logistics required to rob them. Why bother taking off celebrities in the first place? When Willie Sutton was asked why he robbed banks, he said it was because that's where the money is. Well, the rich and famous are where the jewels are.

Good prospects were easy to spot because celebrities, especially those in the entertainment professions, live in a culture where it's not only acceptable to show off, but expected and encouraged. Five minutes watching an Oscar telecast is all you need to prove that to yourself.

The problem is that the world is full of crazies, and it only takes one nut to ruin your day. John Lennon's tragic death at the hands of a deranged gunman marked a kind of turning point for those who live in the glare of publicity. If a gentle, peace-preaching guy like that could get gunned down, no public figure was safe. On top of that, they couldn't hope to predict from what direction danger might arise. Ronald Reagan wasn't attacked for political reasons; it was because some screwball was trying to show off for an actress he'd never even met. Who could have seen that coming? So celebrities have been forced to take extraordinary measures to protect themselves.

But prior to the Lennon shooting in 1980, security wasn't quite as tight as it is now.

~

Just before I moved away from Ohio, Robert Goulet was performing at the MusiCarnival in Cleveland, the same place Phyllis Diller had been appearing when I robbed her the first time. He liked to wear a lot of heavy gold jewelry and a flashy rock or two. I'd like to be able to tell you a fascinating story of some wildly creative and daring caper, but I can't because it was such an easy score. I had the system down pat by then.

On the next-to-last night of his run, I followed Goulet's limo from the show to the Blue Grass, the place Diller liked to go to dinner. I rode up in the elevator with him, saw which room was his, came back the next night and helped myself to all his stuff. Frankly, there wasn't too much there; I guess he pretty much wore it all when he was performing.

I fenced the goods to a guy named Richard "Blute" Tomba (more about him later) but broke one of my cardinal rules and kept a piece for myself, a watch. It was a silver Seiko with a blue face, nothing particularly fancy or expensive, but I liked it and wore it for many years. When I went to prison in Florida a few years later, I forgot to take it off before being processed in, and prison officials stuck it in my personal property envelope. When they gave it back to me fifteen months later, the damned thing was still running. I've often thought about approaching Seiko with the idea of endorsing such a terrific product. ("Even in prison, it keeps on tickin'" or "Don't do a second more than you have to.") It ran beautifully for over thirty years, until I finally lost it just last year while river rafting with my grandsons.

6

~~~~~

Scaling the Heights

BARBARA SHARED my dream to move to South Florida. She in particular hated the winters in Ohio; squeezing the kids into snowsuits and then peeling them off several times a day, walking around in dirty slush and mopping it off the floors, dressing against the damp, freezing air every time you just wanted to go out for a paper. I wasn't much of a fan, either, which was not untypical of anybody who managed property. Protecting your tenants from Old Man Winter was a no-win game. If you busted your ass to get everything plowed, shoveled and cleaned within half an hour of a snowfall, nobody noticed, but if there was a dime-sized patch of ice on a walkway somewhere, there was hell to pay.

When we finally decided to make the move, the management company I worked for tried to entice me to stay with offers of a lot more money. When that didn't work, they asked if I'd be interested in helping them identify properties to buy in Florida, which I could then manage. I jumped at that one and, over the next few months, made several business trips (i.e., on the company's nickel) to scout the territory for them, and for Barb and me as well.

On one of those trips I took Barb with me. We visited with Norm and

Janie Tripp, whom we'd known when they lived in Shaker Heights. Norm, a lawyer, couldn't stop singing the praises of Florida in general and the Coral Ridge Isles area of Fort Lauderdale, where they lived, in particular. At some point when we could get a word in edgewise, we told them we were already planning to move down. They were thrilled and insisted on taking us down the street *right this minute* to see a neighbor of theirs named Sam Hyman, who was selling his house. He'd retired down from New York, and though his wife loved Florida, he himself hated it.

The two of us gulped when we saw Sam's place. "Don't worry," Janie said, "once you get past the paint, it's really a nice house."

It was hard to see past the paint, though, to visualize what it would look like once you made it normal. The outside of the house was pink. I don't mean some pale sandy color, or just the trim, I'm talking *pink*, as in shocking pink, and every square inch of the place. It looked like a giant marshmallow Easter candy, or something you might find in Disneyland next to Sleeping Beauty's castle. Inside, everything was lavender, purple and more pink, and that included the ceilings. No wonder Sam hated Florida.

But it really was a fine place otherwise, with three bedrooms and three baths. Norm and Janie, who had kids around the same ages as ours, told us the school system was exceptional, too, and that it was one of the nicest neighborhoods in Fort Lauderdale. I didn't know as much about the real estate scene in Florida as I did about the one in Ohio, but as a result of my scouting trips I knew enough to know that the asking price was reasonable.

After we'd wandered around the place for a little while, Sam got me aside and said, "Look, the wife's bitching we're not going to get enough for the place, but she's just trying to hold things up. If you give me our asking price, I'll slip you back ten grand under the table. You're in real estate, so let's not bullshit each other. You know it's a great deal."

I mumbled something about how, yeah, it was a good deal, but I wasn't sure we could afford to buy it. He said, "You can't afford *not* to buy it. You know what's going on around here. You get stretched, you can re-sell it in a year and make ten, twenty G's." He looked around and shuddered. "Once you get rid of this fucking paint." Then he pressed the keys into my hand and told me he was going back to New York for a week. "Look it over, you and the wife, as much as you want."

During the week, Barb and I went to the house three or four times. On the last visit, we made love on the sofa in the living room. Afterward I said, "Let's do it. Let's call Sam right now, because if we see these godawful colors one more time, we might change our minds, and it's too good a deal to pass up."

Barb agreed, and I called Sam from his kitchen. "Take back the mortgage," I told him, "and we got a deal."

"Done!" You could hear the relief in his voice fifteen hundred miles away. "I'll have my lawyer put together the papers right away. But it's a deal, right?" I assured him we meant it.

Barb and I returned to Cleveland to make arrangements for selling our place there, and Norm called to tell us that Sam had already completely cleared out of the house. This was a week after our verbal agreement, before any papers had been signed. Can't say I blamed him; I couldn't imagine how he'd lived in it as long as he had.

We made several extended trips down to Florida over the next few months. We painted the place ourselves, and I added a fourth bedroom. The house had a secluded pool, and after a hard day's work we'd always enjoy a skinny-dip before dinner.

I also found a two-hundred-unit complex for sale on Bay Harbor Islands, just north of Miami Beach. The people I worked for in Cleveland came down to have a look and liked what they saw. We made an arrangement to start another management company, then they bought the place and rented an office for me right in Fort Lauderdale. Everything was falling beautifully into place, and before long we said our sad good-byes up north and moved into our "new" house. We were an instant hit with the neighbors, even before they got to know us, because they were so enormously grateful that we'd rid the street of that stomach-churning eyesore.

~

We fell right into the suburban lifestyle of Coral Ridge. It really was a wonderful neighborhood, with plenty of kids of various ages running around all over the place. Evel Knievel lived right down the street; Joe Namath was on the next block over.

Before we moved in, the house across the street was sold to a retired New York City cop and his wife. Chuck and Jean were great people, and Chuck in particular was a real practical joker, so it wasn't too long before Suzi, Mark and I started pulling all kinds of gags on them. Our kids were only ten and eight (Laura was barely two years old and not yet in on the fun and games) but had the knack of seasoned pranksters for coming up with wild and crazy stunts and a dad all too willing to help pull them off. The best was when I'd found some newsprint at a garage sale. It was in a roll six feet high and about a mile long. One weekend when Chuck and Jean were out of town, we wrapped their entire house in the stuff, leaving nothing but their television antenna sticking out the top. Watching them drive up on Sunday evening was hysterical, but they knew instantly who'd done it. Just for laughs they left the house that way for two days, until the fire department showed up and made them take all the paper off. They were right, too: One spark and the whole place would've gone up. Chuck and Jean were to become close friends over the next couple of years.

The neighborhood kids hung around our place all the time, because we always had our own kids outside and I'd play with the whole bunch almost every evening. There was very little traffic in the street, and we'd play baseball, hide-and-seek and a lot of touch football, depending on whether older or younger kids happened to be around. We'd alter the rules so as many could play as possible. Laura was too little to join in on her own, so when my team got the ball, we'd give it to her and I'd run down the field with her on my shoulders, everybody on the other team yelling in protest because she was too high to reach and tagging just me didn't count. Barb would occasionally join in if it was a game she liked. The kids also liked to play on a rope I had hanging from a tree in the backyard. I'd always set up something like that wherever I lived, and made it a point to climb up and down several dozen times a day, using only my arms. The littler kids liked to climb onto my back while I did it, which made it an even better workout.

The only other adult to regularly join in the games was my buddy Bill Welling, who by then had started spending his winters in Florida and was a frequent visitor to our house along with his brother, John. Welling was a bear of a man, huge and muscular—"Irish truck driver" comes to mind—and sometimes when there were kids on the other side big enough to tag Laura even on my shoulders, Welling would pick *me* up and carry both of us around, and nobody could touch her.

There wasn't a lot of excitement in our little area, so when something did happen, it got our attention. One Sunday morning I heard some glass breaking. At first I thought it might have been a baseball hitting a window, but a few seconds later there was another crash, so I went outside to have a look. Chuck had heard it, too, and was already on the sidewalk. He saw me and pointed up the street, where some guy was beating the crap out of a Mercedes with a baseball bat. Just hitting it over and over, smashing glass, cratering the hood and roof, trying to knock the fenders off. I recognized the guy, although I didn't know him other than to wave hello in passing. He was in his own driveway, and I'd seen the car there before, too. After the police came and calmed him down, they told us there wasn't much they could do. It was his wife's car, but in his name, and if he wanted to destroy it, that was pretty much his own business. Although it was the big talk of the neighborhood for weeks, let's face it, it wasn't really much of a story. I mention it only because a few years later I'd have cause to remember it.

Later that year we bought a boat and spent a lot of afternoons running up and down the Intracoastal and venturing out into the ocean to fish. On long weekends we'd go to the Keys or the Bahamas, and Bill and John Welling and I went on diving trips when they were in town.

None of us adults kidded ourselves that all was well in South Florida outside of our sheltered little neighborhood. The use of recreational pharmaceuticals had exploded in the United States following the "Summer of Love" in 1967, and the eastern shore of the Florida peninsula had become the prime point of entry for merchandise imported from Mexico and Central and South America. Otherwise legitimate freighters tooling up and down the coast dropped off bales of stuff to fast boats dispatched from shore to pick them up. Federal drug enforcement officials chased them around all the time and even caught a few occasionally. In a lot of cases, the pickup boats would just dump their loads over the side if the authorities got too close. Packages of marijuana, cocaine and hashish

Bill Welling (right) and me on Antigua.

were washing up on shore all the time. People who went out fishing were always on the lookout for "bale fish," or wayward bales of dope. Sometimes these were turned in to the authorities, especially if it was something crazy hard like heroin. The amount of marijuana turned in was, so I was told, close to zero.

There were some funny and colorful things about the drug trade, at least from a distance and in retrospect, but up close and personal there wasn't a damned thing funny about it at all. Cocaine cowboys were shooting it out with each other all the time, sometimes in shopping malls and other places crowded with innocent bystanders. Drug runners didn't give a rat's ass who got in the way when things got violent. There was too much money in the trade, and too much money can turn people into monsters. There are few things I find more terrifying than a human being without a conscience, and South Florida was filled with them.

I spent most of our first year there working on the house, managing the properties that had been put in my care and hunting around for other places for the company back in Cleveland to buy. It was an idyllic life. Barb and the kids were deliriously happy to be there, and I loved it, too.

Naturally, I started looking around for a way to fuck it all up.

⁓

There was something about all those glitzy high-rises on the beach that was just tugging at me, and after a year of doing the Ozzie and Harriet thing, I was getting itchy, although not itchy enough to crank up a full-scale operation starting with cold prospecting. I needed a silver-plattered opportunity to practically fall into my lap to really get the old juices flowing.

My neighbor Tata Leslie, who lived next door to Chuck, the retired cop, was very well off and spent most of her time doing the social circuit with all kinds of famous people. She and I got along well, and once she found out I was handy, she had me fixing little things for her all the time. I didn't mind, and it gave me the opportunity to occasionally rub elbows with some of her tonier acquaintances, which was kind of fun.

She was close friends with Johnny Weissmuller and his wife, Maria. Although the accomplishments that made him famous were long past, Weissmuller couldn't seem to abide no longer being at the center of things. He was somewhat showy and liked to be recognized, and he was good at getting himself photographed. Once in a while he'd even stand on Tata's lawn and do his famous Tarzan yell, which tickled the hell out of the kids in the neighborhood who'd seen those movies on Saturday-morning television.

He and his wife both wore a lot of jewelry.

I suppose I should have left it alone—for one thing, it was inevitable that there would be a lot of publicity if Tarzan were to get robbed—but I didn't. I've always thought of myself as careful and calculating, even though my avocation was more about thrills than business, but to this day I'm not sure how much of this particular score had to do with the thought of how cool it would be to take off Tarzan, along with his Jane. I rationalized to myself that it would be a good haul and that the security would be on the light side, because I assumed Weissmuller was the kind of guy who would find it hard to believe that anyone would dare to rob him. I determined early on that I wouldn't pursue the job if it looked like a long and intensive effort was needed.

Weissmuller lived at the very north end of the Coral Ridge Country Club, on the third floor of a small condo. As luck would have it, his patio looked out over the golf course. I wonder if people with those highly desirable views realize how vulnerable they are. Golf courses are pitch-black at night, not only because there's no reason to light them but because they're a few hundred acres in size and little light encroaches from distant commercial establishments. All that acreage is utterly deserted, too, there not being much to do out there after the sun goes down. It's about as ideal a setup as a thief could want—cover so perfect you could mount a small military invasion without anybody catching wise.

It looked to me as though it would be an easy task to climb up one corner of the building and then walk from patio to patio until I got to Weissmuller's. It was just a matter of making sure there was nobody home in the correct combination of units. That was easy, too; all I had to do was hang out on the golf course and watch the interior lights. To top it all off, there was excellent parking available. Commercial Boulevard was only some five hundred feet away, and because it was a major thoroughfare, no individual car would be out of place and therefore noticeable.

Don't laugh: When you get past all the sexy tools, clothes and acrobatics, you've still got to worry about where to park, about whether your vehicle is going to be conspicuous, about whether you'll be able to get your tools in and out and then leave without arousing suspicion. Getting away safely is the number one planning priority. Getting away with something worth taking runs a distant second.

It took only a few nights of sitting out on the golf course to figure out who was home and who was out of town, and therefore who was just out for the evening if the lights were off. By the time Saturday night rolled around, I was ready. I loaded my backpack with tools to jimmy a patio door, disable or bypass an alarm and work my way through a small safe. I sat on the golf course for about ninety minutes, until I was sure I had a clear path across the patios of unoccupied units, then climbed up the wall and got quickly to Weissmuller's place. I was no longer capable of being surprised by outside doors left open and had also learned that nobody who left them open bothered to set their alarms. I slid the door open and walked in.

It was dark inside, but it took me less than two minutes with a pen-light to locate the very ordinary jewelry box in the bedroom. I dumped the entire contents into my backpack, right on top of the tools I hadn't needed. Less than fifteen minutes after I'd entered the apartment, I was back in my car, and ten minutes after that I was dropping the loot off at my office. I didn't take the time to look it over because I wanted to get home so Barbara wouldn't wonder what I'd been up to.

~

It wasn't much of a take, maybe forty thousand dollars if my fence Blute Tomba was feeling generous, which he never was. The monetary value, however, paled in comparison to what I found at the bottom of the hastily deposited pile of shiny baubles.

An Olympic gold medal.

I learned from the papers the next day that Weissmuller had won it for the four-hundred-meter freestyle swim at the Paris Olympics in 1924. It was one of three gold medals he'd won that year, and one of the five he'd gotten altogether from two Olympiads.

I'd never had one of those in my hands before. I'd never even seen one up close. I was mesmerized, more so than by any jewel I'd ever held, and I've held some lulus. It seemed to carry its own history with it, and I had this really eerie feeling that there were people looking at it over my shoulder. All kinds of emotions shot through me that I was having trou-ble sorting out, and after about two minutes of not moving a muscle I re-alized that I felt absolutely terrible about having taken it, even though I hadn't intended to. It meant nothing to me—for one thing, its monetary value was zero because, despite its obvious appeal, there's no way to sell something like that—but it undoubtedly meant the world to Weiss-muller.

Despite how much it must have traumatized him, reporters couldn't seem to help but crack wise about how someone had pulled a Tarzan-type robbery on Tarzan. They suggested that the police look for the hanging vines the thief must have swung from, or that maybe it had been done by a chimpanzee . . . a predictable, and predictably lame, string of jokes.

I was sorrier than I'd ever been as a thief. Although I wanted to give him back his medal, I wasn't about to do anything risky to make that happen, yet I couldn't seem to shake off how bad I felt.

About a month later I went to Cleveland to sell the jewels to Blute. It was a much shorter interval than I was comfortable with, but since there were no remarkable pieces in the haul, I thought it safe to off-load them quickly.

I planned the flight so I'd have to change planes in Atlanta. Before leaving, I carefully wrapped and packaged the medal, making sure to wipe everything clean of prints. I dropped the package into a mailbox at the Atlanta airport and felt much better after reading in the papers that Johnny had received his medal.

Especially the part about his gratitude to the *thieves*.

~

I first noticed Elizabeth Bender in the society pages of the Fort Lauderdale newspapers. She was on the Ten Best-Dressed List, but I don't remember how big a geographical area that included. Didn't matter, really, because the ten best dressed in Fort Lauderdale were like the ten richest in Beverly Hills: You were way the hell up there no matter who else you were compared to.

What appealed to me about Bender was that she was older than the others on the list. To me that meant she'd had more time to accumulate goodies during her life. When I saw in a notice that she would be attending a luncheon at the Bahia Mar Hotel for the ten best dressed, I decided it might be worth having a quick look.

I waited in the lobby of the hotel, which was filled with other onlookers. When Bender arrived, she wasn't wearing very much jewelry. It looked to me like she had too much class to be flashing it in the daytime, but there was no doubt in my mind that this woman had some serious trinkets. Over the next few weeks I watched for photographs of her at various benefits, and while she never drenched herself in a whole lot of stuff, there were different pieces in every picture.

She was listed in the phone book as living on Galt Ocean Mile in Lauderdale-by-the-Sea. The building, called the Fountainhead, was a well-known, well-secured seventeen-story high-rise right on the beach and just across the Intracoastal from the Coral Ridge Country Club.

I needed only one element to be in place to make this an opportunity worth pursuing further. I held my breath as I opened my trusty city directory, then exhaled with satisfaction and relief as I read her suite number: Penthouse J. The top floor.

~

Nothing works more in a thief's favor than people feeling secure. That's why places that are heavily alarmed and guarded can sometimes be the easiest targets. The single most important factor in security—more than locks, alarms, sensors or armed guards—is attitude. A building protected by nothing more than a cheap combination lock but inhabited by people who are alert and risk-aware is much safer than one with the world's most sophisticated alarm system whose tenants assume they're living in an impregnable fortress.

I came to understand that there's something about altitude that seems to give people a sense of security. I first noticed this when I managed apartment buildings that were over eight or nine stories high. It's not just a metaphor when people on the upper floors say they feel above it all. They really are, and when you think about it, the higher up you go, the fewer avenues of access there are connecting you to the rest of the world. It's not an altogether unreasonable view of things that, aside from a stairwell and an elevator, there's no way anybody can get to you, and I was to exploit that complacency many times.

I did a bunch of walkarounds at the Fountainhead over the next few weeks and decided it ranked high (no pun intended) on the altitude meter and low on the attitude. There was plenty of highly visible security, including cameras all over the place and twenty-four-hour doormen and guards. There was also an atmosphere of "What could possibly happen?" that was unmistakable in the offhand manner with which the tenants treated the guards, as though they were errand boys and hand servants instead of security professionals. It was kind of like the way airline passengers view flight attendants, as though their primary function is to serve martinis and peanuts instead of what the job really is, which is to save your life in an emergency.

Still, even the simple presence of all those doormen and guards would make getting into the place a challenge, especially at night, when foot traffic was light. On the beach side of the building there was a sheer wall about forty feet high, with a setback that formed the pool deck. (Beach buildup over the years has lowered it considerably since.) Not only would it make for a tough climb, but it was visible to the rear units of the building as well as to anyone wandering along the beach. It could probably be done, but I had to get inside the building for a detailed look around before I could determine exactly how.

I waited until an ad for a unit for sale appeared in the paper, then made an appointment with the real estate agent. Dressed in my Sunday best, I showed up and explained to her that I was looking to buy a retirement place for my parents, who were moving down from the Northeast. Impressed that I had enough money to be so casually generous, the agent latched on to me like an eager-to-please remora.

I tried to look unimpressed as she ticked down all the building amenities and services—the pool, the soundness of the construction, the quality of the other tenants. . . . Like too many salespeople with too little skill in their profession, she made a raft of assumptions about what I would think was important, and never thought to simply ask me.

She babbled on about the incredible views, which I could see for myself, and the great tile in the kitchen, which I could also see for myself—what is it about real estate people that seems to compel them to describe in glorious detail what you're already looking at?

I waited until I was sure she sensed that she was losing me. "Tell you the truth," I said, hoping to convey how little I cared about the "fabulous" bathroom and "utterly marvelous" walk-in closets, "my real concern is good security for my parents."

"Oh!" she nearly screamed in relief, and then started in. "It's the most sophisticated and up-to-date system! There's ultrasonic and infrared and—"

But I was shaking my head and trying to look grim. "Somehow doesn't seem as secure as some other places I've been looking at. They told me about all these really modern systems, the security people . . ."

And thus opened the floodgates. The agent, who was surprisingly well versed in such matters, told me exactly how many guards the building employed, how many were on each shift, even the procedures they followed, right down to how they checked individual floors according to a schedule in addition to random roving around the building. They used a time-clock system in which the guard on duty had to insert a key at various stations around the building to prove he'd done his rounds and to make a record of where he'd been. The agent described how all the surveillance cameras were tied into a central recording system, what kinds of sensors monitored the doors, and how vehicles and driveways were secured in the valet-staffed underground garage. We went on a tour, during which she pointed out virtually every camera in the place, including three on the pool deck. I was starting to wonder if I shouldn't cut her in for a piece of whatever I got on this score.

I noticed three windows covered with heavy wire mesh near the pool, low down on a wall. The agent said that was the boiler room. I didn't want to appear too interested, but I did manage to get a quick look. The windows were at the very top of a huge room that was two stories high.

I began nodding so that the agent would keep yammering as I checked out the poolside cameras. They were fixed in place, and there appeared to be a dead zone near the top of the sheer wall very close to the boiler room windows. It was tight, though, and the guard station wasn't all that far away. There was also a time-clock station by the pool, which meant the area was part of the scheduled patrols.

When we were back inside, I asked about the layout of the floors, and the agent pulled out detailed drawings showing me not only the unit for sale but all the other ones on the floor. I pointed to things so she would have to look down at the plan and wouldn't see my eyes studying the layout corresponding to the "J" line of apartments. I began nodding occasionally and asked a few questions realtors consider "buying signals": Would the seller take back a mortgage, how was the homeowners association organized, how many parking spaces were included?

I listened on autopilot as I thought about everything I'd learned, and maneuvered us back to the pool area because the rear wall presented a timing problem and I wanted one last look. I'd be able to use it only on a moonless night, and it would have to be fairly late so that there were no people on the beach, at least no sober ones. Things were going to depend heavily on what Ms. Bender's evening schedule was. I badly wanted to get a long look inside that boiler room, too, but there was no way to do that without arousing suspicion.

Luckily, Bender's unit faced the ocean. I spent a lot of time out on that beach over the next few weeks. Barb must have thought I'd gone romantic or something, what with all the moonlit walks we took together. Good thing she wasn't making a connection to the last time I'd taken a sudden interest in a particular location, the miniature golf course. I learned that Bender went out nearly every evening, left between six and seven and never came home before ten-thirty or eleven.

The next moonless night, I went for a walk by myself. This time I was carrying a grappling hook and a flashlight. I was also wearing a bathing suit and had a towel with me. If I were to get caught by a guard, I could just say I was going for a swim. To make it more realistic I was prepared to say I'd sneaked in to go swimming in this pool dozens of times late at night.

Throwing the hook over a wall that high wasn't easy; I missed with my first three tries but caught the ledge on the fourth. Soon I was up and over, and got my detailed look at the boiler room and the wire mesh covering the window.

I decided it could be done.

~

The next new moon came on a Friday night. I would have preferred it midweek, when Bender would be less likely to be wearing her best stuff, but there's no negotiating with nature.

I had all my tools and gear in a backpack, which would make the climbing less awkward than using a shoulder bag. This time I got the grapple to grab the pool-deck ledge on the first throw. Some might take that as a good sign, but I didn't take it as anything other than less noise I'd be making.

The climb was tougher with the weight of all that equipment hanging on my back, but I had been diligent about staying in shape. It wasn't any harder than going up the rope in my backyard with an eight-year-old hanging on to me, and I could use my legs against the wall to help. I kept it slow and careful so as not to make any noise. Soon I had both hands on the ledge and began pulling myself up the last yard. As my head cleared the ledge, I heard a scraping noise and came to a stop just as the door on the other side of the pool opened. I watched in shock as a guard came out of the building and onto the deck.

The first thing I did was nothing. A heavy dose of adrenaline had shot into my bloodstream and I fought back the primal urge to do something—anything—to protect myself. But the best thing was just to keep still, for which adrenaline, that instant boost of pure energy that evolution had conjured up for running away from lions and the like, was not only useless but potentially harmful.

I dropped back as slowly and carefully as possible, then hung there so only my fingers would be visible should the guard cast his eyes this way. I figured that his seeing my hands wasn't a risk I had to worry about, considering that a triple-pronged grappling hook was still straddling the ledge and ought to be plenty to get his attention on its own if he chose to look in this direction.

I heard him walking, and strained to make out the direction. He was heading right toward the wall. I looked down, craning my neck to see over my shoulder. What would happen if I just let go and dropped down? I rejected it instantly. Even onto soft sand, a forty-foot drop would probably result in a broken leg or two. No, if I decided to take off, I'd have to shinny down that rope. The guard wouldn't be able to easily dislodge the grappling hook with my weight on it, and I could probably make it down before he even figured out what was happening.

His steps didn't sound deliberate, nor did they sound hesitant, and I didn't get the feeling he'd found something amiss. He wasn't walking right toward me, either, but seemed to be heading for a spot further along the wall. His footsteps stopped, then came a rustling sound, then . . . a match being lit? The guy was lighting up a smoke.

I heard him exhale lazily. He was probably just staring out at the ocean. My arms were starting to ache a little, but I kept still. Aside from the waves breaking on the shore a hundred yards away, I couldn't hear a thing. For all I knew, the guard was staring right at the hook, right at my fingers. Maybe he'd figured it all out and was tiptoeing back to grab a chair to smash onto my hands. Maybe he was motioning at the camera to get another guard's attention.

A thin cloud of blue smoke passed over my head. My arms were really hurting now, and I wanted desperately to transfer over to the rope so I could wrap my legs around it and take a rest, but no matter how careful I was, one of the prongs would probably move and make noise. There was nothing below the top edge of the wall I could get a foot or elbow onto, either, so I just hung there, dangling by my fingertips four stories up in the air. I tried to shift the bulk of my weight from one hand to the other to give at least one arm at a time some relief, but it didn't do much good. I was better off keeping my weight equally divided.

Fuck me . . . how long could it take to smoke a goddamned cigarette! I tried to imagine how much remained, and prayed this guy wasn't a right-down-to-the-filter type. Who was to say he'd even leave once he'd finished it? What if he was a hard-core nicotine addict and lit another one? Then it occurred to me that maybe he wasn't my only worry. I'd been hanging here for at least three minutes, although it seemed more like half an hour. What if somebody on the beach had spotted me? What if I'd been spotted from one of the rear-facing units in the building itself? What if—?

A shooting star caught my eye and I turned my head to see it, watching as the sparks flew from a cigarette butt that was hurtling down toward the beach. Then a shuffling sound, the guard pushing away from the wall and turning around. Footsteps, the scrape of the door again, the sound of a latch clicking into place.

My muscles screaming in protest, I hauled myself up once more until I could get one hand across the ledge, then the other. My arms now parallel to the ground, I waited a few seconds for some blood to start flowing again, then swung a leg over and dropped onto the deck. I rolled toward the boiler room windows and lay there for about a minute. The pain of my arms coming back to life was worse than when they'd been above my head bearing my full weight with blood draining out of them. When I was finally able to move them around, I rubbed my shoulders to try to relieve some of the stiffness. It hurt like hell, but I forced myself to keep massaging my arms because I was in a dangerous position and needed to get going. I had no way to know if I'd been spotted. I wasn't about to abort the job on that kind of flimsy possibility, but I did need to get away from the area quickly.

Once I had enough range of motion back, I shrugged off the backpack and crawled back to the wall to pull up the rope. Using a heavy-duty cutter I'd brought, I clipped enough of the wire mesh covering the window to make a hole to crawl through. There was a narrow sill on the other side, wide enough for me to kneel on with my backpack next to me. Balancing on the sill in the pitch-black darkness, I tried not to think about the boiler room floor far below me—it was concrete, not sand—as I used some stiff wire to put the cut-up mesh back in place. It wasn't a neat job, but it was good enough so a casual observer wouldn't notice that anything was wrong. I tied the rope onto the part of the mesh I hadn't cut, put my pack back on, then lowered myself down to the floor. I kept my eyes closed; for some reason it's much easier to visualize things that way, even in a room so dark you can't see a thing anyway.

Once down on the floor, I gave myself a moment of inactivity just to recover a little. This was a safe time, because there were no visible signs that anybody had gotten into the building. And if I'd been spotted, I could probably hide somewhere in the boiler room for a while. One thing about South Florida and its elderly population: People were always thinking they were seeing thieves and murderers engaged in nefarious pursuits, and oftentimes the police were less than prompt in responding and less than zealous in checking things out when they did arrive.

I listened for any noises that might indicate the guards had been alerted to something—shouts, running, doors slamming, sirens—then got my breathing back to normal. By then my eyes had adapted enough for me to make out vague shapes in the room. I crossed over to the door and cracked it slightly, waited, then stepped out into the lower hallway and walked toward the stairwell. At the bottom there was a door leading outside to the beach. It was for emergency use only and was alarmed.

I began the seventeen-story climb to the top of the building, pausing below each landing to listen for sounds from the hallway. There was a time-clock station on every second floor. My guess was that there was one on each intervening floor as well, but somewhere else other than the stairwell. That way the guard would have to walk the halls to hit all the clocks, instead of just going up and down the staircase. That was good: The last thing I needed was to bump into some guard making his rounds, but if one should happen into the stairwell, the odds were that his next move would be up or down one flight and back into a hallway. I'd be able to get around his floor without being spotted.

I made it to the roof level without incident and jimmied open the door with a strip of celluloid. Once again, a cheap lock protected a door that everybody assumed didn't really need any protection in the first place.

The night air felt cool and sweet. Even the breaking waves sounded soothing, despite the fact that they would tend to drown out any slight sounds that might be useful to me. I looked around to find the lineup points—stacks, wires, antennas—that would orient me to where Elizabeth Bender's balcony was, then tied one end of the rope around a vent pipe and peered out over the edge.

It doesn't matter how many times you do this; looking straight down from nearly two hundred feet in the air is a knee-weakening experience. Looking back on it now, I still don't know how I managed to climb over the low protective ledge and onto the outer wall, with nothing but my hand and arm strength and a single strand of rope between me and an unpleasant death. I don't know how I managed to do a lot of the things I did, but I guess I was younger then. Sure as hell I was crazier.

This particular situation was somewhat less precarious than others. The way I was lined up, even if the rope broke or I slipped, there was a good chance I'd end up on the balcony that was sticking partway out from the side of the building just fifteen feet down rather than on the concrete at ground level, if I didn't get too far from the wall. It only took a couple of seconds to reach the balcony the safe way, though.

Sure enough, the sliding door was unlocked. I can't say I blamed Bender, or anybody else living that high up. In fact, locking a door like that might even look to some people like paranoia. Even if you stretched your imagination to consider someone trying to come in from the roof, there was still the assurance that nobody could get on the roof in the first place. The real estate agent had made that impossibility perfectly clear. I didn't care who called *me* paranoid, and did my standard check of the entire suite to make sure it was really empty.

As experienced at this as I was by now, I still couldn't shake that feeling of violating someone by snooping around in their private space. That feeling was a little bit stronger right now because this was a woman living alone, which heightened the sense of her vulnerability.

She had locked the front door and also set the alarm. Is there something at work in us that makes us assume that the bad guys think as we do (well, as you do, anyway, me being one of the bad guys)? *Surely if someone were to rob the place, they'd come in as respectable people would, through the door provided for the purpose.* Maybe that explains why people will have four heavy-duty locks on a solid oak door that's right next to a glass window.

When I was sure I was alone, I headed for the bedroom, always the first place I looked. There was a big jewelry box right out in plain sight. You could almost see a sign on the side of it: "As long as you made it this far, help yourself." (Here's a little tip: Put a few minor trinkets in the bedroom jewelry box, and the really good stuff in the laundry room or the garage.) I flipped open the top of the box and gasped aloud at what was inside.

Elizabeth Bender apparently liked heart-shaped diamonds, and she had some extraordinary examples. Earrings, necklaces, bracelets and a ring with a ten-carat stone that I was sure was flawless. It was absolutely gorgeous, first-rate stuff. The lady had seriously good taste.

I didn't waste much time admiring the goods, but scooped them into a bag, closed the top of the box (it might delay the discovery of a theft only by five minutes, but if I needed four minutes somewhere along the line, it could make all the difference) and got the hell out. The front door was alarmed, so it was back out onto the balcony, up the rope and onto the roof. I put my ear to the door and didn't hear anything, so I entered the stairwell and had gotten down only one floor when I heard a door open somewhere below me. I froze, then heard the sound of a key being inserted into a time clock. These were special keys, attached by a chain to a box the guard carried around with him. Thankfully, they made a lot of noise. I figured he was about five floors below me.

When I heard his descending footsteps, I knew the guard would drop down one flight and then head back into the hallway to hit the next box elsewhere on that floor. I figured that I could get almost to the bottom level by the time he came back into this stairwell, the way he seemed to be shuffling around.

I counted his agonizingly slow steps, knew just when he'd hit the next landing, and got ready to go. But instead of hearing a door opening, I heard the sound of more descending steps. What the hell was this?

It took forever for the slow-moving guard to get down to the next landing. I heard the chain on his key rattling, then the time clock being punched. *Please go into the hallway!* I begged him in my mind. But no dice. One painfully slow step at a time, he started down the stairs again. It looked like I'd guessed the time-clock configuration all wrong, and there was one every two levels in this stairwell only. It didn't make a lick of sense—the guard would be able to check in at every station without even once setting foot in a residential hallway—but that's the hand I was dealt.

Still, I couldn't assume anything about what this guy would do. He'd entered the stairwell on about the twelfth or thirteenth floor, not the seventeenth, so I had no idea what his standard procedure was. He was humming to himself now, in that style peculiar to very bored people: tuneless, nonspecific, limited in range and annoying as hell. I was starting to get the impression that this guy was maybe ninety years old. What in the world did anybody expect him to do if he actually came across a bad guy? Of course, he wasn't expected to do anything; the simple fact of his presence was supposed to serve as a deterrent.

I began making my way down as quietly as I could, figuring to stay at least three floors above him as he continued down. His hearing probably wasn't the best, but I didn't want to take any chances. I'd be patient and soon be back on the boiler room level.

Which sounded good on paper, but at the rate we were going, I thought I'd be out of there sometime around Christmas. I started to worry that Bender might come home, discover that she'd been robbed and sound the alarm. If the guards had any brains or experience at all, the first thing they would do was block all the exits, and then I'd be good and fucked. I briefly considered just walking down past the guard, like I belonged there, but it was way too risky. And if he put up a fuss . . . well, it didn't matter how old and helpless he was, it wasn't my style to get physical. So I looked at my watch, confirmed that there was still some time before Bender got home, and forced myself to be patient as we continued the slow descent.

By the time I got to the boiler room level, I was practically exploding from the tension that had been building up in me. Every time I'd heard a door close in a distant hallway, I was sure somebody was about to enter the stairwell overhead and trap me. I'd have to go into a hallway and there would be no place to hide until the stairwell cleared, and no other way out I could depend on.

But there we were, this old geek so slow he was still shuffling his way down the hall past the boiler room when I got there. I didn't know where he was headed after that. Maybe it was the end of the line and he was going to turn around. What if he decided to walk all the way the hell back up the stairs? No way was I going to do that right along with him.

The stairway to the beach level was practically at my elbow. The door at the bottom was alarmed, but I said "Fuck it" right out loud, flew down the stairs and slammed my elbow into the latch bar on the door. The sound of that incredibly loud bell going off right near my ear rattled my head, but I hit the ground running and headed straight for the dark beach, turning only when my feet were practically in the water, trying to look like a jogger as I sprinted away.

It was one of the biggest hauls I'd ever taken, in one of the smallest packages. Because of the Fountainhead's prestige in the area, Bender's reputation and the value of the stolen goods, the theft got a lot of press. As usual, reporters referred to multiple perpetrators, and the guards, doubtless facing questions about how this could have happened, started in with the typical backpedaling about phantoms and human flies. There was even speculation about whether Bender had robbed herself, for the insurance money, but I'd inadvertently saved her from that ordeal: Ghosts and goblins aside, *somebody* for sure tripped the alarm on that door leading to the beach.

Of course, one eyewitness swore to the police he'd seen the door fly open but never saw anybody come out. At least not anything human.

You gotta love it.

7

Heat

Pompano Beach, Florida. Christmas. A straightforward, no-nonsense score, at least if you don't count the drop down to the fifteenth-floor balcony from the roof of the high-rent apartment building. Pretty good haul, too, with one major surprise: a ring sporting a truly huge marquise-cut diamond. It's so brilliant, I'm worried it's shining right through my jacket.

Still wearing gloves, I pull the apartment door closed behind me and head down the corridor. Nobody around, no need to fake like I belong there, so I walk faster than I usually would but well short of a run.

"Halt!"

I'm certain my heart actually stopped beating for a few seconds. Raw adrenaline erupts in my chest, and the rush is so powerful I feel weightless. My reaction to the shouted order is instantaneous: I break into a run, the door at the end of the hall suddenly ten miles away.

Nothing happens, no more shouts. Just as I'm about to connect with the door and twist sideways to push a shoulder into it, a tremendous explosion threatens to rupture my eardrums. Sounds like a bomb, but I realize it's a gunshot amplified by the close confines of the hallway. It comes to me at the same time that something traces a line across my stomach. It feels hot, but not really painful, and I envision the bullet that must have just barely touched my skin as it streaked by. If I hadn't twisted away at the last moment . . . ?

I crash into the door and keep going, flying across the top of the staircase and downward before my feet finally find a step and I can grab the banister. I take the stairs four and five at a time, swinging wildly around the landings, expecting another shot any second.

Nothing happens. By the time I hit the bottom floor I'm dizzy from spinning down all those flights, but I've made it to the door leading outside and I'm not being followed. I try to remember: Are there windows in the stairwell? Is the shooter up there standing at one of them, just waiting for me to emerge so he can pick me off?

But he's fifteen stories above me and surely armed with a handgun rather than a rifle. Nobody can hit a moving, weaving target from that distance with a handgun, right? Especially not at night.

There's not much of a decision to be made. Sure as hell I'm not staying inside to be trapped like an animal, and I'm not going to start a search for another exit, either. Besides, how fast could the guy have made the decision to get to a window rather than chase me, and then actually gotten himself positioned there?

I don't even slow down but throw the door open and start running, fighting the temptation to go as fast as I can in a straight line, taking the time to move from side to side, wincing in terrified expectation of another shot, or a whole volley of them, because the more shots he fires, the better his odds of hitting me.

Still nothing. No sounds from behind. I'm sweating so hard, my entire middle feels soaked, but finally I'm around another building and out of the guy's sight. My next worry is how many people that shot must have woken, and that's when I thank whatever deity might be watching over me that I brought a bicycle and not a car.

I no longer give a shit who sees me. No way they can identify me in the dark, at a distance, and there won't be any license plate number to jot down, either. I've never wanted to be someplace else so badly in my life.

The bike is leaning against a telephone pole. It looks locked but isn't, the hasp not fully snapped into place. I yank the chain away, grab the handlebars and push the bike forward, jump on while it's moving and start pedaling furiously. I'm spinning like crazy but don't want to pause even for the short time it would take to shift to a higher gear. I just want to pedal as hard as I possibly can and put some real distance between me and that building.

It's at least a mile before I finally slow down to catch my breath. I can't believe how much I'm sweating. I can feel it dripping down my belly. I can also feel the bullet's path across my stomach and wonder what that's going to look like, and how the hell I'm going to explain it to Barbara. It isn't painful, exactly, just kind of warm and strange.

Then I run out of adrenaline and my legs and arms suddenly turn to jelly. I barely make it off the bike without falling over, I'm so weak and un-coordinated.

I sit down on the sidewalk and pretend to tie my shoes as I wait for control over my limbs to return, my fingers fumbling uselessly at the laces. Some minutes pass and then I struggle clumsily to my feet, walk the bike for about a block, then get on and slowly pedal for home. I stop to stash the goods in Chuck and Jean's garage across the street. He's the re-tired New York City cop I told you about earlier; they're away for the hol-idays and I'm keeping an eye on the house for them. I don't want to turn the overhead light on, so I hide the stuff as best I can in the dark.

I head for my garage and it's not until I'm inside and turn on the light that I realize I haven't been sweating. My shirt and pants are full of blood. As I stand there, staring down in disbelief, it's running onto the floor and slowly pooling at my feet.

~

Later in the bathroom, after loading my clothes into a plastic bag and finding the spent bullet in my jacket lining, I mopped up the garage floor and took stock. There was a clean round hole just below my lowest left rib and a more jagged one on my right side, and things were starting to hurt. I realized I hadn't been quite as fortunate as I'd first thought, but I was still damned lucky. The round had passed clean through without hitting anything vital. I'd seen plenty of old Westerns, so I knew I'd be okay.

The bleeding had slowed considerably and I set about cleaning up the wounds, trying desperately to stop myself from crying out as I dabbed at the holes with antiseptic. The pain was getting real bad, real fast, and I re-alized trying to do this myself wasn't going to work. Reluctantly, I woke up Barbara.

"What's the matter?" she murmured groggily.

"Don't worry, I'm okay," I said quickly, which was when she realized I probably wasn't and came fully awake. "I had a little accident."

"What kind of accident?" She was already peeling back the covers and sitting up.

"I got shot."

She knew better than to waste time asking questions. She was scared half to death but kept a tight grip on herself as she finished cleaning up the wounds and put on bandages, tightly in case more bleeding was on the way. I threw down a couple of shots of vodka and got into bed, trying to sleep even while Barbara quivered in anxiety beside me. But it hurt too bad to lie down, and the only way I could get a little relief was to sit upright in a chair.

Barb called her brother Augie, who had recently moved to Florida and lived nearby, and he came to the house right away. The unusual sounds in the middle of the night woke Suzi and Laura up, and they came padding down the hall just as Augie walked in. Barb intercepted them before they could reach our bedroom and told them that Daddy had a little bellyache.

"Why is Uncle Augie here for just a bellyache?" Laura wanted to know. You could never get anything past that kid.

"In case we need something from the drugstore," Barb answered.

"How come he didn't get it on his way over?" Suzi chimed in.

Barb hustled them back to bed and then came back to the bedroom. There was really nothing for Augie to do at the moment, but he understood why Barb would want him to be there, and he eventually fell asleep at the foot of the bed. Barb stayed up with me for the rest of the night, both of us hoping that my misery would subside after a few hours.

It only got worse. As the sun came up, I was in terrible pain and couldn't begin to think about going to work or even eating. Mark knocked on the bedroom door, wanting to know what was going on. He'd slept through the previous night's commotion.

"You answer him," Barb said, a wise piece of advice.

"Bellyache," I replied, as lightly as I could. "Something I ate." The pain of calling out like that was so bad, I almost passed out.

Barb and Augie went to the kitchen to make breakfast for the kids, who knew from the way their mother and uncle were behaving that it was more than an upset stomach.

After going across the street to see if any blood had gotten onto Chuck and Jean's garage floor, Augie went to get me some antibiotics, but they didn't make any difference I could notice. I stayed in the bedroom all day so the kids couldn't see me, then took something strong that night that forced me into a fitful sleep. I awoke about four A.M. in agony I never would have believed possible. It felt like someone was waving a blowtorch around inside my gut. I started thrashing and left the bedroom in order not to awaken Barbara, and found myself alone with feverish thoughts whirling around in my head.

Had the crime been reported? The apartment's occupants had been out of town, although I didn't know exactly how long they'd be gone. Had the shooter, who was probably a security guard, seen which unit I'd come out of? Did he even know a burglary had been committed? Maybe not! Except who the hell would shoot some guy who was just walking around, even if he didn't live there? So he must have seen me coming out of the apartment, must have concluded I'd robbed it, and therefore must have reported it.

Wait a minute. How could he tell if anything had been taken if it wasn't his place? Well, even if he didn't know for sure there had been a robbery, he knew for damned sure he'd fired that shot at somebody, and he probably traced my steps and saw blood. So he must have alerted the authorities to be on the lookout for someone seeking medical attention for a gunshot wound. Damn!

Wait again. Maybe he didn't know how bad it had been. Hell, even I hadn't known until later. Except he'd seen the blood, probably a lot of it, so he knew he'd hit me good. Or had my clothes soaked it up so thoroughly at first that none had dripped off? On the other hand, wasn't it illegal to shoot at a fleeing suspect? Did that apply to civilians protecting their own property? Except it probably wasn't his. Would he therefore keep quiet about the whole thing to protect himself?

Was I even thinking about all of this coherently?

Limp with fatigue after hours of struggling against the awful pain, I came back to bed but was writhing uncontrollably within minutes. The light snapped on and Barbara sat up, pulling the covers off me before I had a chance to snatch them back.

"Jesus Christ!" she cried after one look.

My belly had swollen up so much, I looked six months pregnant. The bandages were soaked with blood and some had seeped onto the bedsheets. Barbara's eyes were huge and horror-stricken as her hand flew to her mouth. She was paralyzed with fright, and tears began to run down her face. I rolled over and tried to stand up, but it was absurd even to try, and I fell back onto the bed.

Barbara unfroze and reached for the phone on her nightstand.

"What're you doing?" I croaked with no small effort.

"Calling an ambulance," she replied as she picked up the receiver.

"No!" Despite the pain, I stretched across her and pressed the receiver back onto the cradle. "Are you crazy?"

"Are you?" she shot back.

I couldn't let her call for an ambulance. This wasn't a cut from slicing bagels, it was a gunshot wound, and you don't get gunshot wounds fixed up without people asking a lot of questions. Doctors have a legal obligation to report such cases immediately.

A lot of people in dangerous criminal occupations—bank robbers, Mob buttons and the like—have lines into crooked doctors who get paid enormous sums of money to treat injuries suffered in the commission of crimes. I'd never inquired into those sources because there was no way to do so without giving an awful lot away, and that would have violated my self-protection strategy. Besides, it never really occurred to me that I might get hurt on a score, except for maybe falling or cutting myself, injuries that could easily be explained and passed off as routine. I wasn't a violent criminal, I didn't carry a weapon and I never did a job when people were present, at least not on purpose. There was always the possibility of getting caught, of course, and it would be my intention to do everything possible to get away, but I'd never envisioned hurting anyone to do it.

Now I was in a serious fix. I could no longer pretend this was a flesh wound that would pass, given time. My gut was badly infected and seemed to be getting worse by the second. The pain was unbelievable, and no amount of alcohol or home therapy was going to help me deal with it.

Barbara wisely stayed quiet and let me come to the inevitable conclusion rather than provoke me into a useless debate. It was fairly self-evident: If I didn't get some help, I was going to die.

On the other hand, if I went to the hospital, I was definitely going to jail.

"What's it going to be?" Barbara finally demanded.

"Help me up," I said, taking a deep breath. "I'm going to Cleveland."

⌣

It wasn't some damned fool notion of going home to die. Uncle Rudy's son, who was not just my cousin but a good friend as well, was a surgeon in a prestigious hospital in Cleveland. He was also part-owner of some of the buildings I managed. Barbara called him and told him what was going on, as vaguely as possible but enough for him to know it was a genuine emergency. They made some arrangements, then she pulled two suitcases out of a closet and brought them into the bedroom.

I shook my head at the larger one. "I'm going alone," I told her.

She didn't take me seriously, probably thinking it was some kind of obligatory protest I didn't mean. She hoisted the suitcases onto the bed and flipped them open. "You can't go," I said, and this time she stopped moving and asked me again if I was crazy.

Maybe, but I knew what I was doing. "Christmas," I said, trying to minimize my words because it was too painful to talk. "The kids . . . we can't both be gone."

"You can't go alone," she replied, waving a hand at me as though taking in the totality of my condition. "You can barely stand up. You won't make it."

But I knew I'd won that argument before it had barely begun. The kids still didn't know the truth about what had happened, and it was important that we not alarm them any more than they already were. In a family as tight as ours, for even one of us not to be home with them over Christmas was unheard of. For both of us to be gone was unthinkable.

"We can take the kids with us," Barb said, but it was perfunctory and halfhearted and the decision had already been made.

Barb tried telling the kids that it was just another business trip to Cleveland, but that didn't fool them for a second. I always knew in advance when those trips were coming up and made a lot of extra fuss over the kids for a day or two before I left. This time I hadn't even said goodbye. Barb finally told them I was very sick with a stomach ailment and wanted to go to a doctor I trusted back home. Laura was only five and might not have understood the specifics, but she understood her mother's voice and sensed the fear in it. Suzi and Mark, despite their own anxiety, did their best to console her, but at thirteen and eleven years of age, they still had a few days of school before the holiday break, which left Laura at home with Augie while Barb took me to the airport. His somber mood and the muffled phone calls all day long would only contribute to our youngest daughter's growing unease.

Barb had booked me on a midmorning flight. It was one of the worst days of my life. The pain was utterly unbearable, but I had to put on a good front so as not to arouse any suspicion or prompt some well-intentioned airline employee into offering too much assistance. Barb had packed a small carry-on for me, with the lightest stuff she could find, but I would have been better off traveling with nothing. Just lifting it off the ground was torture, and getting it into an overhead bin was out of the question. Rather than ask for assistance, I kicked it under my seat.

As the plane rose, the pain got even worse, which I wouldn't have thought possible. I didn't know it at the time, but it was because the lessening cabin pressure caused the trapped gases from the infection to expand, swelling me up even more. The slightest bit of turbulence that other passengers barely noticed—even someone in the same row shifting around and jostling the seats—was like a spear jabbed into my inflamed belly, and when the plane dropped heavily onto the tarmac at Cleveland's Hopkins International, I felt myself starting to faint.

My cousin Dan Renner was waiting at the gate. When he spotted me, he broke into a smile and raised his hand, but in a few short seconds the smile disappeared and his hand came down slowly, as though he'd forgotten about it. From the way *he* looked, I could only imagine how *I* must have looked.

Dan had left his car at the curb, which you could still do in those days, and if your car sported M.D. plates, you could let it sit there as long as you wanted. Once we were in it, instead of immediately driving off, he twisted to the side and reached for my shirt. His fingertips merely grazing the fabric caused a stab of pain to shoot through me, and I pushed his hand away. He waited while I unbuttoned the shirt myself, then he took a look.

"Holy fuck," he muttered, which is not something you want to hear from a physician who's seen it all and isn't supposed to get fazed by anything anymore. Then he said, "Don't move," and got out of the car. I watched him go to a pay phone, dial a number, wait a few seconds, then begin talking and gesturing with his hands. He looked at his watch a few times during the conversation, then hung up and came back to the car. I asked him what that was all about.

"Getting an O.R. set up," he answered.

Surgery? "How bad is it?"

He didn't answer right away, probably thinking about how to put it into layman's terms. "You're ripped to shreds inside," he finally answered, and let it go at that.

So much for old Westerns and bullets passing clean through. "It's a gunshot wound," I said, worried about his reputation and professional standing. "You're going to have to report it."

He shook his head, then pointed to the places on my shirt that sat over the two holes on either side of my rib cage. "Damnedest speargun accident I've ever seen."

Less than an hour later I was on the table.

At some point while I was under in the O.R., something extraordinary happened to me. I dreamed that I was in a long tunnel heading toward a blinding white light. I felt more at peace than I ever had in my life, perfectly at ease, perfectly content. I was drawn by that light but in no particular hurry to reach it. Then, without warning, the light began to dim and I felt my tranquility waver. The light kept dropping in intensity, the tunnel began to dissolve, and that was all I could remember.

I told Barbara about it by phone that night from the ICU, and she passed it off as a nice anesthesia-induced dream after two days of nonstop suffering.

Once I was safely out of the woods, Dan revealed something to me about how the surgery had gone. "You were clinically dead for a few seconds," he said. "We couldn't get a heartbeat. Gave us a helluva scare." It wasn't until years later that I put those two things together and realized I'd had an absolutely classic near-death experience.

In forty-eight hours I was out of the ICU but stayed in the hospital for another eight days, missing both Christmas and New Year's with my wife and kids. My good buddy Bill Welling and his wife went to our house to help out. I had a lot of time to think, and one of the things that struck me was that all of a sudden my little hobby wasn't quite so much fun anymore. With all the good luck I'd had, it had only taken one tiny turn of events, a two-second accident of timing, for me to get smacked across the face with the reality of what kind of danger I'd been subjecting myself to.

I also couldn't help thinking about what it was doing to Barbara. The look on her face when I told her I'd been shot was one I never wanted to see again, but I'd seen it two days later when she peeled back the covers from my devastated midsection, and I imagined it yet again when Dan ran down the details for her by phone. As to the confused and panicked faces of my kids, not even the intense physical pain was enough to force those images out of my mind.

After ten days of wallowing in such troubling introspection I was crazed to get out of the hospital even though I still didn't feel so hot, and reported to Dan that I felt great. The next day he released me with a stack of post-op care instructions and enough medicine to ensure I wouldn't have to get any prescriptions filled in Florida.

Barbara didn't say much when I got home. I'd lost twenty pounds in ten days, but she'd been worried to death about whether she'd ever see me alive again and seemed as drawn and spent as I was, and I could only imagine what was going through her mind. At least we didn't have to worry about my business; Augie had jumped in and was handling things for me.

She didn't crash down on me over the next few days, either, but I developed pleurisy and my gut got as bad as it had been two weeks before.

When I insisted on flying back to Cleveland alone, she didn't bother to argue but just began packing two bags. It was hard to read the expression on her face. Even if I survived, how long would it be before something else happened and she had to go through it all again, and how many times would there be before finally she lost me altogether?

I never did find out who shot me. Chuck the cop and his wife passed away many years later without ever having learned that stolen, blood-stained loot had once been stashed in their garage.

All in all, a horrendous experience. Needless to say, I got over it and didn't learn a damned thing.

8

Prospecting

THAT'S WHAT professional salespeople call it. "Prospecting" is what you do to locate potential customers. Unless you work at a retail store with a lot of foot traffic, if you depend upon customers for your living, you have to work to identify who might be likely to buy something from you before you can begin selling to them. If you hawk aluminum siding, maybe you drive around a neighborhood looking for weather-beaten walls, or if you're a caterer, you keep your eye on engagement announcements in the local papers.

Another important part of the standard sales cycle is called "qualifying" the prospect, making sure the potential customer is worth selling to. If you're pushing Cadillacs and the guy you just lured in asks you to cash his unemployment check, you're probably wasting your time.

In my case it was a little different. I wasn't looking for customers but for people I could steal from. This was a surprisingly difficult part of the job. There were a lot of well-off people in South Florida, but just because somebody looks rich doesn't mean he's a good prospect. A lot of nouveaux riches wear everything they own at one time, giving the impression there's more stuff at home, but it's like the guy who wraps a hundred-dollar bill around a roll of ones: All glitter and no gold. That's okay if you're the type who likes to stick people up face-to-face, but that wasn't me. I didn't use weapons and I never thought a handful of jewels was worth somebody getting hurt, including me.

Most high-end thieves are well known in criminal circles and get bombarded with all kinds of leads. The better leads are those specific to a thief's specialty. Somebody who is an expert in lifting valuable paintings might get a tip that a collector is in the process of moving, meaning his collection might be vulnerable for a few days. Somebody who specializes in the theft of high-tech secrets might hear from somebody inside a company who knows the security systems inside and out. Same goes for armored-car robbers and truck hijackers. However it comes about, the tipster expects to get something out of a successful score, usually some kind of commission as a cut of the net proceeds. The amount will depend on how specific and reliable the information is. The thief's problem is to separate the good tips from the ones that are junk, or the ones that are stings, meaning that the police planted a false tip to try to trap the thief in the act.

Some of the best sources of leads are fences. A fence is someone who specializes in turning stolen property into cash. Some things are harder to fence than others, and the size of the cut the fence takes on the deal is related to the difficulty and risk of laying off the loot. As an example, gold is fairly easy to convert because it can be melted down, completely concealing its source, and sold off in chunks through legitimate precious-metal dealers. Illicit drugs in bulk are also pretty easy, because dealers are always ready to pay top dollar in cash with no questions asked.

Fine art, on the other hand, is extremely difficult to get rid of. It's easily identifiable and therefore has to be either ransomed back to the original owners or sold to private collectors who have no intention of ever displaying the pieces in public. The middleman's take on these kinds of deals is tremendous, because his job in turning the art objects into cash is almost as difficult and risky as the thief's was in stealing it.

The point here is that fences have a vested interest in keeping their supply lines flowing and therefore are motivated to provide thieves not only with lots of leads but with well-qualified ones. After all, they don't want their best sources wasting time on small scores, and they sure as hell don't want them getting busted and put out of commission. That cuts off a revenue stream *and* presents a significant danger should the thief decide to give up the fence in exchange for a lighter sentence.

This doesn't mean that fences are always reliable, nor are they necessarily tuned in to the specific eccentricities of the people they're dealing with. Blute Tomba, my primary fence in Cleveland, knew how I felt about meticulous planning and avoiding violence but once tried to talk me into ripping off a New York jewelry salesman who called on him about once a month. In addition to the fact that Tomba didn't have much information we could use in planning the job, it would have involved a weapon, so I refused, although I continued to do a lot of business with him.

Many of the traditional sources of leads were closed to me. For starters, I was a loner, with a strict policy of never taking on partners. That's how I managed to stay out of trouble for so many years. As a result, few people on the street had any idea I even existed, so nobody ever came to me with a great "nick." That may have made prospecting a little tougher, but on the other hand, I wasn't walking into any setups, nor was I likely to find that someone else had done the job while I was still planning it because he'd gotten the same tip from the same source. And I didn't have to share a cut of the proceeds with anybody except the fence.

It wasn't my style to wake up one day and decide I had to pull off a job. I was in good enough shape financially, between stealing and my legitimate real estate businesses, that I never had a material need to commit a robbery. It was more of an opportunistic thing, keeping my eyes and ears open during active but relaxed canvassing.

I read all the society pages carefully, studying who was who in town, what was going on and what was coming up. I also frequented a lot of society functions. I "cleaned up nice" as recruiters liked to say about promising job applicants. In a business suit or formal evening wear, and without my wedding ring, I was usually able to waltz right into a large private party or gala event. It got to the point where my presence was not only tolerated but expected, and mine became a familiar face among a large segment of South Florida's social elite.

I grew attuned to these people and, when presented with a new face, was able to ascertain fairly quickly what I was dealing with. Separating the upwardly mobile wannabes from the seriously moneyed was a matter of observing not only how people handled themselves but how other people behaved in their presence. When somebody new showed up draped in what appeared to be diamonds and emeralds, I wouldn't assume anything until I saw them at a number of subsequent soirées. Of the ones who reappeared, I tried to note whether they wore the same or different baubles. Did they mingle with the same people; did people who'd snubbed them earlier now show more deference; where were they seated and how did that change over time? What I was trying to determine was whether they were worth the tremendous amount of investigation and planning it would take to relieve them of some of their more burdensome possessions.

Prospecting and qualifying. All part of the job and not much different from that Cadillac salesman. Sort of.

~

> ### "Ghost Thieves" Rob Sleeping Woman of Millions in Jewels
>
> ---
>
> **Astonished police rule out inside job, say victim had no reason to set up "impossible" robbery**
>
> ---
>
> "I never even knew someone was there until I woke up and found everything gone," says badly shaken victim

Truth is usually a whole lot less strange than fiction. I almost hate giving away what really happened because of how it's going to disappoint all those people who thought it had been done by Martians or something.

After we moved to Florida, I visited Cleveland roughly once a month. I would spend a day or two working on my properties and also meet with the Cleveland Management Company, whose properties I handled in Miami. If I'd had any successful scores, I would also bring along some goods to sell to Tomba.

My visits were purposely irregular. I never told anyone but my family when I was going, and I didn't make appointments to meet Tomba until I was already in Cleveland. I also didn't carry a lot of stuff with me, but would spread it out over several visits. All of this was to minimize the possibility of getting set up or ripped off by some cop or crook who would have the gall to rob me of stuff I robbed from somebody else.

A secondary reason for fencing loot in small quantities was to get a better price, but there was an attendant risk in breaking stuff up this way. It meant that I was carrying stolen property almost every time I went to Cleveland. I liked to maintain as much distance as possible between me and my ill-gotten gains—like keeping stuff in work lockers, never at home—so traveling around with it was pretty nerve-racking. I liked to check the stuff through rather than carry it on my person. That way, if I saw that there were a lot of cops hovering around baggage claim, I could always walk away and leave it.

One time I landed in Cleveland and found myself the last person standing at baggage claim after all the bags had been picked up. I made my way to the lost-luggage counter and met up with a steely-eyed woman of considerable bulk who looked at me the way I imagined a rattlesnake looked at a rabbit. Can't say I blamed her much. How would you like to work in a job in which every single person you dealt with was pissed off and hostile and had nobody to take it out on except you?

She stared at me without saying anything, so I took the initiative. "My bag didn't show up."

No shit, said her world-weary eyes as she slapped a form and a pen down on the counter. After I filled it out, she took it without a word and got on the phone.

"It's in Pittsburgh," she said upon hanging up.

I waited. She waited.

"So what happens now?" I finally said.

"Until the plane gets here, nothing!" Like she'd rehearsed the script and had been itching to pounce on me.

I hated being at the mercy of people who had me by the balls, but I held any smart remarks in check. "When will that be?"

She consulted a piece of paper and said, "Four-thirty." Two hours from now.

"Is that certain?"

"I said it'll be here." Pure ice. She picked up the form again. "Is this your correct address?"

"Oh, you didn't say you wanted my *correct* address." My charming little attempt to soften her up.

It failed miserably. "If this is your correct address, we'll deliver it when it arrives."

"I'd rather wait for it," I informed her.

"We can deliver it."

"I can wait."

"Suit yourself." She turned away, through with me. "But if it doesn't show . . ."

"I thought you said it'll be here." Dumb move! Backing one of these spitting cobras against the wall almost guaranteed a full frontal assault in exchange. As she started to get her hackles up, I raised my hands in helpless surrender and backed out of her space.

Two anxious hours later the flight from Pittsburgh arrived, but my bag didn't appear on the carousel and nobody came by to give me any information about it. There was no way I was going back to confront the baggage monster, so I started wandering around and eventually found it sitting alone in a corridor. I picked it up and walked out, unchallenged, just as anybody else could have done.

I'd usually go straight from the airport to my mother's apartment and call Tomba right away. Within fifteen minutes I'd be in my mother's car on my way to either his store or his house. This hello-gotta-run greeting kind of threw Mom the first few times, but she got used to it.

Richard Tomba was one of the few good things—actually the only good thing—to have arisen out of my thirty-day incarceration in the Cuyahoga County shit hole some twelve years prior. I was very quiet and had determined to mind my own business, but I quickly found out that things inside aren't the same as they are outside. Inside, there's no place to go to be by yourself, so you'd damned well better form the right associations, or things could get ugly in a hurry.

One of the other prisoners was a guy named Vinny "Big Head" Garamendi. I never asked him why he was in jail, because I was afraid he might tell me. Big Head took a liking to me and was always chatting me up on the exercise range. He would laugh and tell me how I should be a gigolo and not a crook, as though there was some kind of difference. As my brief stay drew to a close, he told me about the bar he hung out at on 105th and Euclid, and said I should come look him up after he got out. A few months later I did; Richard Tomba happened to be there that night and Big Head introduced us.

"Blute" Tomba and I struck up a conversation and I learned he owned what was then one of the biggest and most prestigious jewelry stores in Cleveland. (Speaking of "biggest," I should also mention that Tomba was called "Blute" because he weighed about four hundred pounds and looked like Bluto in the *Popeye* cartoons.) It wasn't too big a leap, based on his presence in this spooky bar and the friends he seemed to have, that Blute was into more than advising young couples on engagement rings. When he told me he did a large business in "family jewelry brought over from the old country by immigrants"—in other words, completely untraceable stuff—it was pretty obvious that he was a fence. At the time, I found it irrelevant yet fascinating, but Blute and I became friends and stayed in touch, and later I found him extremely useful.

It was also a good lesson in the utter uselessness of surface appearances. After Blute, I was never again shocked by the corruption that lurked in the dark waters just below glittering respectability.

～

By this time I'd known Blute for years, but I still checked around carefully whenever I went to his house or store, looking for signs of a setup. Once you're a crook, you tend to think like a crook all the time, and it becomes more and more difficult to trust anybody completely. Like a stage actor who gets butterflies night after night, no matter how many times I'd visited with Blute to fence stolen goods, I never got used to it. Because of that, as well as the danger of being in possession of illicit jewels, I liked to get it out of the way as soon as possible.

Blute and I would retire to the back room of his respectable jewelry store and go through the stuff I'd brought him. A precious metal like gold went quickly, because that was based strictly on weight and purity and what the market conditions were on the street. Gems, however, were a different story. We'd spend two or three hours weighing stones and examining them carefully. We each had our own jeweler's loupes, handheld magnifying glasses with high-quality optics. Blute would peer at a stone, then hand it to me with a detailed rundown of why it was junk.

"Loaded with inclusions," he'd say of a diamond.

"Barely noticeable," I'd come back, "and the clarity is outstanding."

He'd shake his head. "Yeah, maybe, but there's this yellowish tinge . . . ?"

Blute was a certified gemologist, a credential I chose to forgo myself rather than someday have to explain why someone in real estate would have undertaken the training to evaluate gems. Nevertheless, I'd studied intensely on my own and was as good at it as he was, and he knew it.

My specialty was diamonds. The king of all jewels, and the most expensive despite their rarity being almost wholly artificial—De Beers SA tightly controls how many come onto the market each year in order to keep prices high—diamonds are evaluated according to the four C's. "Carat" is the most objective quality factor, and refers to the diamond's weight. It's a very old term derived from "carob," a seed that doesn't vary much in weight and was used as a unit of weight going all the way back to ancient Greece. It takes about 142 carats to make an ounce. Because larger diamonds are more rare than smaller ones, the value per carat is much higher in a larger stone, so a two-carat diamond is worth much more than two one-carat diamonds of identical quality. ("Carat" shouldn't be confused with "karat," another jeweler's term that refers to the purity of gold.)

The second C is "clarity." Most diamonds have internal flaws, called inclusions, usually caused by traces of minerals. Clarity is graded based on the number, size and type of inclusions. A "flawless" diamond, one that has no internal or external faults, is very rare and very valuable. These days a one-carat ideal-cut stone with inclusions barely visible to the naked eye might be worth just under five thousand dollars, whereas a flawless diamond of the same size and cut could go for over seven thousand dollars.

Speaking of "cut," that's the third *C* and refers to how the final stone was shaped from the chunk that was originally mined. A diamond in the ground isn't very impressive to look at, and the final gem-quality stone must be liberated from within. Extreme care needs to be paid to the roundness, depth and width, as well as to the uniformity of the "facets," the flat planes that form the diamond's surface. A classically cut diamond is roughly the shape of a child's spinning top, except that all the edges are straight rather than round. Light entering the diamond bounces around inside and then reemerges through the top. If the diamond is cut too squat, light will leak out the sides and the stone will lose brilliance. If it's too deep, light will escape out the bottom and the appearance to your eye will be dull.

But if it's cut just right, with all the facets at exactly the correct angles to one another, most of the light that enters the diamond will come shooting out the top surface, and the stone will look almost as if the inside was generating its own fire. The classic cut is called "ideal," but there are also a lot of "fancy" cuts, such as the oval, emerald, radiant, marquise and pear.

The fourth *C* is "color." A diamond reflects light in much the same way as one of those triangular prisms you might have toyed around with in science class, except that it's much more complicated. Internal reflection breaks normal white light up into the various colors of the rainbow, which sparkle in your eye as "fire" when they emerge. If the diamond has any color in it, usually a yellowish tinge, it's like looking at it through sunglasses. The color acts as a filter and reduces the fire. So, traditionally, the most beautiful and valuable diamonds are the ones with the least color. A nearly colorless one-carat ideal-cut diamond with slight inclusions might go for about forty-five hundred dollars, whereas an absolutely colorless stone with the same inclusions could fetch nearly twice that. I say "traditionally" because, as with a lot of extremely expensive things that essentially have no intrinsic worth whatsoever, fashions come and go. Diamonds with some color are usually considered less valuable, but those with a lot of color are often highly coveted if the color is uniform throughout. This is especially true of yellow diamonds, but other colors have gone in and out of style over the years. Regardless, however, clear or blue-white diamonds have always been at the very top of the quality heap. (Diamonds sure do make you wonder about people: Why would someone pay thousands extra for quality only a trained gemologist could detect, and even then only with a magnifying glass? No wonder scam artists and advertising professionals are never at a loss for work.)

Aside from the carat weight, all of these quality factors are, to a certain extent, a matter of judgment, so it's easy to see how Blute and I could go around and around arguing about individual stones. Neither of us really had the upper hand in these negotiations, but we were both motivated to come to an agreement. Maybe he had other guys who came to him with goods, but I was right there, right now, with top-quality merchandise, and he didn't want me to walk while there was plenty of profit to be made. He also knew that I brought him much better gems than most of his suppliers, and he wanted me to remain a continuing good source.

As for me, I had other fences I could go to, but I didn't like the idea of carting gems around all over town. Besides, given the volume of business I did with Blute, there was less risk than with other guys I didn't know as well. He also knew my ability to grade stones and didn't waste too much time trying to bullshit me.

So it was in both our interests to act reasonably and get the deal done, and our debates were a pretty logical give-and-take based on the true merits of the stones. Where we couldn't agree, or when there were items he just didn't want, we'd set those aside and he'd make a lump-sum offer for all the rest, and then we'd bat that number around a little. In the countless times I'd brought stuff to Blute, we'd never once failed to make a deal, and did so again on this occasion.

With that out of the way, and my red-hot booty converted into cold, comfortable cash, I was free to spend the next few days visiting with Mom and my aunt and attending to my real estate affairs.

~

Let's get back to prospecting.

Most evenings when I was in Cleveland, I'd take my mother and aunt out to dinner. I'd always felt bad about abandoning them when I'd moved the family off to Florida, especially since they'd both lost their husbands and were alone. I felt an obligation to spend as much time with them as possible and was glad that I had reasons for getting back there so often.

Once in a while I'd head down to Bill Welling's shop on East Forty-ninth Street. His bank-robbing days were long over and he'd become downright respectable. Never having been arrested, he had no record and went to work for Cleveland's school board, where he was to serve for over thirty years. Always a hard worker, he eventually got into a position where he traveled to various schools all over the city. That left him with a lot of free time, so he turned some of his less than savory skills with his hands to legitimate purposes and started up a business with his brother, John, making prehung doors and doing the occasional kitchen remodel. Because nearly all of his employees had other day jobs, most of the work was done at night, and the little shop became a hangout for friends. Welling always had a cold keg of beer set up, and everybody who showed up pitched in to help out with the carpentry.

Welling may have gone legit, but a lot of his buddies were still in the life. Some of them came by the shop for the camaraderie, but a lot of others really needed the few bucks they could make sawing lumber and assembling frames for Welling. Makes you wonder about the net benefit of being a criminal, but a lot of these guys are like degenerate gamblers who think they have to hit only one big score and they'll quit. Yeah, right. Truth is, no gambler or crook I ever knew—including me—ever actually had in mind a number he was trying to hit. So no matter how much they won or stole, they had no way to know if they'd crossed the magic threshold and could quit. This was purposeful, of course, and subconscious: For gamblers and crooks, it's rarely about the money.

One evening, about five years after we'd moved to Florida, I'd been at Welling's relaxing over a cold one and struck up a conversation with a guy named Wayne, who worked with Welling at his school-board day job. He was a talker, this guy, and me being a listener, it was a natural match. As we worked through a few more beers, Wayne got more and more chatty and didn't seem to notice when my attention occasionally drifted. Eventually he got around to telling me he had a second job, washing windows at some luxury apartments in Shaker Heights and Beachwood. That got him into a series of boring stories about how he wasn't paid enough, worked too hard, wasn't appreciated and so on. Seems he wasn't particularly grateful that these overstuffed swells were supplementing his income. Behind his tales of slow payment and niggling complaints I could sense some self-pity, and suspected that the residents of those posh digs probably had one or two problems with Wayne's work. I had nearly nodded off when he started to rant about one lady who particularly rankled him.

"Old biddy," he spat. "A widow, with too much damned money and too much damned time. Does nothing but drink all day and bust my balls, bitching about this and that. I miss one little spot, she tells me do the whole thing over, but when I come to collect? Always a problem. Ain't like she's gotta wait for a welfare check, the rich old bitch."

My eyelids reopened. I grunted something to indicate that I was still listening, and it didn't take more than that to send Wayne off on another tear.

"You wouldn't believe it," he said bitterly, "all the dough this old broad's got. Closet full of jewelry, necklaces and bracelets scattered all over the damned place—"

"Ah, bullshit," said a voice behind me. I turned to see Welling drawing some beer from the keg. He let the handle on the spout snap back, winked at me with a slight smile, then gestured toward Wayne with his glass. "Probably all fake." Welling knew exactly what was going through my mind.

"Bullshit on *that!*" Wayne shot back. "I seen the stuff, and I'm tellin' you, it's the real deal!"

After Welling walked away, I plied Wayne with a few more beers and kept him talking, asking harmless-sounding questions about what the apartment looked like, and did the lady ever go out, that sort of thing. He was happy for the willing ear and gushed on for another forty minutes or so, knocking back beers while I nursed only one the whole time.

When I was sure we had some good rapport going and that he was pretty soused, I said, "I know a bunch of people over at Blair. Who is this lady, anyway?"

Sometime later Wayne finally staggered his way out of the shop. I took Welling aside and asked him if Wayne had any idea what he was talking about when it came to jewelry.

"Probably," Welling answered. "His brother's a jeweler."

I hoped Wayne would wake up the next morning with a vicious hangover and forget everything we'd talked about.

⌣

Having thus prospected a new customer, it was time to qualify her.

I had another few days in Cleveland working on my properties. I freed up my nights after telling Mom and my aunt that there was a lot to be done before I went back to Florida, and spent those evenings researching this miserly old lady with an apartment full of jewels.

First stop was the Shaker Heights Public Library to check out the city directory. Wonderful things, city directories: They were like reference books for thieves published at public expense. From that single volume I learned the woman's phone number, how many phones she had, her suite number in Blair House, her dead husband's occupation and similar information for all the people who lived over, under and around her. That took all of half an hour, then it was off to the building itself for a look-see.

Blair House was one of a row of upscale apartment buildings in eastern Shaker Heights. I guess its pretentious name was supposed to evoke an image of the U.S. State Department's official Washington residence for visiting dignitaries, but this was a pretty posh place in its own right. It faced onto Van Aken Boulevard, while the back overlooked the exclusive Shaker Heights Country Club, which had been built in 1913 and was considered one of the outstanding gems of famed golf course architect Donald Ross's career. The whole neighborhood smelled of old money.

Blair House's security system consisted of an intercom and a television camera by the front-door reader board. If you rang somebody, they could look at you on television if they wanted to or just buzz you in based on your voice. Of course, if their television didn't happen to be on and tuned to the right station, they couldn't see a thing. In those days most televisions were still running on tubes rather than transistors, which meant it was doubtful a lot of people turned on the television and sat around while it warmed up whenever they got a call from downstairs. It would be easy to bluff my way in if I had to.

But I didn't want to, and hunted around a little instead. First thing I came to was the service entrance. Using a screwdriver, I put some pressure between the door and the jamb and they separated easily, exposing the latch mechanism. I had with me a tool I'd made, a thin but strong piece of metal curved into an S shape. It slipped easily around the door and behind the spring bolt. Pushing it slightly shoved the bolt back and the door popped open. I now had the run of the building. (I could just hear the police questioning building management about why they didn't have better locks, and the inevitable king of dumb-ass responses: "But we'd never been robbed before!" As though good security was something you needed only *after* you got hit.)

There was nobody around, and a few seconds later I was at the lady's suite, which had two doors, neither of which was closer than fifty feet to a neighbor's. The main door had three sturdy locks on it, but the service entrance had—you guessed it—one. I guess the thinking was that if somebody tried to rob the place, they'd opt for the main door. It was the kind of thinking that could make my life easier, but I also had to assume that the tenant wasn't stupid. Maybe the reason the service entrance had only one lock was that it was dead-bolted from the inside. If that was the case, I might not be able to get in through the inside doors.

The suite was one of the apartments facing the golf course, so I went back outside and around the building. It was a moonless night with little light trickling in from the street, and I was able to take my time as I looked around. The only units with patios were the penthouses on the top floor. If I were to drop down and go through a window, I'd have to pass by one of those, another chance of being seen, which meant I'd have to do the job when neither the lady nor her upstairs neighbor was home. As it happened, she was home right now. I made a mental note of the day of the week and the time.

I got just one more chance to go back there during that trip to Cleveland, and then I had to return to Florida. I tried to push Blair House to the back of my mind, but it was difficult. Once a potential score got into my brain, it lodged there like a virus until I either pulled it off or rejected it as too risky. On my next three trips I revisited the place several times.

This was a lousy way to case a job, dropping in months apart. I couldn't establish any kind of schedule for the woman—were there nights of the week she regularly ate out, or played bingo, or went to the movies? Hell, I didn't know if she drove a car or even owned one. I didn't want to enter the building any more than necessary. Had I run into anybody, I had plenty of good reasons ready for being there, and I always took care to dress neatly so as not to arouse suspicion. But I don't care if you're Laurence Olivier: When you know in your mind you're up to no good, there's no way in hell to act completely natural, and you're too nervous to accurately assess whether you're giving yourself away.

I did have to find out about a car, though, so one ice-cold morning just before dawn I went into the building again and down to the garage. The parking spaces were numbered by unit. (Blindingly obvious security tip of the day: Don't do that!) There was an attendant on duty, but he was asleep, so I was able to find the right spot and check out the car. It was a four-year-old Cadillac, in pristine condition, no scratches anywhere. I might have been tempted to conclude that she rarely drove it, but I figured she just paid the attendant to clean it regularly and probably busted his chops about it the same way she busted Wayne's about the windows. Now that I knew what the car looked like, I could watch for it going in and out and see if some kind of pattern made itself evident.

I went back upstairs and planted myself in the far stairwell on the lady's floor. It was about six-thirty A.M. now, just before a normally high traffic time when people would be going to work and maids and service people would start arriving and puttering around. They'd be taking out garbage, bringing in groceries, carrying around tools, delivering things. . . . Having worked in and around apartment buildings for years, I was very attuned to the patterns of life within.

I sat there for three and a half hours, all tensed up and alert, and never saw or heard a damned thing. Was everyone in this place dead? When I'd had enough of that, I walked right up to the elevator, down to the lobby and out the front door to my car. Never saw a soul the whole time. That might sound like good news, but it was just the opposite. Lots of traffic was good, for several reasons. First, it made the presence of one more body less noticeable. Second, it allowed you to zero in on a pattern and assess its regularity. But seeing absolutely no movement at all meant that whatever movement did occur would be random, unpredictable and potentially dangerous.

Months more of this kind of frustrating casing gained me little new knowledge. Seems that I'd simply have to come to the building, fully prepared, as many times as necessary, and just keep going home until she finally went out one night. And when she did, I'd have no idea how long she'd be gone. This was one I'd really have to think hard about before I committed. I'd given up on plenty of scores I'd spent much more time and effort on when the stars simply refused to line up correctly. One decision I did make, though, was to target the service door to the apartment rather than the front door. I didn't want to screw around with three separate locks, and it would be easier to talk my way out of monkeying with the service entrance should I be confronted.

~

Winter passed slowly into spring, and still I hadn't moved on this job. I'd gone by the place dozens of times and she was always home. It was starting to seem as though the only way to get this done would be to camp out with the place in view twenty-four hours a day for a week, and there was no way I could do that. Besides, as far as I was concerned, this still wasn't a "fully qualified prospect," and I wouldn't put that kind of effort into it.

I was back in Cleveland again in late May and decided to stick around over the Memorial Day weekend. I came in on Thursday evening and made my usual trip to Blute Tomba's jewelry store, unloading a small chunk of a recent score and walking out with ten thousand dollars. Normally I'd want to dump the cash in one of my work lockers as soon as possible, but as I drove along Warrensville Center Road, I caught sight of the Shaker Heights Country Club and impulsively turned toward Van Aken Boulevard. I left the car about a block from Blair House and took a casual stroll to see what was going on. Same old shit: The lights in her apartment were on and I could detect some movement within.

I came back Friday night. Same thing. This was really turning into an exasperating waste of time and I started to think about how I could get rid of this irritating stone in my shoe and just forget about it. That wasn't easy to do, though, unless there was some obstacle that couldn't be overcome. But if the problem was just lack of information or a timing issue, it was hard to call the whole thing off, because the solution could be right around the corner.

I went back again about eight o'clock on Saturday night and blinked hard as I looked up at the building. Her lights were off. So were those in every apartment near hers, and nearly every other one in the building. What the hell was this, a flock of rich people all taking off at the same time? I wondered crazily if they had all gone to the same place.

The shock of seeing those lights off after so many months set my head spinning. Just making a mental note of it and moving on made no sense at all. This wasn't part of any kind of pattern. One Saturday night out of ten or twelve? That told me nothing. So what was the point of even going back there night after night?

I turned around and walked a few steps, shook my head hard a few times and turned back to look again. Still dark up there, and there was no use kidding myself. If I didn't do this right now, I never would, and suddenly time became my enemy. I had no idea where she was or when she would return. Come to think of it, I wasn't even completely sure she was out.

I ran back to my car and drove to the building where I'd stashed the tools I'd been setting aside as I'd thought about how to do this job. I dialed the woman's number and held the phone to my ear with my shoulder as I threw the stuff into a bag. Ten rings, no answer. I dialed again, slowly and carefully, to make sure I'd gotten it right. Nothing.

The tools were all packed and ready to go, but I took the time to dial the numbers of every apartment on either side of hers, upstairs and downstairs as well as on the same level. No answer anywhere. I checked my watch: 8:45. Where the hell could she be? Dinner? But it didn't really matter, because I had no idea when she'd left and therefore no guess as to when she'd return. Maybe I should wait until another Saturday night and start staking out the building earlier in the day. But I'd been at this for months and this was the first time I'd found her away. It could literally be years before another opportunity arose. And what if at that point I got inside and found nothing but photos of her grandkids and drawers full of fake jewelry?

I already knew there was no way I could turn my back on this one. What the hell would have been the point of all those months of reconnaissance if all I did was abandon the score the one night I found the woman gone? So I could either stand there and argue with myself while precious minutes evaporated forever or just turn my concentration toward getting it done.

Less than fifteen minutes later I was on Farnsleigh Road, a slight jog off Van Aken. My clothes were dark but perfectly respectable as I made my way to the service entrance of the building and used my special tool to get in. A few seconds after that, I came face-to-face with the service entrance of the apartment. I turned away from it, walked to the main door and pressed the doorbell. No answer, so I pressed it again and put my ear to the door. I have to admit that part of me wanted her to answer. I could tell her I was a Bible salesman, fumble around about why I was hawking the Good Book at nine o'clock on a Saturday night and then get the hell out of there, rid of this job once and for all. But nobody answered and I didn't hear a thing from inside, and rang the bell four more times in quick succession for good measure. Then it was back to the service door.

I examined the lock with a practiced eye, suavely whipped out my butter calfskin wallet and carefully selected a pick from a row of variously sized tools. Once I'd done that, it was simply a matter of inserting the gleaming pick into the lock and jiggling it a few times as I looked away and let my sensitive fingers do their thing. Three or four seconds later I was rewarded with a loud and satisfying click as the lock succumbed to my extraordinary expertise.

Just kidding. In real life, picking a lock is a bitch. Even when it works, which isn't all that often, it takes a long time to get each of the pins lined up just so, one at a time without disturbing the ones you've already worked. There are only two reasons to go through all that trouble in the first place. One is that you save the lock—and if all you did was forget your keys somewhere, that might be worth it. The other is that you can get in and out without anybody knowing you've been there.

If neither of those things is relevant, there are faster and surer ways to defeat the lock. You can usually dismantle most of the surrounding and cosmetic hardware from the outside and work the mechanism with a small screwdriver. Or, if a little noise isn't an issue, you can drill right into the keyhole and straight through the pins, and then the core of the lock will turn freely. Both ways are much faster than picking, if you have the leeway to do it, and no one will notice the slight amount of visible damage while you're inside.

I didn't know what kind of leeway I had, so speed was my top priority. Luckily, the lock on the service entrance was an ordinary key-turned Schlage. The easiest way to get through one of those was to grip it with a heavy pair of Channellock pliers and just turn it, like turning a doorknob. It takes a lot of pressure, but eventually the whole lock breaks apart inside the door. When you turn it back to the original position, the latch that holds the door shut releases.

I got the pliers in place and then paused, listening, but got only silence in return. A few seconds of hard twisting and the inside of the lock fell apart with a muffled snap. I held my breath, hoping there'd be no dead bolt on the other side, but the door moved easily. Not unexpectedly, it stopped after three inches, held in check by a security chain. A few vigorous twists with the pliers and it broke apart, scattering loose links on the floor with a clatter. That was it; I was in.

I picked up my tool bag and pushed on the door. One inch later it came to a dead stop. What the hell was that all about? I reached my gloved hand around the edge of the door and felt around. Something big and solid, with a bunch of thin parallel rods . . .

No wonder the door had only a simple lock: There was a refrigerator backed right up to it. Shining a flashlight in and upward, I could tell by the height of the thing that it was a brute.

No way was I going to the front door to wrestle with three separate locks. That would take forever, and the odds were pretty good I'd have to mangle at least one of them so badly, it would be instantly noticeable by anybody passing by. That somebody *would* pass by while I was inside was a working assumption that I had no intention of abandoning when the chips were down.

I pushed on the door, but it didn't budge. I put my shoulder to it and shoved harder, and was rewarded by about a half inch of movement. Then I turned around and got my back on the door, inching down a bit to get maximum leverage from my legs. My shoes found good purchase against the carpet in the hallway and I pushed once again.

The noise of that massive fridge scraping along the linoleum as I pushed against the door was horrific, like two cats in a blender. I stopped and listened; surely that must have woken up people a block away. I pushed again, then waited for a good minute. If the first sound had gotten anybody's attention, they'd be listening for a repeat, and when they

got it, they might decide to investigate. But there were no sounds in response, so I leaned into it again and kept it up until there was enough
room for me to squeeze through the doorway. Once inside with my tools,
I quickly began a canvass of the apartment to make absolutely sure I was
alone. After that I'd stop moving and take a breather, prepared to bolt if I
heard anything unusual.

The apartment had the unmistakable smell of booze. That was good
news, because it confirmed at least one thing Wayne had told me about
the old lady. I crossed the living room and stepped into the master bedroom and came as close to a coronary as I ever had in my entire life.

There was a woman in the bed, either sleeping or doing a damned
good job of faking it.

There were so many thoughts rocketing around in my head I couldn't
sort them out, but one was so strong it kept pushing its way to the fore-
front: A simple B&E, Breaking and Entering, which might have meant a
couple of years in prison, had suddenly turned into Burglary of an Inhabited Dwelling, which carried a mandatory ten-year sentence in Ohio.
Something was screaming at me to split and chalk it off as a learning experience, and I was in no frame of mind to argue. Everything else aside, I
should have known from my background managing apartments that
heavy-boozing tenants who drank alone rarely went out. I'd also been
dead wrong about her prissy-clean car indicating that she had the attendant take care of it. More likely she just never drove it.

How many other mistakes had I made?

I began stepping backward as quietly as I could, the absurdity of it
dawning on me only much later: Did I really think my footsteps would
wake a drunk who'd slept through all the racket I'd already raised?

Back in the kitchen I picked up the phone and listened to it. What if
she was faking being asleep and tried to call the police? What if she'd done
that earlier, and they were already on their way? I got a dial tone and left
the phone off the hook. If she hadn't yet made a call, she couldn't do it
from the bedroom now.

There was so much adrenaline pumping through my veins, I could
barely keep my hands steady. If you were watching this on videotape, all
you'd see is some guy standing in a room, with nothing else going on and
everything quiet. But in my mind the world was moving at ninety miles
an hour. The darkness itself seemed to rush around me, and even the
floors and walls were vibrating. Despite all of that, I struggled to think rationally, to imagine what I'd look back on later and wish I'd done.

I had to get out, but there was no sense in the old lady ever learning that her apartment had been broken into. I couldn't leave through the service entrance because there'd be no way to get the refrigerator back in place, so I'd push it back from the inside and then go out through the main door. I was able to move it back into place with much less noise than before by rocking it back and forth as I shoved it toward the door. Once that was done, I thought maybe it would turn out all right. And then it hit me: What if the old lady hadn't heard me because she was dead! If I got caught, that meant a murder rap, and goddamnit, that was something I didn't deserve.

I crept back toward the bedroom and paused in the doorway, listening hard. Turned out I didn't have to strain, because I was greeted with a faint snore from the bed. Not only wasn't she dead, she wasn't faking sleep, either, because no lady would purposely snore. It was too unladylike. She was breathing slowly, too, and it'd be awfully tough to fake that if you were scared half to death, as she'd have to be if she was really awake. I knew, because I was breathing so fast I was in danger of hyperventilating, at least if my pounding heart didn't blow up and kill me first.

All of a sudden things were looking up. No way in hell was this lady going to wake up in the next few minutes, and even if she did, she'd be so whacked out, she probably wouldn't even realize someone was in her apartment. Maybe I could still make this whole fiasco pay.

I went into the living room, made sure all three locks were locked and opened the window and screen. If the cops should come calling, I'd have some time to get out the window while they fiddled with the door. It was only a three-story drop to the garage roof, a matter of a few seconds for me.

Canvas bag in hand, I got down on all fours and crept back into the bedroom. If she should awaken for a few seconds and happen to glance around, she wouldn't see me. Once I was through the open door of the walk-in closet, I stood up. Flicking on my penlight, I saw that one panel was filled floor to ceiling with drawers. I pulled the middle one open and was dazzled by an untidy mess of diamond jewelry. Sticking the penlight in my mouth, I emptied the contents of the drawer into the bag as quietly as I could, then turned the light off and stepped out of the closet. There was no movement from the bed, and the rhythm of the woman's breathing hadn't changed at all.

Back into the closet and another drawer. Same thing, and into my bag it all went. Back out for another check, then back in to clean out a third drawer. That was it. There was nothing of interest in any of the other drawers.

In the bedroom the woman hadn't budged, nor had her breathing changed. I noticed by the dim light coming through her half-shuttered window more diamonds lying on the night table. What the hell: I scooped those up as well.

Everything back in my bag, I had a long look through the front-door peephole, a few quiet moments listening for unusual noises, then unlocked the three locks and took off.

~

I can't remember ever having been more grateful to hit fresh air. I was so relieved to be out of that apartment that carrying a bag full of stolen jewelry along a street hardly bothered me. I drove to my work locker, watching my speed carefully and resisting the temptation to overdo it, and stashed the bag without looking inside.

Just because I was relieved was not to say I wasn't still wired. I came out of my building at ten-thirty and started walking, fast, almost at random. I didn't stop for nearly two hours and felt better by the time I ducked into a bar on Woodland Avenue. Physically wrung out and mentally exhausted, I had a couple of vodkas and went home to my mother's to try to sleep.

I was up early on Sunday and went to my locker. Opening up the bag in the cold light of day, I gave a silent thanks to Wayne. The stuff was amazing, every piece genuine and high-quality, and far and away the largest haul I'd ever taken. I put it all back and spent the last two days of the holiday weekend with my mom and aunt, barbecuing, going to the movies, drinking in the evenings and generally trying not to think about all the goodies in my work locker.

About three weeks later I was back in Cleveland and went around to Bill Welling's shop. Despite the late hour, there were plenty of guys working, and Bill had put out a second keg. The Blair House burglary was still the hot topic of conversation among the less savory characters in the shop. There had been endless speculation in the local papers about how the thieves were able to pull off such a spectacular job, cleaning out everything of value without the old lady even having known they were there until she'd woken up and found everything gone. The wiseguys in the shop were coming up with all sorts of crazy theories, and I couldn't blame them: It was a seemingly impossible score. Obviously, the victim hadn't said to the police, "I was so snockered, they could have taken the bed with me in it," so they had no way to know she might as well have not even been there.

Welling didn't come out and ask me if I was the one who'd pulled it off, but he knew.

"The cops questioned Wayne," he said without any more preamble than that.

"And . . . ?"

"They let him go. He came by here afterwards."

It had been months since Wayne and I had met and had our conversation. "Think he remembered telling me about the place?"

Welling shook his head. "What I can tell, he's told the same damned story to a hundred other guys, anybody who'd buy him a couple beers and sit still long enough to listen to all that bullshit."

I pointed to the keg Welling had set out. "I didn't even spend a dime on the guy; it was your beer!"

"Seemed to me he was happy as hell *somebody* hit the old broad, and not much caring who. Don't worry about it."

We had a good laugh about that, because that's how I thought about her as well, an "old broad," when I thought about her at all. To me she wasn't even really a person, just a comical character in a play we were both acting in, an unanticipated obstacle to be overcome so that Act X, Scene Y, could be concluded. It wasn't until much later, after I'd been through some tough times myself, that I looked back and began to nurse growing remorse for what I'd done. To a lot of people, but to her in particular. Here was a lonely old lady hanging on to inherited money and possessions because she had nobody in her life, and these were the only things left that defined her. She drank herself into a stupor night after night to blot out the awfulness of having nothing that mattered, only a car she never drove and jewels she had no opportunity to wear, so soured on living that she alienated even the few people she had opportunity to interact with, like the window washer and the parking lot attendant.

Then one morning she awakens to find that all her glittering anchors are gone. She was probably so hungover it took her several nauseated hours to try to piece together what she herself might have done with them, and only when the fog finally cleared did she realize they had been taken from her. Then she had to clean herself up, air the apartment out and hide all the booze before calling the police. I had no idea if she'd been insured, or had other means, maybe a bank account so crammed full of cash that her only real loss was that of sentimental value. That wasn't part of the investigation and planning of a professional thief. But having since come to understand the kind of psychological trauma that being burglarized induces, I have no doubt it was a severe blow, especially considering the nightmares that must have resulted, torturing her with visions of strange men hovering within inches of her as she lay there, inert and vulnerable. For all I knew, it might have even shortened her life, if she boosted her alcohol intake because of it.

I didn't think about any of these things at the time, and tried not to the whole time I was a thief. I needed to keep a distance from the victims, or it all would have been impossible. I worked at not liking them, at begrudging them the money they had and I didn't. If I allowed myself to see them as decent and sensitive people, if I gave in to contemplating how, but for accidents of birth, they could have been family to me, my career as a criminal would be over. One time I'd been planning for weeks to rob a condo and happened to catch sight of the owners, an elderly couple, holding hands when they didn't know anyone was looking, and it did me in. It was so touching, I could no longer convince myself it was just a job and that the victims were unworthy of consideration. I abandoned the plan, then tried to put it behind me and move on.

The jewelry from the Blair House score sat in that locker for over three years. It was only after I'd become a fugitive and needed some money that I finally took steps to cash it in.

Part
II

9

On Doing Time

A MAGAZINE feature writer once wrote that I didn't like jail. Really? I was shocked. I always thought jail was so comfy and relaxing that you were supposed to like it and want to come back again as soon as possible.

Of course I didn't like it. A basically solitary guy who had everything he could want on the outside now in a place with no privacy, constant noise, awful smells that never went away and sociopathic degenerates who would cut your throat for a pack of cigarettes . . . What the hell was there *to* like?

Some guys were used to jail and could do a stretch easily. "Easy timers" didn't have much of a life on the outside. They spent most of their time hanging out with their buddies, bullshitting all day and never doing anything except the occasional idiotic convenience-store robbery or mugging or B&E of a house whose occupants didn't have much more than the burglar did. For these guys, jail wasn't all that different from the street. A few more rules, sure, but "three hots and a cot" and no worries about drive-bys or bill collectors.

That wasn't me. I was the kind of guy who was said to pull "hard time." I had little fear of other inmates because I could take care of myself and they seemed to sense that, but for someone as fun-loving, outdoorsy and family-oriented as me, jail was like a living death. I wasn't afraid of anything *in* prison, just of *being* there. It was the only thing in the world that truly terrified me.

There are a lot of common conceptions about incarceration, some very true, others less so. For one thing, it's widely believed that you can't just keep to yourself and do your time quietly and expect to be left alone, that it's vital to form alliances, to hook up with the right people, so you have a protective "family" that will ensure that you come to no harm. As it happens, this is largely true, except that it's not a universal truth. It depends on which institution you're in and, even more important, who you are and how you handle yourself.

Some guys come into the joint so scared, they're practically peeing in their pants. Sometimes they *are* peeing in their pants. They're not career criminals and all they know is what they've seen in movies and on television. Those dramatic forms are not real good at communicating the basic truth of prison life, which is grinding, maddening, excruciating tedium, so they tend to concentrate on moments of high drama and action. The newcomer is terrified of being gang-raped on his first day by half a dozen three-hundred-pound psychotic black guys who've been without fresh white meat for weeks, and who will follow up the party by beating the guy to death just for laughs.

Things like that happen, sure. There are stabbings and murders, too, but not nearly as often as sensationalistic media portrayals would have you believe. Fights are another thing, though, and there are plenty of those, but the most depressing reality of prison, other than not being able to be with your loved ones, is boredom.

I came into the Broward County Jail in Florida for a three-month stretch (I'll explain why soon) at the age of thirty-six with my back straight and showing no fear. I cast dirty looks at the more intimidating of my fellow inmates, which got me a lot of catcalls and derisive remarks at first, but I kept it up and didn't look away. The jail wasn't well designed, and was kind of just an afterthought extension to the courthouse, so there was no exercise yard—in effect, we were on twenty-four-hour lockdown—but I did chin-ups by the hundreds on the cell-block bars to demonstrate my upper-body strength. It wasn't to show off but to make sure guys knew I wasn't some couch-potato white-collar embezzler who couldn't and wouldn't defend himself. Early on I established that I wouldn't take too kindly to someone trying to fuck me in the ass, that I'd rather get killed fighting back and would make sure to seriously damage my attackers in the process. In short, I gave the impression that I would be more trouble than I was worth, and I was left alone.

Time goes ever so slowly on the inside. If you just dwell on your situation and your problems, it goes even slower and you can easily drive yourself crazy, so occupying your mind is the first order of the day. Because of the virtual twenty-four-hour lockdown, food was passed through the bars into the cell blocks by trustees ("model" prisoners with jobs that let them move around more freely), so you couldn't even break up the day by going to a dining hall for meals. Gambling was the big thing to do, and cigarettes and food, especially desserts, were the big items to gamble for. Most of the fights arose over gambling losses.

I was lucky in that I loved to read, and while there was no prison library in that underfunded, undermanaged facility, there was also no objection to prisoners having books brought to them by visitors. I also spent a lot of my time figuring out how to escape. I didn't plan to actually break out, I was just trying to keep my mind occupied, but I was intrigued by the possibility and drew up a lot of detailed plans, if only to pass the time. The conclusion I came to was that it would be a relatively easy thing to do if you had the right help on the outside. Alone, it would be very difficult.

Not impossible, though. Because of my experience managing buildings with elevators, I knew that the elevator doors on every floor had small emergency overrides at the top. It took a special U-shaped key, which you pushed in the slot or keyhole and flipped to release the sliding door and open up the elevator shaft. This also automatically stopped the elevator car if it was in motion, no matter where it happened to be located at that time. While I was especially bored one day in the prison, I made a key out of metal ballpoint parts. During my trustee shift on the fifth floor, I tried it out when nobody was around and I was sure none of the cars was moving. The doors popped right open, and I saw that it would only be about a four-foot jump to reach the cables. If you held a towel in your hands, you could slide down one of the cables to whatever floor any of the cars happened to be on, jump to the top of it and ride it until it stopped on a floor below the jail. Kids in the Bronx do this all the time; it's called "elevator surfing," and aside from the fairly frequent deaths that result, I suppose it's fun. Once you were stopped at a lower floor, you could open the door above the one the car was stopped at and, assuming you didn't run into a judge or some cops that knew you, out you'd go, looking like just another greasy elevator repairman. In that antiquated jail everybody wore street clothes.

As it turned out, my escape plan was probably overengineered. About six weeks after I got out, a Cuban wiseguy I'd met briefly when I was inside hid in a supply room near the main phones. In the middle of the night he cut a hole through the floor and wriggled himself right into a judge's chambers, then made his way out of the courthouse. As far as I know, he hasn't been heard from since. Pictures of the hole he cut were in all the papers.

That escape may have been what led to the eventual revamping of procedures in the prison and put it on a more professional footing. Since there were never any prisoner counts, and the guards entered the cell blocks only in extreme circumstances, it was four full days before anybody even realized the guy had escaped. Seems his lawyer came to see him and sat steaming for an hour, only to be told his client was gone. The newspapers had a field day with that one.

~

Tedium was just as much a factor for the guards. They were basically underpaid civil servants trying to get through the day without going crazy, getting hurt or losing their jobs. The only thing that broke up the monotony for them, other than disturbances or the occasional beating, was when they had to move an individual prisoner around. You'd think a guard could just go directly to the correct cell, but this place was so badly organized that prison officials didn't know which four-man cell a guy was in, only which block he was on.

The prisoner being called would go into a little holding cell that led outside the block. Sometimes the guard would have to wake him up first or wait for him to get dressed. Any kind of delay and the guard would harangue him to hurry up. I don't know why they always did that—what the hell else did the guard have to do that was so important?—but they always did. The prisoner would then be released to the walkway and go with the guard. One detail that struck me funny was that the prisoner's name was always written on a piece of paper the guard carried. Maybe it was so the guard wouldn't forget who he was after on the long walk down the outside tier.

Isn't that incredibly exciting? And that was generally the highlight of the guard's working day.

Which was just fine with them, because the only other thing available to break up the day was trouble. Guards genuinely fear trouble and therefore have a tendency to overreact to it. It's not that they hate the prisoners; they may have contempt for them and little respect, but it isn't about hatred. It's just that when trouble starts, it ups the probability that something is going to go wrong and the guard is going to suffer for it, either an injury or a reprimand on his record or outright loss of his job. So they like to quell disturbances quickly, and they really, *really* don't like troublemakers.

Most of the guards in the Broward County Jail liked me. I never made trouble and was always polite and cooperative, but I never sucked ass, either, which they understood. They also understood when I had to stand my ground against an inmate who was bothering me, and there were never any consequences from those occasional confrontations. It was a good "working relationship," I suppose, and it paid off. When I needed something, like a phone call or some other special privilege over which the guards had control, I was rarely denied.

Not everybody in the jail was under sentence. Some were being held in custody pending trials or hearings because they couldn't make bail or bail had been denied them. There was no telling how long those guys would be there, so they weren't given any kind of job.

I was under sentence and so I was made a trustee on the fifth floor, the main receiving center for all the new prisoners coming in. The fifth floor was run by a decent guy named Sergeant Richard Howard. He had about half a dozen other guards under him. My job was to answer the phone, take messages as to who was wanted where, make sure all the new prisoners got some sandwiches and things like that. Not very taxing work, but it filled the day. There were always four or five guards standing around doing zilch, telling stories and generally trying to pass the time. They never seemed to mind that I was always on the phone, and never asked whom I was talking to. It had taken me about an hour to figure out how to use the phone to make outside calls, so I talked to Barb quite a lot.

One of my most important jobs was to make sure I didn't get blamed for the dopey jokes the guards liked to play. Their favorite was to take a new guard and have me give him a slip with the name of a prisoner in the furthest block, a guy named "Jack Meoff." So here goes the poor innocent greenie, who is determined to do a good job on his first day, walking down the whole tier calling out "Jack Meoff!" in front of all the degenerates located in the blocks. They would get the biggest kick out of this, and the old-timers who were in on the gag would yell things like "Jack's asleep. We'll get him up." When the new guard finally realized what he was doing, he'd assume it was something I'd put him up to, especially since all the other guards were looking so innocent. Shows you how truly monotonous it was when dumb gags like that could spice things up.

They loved to pull any kind of joke, however cruel. One involved a prisoner named Steven Simonson. I knew him because we had the same lawyer, Ray Sandstrom, and I had a bit of a beef with him because his sentence and mine were kind of intertwined, which I'll get to later. Simonson had some notoriety as a thief, and he'd been sentenced to two years for a robbery in which he'd posed as a priest, knocked on some lady's door and then stolen her jewelry when she answered.

Simonson was one of the most nervous guys I'd ever seen. He was scared to death of jail and was always trying to talk to me in order to calm himself down, to the point where it got really annoying. One day a guard and I concocted a plan to pester him back. We sent another guard to tell Simonson to get all his things—"bag and baggage," as we called it— because he was being sent up the river to Chattahoochee, known in prison circles as "the nuthouse." The place had a horrendous reputation, and this poor guy stood by the door for two solid hours quivering in terror, until I finally took pity and told him it was a joke. It was mean, sure, but remember that this was no summer camp. Simonson was later moved to another prison, and Ray told me he'd been raped there.

All of this idiotic fun aside, there was an incident very early in my incarceration that was very disturbing but also instructive. Incoming prisoners would arrive at the booking desk in all kinds of conditions. Some would be drunk, some would be in drag so elaborate it was hard to believe they were really men, and some were belligerent. On my second day there, an especially stupid guy swaggered in, confronted one guard and pushed a second one. As though some secret radio signal had flashed from one guard to another, four uniforms immediately set upon the guy, clubbed him to a bloody pulp, then threw his unconscious body into a solitary cell. From what I could see, one token poke in the ribs would probably have shut the guy up, but what he'd run into was the standard operating procedure when a new guy thought he could throw his weight around. It helped explain why most of the inmates were so well behaved all the time, and it also taught me a valuable lesson: It was okay to chum around with the guards so long as you never, *ever* made the mistake of assuming you were buddies. Over the next couple of months I saw some severely beaten prisoners who barely knew what hit them.

That old jail has been torn down and a modern one built in its place. Brings to mind some lines from one of my favorite films:

> BUTCH: What happened to the old bank? It was beautiful!
> BANK MANAGER: People kept robbing it.
> BUTCH: Small price to pay for beauty.

I should probably tell you how I got there. . . .

~

Life was good for me in Fort Lauderdale in the mid-seventies. My real estate company was doing well and I was busy overseeing property in Miami and visiting potential acquisitions on an almost daily basis. I checked out larger complexes for the investment group back in Cleveland and smaller properties for myself.

I'd completely recovered from my gunshot wound, although the entry, exit and surgery scars were still quite prominent and took a little explaining around the pool. As far as Barbara was concerned, I'd learned my lesson, but all I really did was push my sideline further under wraps. I was still regularly scanning the society pages for opportunities of a distinctly non–real estate nature.

As quiet and private as I tried to be about that sideline, there was no way to keep something like that completely to myself unless everything always went exactly right, and life isn't like that. One person who'd figured a few things out early on was Barb's younger brother, Augie. Although he'd come to do some dumb things in his life, Augie was no dummy. About six feet tall, extremely handsome and multitalented, he was a hard-partying type but also thoughtful and a bit enigmatic. I liked him a good deal and also trusted him, although his judgment sometimes didn't measure up to his personal loyalty, which was never in doubt.

Augie had a fraternity brother named Calvin Johnson who lived in South Florida. Augie told him a few stories during some college beer blast or whatever, and Calvin probably passed them on to to his older brother, Derek. It didn't take me long to figure out that old Derek wanted something from me.

Derek began hanging around my house on weekends, sometimes with his wife. He'd swim in my pool, drink my booze and generally make small talk loaded with innuendos. Finally, lying around the pool one particularly warm day, he scratched himself, heaved a great sigh and said, "Seems I need some dough, Bill. A lot of it." He rolled over and looked at me. "You happen'a know any way I could lay my hands on some money real quick?"

He couldn't have asked at a better time. Or worse, depending on how you looked at it.

About a year before, I'd been out in my boat, tooling along the Intracoastal Waterway. In case you're not familiar with the geography of southern Florida, the Intracoastal is a narrow waterway dividing the main body of Florida from a strip of land that runs parallel to the coast. That thin sliver of land is where all the famous beaches are, like Miami and Laud-erdale. The Intracoastal carries some heavy boat traffic, because you can cruise for miles without having to venture out into the ocean. While most people in Florida tend to think of it as a local feature, it actually runs all the way to Boston, in one form or another. It was created during World War II so barges could travel up and down the East Coast protected from attack by enemy submarines.

It's also the body of water you're talking about when you talk water-front homes in that area. There are thousands of homes and boat docks fronting the Intracoastal, and those are what I was admiring as I motored quietly, going nowhere in particular. Houses there can run into the many millions, and there are private boats that can easily accommodate dozens of party guests.

I heard some music from somewhere off to my left, and looked in that direction to see a hundred-foot yacht looming up from behind me. There was a party going on, with about fifty people clad in tuxedos, evening gowns and—even from a distance it was easy to see—a whole lot of fine-looking jewelry. As I let the boat pass by, I recognized some faces. One was that of Bert Parks, the perennial and ageless host of countless Miss America pageants.

Intrigued, I followed at a respectable distance. They went up the In-tracoastal to Port Everglades, then turned east into the ocean, north again and all the way to Palm Beach. Altogether it was a trip of about fifty miles, but nobody on board seemed in much of a hurry. They finally docked alongside some extremely fancy digs and disembarked to join hundreds of other similarly clad swells at what turned out to be the annual Red Cross Ball.

With a little digging I found out that the yacht belonged to the lady who owned Hollywood Bread, which was pretty famous stuff at the time. Henry Miller even mentioned it in an article he wrote just after World War II. They were later to have some trouble with the FTC over weight-reduction claims they made in advertising, and I think they eventually went out of business. The old Hollywood Bread building in downtown Hollywood, Florida, is still a local landmark.

Anyway, each year this lady invited a bunch of people who were going to the ball to join her on the yacht and thereby avoid the maddeningly in-terminable drawbridge delays that were a fact of life for motorists down there. She made a party out of it, and people would begin angling for in-vitations for the next year barely before the current year's ball had even wrapped up.

That yacht looked to me like a wounded seal must look to a great white shark. Once I'd gotten it into my head that it might be possible to pirate the thing, I couldn't shake it loose. I quickly came to the conclusion that there was no way to do it solo, which cooled me on the idea. It would also involve guns, which I didn't like one bit. You'd have to keep fifty guests under control, along with four crewmen, and it would only take one wannabe hero in the crowd to do something really dumb and screw the whole thing up. Without some serious ordnance pointing at them, it would be too risky.

The plan would be to come up to the boat from behind once they were in open ocean, climb aboard with grappling hooks and generally take over. We'd disable the radios first, then the engines, then relieve everyone on board of their goodies. Back into our own boat and off to a spot where we planted a car, then sink the getaway boat and be on our way with millions in jewels. It would be a whole lot more complicated than that, of course, but the concept of being a twentieth-century pirate was simply too inviting to let go of completely.

Inviting enough that I was willing to reconsider some of the rules that had served me so well in the past? Maybe I'd been too much of a hard-ass about not using partners or weapons and never robbing premises with people on them. Had I unwittingly been passing up some fabulous opportunities because of an antiquated code of proper procedure?

I'd already run it past Augie and my buddy Bill Welling, just for laughs. They joked back and we had some fun discussions, and after a while I knew they were in. Now here was Derek Johnson, asking if I knew of a way to make a bunch of dough, both of us knowing exactly in which direction he was looking. I'd already come to the conclusion that to do this job right would take four men. Now, I didn't trust Derek—it takes me a helluva lot longer to get to that point than I'd spent with him—but I sure as hell trusted Augie and Welling.

Trying to sound as casual as I could, I told Derek I didn't really know of anything specific, but how would he feel about driving a boat for a few hours for a flat ten grand?

He sat up. "Driving it where?"

"What's the difference?" I answered, staying on my back with my eyes closed. He knew what I meant. First, if someone offers you that kind of money to drive a boat, it's probably not to deliver a load of stone crabs. Second, if I'd wanted him to know, I would have told him.

He saw the point. "Sure, no problem," he said eagerly.

What a jerk. I should have known from that alone to stay as far away from him as possible. In the movies guys are always walking into risky situations on no more data than a wink and a touch to the side of the nose. In the real world, if you want to stay alive and out of trouble, you ask a million questions until you know the color of the shoelaces your backup driver is supposed to wear. But here's Derek, not knowing if I plan to dump a body or run a load of drugs or God knows what, agreeing to take part. Dumb as I was for including him in the caper, at least I had the good sense not to let him know what was going on.

~

It was about that time that the Fort Lauderdale Tactical Squad started following me, although I had no idea at the time.

That unit had been formed by the police in response to the state's Career Criminal Program, which mandated local police departments to target known habitual offenders and make an attempt to apprehend them in the commission of serious crimes. Needless to say, I fit the mandate perfectly, but how on earth could they have known that?

They began following me day and night, and those TAC boys were very good. It's not hard to do good surveillance if you've got the budget for it. It just takes a lot of men. Contrary to popular belief, the more crowded and busy the city, the easier it is to maintain a tail, because it's more difficult to spot the guys who are watching you. It's when you're out in the boonies that it's nearly impossible to follow somebody without him copping to you.

The TAC Squad constantly changed personnel and cars so I wouldn't be likely to notice the same vehicle in two different places. It was nothing for one team to sit still as I left an area and radio ahead for another team to pick me up, then leapfrog them to be ready for the next handover. I drove them crazy anyway, because I was always out inspecting properties. I'd stand in front of a building in an upscale neighborhood, walk around, check out entrances, maybe even take a few pictures. Radios would start to crackle all over the place, the TAC guys certain I was about to hit the place. They'd have as many as six unmarked cars gathered to pounce on me as soon as I made my move. Then I'd just leave and go somewhere else. One afternoon Augie and I took my boat out for a long ride, and there were plainclothes cops stationed on every bridge between Fort Lauderdale and Miami, tracking us and radioing in our position.

Like I said, I didn't know any of this at the time and had absolutely no idea that I was being tailed. Later, when the shit finally hit the fan, my lawyer got hold of all the surveillance reports and I eventually pieced it together. It was interesting reading, too. The most utterly innocuous things I did were seen as preludes to evil by the jumpy police. Ever since then I've cast a pretty skeptical eye on news reports dealing with someone suspected of a crime. Any high school newspaper reporter can dig up stuff that would make anyone at all look guilty if presented in the proper accusatory light. Just look what the media did to Richard Jewell, wrongly accused of being the Atlanta Olympics bomber. They made the guy look like a professional terrorist and he was completely innocent.

The most tense moment of all, unbeknownst to me at the time, came when Barb and I attended a swank fund-raiser for the Florida Republican Party. Then-president Gerald Ford was there, and at one point he and I shook hands and spoke for a few seconds. Seems about two dozen ear-pieces went into overdrive as that happened, the local cops begging the Secret Service guys not to intervene lest their entire surveillance get blown, the Secret Service guys yelling for instructions from their agent-in-charge, the AIC yakking with the head of Fort Lauderdale TAC to determine how dangerous I might be. It all passed quickly and, at least to the guests, quietly, but imagine what heads would have rolled on that decision had I really been up to no good.

I suppose I should have known something was up, but I wasn't actually doing anything wrong, so my guard was down. My calm exterior might have saved my life, too, or at least prevented some broken bones, because if I'd been nervous as I approached President Ford, I might have ended up at the bottom of a pile of Secret Service agents, who are famous for overkill when protecting their man. (They almost crushed President Reagan to death on the floor of the car after he was shot, and are reputed to have actually broken one or two of his ribs in the process. Must be cool to say you roughed up the president, even if it was for his own good.)

The Red Cross Ball was still a long ways off and I was getting restless. I'd found out from a broker in Fort Lauderdale that a Ramada Inn right on the beach had quietly gone up for sale. I was in no position to buy a hotel, and the real estate company in Cleveland wasn't interested in it either, but it was a good excuse to do a little prospecting. I'd actually cased the place once before and, courtesy of the Schlage lock company, already had master keys to every room.

I'd sneaked a peek at a master key on a cleaning cart during an earlier visit and memorized the code number stamped on it. I wrote to Schlage on "Bay Harbor Management Company" stationery and told them I'd lost the master key to one of our apartment buildings but had wisely written down the code and put it in our corporate safety-deposit box. Those dear customer-service-oriented people overnighted a new one to me. (I do believe I sent a nice thank-you note.)

But it only worked on the first floor. However, in that particular key system, a cheap one, the master for each floor differed from the other floors on just one pin of the five-pin lock. I knew that it was virtually certain to be either the first or the last pin. Since I already had one master key, all I had to do was obtain some Schlage blanks and copy the master a few dozen times, moving just one tooth, the first or last, slightly up or down with each new copy. I ended up with about forty keys representing every possible master for that particular hotel and tried them on a bunch of doors until I found the ones that worked.

Even now I shudder when I think back on that day. There I was, blithely going off to case a hotel, not knowing that an entire platoon of cops was watching my every move. Had they been dumb enough to accost me as soon as I'd shown up, or somehow given themselves away, I could easily have proven that I was there to look over an available property. But they weren't one bit dumb. Impatient, maybe, but not dumb.

I hadn't been on that beach for two minutes when I spotted a middle-aged couple in side-by-side lounge chairs. The lady was sporting a load of gold jewelry and a diamond that had to have weighed in at six carats, minimum. Who the hell wears that kind of stuff to a beach? you might ask. In Florida, maybe half the population. I assumed these two were hotel guests, and that was confirmed when a waiter came around with drinks and they signed for them.

There were only about two dozen people on the beach area just behind the hotel. I sat down in another lounge chair and tried to look as much like a nondescript tourist as possible. I didn't need a good view of the couple, just enough to see when they got up so I could follow them and try to determine which room they were in. I'd return at night to see if the wife was careless enough to leave her goodies lying around the room.

During the next two hours, the beach began to fill up. At least fifteen people strolled onto the sand, all of them in their twenties and thirties. I was surprised to see that much business in a hotel that was being sold. I would be even more surprised later when I found out that every one of them was a cop. There were more in the lobby, more in the parking lot, and two on the roof. They were all there watching me, convinced I was up to something, and they were right.

Finally, the two people I'd been watching started moving like they were preparing to pack up and go to their room. Not wanting to trail right behind them and be obvious, I rose quickly and walked to the hotel first.

There was one door opening onto the beach. Inside, you could go left and up the stairs to the second and third floors, or go straight and then left to stay on the first floor. When I got to the door, I politely held it open for an exceptionally pretty young lady who was just coming out, then I walked straight through and onto the first-floor corridor. I was delighted to find that the doors to the first three rooms on either side of the hallway were wide open, probably because the rooms were being aired out for incoming guests. The hallway carpet was wet, which was not unusual in beachfront hotels, where people and their kids come in dripping after swimming, and the breeze blowing through would probably help to dry it out faster.

I ducked into one of the open rooms and swung the door closed to within an inch, leaving it ajar just enough to be able to see into the hallway. As soon as the couple came into the hotel, I'd know right away if they were going up the stairs or heading for the first floor, where they'd have to pass right by me. I could then follow at a discreet distance and see which room they were in.

A short time later they came in and walked right past the room I was in. I waited about ten seconds, stepped out, followed quietly, saw their room, then came back that night and stole a fortune in gold and diamonds and got away free and clear.

At least that was the plan. What actually happened was something quite different. As soon as I opened the door and prepared to step into the hallway, I saw the pretty lady for whom I'd held open the door. She was standing right in the doorway, looking straight at me, a .38-caliber Police Special in her hands pointed at my head, and she was screaming for me to hit the ground, facedown. It was hard to make out her words because there were three other cops behind her also pointing guns at me and screaming the same thing. The only thing that came through clearly was my name: These guys knew who I was.

As I'm lying facedown on this soaking-wet, musty-smelling and sandy carpet, one of the cops jams his knee into my back and handcuffs me. Only when I'm securely bound do the others back off with their guns. Two of them drag me to my feet and begin searching me, while the female and the remaining guy start teasing me about peeing in my pants, because I'm dripping from the wet carpet. This would be one of the favorite stories the Fort Lauderdale police would tell reporters about me for years.

I didn't really give a shit what they were thinking. My mind was racing ahead trying to see what they had on me. I couldn't imagine why, if they'd been following me, they'd jumped the gun like that instead of waiting to catch me red-handed in some blatantly felonious act. What did they have that I didn't know about? They were sure to find the master keys to the hotel on me, so they could make a case for possession of burglary tools, and I was pretty good for trespassing, too, but these were awfully chintzy charges. How would they explain that truly enormous expenditure of law enforcement manpower? If there were any serious crimes going on that the police were unable to respond to because of this business in the hotel, the department would surely suffer.

Other cops started showing up, everybody congratulating everybody else for having gotten their man. None of it made any sense. Then I heard an older detective speak into his radio and tell someone that I was in custody and that they'd found burglary tools on me, so they could go ahead and execute the warrant.

"What warrant?" I asked the detective.

He grinned at me. "The one to search your house, buddy-boy."

Shit.

~

They walked me out to a prowl car and took me off to the station. Given the size of the caravan, you'd have thought they had the president in there.

Except we weren't heading for the station. We were going in entirely the wrong direction. I had a moment of panic, wondering if they were going to take me out to the Everglades, shoot me in the head and feed me to the alligators or something. I calmed down quickly, though. It made no sense to do something like that to a nonviolent criminal, no matter how much I'd frustrated them, and too many cops had been at the arrest scene to keep a secret like that.

Then I realized we were heading for my house. As soon as we got there, they pulled me out, walked me up to the door and politely rang the bell. We all have certain images so crisply seared into our brains that nothing can eradicate them; one of mine is that of Barbara's face when she opened the door.

You read in books about how different emotions run around somebody's face all at the same time, and it sounds like bullshit, but it isn't. Shock—the dizzying kind—and confusion were the first things I noticed on Barb's, and then fear so powerful she seemed to shrink. She looked from me to the cops and back again, very rapidly, as though trying to read the answers to every question she had. I felt so awful for her, I could barely breathe. Her eyes finally settled on me as she realized why my hands were behind my back.

It was excruciating for me; when Barb needed me the most, I was the cause of that need. Humiliation and helplessness were all I had to offer her.

It would have been different had she colluded with me and participated in my thievery, but she was completely innocent and didn't deserve this. I knew she strongly suspected that I hadn't gone straight even after I was shot, but what, specifically, I'd been up to, she had no idea, and I don't think she wanted to know. The kids and the house occupied most of her time, and while money was never an issue, she didn't ask any questions about where it was coming from. Maybe she thought the property business was a gold mine, but Barb was pretty bright so I doubt it. My frequent nighttime absences might have become an issue under other circumstances, but I spent a great deal more time with my wife and kids than nearly any other father I knew, so it wasn't like I was neglecting them. "Dad likes to go off by himself once in a while" is something they just got used to.

That was about to end. Barb's reaction to what she was witnessing as she stood in our doorway may have been agony for me, but the cops were used to that kind of thing, and they used it to their advantage. The detective must have instantly sensed that Barb was easily intimidated; rather than let her have a few seconds to recover and compose herself, he held out his badge, stuck out an envelope and said, "Warrant to search the premises, Mrs. Mason. I'm Detective King. May we come in?"

Barb struggled to gain some kind of control. "I haven't read this yet," she said, without much conviction or authority.

"Doesn't matter if you read it or not," King replied, waving Barb to the side as he stepped forward. "It's still valid."

Despite her fear, Barb was fairly confident that there was nothing to find. After all, she was the one who cleaned and took care of the place, so she would know if something was amiss.

I was a little less confident. I had been just about to leave on one of my Cleveland trips and had brought some things home to take with me to fence to Blute Tomba. I had some hope the cops might not find that stuff, but that dimmed quickly as I watched them work. These guys were prepared to spend the rest of their careers in my house if that was what it took. Not only did they badly want to bust me, although I still didn't know why, they wanted to make damned sure they didn't go limping back to the station house to explain why they'd mobilized an army against a citizen with only one very old line on his rap sheet and then shown up empty-handed. It wasn't the cops I was afraid of, though. What was giving me the most anxiety was the thought of Barb's face when she found out that I'd hidden stolen goods in our house.

There was nothing I could do to stop any of this, but there was something I could do to begin protecting myself. "When do I get my phone call?" I asked King, who appeared to be in charge.

"Phone call? Whadda you need a phone call for? You're right here with your wife!"

"My wife's not a lawyer," I said without rancor. "Come on, let me make my call."

He walked me to the kitchen, recuffed me in the front and watched as I brought the phone to my ear and held it there with my shoulder as I dialed with my manacled hands. I phoned my neighbor across the street. He was a lawyer, as was another neighbor, and they were both over in less than two minutes. They'd seen the commotion and were prepared, but told me they weren't criminal attorneys. "We got another guy waiting in the wings," one of them said. I told them to make the call, and a few minutes later a lawyer named Howard Zeidwig showed up.

"Not a word" was the first thing he said to me as he walked into the house. He hadn't needed an introduction to know who was who: I was the only one wearing handcuffs, which were now behind me again.

"Haven't said anything," I told him, and he nodded in approval.

A few minutes later the lead detective reappeared. "So what's this?" he asked as he jiggled a canvas bag up and down.

"For all my client knows," Zeidwig answered, "it's your lunch. Why'd you bring it into the house?"

Detective King had heard it all and wasn't fazed by this wiseacre attorney. "We just found it. Out in the garage."

"Where, exactly?" Zeidwig asked.

"Under a pile of junk. Paint cans, stuff like that." King opened the top and held it toward us. Diamonds, a couple of emeralds and a gold filigree bracelet gleamed out. There was also a large number of silver coins. "Maybe your client can tell us where he got these."

"Yeah," my lawyer responded, "and maybe he can tell you how he killed Kennedy."

I almost blurted out that the silver coins were mine. They were, but that would be as good as admitting the rest of the stuff wasn't, so I stayed quiet.

The detective laughed good-naturedly. Here were two old professional bullshit artists, wary but mutually respectful, playing a game whose sole purpose was for each of them to feel out how savvy the other was. It didn't take them long to figure out that they could skip the usual tricks that worked only on rookies.

"What's next?" Zeidwig asked. "You haven't booked him yet."

"Taking him down right now. You coming?"

The lawyer looked at his watch, and I knew what was going through his mind: It was still early enough in the day to get a bail hearing, so he'd come with me. Had it been later, there would have been nothing useful he could have done and he wouldn't have wasted his time.

He told Barbara to head for the bank and wait there. I was taken to the station and booked, and bail was set at seven thousand dollars. Zeidwig called Barb, who withdrew the money, came down and got me out. Barely four hours after I'd been taken at the motel, I was back home.

Barb had sent the terrified kids to a neighbor's, so the first order of business was to get them back into their own house, show them it was still the same and try to settle them down. I gave them a sugarcoated version of events, about how it had all been a mistake, but the cops were so angry it would take us awhile to straighten everything out. I stayed with them a long time, for obvious reasons, but also because I dreaded going back to the living room to face Barb. I knew exactly how she'd react, and I was right.

She didn't ask what I'd done, didn't speak accusingly, didn't get mad and threaten to leave me or stick my old promises in my face. She asked a lot of questions about what was going to happen, and what she needed to do, and what the likely outcomes were. In other words, she was doing exactly what I'd dreaded, which was being 100 percent supportive.

Which isn't to say she wasn't badly shaken about what had happened that afternoon, or very frightened about what was to come, and that only made it worse. What kind of a complete shitheel would do to a sweet and decent woman what I'd done to Barb? Here was a rock-solid wife who loved me completely, and I couldn't seem to stop myself from causing her pain. I had a million rationalizations ready to tell myself—I didn't know I was going to get caught, it was a bullshit bust and the cops knew it, I was just trying to give us a better life—but all of them were sad and sickening in light of this beautiful, trembling woman with red-rimmed eyes doing her best to hold everything together.

I wanted to explain things to her anyway, and I told her the truth, at least as I knew it at that time and with one or two details slightly modified. On the face of it, everything I told her was plausible because technically I really hadn't done anything at the hotel, and the cops had truly fucked up. It was the same story I would tell the prosecutors later. The hotel was up for sale—true—and I'd gone to look things over. I sat on the beach for a while observing the kind of clientele they attracted and the service they provided. Then I went inside to check the condition of the common areas and guest rooms. A bunch of rooms were open, so I went in one to have a look. It was unoccupied, and not just for the moment, either: Nobody was checked in, there was no personal property in it and the chambermaids were airing it out. I was in there for no more than a few minutes, then opened the door to leave and got jumped by a team of cops. I had no idea what they'd been doing there—that was the truth, too—and no idea how they happened onto me. The fact that they knew my name had floored me, and, thinking back on it, it was clear they hadn't just recognized me on the spot. They'd known it was me in the room before they ever saw me in it.

I couldn't easily explain why I had master keys to the entire hotel on me. There is nothing inherently illegal about that as long as you didn't steal the keys, but the definition of "burglary tools" is fluid and dependent on context. If you have a screwdriver, crowbar and power drill on you and you happen to be in your basement rebuilding a cabinet, you're on safe ground. But if you're carrying those same items near a bank at three A.M., you're in possession of burglary tools. Those are obvious examples, with which few would find argument, but carrying master keys inside a hotel in broad daylight when you're a licensed real estate agent and the property is for sale is not exactly an airtight case for intent to commit a crime. That I was intending to commit a crime is, of course, entirely beside the point, and I hadn't been intending to rob it at that time. I was planning to return at night, but only if I thought it worthwhile, and I hadn't made that determination yet, so was I guilty of anything? You see how convoluted this can get.

There wasn't anything convoluted about one of the other charges, though, and that was possession of stolen property. I didn't know for a fact that they could prove any of that stuff they found in my house had been stolen, but I was starting to think they knew a bit more than I'd first assumed.

I didn't share all of this with Barb as we sat and spoke, and she wouldn't have been interested in the details anyway. I knew there were only two questions on her mind. One was what was going to happen to me this time, and the other was what about next time. I wasn't holding out much hope that I was going to walk away from the bust, and even less that I would learn any permanent lessons from the situation. In my heart I was ready to swear on my kids' lives that I'd finally go straight and stay that way, and I really believed it, too. But my mind was telling me something else, that I'd been at this crossroads before, felt just as committed to quitting the life, held out for as long as I could and then lapsed. It's what a serial dieter must feel like every time he overeats, or a heroin addict right after he shoots up, or a gambler when he loses his last dime for the hundredth time: This is it, man, I've had it. It just isn't worth the grief and I don't need it anymore.

Textbook denial, the standard response of the hard-core addict.

~

I had a ten o'clock appointment with Zeidwig the next morning. I was on time but cooled my heels for an hour waiting for him. When he finally arrived, he apologized for being late and explained it was because he'd been trying to work out a deal with the detectives and assistant district attorney. "I think you're going to like this," he said with a self-satisfied grin and a wink.

We went into his private office and sat down. Zeidwig leaned back in his big leather chair and put his hands behind his head. "They seem to be more interested in closing cases than in putting you away for possessing supposedly stolen property."

Supposedly? "Then they don't know where that stuff came from?"

"Near as I can tell, they're still working on it. Stuff like that, though . . ." He shook his head. "Pretty heavy goods. If it came from around here, from southern Florida, they'll track it down eventually."

He was right about that. Even if the cops weren't interested, insurance company investigators would be, and those guys talked to each other a lot. "So what's the deal?"

Zeidwig brought his chair forward and put his elbows on his desk. "Tell them exactly where it came from and they'll give you immunity in each of those cases. If they have to find out themselves, they'll prosecute you for every one." He meant prosecute me for receiving stolen property, since it would be difficult to prove I was the original thief.

"What about the Ramada business?"

Zeidwig shrugged and sat back once again. "That stands. They'll pursue the case against you. I guess they have to justify all that manpower."

Why justify it using me? "You telling me all those cops at the hotel, they were there for me?"

Zeidwig blinked, confused by my question. "Obviously."

"But why would they be tailing me?"

The police, Zeidwig explained, told him that they'd first become aware of me while investigating an unrelated matter at Lago Mar, a very swank place in Harbor Beach just east of Fort Lauderdale. I'd been there over a month before. "They saw you back your car into a parking space and then walk around to the hotel."

I waited for him to continue, but he didn't. "And . . . ?"

"And . . . that's it."

I was starting to wonder if my lawyer had asked them any follow-up questions at all, or just believed every single thing they told him. "So you're telling me they saw a guy back a car into a parking space at some hotel and decided to assign half the police force to follow him for a month?"

"They said you backed in to hide the rear license tag." Zeidwig must have realized how utterly ridiculous he sounded, because he tried to get off the topic quickly. "Who'd you think they were at the Ramada for?"

"How the hell should I know? I wasn't doing anything!"

"So how come you were wiping your fingerprints off an inside knob in a guest room?"

I was too stunned to answer right away and preferred to let the implications sink in first. Wiping fingerprints? "Howard, I have no idea what the hell they're talking about!"

Zeidwig's expression began to devolve into the standard we-both-know-you're-full-of-shit-but-I'll-be-polite-because-you're-my-client mask of studied neutrality, but I wasn't having it. "Goddamnit, I wasn't doing anything of the kind! They're blowing smoke up your ass!"

"What can I tell you? True or not, it's four cops against one alleged perp, and there wasn't anybody else who saw you in the room." He was right about that. "Although they do have a civilian witness. A woman from Connecticut named Jean Tierney."

Connecticut? "What does someone from Connecticut have to do with—"

"That was her room they found you in, number 127. She'll come down and testify that she was registered to it, which establishes that it was occupied, which makes it a lot easier for them to prove you were committing robbery."

"Howard, that room was completely empty," I tried to explain. "The door was wide open because they were airing it out. Chambermaids don't do that with occupied rooms."

"I believe you," he protested, holding up his hands like I was wasting my breath trying to convince him. "But maybe she was exceptionally neat and kept everything in drawers."

"Bullshit!"

"Perhaps. But how are you going to argue with them? If you tell them you looked in the drawers, then you *were* robbing the room." He waited for that, his only triumph in this irritating conversation, to sink in, then said, "I recommend you take the deal, Bill."

Sure he did. He would walk away with a fat fee and no loss at trial on his record. His failure to poke at the police at all—a standard tactic to let them know you thought their case was hogwash and planned to fight them tooth and nail—let me know I was on my own to analyze this in terms of my self-interest, not his.

It took about ninety seconds. "I want it in writing that I walk on any case I tell them about, and I want all the silver coins back they took from my house. Those are mine."

Zeidwig, relieved that I was going for it and no longer challenging his commitment to my case, ushered me back into the waiting room so he could make the call. Less than a minute later he came out. "We have a deal."

He didn't know the half of it.

~

We met with Detective King early the next morning. He handed me two copies of the written agreement and a pen. "Sign these and let's get to it."

When Zeidwig didn't do anything, I took the papers, ignored the pen and sat down to read. Without looking at him, I could sense King fuming as I took my time.

"It's pretty standard wording, Bill," Zeidwig said.

"How would you know?" I said without looking up. "You haven't read it."

"Listen—" King began, but I reached out for his pen and he quieted down. As soon as I had it, I began crossing out sentences and paragraphs and writing in the margins.

"What the hell are you doing!" he snarled.

"Just want it to say what we agreed."

"It already does. What are you trying to pull, Mason?"

"Pull?"

"*I* signed it, didn't I?"

"You wrote it!" I stopped writing and looked at him, then at my lawyer. "Does anybody in this room expect me to put my signature to a document I don't agree with?"

Zeidwig, who clearly just wanted to get this whole episode over with, nevertheless didn't have much choice in answering that question. "Course not. So what's the problem?"

"Couple of things. For one, there's all this legal gobbledygook I don't understand. I want this in plain English." I read from my own writing: " 'Mr. Mason will receive immunity for everything he tells the police.' That's what the deal was, right?"

"And that's what it says," King insisted.

"The hell it does."

King reached out and took the document himself. I think he saw the deal falling apart and was starting to sweat. I was banking on the fact that he'd already had it reported right up to the police commissioner that he was about to close three or four frustrating cases, and all he needed was to go back to them and say that he'd blown the whole thing because of wording problems in the written agreement.

He read for a few seconds, then sat down and started writing his own stuff. "First off, it's not anything you say, it's anything you say *today*, during the ride-around."

"Fair enough," I said. We negotiated for about twenty more minutes, Zeidwig occasionally chirping in because he was, after all, supposed to be my attorney. Truth was, though, I didn't want him too involved. I had an agenda and hadn't bothered filling him in on it.

"Now I gotta go get this typed," King said at last.

"No, you don't," Zeidwig said. "Both of you initial each change, make a photostat and it's perfectly legal."

We did that, and then it was down to the squad car. King drove, I was in the front passenger seat and Zeidwig was behind me. "Okay," King said as we pulled out of the parking lot. "Start singing." He really said it just like that.

Hard to believe, but I kind of liked Detective King. He'd been nothing but polite, even friendly, since this whole business began. I think his attitude was that as long as a perp wasn't giving him any trouble, there was no reason not to be civil. That was a pretty enlightened way to behave, and I felt a little bad about what I was getting ready to do to him. I hoped he wouldn't hold it against me but knew he would. Big-time.

I waited until we were out in the street and said, "Well, there was the Fountainhead job."

King blinked a few times, then said, "The what?"

"The Fountainhead. The one where—"

"I know what the goddamned Fountainhead job is." His eyes grew wide and he turned to me. "You telling me that was *you*?"

"Yep. Hey, watch the road!"

He jerked his attention back to his driving, which had been fine, but I just wanted to throw him off a bit. At a red light he pulled a small black notebook out of his shirt pocket and made a note.

"Armand Hammer, too," I said, as casually as I could.

"Bullshit!" King retorted, anger beginning to sound in his voice. "Like hell you did Hammer! *Bullshit!*"

I decided not to answer right away, to give his anger time to die down, and also to let the implications of what I'd just confessed sink in. The Hammer score had never been mentioned in the press.

"Bullshit," King repeated, but more softly this time. "Nobody even knew about that job. The Hammers, their insurance company and a couple of cops. We kept it quiet. Nobody else—"

"The thief knew," I reminded him.

I didn't care if he believed me or not, so long as he got it all down. King's believing me wasn't part of our deal; I just needed it on the record. But, like I said, he was a decent guy, so I proved my claim. "You know that gold filigree bracelet you found at my place?" I waited for him to nod. "Show it to Mrs. Hammer."

King thought about it, then banged his closed fist on the steering wheel and muttered "Christ!" between clenched teeth.

We rode in silence for a few minutes, then he said, "You have help?"

I couldn't tell if he was simply curious or, since I was no longer liable to prosecution for that robbery, if he was maybe trying to get me to give up accomplices he could do something about, so it wouldn't be a total loss. I told him no, that I was alone. It was the truth and I had nothing to lose.

I turned around to make sure Zeidwig was taking his own notes, in case King conveniently forgot to jot one of my confessions down. Before the detective could get past his shock and figure out what was going on, I told him about half a dozen other scores. Big ones. I directed him to several addresses, gave details only the real thief could know and answered all his questions. I even answered questions that weren't directly related to those thefts. Far as I was concerned, if Detective King was the one who brought them up, they were part of the deal.

I don't think he much cared about that technicality. He looked like he was about to shit his pants and didn't even bother trying to pretend, like he was in control of this situation. He and the assistant district attorney had fucked up, but good. I'd just copped to some of the biggest heists in the county's history, a few of which had made the front pages, and there was no longer a damned thing anybody could do to me for any of them. As we continued driving, I also made sure to connect every single piece of jewelry they'd taken from my house to jobs I was confessing to. So much for any possession of stolen property charges.

When I'd run through everything and we were finished, we headed back to the station house. King was quiet and thoughtful, and I saw no reason to start up any conversation.

Zeidwig, who'd barely said a word since we left the parking lot, spoke up now. "I trust you're satisfied, Detective?"

King didn't answer right away, then looked at me and said, "One more thing."

Zeidwig sat up straight, but before he could mount a protest, King, still looking at me, said, "Tell me how you did Hammer."

"That wasn't part of the—"

King impatiently waved my lawyer back down. "Off the record, Mason," he said. "Strictly between you and me. For all I know, you were holding that bracelet for the guy who really did it."

He turned his attention back to the road, and I glanced at Zeidwig, who shrugged: *Up to you; there's no obligation.* That was true. I'd already confessed on the record, so whether King believed me or not was irrelevant. They could never come after me for it. Why should I tell him anything more?

King sighed and shifted uncomfortably. "I was the lead on that case."

Now I understood. "Off the record, right?"

He nodded, and then I told him.

Except I didn't tell him what he really wanted to know. Instead, I danced around those details. I told him I'd gotten into the apartment without breaking anything, that none of the alarms had been set, that the only trace of my having even been there was the missing jewelry. Of course, he already knew all that, and since I wasn't giving him what he wanted, he was starting to make noises about doubting my confession. King was smart and a pro, and he was working me; he knew damned well I'd done it, and he also knew it didn't make any difference to me whether he believed me or not, so he was hoping to goad my ego into convincing him.

I told him the date I'd pulled the job and described half a dozen standout pieces that were not in my home when it was searched. I told him the layout of the apartment, exactly what the jewelry box looked like, even what time the Hammers had left for dinner. I didn't tell him how I'd gotten in and out. He knew it was useless to press me, so he gave up.

But I had a question for him. "How come there wasn't a single word about it in the papers?" That had been fine with me, because publicity was the last thing I wanted or needed, but I was curious.

King mumbled something about not wanting to embarrass the Hammers and then quickly changed the subject. I think it had a lot more to do with not embarrassing the police. I found out later that there had been some acute humiliation over their inability to make any headway on the case whatsoever before finally giving up altogether. They assumed it was an inside job of some kind, maybe a doorman or a guard, maybe some maintenance guy, maybe even a family member with access to the place. They got so desperate, they'd even entertained the notion that Armand Hammer had done it himself, for the insurance money, but that was so absurd, they wisely got over it. Imagine a multibillionaire pulling that kind of a scam.

There was also the matter of the usual "human fly" and "phantom" theories they'd allowed the papers to trot out with increasing frequency every time there was a baffling robbery. They'd been doing a lot of that lately and had to know there would doubtless come a point at which some savvy reporter would start to wonder if the police were going to fall back on that sorry bullshit every time they failed to solve a crime.

Of course, they had no way to know at the time that nearly every one of those scores had been pulled by the same guy. They wouldn't know that until the day I rode around in a car with Detective King and confessed to them under the cloak of immunity.

I felt bad that King was burning with so many questions he wanted answered. But the fact is that even though I was in some pretty deep trouble at the moment, I didn't know whether or not I'd be back pulling scores on his turf someday. What was the point of revealing trade secrets? There was absolutely nothing in it for me to tell him how I'd done those jobs. Or maybe there was.

"If I tell you how I got into the Hammer place," I said, "will you get the Ramada charges dropped?"

I could see the gears turning in his head. He wanted desperately to get the details. I made it sound like I'd mentioned just the Hammer job as an opening gambit, thinking maybe he'd come back and ask for two or three others, a bit of negotiating. I had no doubt he'd go for the deal.

But it wasn't his call. "No way the D.A.'s office is going to let you off, Mason. Was up to me, sure, what the hell. But not those guys."

As a result, and against my own interests, the idiotic legends only grew. When the papers reported the deal, the same lamebrained reporters started up the human-fly bullshit yet again. (I bet they thought the Amazing Kreskin and Uri Geller were really psychic.) I suspected South Florida was about to dry up for me completely; every time somebody had some jewelry stolen, the cops would come around demanding to know where I'd been at the time.

As claustrophobic and tense as that situation was, it was just as well that I didn't know it would all crop up again, over eight years later and a thousand miles away. But I'll fill you in on that when I tell you about how I robbed industrialist Joseph Mandel.

10

On Doing Time
(continued)

I KNOW, I know, I was supposed to tell you how I wound up in prison. I'm getting to that.

Just because I'd pulled a good one on the police and district attorney didn't mean they were about to slink away and quietly lick their wounds. To say they were pissed at me doesn't begin to capture it. And to think I voluntarily closed a whole bunch of very visible cases for them. Some gratitude.

They also did nothing to discourage the newspapers from printing wild inaccuracies. A magazine feature article I still have said I'd confessed to more than two hundred robberies. A newspaper said it was more than five hundred. The most I saw in any paper was an even thousand, which would have had me pulling a major score every two days for six years; and two publications quoted an anonymous police source as saying I was also suspected in several murders and rapes. It wouldn't have surprised me if they'd pinned the Lindbergh kidnapping on me as well. It turned out later that the two hundred figure in the magazine came right out of a police report, except that the writer had changed "suspected of" into "confessed to."

There were so many police cars cruising up and down my street every day, it was hard to believe there were any left in case there was a real emergency somewhere else in the city. Helicopters buzzed around overhead, including at all hours of the night. My neighbors hadn't minded the police cars—crime in our immediate vicinity dropped to zero—but the choppers were noisy as hell, especially when they dipped down to nearly treetop level. That there was no real surveillance going and their only goal was to harass me was pretty obvious, because what the hell did they think I was going to do after confessing to all those crimes . . . go out and rob a bank?

Sometimes, just for the hell of it, I'd get up around dawn, get into my car and drive slowly down the street with my headlights off. As soon as I got to the intersection, I'd flick on the lights and zoom off, then zigzag around for ten or twenty minutes, half a dozen prowl cars and a chopper or two following me. Then I'd duck into an all-night convenience store, buy a quart of milk and go home. That, of course, would only piss them off more, which made them step up the midnight chopper-buzzings, which made me even madder, and on and on it went.

It made the neighbors mad, too, but when they'd call the police to complain, they were given an earful of what a dangerous criminal I was and how the police owed it to the community to keep me under surveillance. Since the neighbors all knew me—they trusted me to play with their kids and I was always helping out with minor fix-up chores—they assumed the cops were full of baloney. As one of them said to Barb over coffee one day, "If the police really think your husband's another Dillinger, they'd arrest him, right?"

One real consequence of all of this was that the cops and the D.A. were in no frame of mind to cut me a good deal on the Ramada bust. Zeidwig called one morning and said, "I got their offer. You're not going to like it, but it's the best you're going to get."

I don't remember all the details of what the deal was, but, as I expected he would, Zeidwig tried to talk me into taking it. I interrupted him and said, "I thought you were supposed to be on my side."

"I am on your side. I'm just telling you that I don't think there's any way they're going to improve their offer."

What was with this guy? His attitude seemed to be that we do some negotiation over the offer and when the prosecutors refuse to give any more, we just take it. It didn't even occur to him that maybe we should reject their offers and go to trial.

I was annoyed that Zeidwig automatically assumed they had us by the balls and we had no recourse. Of what possible use was this guy to me if all he was going to do was roll over and play dead? I could do that myself without professional assistance.

"They're pretty pissed at how you got a walk on all those scores," he pressed me, "and now they want—"

"I'm pretty pissed, too, Howard," I told him. "So tell them to stick it in their ear. I want a jury trial."

Zeidwig, who I was liking less and less, was dumbfounded at such a radical notion. "A jury trial! You think you can win a jury trial?"

"Well, hell," I responded, "even if I lose, it can't be much worse than the deal they're offering me now." Actually, it could be a lot worse. I was just trying to leverage my negotiating position, something he should have been helping me with.

He wasn't at all happy with this and seemed more concerned with protecting his reputation in the legal community than with aggressively representing me. "You're a criminal defense attorney," I told him. "And I'm the highest-profile client you ever had. Get me acquitted and you can start doing talk shows."

But I knew what his problem was. He was a dealmaker, not a litigator, and his ability to make those deals was dependent on maintaining good relationships with the other side. If he took me to trial, he'd have to do everything he could to paint the police as inept, incompetent, maybe even corrupt. When it was all over and he had to sit down with them on behalf of another client, his reception would be, to put it mildly, chilly.

I wasn't supposed to have to give a damn about his problem. He was being paid to worry about mine and had sworn an oath to that effect. He was legally obligated to do everything possible within the law to get me acquitted. I remember years later being engrossed in the O. J. Simpson trial and utterly dumbfounded when Johnnie Cochran was criticized for "playing the race card" in getting his client acquitted. It showed me how a lot of people, many of whom should really know better, misunderstand our legal system. Had Cochran *not* played that card, he should have been prosecuted for malfeasance. His job was to do everything he possibly could on behalf of his client, even if that meant blaming the crime on invaders from Mars if necessary.

I had a right to expect a similarly zealous effort from Zeidwig, but I was savvy enough about the world to know that I wasn't going to get it. He wouldn't deliberately compromise my interests, but I didn't think I could count on him to go balls to the wall for me. I realized I was going to have to be a proactive client if I had any chance here at all.

The first thing I asked him to do was subpoena all the police surveillance and other reports. "What do you want those for?" he asked.

Tired as I was of fighting him at every turn, I explained anyway. I wanted to know what they were doing at the Ramada. Who were they really watching for and trying to nail? Was I grabbed up by mistake, and was this harassment just to hide their embarrassment at having gotten the wrong guy?

That's what I told Zeidwig. The other half of it was that I had an unprecedented opportunity to find out what the cops knew about me. Even though I was sure they'd been after someone else, I was bothered by the fact that they'd called me by name when they took me down and hadn't seemed at all surprised that it was me.

I'd done my homework and knew I had a right to those reports. There's a legal process called "discovery" by which a defendant can subpoena anything that can be used against him, and the interpretation of what that involves is pretty liberal. The other side usually fights like hell not to disclose anything, and a judge makes the final determination of what is to be handed over. In civil litigation, discovery is often used as a delaying or harassing tactic. It's not unusual in product liability cases, for example, for an attorney to request documents consisting of millions of pages, hoping this will be such a burden that the opposition will try to settle rather than go broke complying with all those requests. In similar fashion, criminal defendants often ask for things that law enforcement would rather keep hidden, for fear of compromising their sources. Sometimes they'd rather let the defendant go than risk blowing their secrets.

So I settled in for a long wait after Zeidwig made the request for the surveillance reports, figuring this would drag on forever. Less than two days later he phoned. "I've got them," he reported.

"Got what?" It hadn't occurred to me that it would be the reports. He offered to drop them off after work, but I was too excited and immediately headed down to his office.

I expected maybe four or five pages of reading material. Cops are not novelists and they hate paperwork and hardly any of them can type well. When they have to write something up, it's usually done in the fewest words possible. So I could hardly believe my eyes when Zeidwig pointed to a stack of paper on his desk nearly a foot high.

"You're the guy they were watching," he said. "And not just at the Ramada."

‿

I took the stack into a small conference room and started leafing through it, intending to get into the details later but anxious to get an overview. This was when I not only confirmed that it really was me they were watching at the Ramada, but also learned that I'd been under intense surveillance for several weeks prior to that, which made even less sense. That story about seeing me back my car into a spot at Lago Mar was so patently absurd, the prosecutor wouldn't dare try to get away with it at trial. And it couldn't be because of all those big scores; they hadn't even known I'd done them until I rode around with Detective King and told him. Truth be told, there was no reason the police in Florida should have been aware of me at all. The only thing on my record was the garage break-in back in Cleveland when I was practically still a kid, and it was such a small and inconsequential matter, there was no way it could have followed me to Florida. So why would the Fort Lauderdale police have undertaken such massive and expensive surveillance of me? Equally troubling to me, why had they done it at that particular time?

I found the answer almost at the bottom of the stack of documents. It looked to me like it had been buried there deliberately, maybe in the hope that neither Zeidwig nor I would notice it. As I read it, I got madder and madder, but only at myself.

Turned out old Derek Johnson, the friend of Augie's I'd spoken with about driving a boat for the Red Cross Ball score, wasn't so dumb after all. Venal, deceitful and traitorous, but not dumb.

Derek had neglected to tell me that he had some legal troubles of his own. He'd hardly made it out of my backyard the afternoon we'd spoken about the job before he ran right to the cops and said he had some information he was willing to trade for a free ride on actions pending against him. He told them he knew about an upcoming score, except he didn't know what it was or when it would take place, just that it involved me. They believed that Derek might have been on to something, because they knew that nobody, especially somebody who was already in trouble, would be stupid enough to lead them into a wild-goose chase, but they were ready to send him on his way anyway because his information was too vague. Then somebody decided to run a quick background check on me and turned up my old burglary conviction, and that got their attention. From there, they considered the few details Derek had given them—use of a boat, ten grand for a few hours' work, a perpetrator they'd never heard of who'd come to town from a thousand miles away—and decided maybe something really big was in the works.

Never use a partner was what I'd learned back in Ohio. That simple concept had kept me out of trouble for years. Then I'd gone ahead and broken that rule, had actually only *spoken* about breaking that rule, and *whammo*: Here I was.

I didn't mention any of this to Zeidwig when I emerged from the conference room some two hours later. I would have liked to let him know that I'd been right about the Lago Mar business being a load of crap and that he ought to be casting a more skeptical eye at what the police were telling him, but I didn't want to get into a conversation about how a guy I'd considered hiring for a hijacking had turned on me. Besides, it really didn't matter, because even though the police had lied to my lawyer, they could always argue that they were just trying to protect a confidential source, and they'd probably get away with it. Instead I told Zeidwig I wanted to subpoena every single cop who was at the Ramada and who had been involved, however slightly, in following me during the weeks prior. I also told him to subpoena the manager of the Ramada, the head of housekeeping and all of the chambermaids. I said I'd draw up a witness list and would include a bunch of real estate brokers from Fort Lauderdale and Miami, as well as guys from the Cleveland investment group who owned the properties I managed, who would testify that I had good reason to be checking on properties for sale.

"And subpoena Gerald Ford, too," I finished up.

Already annoyed at how I seemed to be taking over management of the case, he slammed his pen down on the table and stood up behind his desk. "What the hell are you talking about!"

"I spoke with him while the cops were watching me. Shook hands, too. If they thought I was such a dangerous and reprehensible character, how the hell come they let me walk right up to the president?"

"Listen—" he started, but I was no longer interested in his opinion.

"I got the right, so let's get him in." It wasn't going to happen, of course, but I thought it was a nice touch.

There wasn't even a burglary charge on the table, because nothing was stolen, so the most they had was trespassing and this nonsensical "Possession of Burglary Tools" thing. Were they really prepared to put on a full-bore trial for that petty bullshit? The judge would laugh them out of the courtroom. They couldn't even muster up the standard resisting-arrest baloney, because there wasn't a single hint anywhere in my background that I'd ever been involved in anything violent. Even the records of my bust for the garage break-in years ago had a note stating that I'd offered zero resistance and had been completely civil throughout.

The story the cops were telling about the bust itself was impossible. They said they caught me wiping fingerprints from the doorknob of Room 127 with my handkerchief. I knew they'd made that up because I never did it. That wasn't much of an argument, of course, but what made their story impossible was that they couldn't have seen it even if it were true. I was inside the room and they were outside.

I hired a professional photographer to take pictures of the Ramada, concentrating on getting shots from every angle of the interior and hallways in the vicinity of Room 127. I had Zeidwig notify the Ramada manager that the reason he was being subpoenaed was to testify as to the authenticity of those photos. Damned if I can remember how, but I also got my hands on a list of the prospective jurors and used the trusty city directory as a starting point to learn everything I could about them. I was my own jury consultant before that term ever came into vogue.

I called Bill Welling, who, as I knew he would, came down to help out. We set up shop in my garage and he got to work making a scale model of the hallways around Room 127. When it was done, he practiced assembling it for court and could get it out of the box and all put together in about three minutes. It would prove the police couldn't have seen what they reported. Every time I opened my garage door, we could see one or two police cars parked in the street, guys inside with binoculars and cameras equipped with telephoto lenses, trying to see what we were up to. Welling did most of the work himself, because I was spending a lot of time in depositions.

Part of the discovery process, a deposition is an official statement made by a witness in a criminal case or lawsuit. It's done under oath, under questioning by the attorney for the side the witness will be testifying against. All those great courtroom surprises you saw on *Perry Mason* were largely fictional. In real life, defendants have the right to know what witnesses and testimony are going to be brought to bear against them, in order to be able to prepare their defense. That doesn't mean that the witness has to tell everything he's going to say, but what he does have to do is answer every lawful and relevant question that's put to him by the opposing attorney. That means the attorney has to think of everything to make sure he doesn't get surprised at trial. I sat at Zeidwig's side for every depo and often passed him little notes with questions to ask the witnesses.

Also in the room during depositions was the head prosecutor, assistant state attorney David Damore, representing the people. His job was to protect the state's case, and he had the right to object to any of our questions he thought inappropriate. I chatted with him a lot during breaks, and we got to like each other. For some reason he enjoyed seeing the cops squirm, especially when Zeidwig and I cornered them into giving information they knew contradicted what other cops had said. He was a damned good prosecutor and thoroughly enjoyed putting bad guys away, but he didn't seem to think I was that bad, and he was beginning to see that the people's case wasn't all that the cops had led him to believe. Once when we were alone in a hallway, he confided that he had a thing going with that pretty cop I'd held the door open for at the Ramada.

"Your biggest problem," he said that same afternoon, "is those master keys."

I nodded. No reason not to let him know I understood, but I didn't say anything out loud. When I reported that to Zeidwig, he said, "What he's doing, he's letting you know that their case isn't as hopeless as we'd like to think."

"But what about me wiping fingerprints off the doorknob? Everybody knows that's bullshit!"

"You're right," Zeidwig said. "And that's why they won't ever mention it."

That shook me up, and I asked him what he was talking about. They'd already mentioned it on dozens of occasions, and I'd never given them a hint of how we planned to thoroughly nuke their testimony on it.

"They might figure it out for themselves. We subpoenaed the manager of the hotel, you had a photographer in there. . . . They might piece it together."

"So why don't we bring it up ourselves?"

It was a silly question, as I was to quickly learn. You can't put words in the other side's mouth at trial and then expect to make them look bad for things they didn't bring up themselves. Even if it was in their written reports, they could always say they weren't sure enough to testify to it, which makes them look honest and forthright and makes you look like a schmuck.

"Don't look so down," Zeidwig said. "If they do bring it up, we nuke 'em. If they don't, that's one less thing they have against you."

But it still left us the problem of the keys.

~

By that time the cops and I had a real mutual-hate thing going. I have to say, I don't have a dislike for police. Quite to the contrary, I've had police friends and neighbors all my life, and still do. I respect what they do and have usually been treated civilly by them even when I was in trouble or under suspicion.

But this was different. I didn't hate cops, but I sure hated *these* cops. I knew they were terribly frustrated, having expended enormous resources on me only to come away with almost nothing, but that was part of the game and they should have simply gone on to other matters instead of pursuing this one so relentlessly. I'm not saying I was completely innocent—far from it—but there were an awful lot of really vicious crimes being committed in South Florida, most notoriously by drug smugglers, so no way was I worth the kind of attention being paid to me. If the citizens of some of the more beleaguered communities in Broward County had known about these lopsided priorities, I bet they would have rioted.

I was still playing baseball and football in the street with neighborhood kids every night, and the cops would cruise by several times an hour. Every time they did, it would interrupt the game, and they made sure to go extremely slowly. They weren't making too many friends among the impressionable youth of the area. Once in a while they'd roll down a window and say something nasty to me, just out of earshot of the kids. If I could also avoid being heard by the kids, I'd tell the cops to go fuck themselves. It was getting real petty and juvenile, and I wasn't doing much to help the situation.

I need to point out, in case it's not obvious, that my behavior in this situation was so completely different from the way I'd lived my life up to then that it was as though my brain had been taken over by aliens. I'd always been described as quiet, even somber. I never bragged about or disclosed any of the things I'd done, and in those few situations where it was necessary to let slip a few details, I stuck with the unembellished basics. My entire modus operandi was never to call attention to myself, never to needlessly antagonize anyone and never to make it necessary for someone else to act against me because I'd let something go public. So why was I all of a sudden allowing myself to get drawn into a pissing contest with policemen, knowing full well that they held all the cards?

Part of it was probably that the whole situation had already gone public, and that aspect of it was out of my control. I was also facing charges, which I hadn't had to come to grips with since I'd broken into that garage as a teenager. And these were a lot more serious, with no quick deal on the table. To top it off, some of the charges were completely bogus: In order for the police to save face and justify that ridiculous expenditure of department resources, they had to demonize me and see to it that the charges and subsequent sentence warranted all that effort.

The harder they pressed the case, the harder I felt I had to hit back. Having been on my own for so long, relying only on my wits to protect me, I wasn't at all comfortable placing my fate in the hands of an attorney who didn't appear to have as much enthusiasm for my defense as I did. The harassment the cops were subjecting me to was petty and sopho-moric, and had I been thinking straight, I might have had the resolve to ignore it, to make sure that none of that bickering could be laid against me. But when caravans of squad cars began cruising past my house, scaring the hell out of my kids, and when uniformed officers hurled profanities and threatened me as they drove by, it wasn't in my nature to stand there and take it. I rationalized this by telling myself I had to let them know they weren't dealing with some pansy who was going to lie down in front of their legal juggernaut; they had to know I was going to fight them tooth and claw. Fact is, though, what the police thought shouldn't have been my main concern. What mattered was what the prosecutor and jury thought, and if I'd played it differently, I wouldn't have riled the entire police force into putting pressure on the D.A. to let me have both barrels. If I'd lain low and played nice, it might have faded a little from their memories as they turned their attention to more pressing problems. Instead, their hatred of me kept escalating as I hated them back.

It was about then that I first met Ray Sandstrom, who was to figure large in the rest of my life. I also met his client Steven Simonson, that amazingly nervous guy I told you about whom the guards in prison liked to play jokes on, the one who had disguised himself as a priest to commit a robbery.

Simonson was going to trial on those charges in two weeks, and Sandstrom came to Zeidwig with an idea. I can still conjure up almost verbatim the conversation that followed, because it made such a strong impression on me.

Simonson was out on bail pending trial, as was I, so the four of us met at a bar in Hallandale. Ray Sandstrom looked like a real character, with deeply etched features and a big, droopy mustache. He was given to wearing flashy suits with wide lapels and a lot of jewelry: bracelets, gold neck-laces, fat rings on half his fingers. That was part of the way he thumbed his nose at what he called "the power structure." Much later I'd think back to this first meeting, and the early intimation I had that Ray Sand-strom was the most volatile third rail in South Florida's criminal defense community.

The flashy lawyer wasted no time in laying out his plan. "Thing is," he said to Zeidwig, "your guy [me] fits the description the police have of the phony priest better than my guy [Simonson]." He turned and addressed me directly. "What I want to do, I want to call you as a defense witness and ask you a whole bunch of questions that make it look like you were the priest, not Simonson."

I stared at him like he'd just landed from the planet Bonkers, but Zeidwig never batted an eye. Whatever he thought, he knew Sandstrom wasn't crazy, and he also knew he wouldn't waste our time, that there had do be something in it for us. "Then what?" he prompted.

"Mason gets all pissed off and huffy," Sandstrom answered. "He takes the Fifth and refuses to answer anything I ask." He paused and looked at each of us in turn, to make sure we were following. Zeidwig still had his poker face on, and I have no idea what I looked like because all it was to me was nuts. "At that point I declare him a hostile witness," Sandstrom went on.

"Bet your ass I'd be hostile." Those were pretty much my first words of the meeting.

Sandstrom nodded sympathetically. "And who could blame you? But your refusing to answer means my client isn't getting the justice he's enti-tled to. Asking the judge to declare you hostile means you're not cooper-ating voluntarily. You're fighting me to save your own ass, and there's not much anybody can do about it, because you have a right to protect your ass. Constitution says so. And right there we have a real whopper of a dilemma."

He leaned back on his chair. "My guy is getting the short stick because Mason won't say what he knows. And if Mason is forced to say what he knows, then he gets fucked because he's not supposed to have to incrimi-nate himself. It's like dueling rights."

From the corner of my eye I could see Zeidwig nodding. "Except only one of them is actually on trial," he said, "and that's your guy. So at that moment he's more important, because he's in jeopardy."

"Right." Sandstrom let his chair drop and leaned forward with his forearms on the table. "Better to let ten guilty men go free than put one innocent man in jail. Bible says that somewhere, right? So the only solu-tion is for the judge to grant Mason complete immunity so he can testify."

Now I got it. Sort of. "What the hell do I need immunity from the priest job for? I didn't do it!"

"Fuck the priest job!" Sandstrom shot back with a smile.

Zeidwig grabbed my arm and squeezed. "You still deny the priest job, but it comes off lame. Then Ray here, he says something like 'Who are you kidding, Mason? What are you, some kind of angel? You telling this court you didn't intend to rob that Ramada?'"

"At which point," Sandstrom said, "you cop to the Ramada thing. 'Hell yeah, I was out to rob the Ramada, but I sure as hell didn't dress up as no priest!' Now you're off the hook for Ramada because of your immunity, the jury thinks you did the priest job, too, or at least they're so goddamned confused, they have reasonable doubt about whether Steven here did it, and they acquit him." With a huge, smug grin beneath that walrus mustache, Sandstrom spread his hands and said, "Everybody walks away happy!"

"Except the prosecutor," Zeidwig threw in.

"*Fuck* the prosecutor," Sandstrom snapped at him. "He's not my client!"

I still remember what I was thinking at that moment like it had been laid out in glowing neon: *Goddamnit . . . now* this *is my kind of lawyer!*

Zeidwig shook his head and looked down at his hands. "It's not ethical," he declared.

Sandstrom rolled his eyes at the ceiling, then looked at me like *Where the hell did you find this guy?*

I waved my lawyer to silence and asked Sandstrom a bunch of questions. Zeidwig started fidgeting and at one point said imperiously, "I cannot suborn perjury! If I know in advance my client is going to lie on the stand, I—"

"Show me where he's lying," Sandstrom challenged him.

Here I was fighting Zeidwig again. Like I didn't have enough worry and stress and a mile-long list of things to do, I had to waste energy wrestling with my own lawyer?

~

We broke up the meeting, but over the next few days I met with Sandstrom and left Zeidwig out of it. We had it nailed down pretty good, and then just before Simonson's trial the assistant D.A. made him an offer: two years on some lesser charge. Simonson, so nervous and panicked he hadn't slept right in months, took the deal, so we never got to see if our plan would work. I was enraged at the cowardly little prick, but at least I'd gotten to see a real lawyer in action.

I thought Ray Sandstrom was absolutely the cat's nuts. He wasn't so much about wanting to get guilty people off; he was simply the most rabidly antiauthoritarian human being I'd ever met. "People in charge" who threw their weight around pissed him off. He'd conjured up all kinds of crazy strategies and delaying tactics for Simonson, and whereas I'd had to kick Zeidwig in the ass to get him to think outside the box, you practically had to strap Ray down just to keep him on planet Earth.

I had Zeidwig conduct a few additional depositions, just to make sure David Damore knew how committed I was to the case. One of the people we deposed was Joseph Gerwens, a police officer who'd been at the Ramada that day. He would later become chief of the Fort Lauderdale Police Department. I didn't think about him much at the time, but he was to figure in my life more than once.

Two days before my trial, Damore called Zeidwig and asked for a meeting. We went to the D.A.'s office, got a couple of cups of coffee and sat down.

"Look," Damore said, "we all know our case isn't airtight."

"That's for damned sure," I agreed.

"On the other hand, I'm betting you don't have a very good explanation for those master keys." He waited for us not to comment, then said to Zeidwig, "Your client and the cops may be at each other's throats, but the fact of the matter is, my office doesn't really give much of a shit about this case."

"So drop the charges," Zeidwig suggested glibly.

"Yeah, right. After all that publicity? We're not about to end up looking like a bunch of assholes without a fight."

"You'll look like a bunch of assholes if you lose at trial," I tossed in casually. Big mistake. Zeidwig had warned me to keep my mouth shut, and now he threw me a withering look.

Damore sneered at my naïveté, then explained what Zeidwig already knew. "If we lose," he said with exaggerated patience, "we come out looking all grim and self-righteous and tell the papers how you snookered the dumb-ass jury with underhanded tactics, just another example of what happens when a knee-jerk, bleeding-heart liberal Supreme Court waters down the laws and coddles criminals, et cetera, et cetera."

Zeidwig shrugged, totally unoffended. "That about sums it up."

Now I was thinking, *So why is Damore so reluctant to go to trial? Win or lose, he comes out okay.*

He answered without my having to ask. "But we don't want you getting away with all of it, Mason. We don't want it *seen* that you walked on this. And you don't want to go to trial, because if you lose, you're going to do some very serious time. And you *could* lose. Your lawyer explain all of this to you already?"

He had. Somehow or other, Damore would see to it that the jury knew about all those scores I'd owned up to and gotten a walk on. That would turn them against me, and he'd also bring up to the sentencing judge that I had a criminal record stemming from the break-in at the garage. Put all of that together and I could get convicted and end up in prison for-damned-near-ever.

"So what're you proposing?" Zeidwig asked. All the preliminaries had been for my benefit; he already knew all of it.

"Ninety days in jail, seven years probation. Hell, he could get five years on the burglary tools alone, plus whatever else the jury chooses to buy into."

There was no need for him to go into sales overdrive. It was a tremendously generous deal, and Zeidwig and I both knew it. Nevertheless, Zeidwig said, "Give us the night to think it over."

Damore said that was no problem, and we broke it up. On the way home in my car Zeidwig and I talked it over. The first thing he said was, "If you want this deal, and I think you do, we better get it done today."

"How come?"

"Because it's my guess the police don't know about it. After what you put them through, if they find out about this offer they're going to try to lynch Damore, and he might take it off the table."

"After what I did to them? What about what they did to me!"

"They don't care about what they did to you! They're not on trial and they're not facing prison!"

He was right, of course. And if nothing else, I didn't want my family suffering any more embarrassing publicity. I dropped Zeidwig off and went home to talk it over with Barb, but it was just a formality. She figured she could live without me for three months but not five years or ten or twenty. There was also something about the finality of a deal that seemed to settle her down. I think it was mostly uncertainty that had been driving her up a wall. Same went for me. When I called Zeidwig back to tell him to accept, I suddenly felt a tremendous weight rise up off my chest that I hadn't quite realized had been there.

Once we got that resolved, Barb's biggest concern was the kids. Suzi was fifteen, Mark thirteen and Laura seven. Although not particularly worldly-wise, they were each smart as hell, intensely curious and savvier than most adults. They read the newspapers, too, even little Laura, and while I could pass off most of what they'd been reading about me as baloney, there was no way around the fact that their father was about to go to prison. I did my best to explain the situation, using all the standard euphemistic terminology about "mistakes" and "bad decisions," and I also made sure they understood that the crime for which I was actually about to be punished had never occurred and that it was all a mistake. I could have saved my breath, though, because what I'd done or not done and whether I deserved the prison time was the last thing on their minds. All they cared about was that I'd be gone. The emotions shooting through me as they hung on to me like baby chimps and cried their eyes out are impossible to describe. Needless to say, I made a solemn vow never to do anything that would risk a repeat of that scene.

The next morning I went into court to plead guilty. It was supposed to be a formality, but at one point the judge, Robert Tyson, started reading something and went quiet for several uncomfortable minutes. Just as Zeidwig cleared his throat and got ready to ask him what was going on, Judge Tyson looked up at me and tapped his fingers on the papers in front of him. "Says here—"

"Where?" I asked, because my lawyer wasn't about to.

"Police report," the judge answered. "Says there's a standing order in the police department never to arrest you unless at least four officers are present. Now why's that?"

I knew why it was. Detective King had written up in his report that I could climb four stories up a rope, hand over hand, while carrying a fifty-pound backpack and without using my legs. There were probably very few officers in the Fort Lauderdale P.D. in that kind of condition.

I was struggling to frame an answer when Zeidwig jumped in. "With all due respect, your honor," he said, all humble and subservient, "is the court really asking my client to explain something in a police report? He didn't write it, nor does he agree with it. Mr. Mason has never had a single incident of violence, has never resisted arrest, hasn't once in his entire life—"

"All right, all right," Tyson said, waving Zeidwig down. The judge was a small, gray-haired mousy guy, a big boozer who always looked like the bench he'd rather be on was the one in a bar. "Guilty plea is entered, sentencing to be pronounced in thirty days."

I was released on my own recognizance with no restrictions, as we'd arranged with Damore, and I took Barb and the kids on a weeklong cruise. We had a great time, the most relaxed and happy we'd all been in months. I prepared the kids for my impending absence, telling them again that the police had made a mistake but that I'd agreed to go to prison for a while in order not to risk it turning into a bigger mistake. Three months would pass like it was nothing, I assured them. By then they'd pretty much gotten used to the idea after the initial shock, and were so excited and agog and distracted at being on that giant ship that we managed to have one hell of a time together.

Two weeks after that I appeared in court again and was sentenced to twenty years, with all but ninety days of it suspended and seven years' probation. As expected, the Fort Lauderdale police just exploded when they heard, but there wasn't anything they could do about it except fume to the press. When they took out after Damore, he got his hackles up and lashed right back, letting them know in no uncertain terms that if they hadn't fucked up the bust so badly, he could have put me away for the full twenty. He was right, so they backed off and got on with their business, without holding it against Damore.

And that's how I came to be on the fifth floor of the Broward County Jail, answering the phones, bullshitting with the guards and playing nasty tricks on Steven Simonson, who I figured had screwed me by opting out of his trial and accepting a two-year stretch. If he'd gone along with Ray Sandstrom's wildly creative strategy, neither of us might have ended up in there.

Howard Zeidwig kept his cordial relationship with the D.A.'s office and went on to become a judge.

Ray Sandstrom went on to become my lawyer.

11

The Storm After
the Calm

THAT SEPTEMBER, because of good behavior (I didn't kill anybody while inside), after seventy-seven days of my ninety-day sentence I was processed out of the Broward County Jail at a minute past midnight. Barbara was there to pick me up. I remember us hugging each other fiercely but don't remember that we said much. At home Mark and Suzi had stayed up to greet me, and it was a joyous reunion. Looking at them, so innocent and so unaware of the real world, climbing all over me and not even wise enough to be angry at me for depriving them of their father for so long, I felt pangs of guilt so strong, it was all I could do to keep from breaking down on the spot. They were both teenagers, which would seem to put them beyond too many notions of "innocent," but Barb was a strong and loving mother who made sure that family came first in their lives, and that seemed to be just fine with them. I promised them over and over that I'd never let it happen again, and I meant every word from the bottom of my heart. Barbara, standing nearby, joined in my reassurances to the kids. I wanted to stay up all night just holding them, but they started yawning and eventually dropped off to sleep. I carried them up to bed, and there was no doubt in my heart I was now a reformed jewel thief. "I mean it," I said to Barb, many times.

After barely three hours of sleep, I went back downtown to meet with my probation officer. Walking past the jail, I thought I could actually smell the inside of the place from out there on the street. The building seemed to loom over me, threatening and forbidding, a dark and ominous fortress that was as much an ever-present warning as a place of punishment. I shuddered and turned away, quickening my steps.

My P.O. was a woman named Cheryl, and she was an absolute knockout. Though just in her mid-twenties, she was a thorough-going pro and was quite used to meeting men who were fresh out of jail and hadn't had sex—at least not with a woman—for months or years. She made small talk and shuffled papers around until I managed to put my eyes back in my head, then we got down to business. I found her very easy to talk to, and she seemed to like me as well. After a while she said, "You need to start keeping your nose clean. You know that, right?"

I threw up my hands defensively. "I hear you," I said with great conviction. "And believe me, I'm a changed man."

"Yeah, right. Seen the light, have you?"

"I'm not going to kid you," I replied. "It's not about finding God or suddenly respecting the law. Thing is"—I pointed toward the bleak walls of the jail visible outside her window—"there's no way in hell I ever want to go back in there."

"Good," Cheryl said. "But when I said to keep your nose clean, I don't mean just burglary. I mean don't let a parking meter expire on you. Don't spit on the street, don't even cross against a friggin' light."

Seemed a little strong to me, and I must have shrugged or something, because Cheryl leaned across her desk and said, "Listen. My boyfriend's a criminal defense attorney here in town. He's heard about you and said that every cop in the city is looking for an excuse to nail your ass to the nearest cross. You understand what I'm saying?"

I nodded dumbly. I should have known that anyway, but somehow, hearing it from a public official drove it home just a little deeper and it shook me.

Over time Cheryl and I became good friends. She'd drop by the house periodically and she and Barb hit it off real well. The three of us even went out for dinner or drinks once in a while, and to the Las Olas Art Festival. Obviously, she knew all about my background and would sometimes ask me to come to her condo to fix something. She came to trust me and would always give me permission to go back to Cleveland on business anytime I asked.

She never let us meet her boyfriend, though. We knew his name was Frank and that he was a top-notch defense attorney, but he was also married. Cheryl never mentioned it outright, but I had little doubt that Frank, aware of my criminal history, wasn't about to let himself be put in a position where a known felon could blackmail him by threatening to tell his wife about his affair. Can't say I blamed him one bit, even though blackmail wasn't in my repertoire.

Cheryl wasn't kidding about the cops having it in for me. Our street was still the best patrolled in all of Fort Lauderdale. I was the most cautious and law-abiding citizen you ever saw and wouldn't so much as drop a toothpick on the street. I spent time managing the properties in Miami and my own building in Cleveland, and I got pretty good at knowing when I was being tailed. Of course, with something like that it was impossible to know *how* good, because there was no way to be sure nobody was following you at the moment.

A couple of months after I was released, I got a surprise phone call from Dave Damore, the guy who had prosecuted my case, inviting me out to lunch. Wondering what the hell that was all about, I agreed, and it really was a surprise.

"I quit the D.A.'s office," Damore said. "Going into private practice."

"Don't tell me criminal defense," I responded skeptically. I wasn't aware at the time that this was a traditional career move for assistant D.A.s. They get tons of invaluable trial experience on the county's nickel and make great contacts up and down the line, then let the private firms know they're available and just wait for the best offer, which can be double what they've been making.

We chatted for a while, then Damore looked at his watch and said he had to get going to a meeting. He handed his business card across the table. "You ever need some help, give me a call."

I took the card and grinned. "So what are you doing, trolling your old busts for future clients?"

He laughed. "If I'm ever going to be rich, it'll be off habitual fuckups like you, Mason."

I shook my head and told him he'd be wasting his time with me. "I'm out of it, Dave. Swear to God, I've had it."

"Tell you the truth, I hope so. But you'd better watch your step; cops around here still don't like you."

I told him that I was doing just that, and there was no way the cops could pin anything on me.

He got up to leave. "You never know what can happen, Bill. Hell, one phone call to the IRS . . ."

"One phone call and what?"

"Who knows?" he said. "But if I were you, I'd make sure my financial affairs were all nice and tidy."

I had the definite impression I'd just gotten an important warning, and that afternoon I asked Cheryl if she knew a good accountant. She recommended a tax lawyer instead, a guy named Peter Aiken, and offered to set up an appointment for me.

Aiken was a great guy. He had a big fish on his wall with a sign under it: "He wouldn't have gotten caught if he'd just kept his mouth shut." After I laid out my situation to him, Aiken advised me to put everything I owned in Barb's name. Then he told me to move all my records to his office.

"What for?" I asked him. I wasn't comfortable with someone else having them. What if he got squeezed himself and was forced to turn my papers over to the police?

"Because it's a whole lot harder for the police to get a search warrant for my office than for your house. You can come down here anytime you need to work on them, but nobody else can get their hands on them."

I must still have looked a little skeptical, because he added, "You do understand that attorney-client privilege applies to any attorney, right? Not just a criminal defense lawyer, but me, too."

That hadn't occurred to me. It made sense, and I did just as Aiken advised.

~

This is a good place to relate a little story that will give you some idea of what South Florida was like in the seventies.

With all of this extra time I had by not stealing jewelry, I decided to get serious about my real estate business. I thought it would be nice to have some income property in Florida that I actually owned rather than just managed for someone else.

I found a nice house in Lighthouse Point, just north of Pompano and close to the Hillsboro Inlet coming in off the Atlantic, a great place to watch ships of all sizes sail by. I got the house for a good price because it needed a lot of work and had put it in Barb's name, as Peter Aiken had advised me to do. I hoped to have it ready to rent by the start of the winter season. The house was originally two bedrooms and two baths, and I wanted to add a third bedroom and bath in addition to a new sixty-foot dock. With help from Barb's brother Augie, I did all but the most specialized stuff myself.

When it was done I ran a rental ad in the paper, and it hadn't been on the newsstands for two hours the next morning before our phone began ringing off the hook. The first guy I showed it to loved it but didn't seem to be interested in much else besides the dock. Now, remember that I had put about a thousand backbreaking hours into this place, used quality materials and even partially furnished it, and was thrilled I could get it ready on time. I had no idea that none of that made any difference and I could have saved myself the trouble.

In the ad I'd said I wanted the first and last months' rent and a security deposit, but this guy, who hadn't been in the house ten minutes, offered to pay for six months in advance and started peeling hundred-dollar bills off a huge roll of money. Then he signed the lease without reading it. All this was pretty suspicious, but I didn't see much basis to argue about it, so I handed him the keys, wished him good luck and left.

I didn't hear a word out of him for nearly two weeks, which is awfully unusual for a new tenant, who usually has a list of things he wants fixed. I called information to get his number, but they didn't have a listing, so I decided to go out there and check up on things, and would tell him I was just dropping by to see how he was doing. When I got there, the house looked exactly as it had when I'd last seen it. There was nothing at all on the lawn or the deck, no personal touches of any kind. I knocked on the door and got no answer, and the elderly lady who lived next door called out, "I don't think anybody lives there." I had said hello to her once or twice when I was working on the place, but now introduced myself more formally and explained that I'd just rented the place out. She said that she'd never seen anybody go in or out. I left her my phone number, then went to the mailbox to see if anything had been accumulating in there. I found the keys and a note. It said, "Decided not to take the house. Keep the money for your trouble," and was unsigned. I knew right away that the guy was a drug smuggler and had used the house—and the dock—to bring in one big load and had then gotten out of Dodge.

The amount of money involved in the drug trade was truly staggering. Freighters were going up and down the coast at night, off-loading their cargo onto smaller boats that would ferry it in to various points along the shore. The coastline was too big to be patrolled effectively, and you had to laugh every time the police would display a seized shipment on television, always claiming it was the biggest haul ever, anyone with half a brain knowing it represented an absurdly small percentage of the stuff that was being brought in. The popular line was that all the DEA was doing was raising prices, but the fact is they weren't even doing that. They really weren't making any difference at all. The money my "renter" had paid me would barely be a rounding error compared to how much a single shipment of quality dope would net him, and every shipment that got intercepted by the police was just the cost—and a modest cost, at that—of doing business. Every time the feds trot out a table full of seized dope and claim to have made a significant dent in the drug trade, it's pure deception. If it weren't, it'd be difficult to find dope on the streets, and there's nothing difficult about it at all.

The truly incredible money to be made in the cocaine trade turned a lot of otherwise ordinary people into monsters. The muscle side of the Colombian cartels thought nothing of shooting up crowded public places and killing innocent bystanders when they got in the way of business, and it wasn't just about murdering people who'd crossed them up in deals. They'd kill competitors, aggressive law enforcers, judges, D.A.s, anybody who threatened to come between them and the free flow of dope and money.

I ran another ad in the paper and showed the house to a nice young couple who liked it immediately. They looked pretty straight, even though they gave me the up-front money in cash. I stopped by a couple of times to see how they were doing. They'd wasted no time in filling the house with top-of-the-line furniture and electronics, including sophisticated stereos and the biggest televisions you could buy at the time. They seemed like a very pleasant, down-to-earth couple, and I started to relax a little.

One morning a few weeks later my phone rang. It was the old lady next door, telling me that the cops had been swarming over the house all night. She said they'd missed the couple but were convinced a big load had come in before they'd split. I got out there right away, but by that time the police had left. The house was perfectly intact, including all the furniture, electronics and closets full of very expensive clothing. While I was going from room to room, two detectives showed up and started questioning me, but I couldn't give them much. I wouldn't have, anyway, but they didn't seem to know who I was, so I acted cooperative. I'd never asked the renters for I.D., since they'd paid me in cash, and they doubtless hadn't used their real names. I asked the detectives if they were going to stake the place out in case the couple came back, but these were two experienced guys who weren't about to waste their time. "They're gone," one of them said. "You might as well look for new tenants."

I would do just that but not before I returned that afternoon with Barb, the kids and a truck. We loaded up all the toys and clothes and some of the furniture, and by that evening Mark was happily fiddling with the best stereo rig a teenage kid ever had.

I ran an ad again and, sure enough, rented the house to another couple who paid cash up front and then disappeared. So far I'd rented it three times, pocketed a year and a half's worth of rent, in cash, and still the house was empty. I was starting to like this setup. The fourth tenant was a very nice guy who told me he was in the process of moving his business over from Plant City, Florida, which is about twenty miles east of Tampa. When he moved in, he had another nice couple with him, and I was starting to think maybe I had a straight tenant this time, although I hoped not so I could rent the house yet again. For the next two months he paid the rent right on time and I assumed the gravy train had come to an end, but then I got "the call" again.

This time the cops did a little better. I don't know if they nabbed the original renter, but they got the couple who'd been with him and a few other houseguests. They found over three million dollars in marijuana, most of it in the house and some on a boat docked in the back. One of the houseguests had an even million in cash in the trunk of his car that was parked in the driveway.

The police confiscated the drugs, cash, boat and two cars, and took seven people into custody. I hung around as they went over the house from top to bottom. Interestingly, they hadn't bothered to take a panel van that was in the garage, and also left all the expensive stereos and televisions. They'd also missed a half kilo of cocaine under one of the beds.

The next day a detective called me at home and wanted information about the man from Plant City. He was gruff and insistent, and it got my hackles up. I refused to tell him anything, and he said, "Some of us are starting to think maybe you're involved."

I asked him how stupid somebody would have to be to purposely rent the same house to drug smugglers when the police had already busted the place twice. I also told him I couldn't be expected to run criminal background checks on everybody who wanted to rent the house. The detective and I weren't getting along at all, but I couldn't seem to stop myself from angering him.

Meanwhile, I once again had a house full of expensive electronics, and the detectives never mentioned the van still in the garage. I let two weeks go by before assuming they'd just forgotten about it, then did a title search based on the plates and vehicle identification number. It was in the name of a company in Plant City, which it took me only a couple of phone calls to find out didn't exist any longer, if it ever had. I had a locksmith make up a new set of keys, and then I made myself president of the company by ordering up some business cards. I also "moved" the company to Cleveland the same way, then filed for new title using that address. Any cop who stopped me and radioed in to the station for "wants and warrants" on the vehicle would find that everything matched up and was completely legit. Another week without hearing from the police, and I drove the van a few miles south to Hollywood and parked it at Barb's aunt's house.

And the house was unoccupied once again. South Florida in the seventies was like a custom-tailored paradise for me. Or so I thought.

For a little over a year after I was released from jail, things went pretty smoothly. I was being a good boy, as the cheesed-off cops were still following me, although with nowhere near the intensity as before. It didn't bother me much when I could see them, cruising slowly by the house in official prowl cars or following me when I was driving. It was much more disconcerting when I couldn't see them, because then I didn't know if I was being tailed or not. On the surface it wouldn't seem to make much difference, since I wasn't doing anything illegal, but you have no idea how uncomfortable it is when you simply don't know.

Things were good at home. Once the shock of my incarceration and the events leading up to it had worn off, Barb figured I must have learned my lesson. Looking back over my account of that period, it seems I put a humorous spin on some parts, but I assure you there was very little funny about it. Maybe those cops and reporters who said I "didn't like jail" were more insightful than I credited them for. There really were a lot of guys there who didn't seem to mind it anywhere near as much as I did, and I just couldn't understand that. Ninety days might not seem like much, but think for a second about what the date is right now, think of the date three months from now, and then imagine being locked up in a noisy, smelly, stultifying cell block until that date. Imagine having virtually nothing to occupy your mind and being utterly at the whim of other people with no way to say, "Okay, no more, I give up, make it stop." I never wanted to go back there and, as Barb assumed, thought nothing was worth that risk.

Business was good, too. I'd resumed my regular trips to Cleveland, although nowhere near as often as before, since I wasn't fencing any goods to Blute Tomba. I just went there to work on my properties, kept my nose clean and then returned to Florida.

Out of the blue someone made a great offer on the building I owned. I'd put it in Barb's name and we flew up there together to close the deal. We saw some old friends and had a wonderful few days, then returned with a very comfortable chunk of money in the bank in addition to the steady income I was earning. I was living the typical life of the typical suburban square, and all was well again.

One Saturday a few weeks after we closed on the building, I spent the morning cleaning the pool and washing the car, and the afternoon playing with the kids. Barb and I usually went out Saturday evenings, but Suzanne was out with friends and we were unable to get a baby-sitter for Mark and Laura, so that wasn't in the cards. Long about nine o'clock I was feeling a little restless and decided to take a ride up to Oakland Park Boulevard, about five blocks north of our house, and have a drink. I parked behind a bar on the corner of Oakland and Bayview and went in, but there wasn't anybody there I knew so I had only one drink and then left.

It was a beautiful night, so I didn't bother with my car but walked about two blocks east to a nice place called Christopher's, right on the Intracoastal Waterway. I went in and again didn't see anybody I knew, so I left without even having a drink and walked back toward the first place, then past it and across Route 1 to a place called the Wooden Spoon. Since it looked like I wasn't going to run into any friends, I figured I might as well hear some music, and the Wooden Spoon had a singer I really liked, a four-hundred-pound crooner named Big Mama Blue. I crossed the last street and was less than ten yards from the door, when I heard a crash from behind me. I turned, along with everybody else on the street, and saw two police cars that had just plowed into each other.

The doors popped open and two cops scrambled out of each car. They seemed to be in a big hurry, although it looked to me like there was little danger of a fire. Steam was coming out of one car's radiator and there was a lot of crumpled metal, but it didn't seem all that bad an accident.

The two cops who'd gotten out from the doors opposite me came around the car, and before I knew it, they were standing with feet apart and guns drawn. One of the other two had dropped to one knee, his piece also out, and the fourth was talking into a microphone in his hand. That was about the time I realized that all the guns were pointing directly at me. What the hell . . . ?

Then they were on me, spinning me around and pushing me up against a parked car. I got a thorough frisking and then I was handcuffed behind my back. By that time four more police cars had arrived—without running into one another this time—and I was thrown into the backseat of one of them. So far nobody had told me why I was being arrested, but they started asking questions, and not having any idea what in hell was going on, I didn't say anything. I didn't even tell them my name, which they knew anyway. I was dying to ask some questions, to find out why I'd been taken, but bit my tongue.

At the Broward County Jail we were met by some detectives. They removed my handcuffs, sat me down and started peppering me with questions, but again I refused to say a word. One thing I remember clearly is that I fought the urge to rub my wrists when those cuffs were taken off. It's an automatic reaction whenever anybody comes out of the cuffs, and I wasn't about to give these guys the satisfaction of seeing me behave like every ordinary perp they'd ever brought into the house.

Then one detective I'd never seen before sat down across from me and said, "Mr. Mason, you've been arrested on suspicion of burglary, burglary of an inhabited dwelling, carrying a gun during the commission of a felony, fleeing a police officer . . ."

At that point he paused, then added ". . . and parole violation."

He knew that would get my attention, and it did. Violation of parole, or VOP, was the scariest thing you could hurl at somebody, because there was no bail for it. In essence, you were out of prison not because you were legally entitled to it but because of the good graces of the court. As a convicted felon under a twenty-year suspended sentence and seven years' probation, I had to keep my nose clean or that probation could be revoked. The criteria under which that could happen were very subjective, and the procedures for fighting it were much more limited than for the original charges. I don't know all the legal nuances, but I think the basic theory is that a lot of the rights you have to defend yourself against a criminal charge go out the window once you've already been convicted, and the only question left is how you pay for it.

I was starting to smell an extremely large rat and had to struggle not to lose my resolve in front of these guys. I had a feeling they'd been following me all these months just praying for me to fuck up so they could arrest me and violate my parole. Was it possible that when they couldn't do it legitimately because I'd stayed clean, they decided to set me up? The thought petrified me, but what else could it be? Burglary, possession of a gun, fleeing . . . I'd done nothing of the sort!

I waited a few seconds until I was sure I could steady my voice, then said, "I'd like a phone call."

"A phone call? Absolutely!" the detective said expansively, and waved for a uniform to take me to the phone. I picked up the handset, then looked at him until he stepped back a few paces, and dialed my home number. When Barb answered, I said hello, but before I could get beyond that, she started talking.

"Where are you!" she said, anxiety lacing her voice. "The police are all over the place!" She told me that there'd been half a dozen uniforms camped out around the house since about ten-fifteen, but none of them had knocked on the door or spoken a word to her. "What's going on? What's happening?"

"I don't know," I answered, and it was the truth. "I've been arrested and I have no idea why." I could hear skepticism in her silence. "Barb, listen to me," I insisted. "I'm telling you the truth."

I told her exactly what had happened, and since there was nothing I was trying to hide, something in my voice must have made her believe me. "Call Dave Damore," I said, "and get him down here." That was the same David Damore who'd been the assistant D.A. prosecuting me two years before. Looked like the prospecting for new clients he'd done among people he'd prosecuted was about to pay off for him.

Since I'd been arrested on a Saturday night, the county had no obligation to arraign me until Monday morning, so I stewed in jail. When you know you did something wrong, you can use the time to strategize, to plan a little. You think about what they might have on you, where they might have made mistakes, assumptions they made that you can refute. If you ripped off a store or something but were cooperative when you were arrested, you can get all huffy about a charge of resisting arrest and plan how to counter it. Maybe you could subpoena onlookers, or depose the cops separately, and hope for discrepancies. You could do *something*. If nothing else, you at least know you really did fuck up, and let's face it, your being in jail ain't exactly a gross miscarriage of justice.

But when you didn't do a damned thing, all you can do is worry yourself half to death trying to figure out what the hell is going on. I had nothing to latch on to, because I couldn't even figure a starting point to think about all of this. All I'd done was walk down a street.

After all of that swirled around in my head for a few hours, I decided that the best way to drive myself really crazy was to focus on the VOP charge. Even if everything else went away, I could still get nailed for that. I was beginning to realize that giving the Fort Lauderdale police all that shit two years ago may have been the dumbest damned thing I'd ever done in my entire life.

~

Monday morning finally rolled around, and I was taken out of lockup to meet with Dave Damore. With his years of experience, he didn't even greet me while we were still in earshot of the police, and I followed his lead. He'd probably had some incident where he'd offhandedly said, "How're you doing?" to a client and the guy came back with something like "I'm looking at five to ten, how the hell do you think I'm doing?" which someone might have stretched into an admission of some kind. I did notice that Damore was carrying some documents under his arm in addition to his briefcase. We were taken to a tiny room where we would have some privacy. My first words to him were "You got any idea what the fuck is going on?"

He looked at me in surprise. "I got a damned good idea," he said, waving the documents in front of me. "And I'm your lawyer, remember? So let's cut the bullshit."

I'd seen a movie like this once, or maybe it was a *Twilight Zone* episode, in which some poor sap wakes up and he's in some kind of parallel universe where everything is slightly different than it should be and everybody knows what's going on except him. Without being aware of it, I'd been anticipating this meeting as the time when everything would become clear, and so far it was just getting murkier. But I didn't want Damore to think I'd gone round the bend, so I just pointed to the papers he was holding and asked him what they were.

"Copies of the police reports that were filed in connection with your arrest," he answered as he motioned for me to sit down. I doubt if anyone but a former assistant D.A. in the same county could have gotten them that fast. When I reached for them, he said, "You can read them later if you want. You probably pretty much already know what's in there, so let's just go through your version and see what kind of discrepancies we can come up with." He opened his attaché and reached in for a pad of legal paper.

That was it. I'd about had enough from the cops and didn't need this from my attorney. I reached over and pushed the lid down, making him look up at me.

"Listen," I said as calmly as I could, "I don't know what the fuck I'm doing here. I've been cleaner than Snow White for over a year, which those assholes"—I pointed outside the room, intending for the gesture to encompass the entire Fort Lauderdale Police Department—"know damned well is true, because they've been hounding my ass the whole time. I can barely tie my shoe without looking up to see one of them staring at me, so do me a goddamned favor and tell me what they say I've done!"

I think I got a little strident toward the end of that rant, which I hadn't intended, but it seemed to give Damore some pause. He looked at me for a few seconds and then decided to give me the benefit of the doubt. "You're telling me you really don't know why you were arrested?"

He didn't need to wait for a response. He knew I was savvy enough about how things worked to know not to lie to my own attorney. Do that and there's no way he can help you.

Damore stood up and took off his jacket, then sat back down and picked up the police reports. "A cop named Matt Palmeri . . . you know him?"

"Never heard of him."

"Well, he said he was down on the beach talking to someone early Saturday evening when he saw your car pull up and park. You got out, and just as you began walking away, he saw you put a crowbar up your sleeve. Then he lost you in a group of apartment buildings. Any of this familiar?"

I assured him I had no idea what this guy was talking about.

"He goes back to the beach," Damore continued, "and finds your car gone, so he puts out an APB on it. Then he found it again at the Stouffer's on U.S. 1. Parked."

"Wait a minute!" I needed a moment to digest this. "He goes back to the beach, heads out to look for me and somehow finds my car at the Stouffer's?"

He tapped the sheaf of papers. "That's what it says."

From the look on his face I could see I didn't have to tell him the obvious, which he'd probably not thought about when he did his initial read. The Stouffer's is five miles away from the beach, on the other side of the Intracoastal. In barely the time it would take just to drive up there at full tilt, this guy just happens to come across my parked car when the APB turned up nothing? Damore saw the point, so we didn't have to belabor it, and he went through the rest with increasing skepticism.

"He saw you throw something into a dumpster—"

"What was it?"

"Doesn't say." We never did find out. "Just then a report comes over his radio of a burglary in the same beach area where he saw you with the crowbar. The victims said they saw the guy split. Wearing a green jacket."

I still had on the white jacket I was arrested in, which Damore took notice of. "You could have stashed the green one. . . ."

"Yeah," I said sarcastically. "I planned on getting spotted and caught, so I brought a change of clothes. Keep going."

"Okay. So he follows you in his car—"

"He let me get into mine and drive away?"

"Whatever. Says he pulled you over, but when he got out of his car, you floored yours and took off. He goes out after you . . . 'high-speed pursuit,' it says . . . on streets close to where you live. Then you tossed a paper bag out the window—"

"He could see that? At high speed at night?"

Damore leafed through the papers. "Seems you threw it at the exact moment you passed under a streetlight."

He couldn't suppress a smile at that. I had my lawyer back.

"He finally lost you in a parking lot on U.S. 1," Damore continued. At the time that actually sounded plausible. Later he and I would visit that parking lot, which still exists on Federal Highway between Thirtieth Street and Thirtieth Place. It has a grand total of six rows of fewer than twenty-five cars each and is completely empty on Saturday nights. Helen Keller couldn't have lost me in there. "Then later on he sees you walking across Oakland Park Boulevard. Jeez, this must be the luckiest god-damned cop in the world, the way he keeps running into you. Anyway, after they arrest you, he goes back to where you tossed the bag and re-trieves it. Inside they find jewelry and a gun, which they determine had been taken in the robbery. Then they came and got your car and towed it to the impound lot."

"Where'd they find my car?" I asked, a shot in the dark. Damore gave me the location. Why wasn't I surprised to find out that it was a parking lot across the street from where I'd actually left it? The report also said that when they went back to the burglary site to look for the green jacket, miracle of miracles, they found it. It was a size small, which I couldn't get into if I lost fifty pounds. As Damore finally flipped the pages closed, I didn't know whether to laugh or cry or tear the door off its hinges.

"I take it this is all bullshit?" he said.

"No. The part about how they arrested me was real. The other stuff is bullshit."

He nodded but didn't say anything, and I knew what he was thinking: If the cops had it basically right, he could dig right in and start hunting for small discrepancies to exploit. But if I was maintaining that their entire account was a fabrication, where did he start to counter that? The only thing to do was figure out how I could establish that I'd been somewhere else at the time, or come up with any other evidence that would directly contradict the report.

After a minute of thinking he said, "There was a burglary. That part was real."

Good point. "But I didn't do it." Actually, that didn't really make much difference. Damore didn't care if I'd done it or not. He was only interested in what we could prove. "Maybe we'd better talk about the arraignment," I suggested, and that's when he gave me the bad news: There wasn't going to be an arraignment, at least not a timely one. That threw me into even more of a tizzy, which was about the time there was a knock on the door. Damore opened it and Cheryl, my probation officer, waved and asked him if she could have a few minutes with me. Damore got up quickly, as though relieved to pass the baton to someone else.

⌣

Cheryl was a good person and a good friend. So my heart—and I wouldn't have thought it possible—sank even further when I saw the hard, all-business look in her eyes. It wasn't hardness toward me; it was Cheryl keeping a tight grip on herself so she could get through the next few minutes.

"You got serious problems, Bill," she said, getting right to the point. "I can't let you out." Then she waited, probably to allow the panic she saw rising in me to set in. Even through my fear I could see the kind of determination she'd worked up, and I figured she must have rehearsed all of this. "On account of the VOP charge. And if you get convicted of everything, you're looking at life plus forty-five years."

Before I could stop myself, I blurted out, "But I didn't do anything!" It was a dumb thing to say for several reasons. For one, Cheryl was now my P.O. and not my friend, and she couldn't do anything for me unless she could defend it to her superiors as reasonable under the circumstances and no different from what she'd do for any other person in my position.

"Personally, I don't think you did," she said, "but if I let you go, they'd throw my ass into the street and keep you here anyway."

Maybe you noticed her strange phraseology, about how *she* couldn't let me out, *she* couldn't let me go, as if she were the supreme authority here and due process and civil rights didn't enter into it. Well, she was and they didn't, because in Florida you could get your parole revoked just for being arrested, even if you weren't convicted. And since the court based its decision almost entirely on a report submitted by the P.O., she had your life in her hands. There were no "beyond a reasonable doubt" kinds of criteria and few procedures available to fight back. The whole thing was purely judgmental, like the probation condition that forbids you to consort with undesirables or known criminals. "Known" meant known to the police, even if the supposed criminal had never been convicted of anything or even arrested. How do you defend yourself against something like that?

I asked her about this life-plus-forty-five-years business, and she explained that as well, starting off with a real gem: "If you get violated, you have to do the whole twenty years of your original sentence."

This was getting worse by the minute. "But that sentence was suspended," I protested. "Probation was for seven years!"

"Suspended doesn't mean dismissed. It's technically still in effect. You're out but still under parole, and if you fail to keep your nose clean during the parole period"—she flipped a hand up and let it drop back onto the table—"back you go for the whole stretch."

I couldn't believe this and was unable to say anything for the moment as it all bounced around in my head. She let me have the time, and then said, "Just between you and me, pissing off Joe Gerwens and the TAC guys wasn't your smartest move."

That was the last thing I wanted to hear from someone who was in a position to know, because it let me give full rein to a thought that had been nagging at me for the last two days and which I'd tried hard to suppress.

The TAC Squad was composed of a bunch of very gung-ho, publicity-loving macho cops with a reputation for always getting their man. What they didn't add to that quaint expression was "dead or alive." Shortly after my first arrest they'd been following two suspects along a beach and ended up shotgunning them both to death. They claimed the suspects had tried to run, but since there were no witnesses and the suspects were dead, there was no one to dispute it. There was little in the way of public outcry about their itchy trigger fingers because there was so much crime in the area that the citizens were in no mood to concern themselves with the rights of suspects. It seems that, for many people, civil rights are a luxury you indulge in only when they're not necessary. As soon as things get tough and people really need protection from overzealous law enforcement, the citizenry tends to get a little complacent. Someone once said that a conservative is a liberal who just got mugged, and a liberal is a conservative who just got arrested. How true.

A few minutes before Cheryl had come in, Damore was telling me about how the police report said my car had been found across the street from where I'd really parked it. I'd automatically assumed they'd falsified the report, but now something else occurred to me: What if they'd moved the car to the lot across the street? And why would they do that?

I don't remember if Joe Gerwens actually headed the TAC Squad or was just a higher-up within it, but either way it wasn't good. He'd been at the Ramada when I was busted and was one of the people we'd subpoenaed for deposition. Since he was a prominent and well-respected member of the force who'd carry a lot of weight at trial, we'd given him a particularly tough grilling, pressing him on discrepancies no matter how inconsequential and not letting him get away with anything. I knew he'd been nursing a hard-on for me ever since, and now I couldn't help wondering if they'd moved my car, because the lot across the street was much more secluded than where I'd parked. If I'd walked down a less busy street, or if those two police cars hadn't run into each other and startled everybody in sight, including me, was it possible that I'd have been gunned down just like those two guys on the beach? And that it would have been a planned execution?

That was just one of the scenarios I entertained as I sat alone in a cell, where I was to spend quite a bit of time because I wasn't going anywhere for a while. I worked hard at not letting on how I was feeling, but inside I was tearing myself to pieces. Barb could see it easily and was giving my lawyer Librium to smuggle in to me during our visits, but it wasn't doing much good. Now, I suspect that a lot of people will think I deserved what was happening to me because of all the scores I'd gotten away with and how I'd screwed the police into giving me a free ride on a few, but this was way out of proportion. Murderers, pushers, child pornographers and wife beaters were getting light sentences or being let go altogether, while I'd never laid a hand on anybody, but because I'd opened my mouth and gotten the wrong people angry, I was facing a lifetime in a cell for something I didn't do. Whether you agree with that assessment or not, that was how I felt, and I was falling further apart with each passing day.

I spent the next month drowning in my own fears and leaving the management of my case to Damore. I was beginning to wonder whether this former prosecutor had too many friends in too many places for him to risk getting really aggressive and creative on my behalf. He would never do anything sneaky or wildly clever, because those kinds of tactics by their very nature would embarrass the other side, and he had to work with those people on a daily basis, on a lot more cases than just mine. In that pulp mill of a system, one hand washed the other, and the trading of favors was the fuel that powered the efficient resolution of cases. ("In the halls of justice, the only justice is in the halls.") I could easily see things going south in a hurry and decided that, with what I was facing, there wasn't much downside to painting outside the lines a little. The last thing I needed right now was a respected and well-behaved navigator of the system. What I needed was Godzilla.

"You happen to know a lawyer named Ray Sandstrom?" Cheryl asked, out of absolutely nowhere.

As shocked as I was by that question, I held any outward expression of it in check. This was my P.O. I was talking to, not my friend, but why would my P.O. ask me that question? The only thing that came to mind was that Sandstrom was in some kind of trouble and the police, knowing I'd met with him a few times, were trying to link me to him. But there was no denying that I knew who he was; he was a legend and *everybody* knew who he was. "Heard of him. Why?"

She stood up and grabbed her jacket from the back of the chair. "You know that guy I'm seeing?"

"The lawyer? Frank?" Cheryl had never gotten us together or even mentioned his last name.

She shook her head. "Not Frank. Fred. Fred Haddad."

That sounded awfully familiar. "How come I seem to—?"

"He and Ray Sandstrom are partners."

Good ol' Godzilla. Shows up just when you need him the most.

12

<div align="center">~~~~~~</div>

The Ballad of Ray
and Fred

WHEN YOUR own parole officer, who, after all, is working for the people who put you in jail, suggests that you change attorneys and then actually recommends one, and when the one she refers you to is her boyfriend's partner, that is not advice you take lightly. Cheryl knew the system inside and out, knew all the players in it, and she knew me. From the interaction I'd had with Ray Sandstrom, and that incredible courtroom strategy he'd concocted before his client Steven Simonson wrecked it by copping a plea, I had a feeling he'd want to take on my case, and I also had a feeling Cheryl had run the idea by him before she suggested I call him.

Ray and Fred showed up at the jail and I could hear them throwing their weight around when I was still two cell blocks away from the private rooms where lawyers could meet with inmates. If a guard took more than ten seconds to get a gate opened, Ray would start accusing him of harassment, hindering the legal process and interfering with his client's civil rights. Having to open his briefcase for inspection made him even angrier, and he'd threaten to file affidavits the whole time they rummaged through his papers, while Fred shouted that they were violating lawyer-client privilege. Hard to believe, but the guards were actually intimidated

Fred Haddad and Ray Sandstrom.

by these displays, because they knew that these two attorneys weren't above really lodging formal complaints.

At this first meeting they brought along a bombshell of a secretary who didn't seem to have anything of substance to do. I think they were just taunting the guards, trying to throw off their concentration, maybe daring them to pat her down. After we sat down, I started to tell them what Damore had done so far, but they waved it away. "We read all the papers," Fred said. "That rate, you'll end up serving twenty-five years of your twenty-year sentence. We gotta do something different."

"But they got me on parole violation," I said. I didn't understand what they could do about that other than what Damore had been doing, which was to request more hearings and try to out-argue the prosecutor over whether violating me was reasonable. The standard the county had to meet to keep a convicted person inside wasn't nearly as strict as getting the conviction itself. "Doesn't that mean they can pretty much lock me up at will?"

Ray lit up a cigarette and flicked the spent match at a "No Smoking" sign on the wall. "Yeah, it does. So what we gotta do, we gotta get your original conviction thrown out. Once we do that, your probation doesn't exist anymore and we can get you the hell out of this shit hole."

"Thrown out? How can you do that?" After all, I'd agreed to the deal.

"By showing that the deal was bullshit from the very beginning. Bad faith, deception, you name it. We demand a jury trial on the original charges, and while that's pending, you're not on probation anymore.

You're back to being innocent until proven guilty, and we'll get you out on bond."

Fred explained that a full-scale trial was really our only chance. "If you're already convicted and the only question on the table is how you get punished, the state has enormous power, because you're no longer an innocent citizen. You're officially guilty, and most of your rights fly out the window. But when they're trying to convict you, you have every constitutional protection under the sun. You can confront your accusers, cross-examine their witnesses, and instead of this vague set of bullshit criteria for violating your parole, they have to prove you guilty beyond a reasonable doubt."

"We get a new trial," Ray said, "there's no way they can make that case. Their evidence sucks, their witnesses suck. . . ."

It sounded too good to be true, and I wondered out loud why the hell Damore hadn't thought of that.

"Speaking of him," Ray said, "the county can't get any help from him, because he's been your attorney and there's privilege there."

"He wasn't my attorney when he was prosecuting me."

"Doesn't matter. You guys had all kinds of conversations, and if anyone in the D.A.'s office even says hello to him over a cup of coffee, we'll scream bloody murder all the way to the Supreme Court."

"But he can't do his job without talking to the D.A.," I observed.

"No shit," Ray said, laughing and stubbing his cigarette out right on the tabletop. "But how's that our fucking problem?"

I was liking this better all the time, but there was still the small matter of getting my plea bargain overturned. Ray and Fred had some interesting ideas on how to go about that.

This would probably be a good time to tell you a little more about these two larger-than-life characters, two of the best criminal defense attorneys I'd ever met or even heard of.

~

From all of the stories I'd heard about Ray Sandstrom, it was a wonder that he was still alive and had his law license when he came into my life. He was older than his partner, probably in his late fifties, but looked even older because of a lifetime of heavy drinking, smoking and Lord only knew what else.

As I've said, Ray was the most antiauthoritarian, antiestablishment human being I'd ever met on this side of the bars. He hated cops, judges, wardens and just about anybody else in a position to exercise authority over other people. He believed that nobody who had the power to control somebody else's life did so without somehow asserting himself as superior and enjoying, however subconsciously, the subtle humility he was inflicting. As far as Ray's methods were concerned, his philosophy seemed to be that you used whatever worked. Period.

A classic example of that occurred on the first day of a trial in which Ray was defending an armed robber. He walked into the courtroom and spotted the only piece of physical evidence, a handgun, lying on the prosecution table with a property tag dangling from it. Ray opened his briefcase and set it on the floor next to the table, and casually brushed the gun off and into the bag when nobody was looking. After exchanging a few pleasantries with the assistant district attorney (think of a cobra telling a bunny rabbit, "Have a nice day"), Ray slipped the gun to the defendant's wife, who then left the courtroom. Ray sat down at the defense table and calmly began preparing his notes, taking little notice as the prosecutors discovered their evidence was missing and went nuts trying to find it. When they couldn't, Ray made a motion for the charges to be dropped, and that was the end of that. It was vintage Ray, and if his name hadn't been dirt in the D.A.'s office beforehand, it sure was afterward, even though there was no proof he'd taken the gun.

A womanizer who hated women, Ray was on his eighth wife—at least I thought they were married—an outrageous flirt named Lollie, and it was beyond me why she married him in the first place and why she stayed. Maybe it was all the money he had, hard currency he'd gotten as fees from drug dealers and had stashed away in dozens of hiding places all over the city. He sure didn't spend a lot of time with her. If he wasn't in court, the last place anybody would ever think to look for him was his office. He loved boating, fishing and flying airplanes but was forever fighting the FAA over his pilot's license; they claimed his eyesight was failing, which it was, but he refused to admit it, including to himself. He refused to wear a tie in court, which got him into endless trouble with judges, who also didn't much like all the gold jewelry he liked to drape himself with, either.

I never saw Ray actually read a single document or open a case file, but once he got into court, you'd swear he'd memorized every line of every piece of paper that had ever been filed in the case at hand. Cross-examination was his specialty; he'd start off in a slow, thick southern drawl that was barely understandable and practically put witnesses to sleep, then pounce after he'd used their inattention to trick them into inconsistencies that seemed innocuous until he strung them together and made them seem like purposeful lies.

Fred Haddad, who'd started out as Ray's protégé, although he would never admit it, was even more brilliant than his onetime mentor. His raw brainpower was almost frightening, and he was always a dozen steps ahead of anybody else in the room, instantly seeing implications it would take others hours to come around to. This was all the more amazing because Fred was a heavy-duty drinker who practically needed a beer before he even got out of bed, which wasn't always in the morning. Though he was happy-go-lucky and gregarious among friends and family, his cheerful Middle Eastern face would go dark and menacing as soon as he stepped into a courtroom.

He loved cars with blacked-out windows and always owned several at a time, and he wore even more gold jewelry than Ray. He genuinely liked women but had a lot of trouble hanging on to one, because by eight o'clock most evenings he could barely talk. (His relationship with my parole officer set some kind of endurance record for him.) I think if he hadn't worked so hard on pickling his brain, he might have won a Nobel Prize or been a senator. Fred's standard courtroom tactic was to pepper witnesses with a barrage of questions, confusingly out of sequence so the witness couldn't stick to a cohesive story and kept getting tripped up on details. Unlike his victim, Fred could follow the various threads at once and then play them back to the jury, in the correct order, so that glaring inconsistencies jumped out all over the place. When the prosecution attempted to rehabilitate the witness during redirect, Fred would look on happily as the poor guy attempted to recant half his statements and still maintain some kind of credibility.

Ray and Fred loved drug-smuggling cases. Prosecutors were rabid about getting convictions, which made for some very intense battles, and clients would always come in with huge amounts of cash to pay for their defense. Ray and Fred were fiercely competitive with each other as well, and fought all the time, but I think they genuinely loved each other. Unfortunately for me and some of their clients, their inherent combativeness sometimes got in the way of their legal judgment; if I thought the Fort Lauderdale police had it in for me before, they were practically ready to kill me once these two waded into the fray. Before it was over, my little feud with the cops would escalate into a full-scale vendetta in which any notions of justice and fair play were but distant memories. I fully shared the blame, of course.

I'm not certain how I came to be so attached to this strange pair, and have given it a lot of thought. In retrospect I'm dumbfounded that such a deep friendship could have developed among us. They were outrageous, flamboyant and totally crazy, which was the complete antithesis of my personality. I'd spent a lifetime staying quiet, keeping to myself, never bragging to anybody about the things I'd done, barely even mentioning them to anybody else except, once in a rare while, Bill Welling. My tack with law enforcement was not to become a pain in their collective asses but to stay as invisible as possible. I didn't hate the police, never rubbed my successes in their faces and only fought them when I felt I needed to in order to defend myself. Even when I was in the thick of my drawn-out tussle with Joe Gerwens and the Fort Lauderdale police, all I really wanted out of it was to be left alone, to get out from under the gun and to do only what I felt was necessary to show them I couldn't be trifled with. I wasn't out to make them mad or show them up.

Slowly, though, I found myself drawn into Ray and Fred's style of doing things. They fought so hard for me, even seeming to compete with each other to win my approval, that I unwittingly became as outrageous as they were. With the benefit of hindsight I can trace exactly how I changed during that period from a secretive, self-contained loner into a publicly contemptuous smart-ass too goddamned dumb to see all the harm I was causing myself and those close to me.

If there was ever a situation that did more damage to my marriage, I don't know what it was. The crimes I'd committed and the trauma of getting shot had been bad enough, but this period beat them all in driving Barbara away from me. Maybe it was the booze, which was a constant companion to my lawyers and me, or maybe it was temporary insanity on my part, but I look back at those years and wonder not just how I made it but how I'm still alive and not lying in some alley shotgunned to death by the TAC Squad or some other unit of Broward County law enforcement.

~

After the exhilarating flurry of creative ideas during our first meeting, the gloomy fog of the real-world legal process quickly descended on us. Often over the next few months I'd feel like a POW who thought he'd made good his escape but was quickly recaptured; sometimes it's better not to have had that little taste of sunlight at all.

It started off well enough. Ray and Fred demanded and got a hearing in front of Judge Robert Tyson to contest the deal I'd made with Damore that had led to my twenty-year suspended sentence for the Ramada nonsense. They subpoenaed my first lawyer, Howard Zeidwig, whom they had too much contempt for to even bother disliking, and got him to testify about how he'd pressured me into taking a deal whose implications I didn't fully understand. By the time they got through with him, he might as well have admitted that he'd pointed a flamethrower at me and threatened to incinerate me if I didn't give in. Ray ticked down a list of about fifty pieces of legal trivia and, one at a time, asked Zeidwig if he'd explained it to me. The answer most of the time was, of course, no, generally because it wouldn't have made any difference, but Ray's feeling was that the sheer number of such "lapses" would carry weight with the court.

They also subpoenaed all the cops who were at the Ramada bust, and others who'd had a hand in setting up the surveillance but weren't even there. They did a pretty good job of humiliating them and clearly demonstrating what a weak case it was, implying that I'd been arrested mainly so the police would have something to show for their misguided efforts.

Our very best shot to prove we'd been misled had to do with this Jean Tierney character from Connecticut, the woman who was supposedly registered in the room I was caught in. Then-prosecutor Damore had told us that she was planning to come back to Florida and testify that her suitcase had been ransacked. Ray argued that this was complete bullshit (using more legal terms than that, but the same sentiment). He also told the court that Mrs. Tierney had informed Damore that in fact her suitcase hadn't been touched. "The plea bargain proposed by Mr. Damore," Ray concluded, "was a reasonable deal only if it was true that Mrs. Tierney had really been robbed and only if she was really planning to come back and testify. And neither of those things was true!" What he couldn't say, without admitting that I'd searched the room, was that there hadn't been any suitcase in there at all.

My guys were good, but so was the assistant state attorney, William Dimitrouleas, a real straight arrow who had replaced Dave Damore on my case. Heavyset and studious-looking, Dimitrouleas was a career prosecutor with no ambition to go into private practice. He genuinely felt he was providing an invaluable public service to the citizens of Broward County, and, to be candid, he was. (He would eventually be appointed a U.S. district judge by President Clinton.) He didn't rise to Ray's bait and make an attempt to retry the original case in front of Tyson, but stuck to showing that everything the police had done was appropriate and lawful. Whenever Fred would try to demonstrate that the police had exercised bad judgment and been overzealous in their pursuit of me, Dimitrouleas would calmly reply that even if that were true, it was irrelevant. If Zeidwig and I had wanted to go down that road, we should have done it at trial. Instead, we willingly accepted the deal offered by Dave Damore, so how could I now claim that justice hadn't been served?

It wasn't much of a surprise that Judge Tyson agreed with Dimitrouleas. After nearly a week of testimony and argument, Tyson didn't even bother to leave the room to go off and consider what he'd heard, but made his decision on the spot—or, more likely, had made it days before—and declared that we had no case. "Testimony by three police officers yesterday," he said, "that Mrs. Tierney said her luggage had been disturbed outweighs a purported later comment to Mr. Damore, by phone, that it had not." He put special emphasis on *by phone*. "Also weighing against the defendant is his de facto admission of guilt when he agreed to the plea bargain."

I thought Ray would go for the judge's throat when he heard that last remark, a piece of reasoning that would have made Kafka envious, but Fred held him back, reminding him that we still had to go through an appeal process and didn't want to hurt our case by behaving badly.

We immediately filed an appeal with the Fourth District in Palm Beach, but by that time I'd already been in custody for five months and was not handling it well.

Barb came to see me as often as permitted and was also at every hearing. I could see that she was sinking as rapidly as I was, as much from the uncertainty of everything as from the absence of her husband and the kids' father. It was impossible to predict the result of each legal maneuver, and afterward things weren't any more clear than they'd been before. Neither of us had any idea if I'd be out in a week or if I'd spend the rest of my life inside, and the awful toll of being in that kind of limbo is impossible to put into words. Worst of all, I had no one else I could blame. Sure, the police had overdone it and were pressuring the D.A.'s office to keep putting the screws to me, but even in my bitterest moments I couldn't pin it all on them. It wasn't like they'd picked out an ordinary citizen at random. I was a criminal, and their failure to catch me actually committing a real crime had embarrassed them on more than one occasion, as had my confessions to a slew of highly visible burglaries they'd been unable to solve. While it was true that the charges they were holding me on really were bullshit from a legal point of view, it was equally true that had I never broken the law in the first place, I might have been on the same bowling team as Police Chief Joe Gerwens rather than top dog on his official shit list.

Never was that driven home to me more than when Barb came to visit. She was drawn and haggard and could barely meet my eyes. Sometimes her hands shook, and she'd put them in her lap so I wouldn't see. She was holding it together for the sake of the kids, trying to create some semblance of normalcy at home.

Barb had taken over the job of renting out the Lighthouse Point house. On one of her visits she reported this terribly strange occurrence: two people who'd rented the place, paid in cash and then disappeared. What was going on and what was she supposed to do now?

"They were drug smugglers," I said across the table that separated us. "They only wanted the house to bring in a single shipment."

She looked at me with her mouth hanging open. "How do you know that?" she finally managed to say, and I explained how it had happened to me several times. That threw her for a loop, and it took me a while to convince her I hadn't done it on purpose. I didn't bother to mention that I'd spoken to the police about it on several occasions.

"So what do I do now?" she asked.

"Rent it again."

"But those people paid for three months in advance. What if they come back?"

I assured her they wouldn't. She rented it again, and damned if the same thing didn't happen. Despite the very helpful money it was putting into our bank account, Barb said she didn't have the stomach for it and wanted to sell the place. I didn't argue.

~

Until I'd been thrown in jail with nothing but time on my hands, I'd never really stopped to consider the impact my self-indulgent ways were having on those close to me. The kids were confused and fatherless; Barb was torn up inside and getting worse; my mother and aunt were anxiety-ridden. . . . As quiet as I'd tried to be about the shadowy part of my life, several other lives were now being affected by it, drawn into my predicament to the point where their own lives were being put on hold.

One interesting thing I learned in jail: Rarely does a member of an inmate's family weigh the crime, weigh the time and determine that the loved one is getting just what he deserves. No matter what you did to get yourself there, everybody in your family hurts for you. Helpless, afraid and in pain, they feel that you're completely at the mercy of a dark, shadowy system peopled with dark, shadowy custodians. They spend sleepless nights worrying about what "they" are doing to you when nobody is looking and what an agony it must be to be locked up. When they sit down to a nice meal or go to a movie or just read the paper with a cup of coffee, the fact that you can't do those things nags at them, and they feel guilty, even though it's not their fault. It doesn't much matter to them why you're inside. They hurt for you, regardless.

I was and still am deeply ashamed about this period, about the awful impact it had on people who hadn't done anything wrong. Even if I'd kept on pulling the occasional score—in retrospect I'm not sure I had the ability to stop doing that—there was no reason for me to have taken on Gerwens and the entire Fort Lauderdale police force. My arrogance and outsized self-confidence prevented me from realizing that you don't fuck with real power, with people who have state authority, vast resources, licensed guns and an institutionalized hatred of outlaws like me and everything we represent. I should have been smart enough to realize I would be set up, because Gerwens and his trigger-happy minions weren't going to be satisfied until I was either under a life sentence or dead. And whether their resolve affected innocent people or not wasn't their problem.

I actually had it better inside than most of the other prisoners. When I'd first been locked up in that same jail for those seventy-seven days two years before, I'd gotten along well with the guards and never given anybody a hard time. They remembered that and routinely afforded me privileges, such as phone calls, that other inmates had to beg for. It seems like a small thing, but I was locked up twenty-four hours a day with nothing to do but write long, rambling letters to Barb and add up how many years I would get if convicted of all charges (it was 104), and little things could make a difference.

Not enough of a difference, though. It was still hell for me being caged like that with no idea how long it would go on. I began to develop stomach pains, not an unusual situation for inmates getting bad food and a lot of stress, but these were different and wouldn't go away. There was no doctor in the jail, just a jaded nurse who had heard every kind of malarkey you could possibly imagine and didn't believe anything was really wrong with somebody unless he'd already lost most of his blood or a limb. She gave me a handful of Rolaids and sent me away, but the pains got worse and I told Fred. He raised some holy hell and got permission for me to see an outside doctor, who examined me and then said to the two guards who'd accompanied me, "I want to see him again in three weeks," and named a specific day and time in late September. He must have been new to examining prisoners, because he'd violated a basic tenet of prison procedure: Never let an inmate know exactly when he's going outside. Excursions outside the walls were prime escape opportunities, and knowing when it was going to happen made the job infinitely easier.

When we got back to the jail, I found out my appeal to the Fourth District had been turned down. My desperation level jumped right off the scale and I got in touch with Bill Welling, who by then had moved to Florida.

When he came by the next day, I knew he'd sensed instantly what I had in mind from the way he looked around to make sure we couldn't be over-heard by a guard. "So what's up?" he asked as he took a seat opposite me.

"I'm going out," I told him. "Three weeks from yesterday, to see a doctor."

"You been there before?" he asked, ever savvy.

I told him everything I could remember about the layout of the building where the doctor had his office. "If you could somehow get in the elevator with me," I said, "we could take the guard on the way up. He'll have the keys to the shackles, and we can get them off me and onto him, then tie him up somewhere." That was assuming only one of the guards would be taking me up.

"Lot of scuffling," Welling mused. "Patients going in and out . . ."

"From what I saw, it's mostly elderly people. We do it fast, there's con-fusion, nobody knows what to make of it until we're gone." It wasn't the best of plans, but I didn't see a lot of options.

We talked some more, then Welling left and came back two days later. He'd been to the doctor's building and had a thorough look around. "There's a back hallway behind the patients' entrance to your doctor's of-fice," he reported. "It's less than twenty feet from the elevator. If we get the guard under control before the door opens, you can go see if the coast is clear before we bring him out and stash him in the hallway."

For the next three weeks I agonized about whether to attempt an es-cape. Not only was it a pretty risky proposition, but even if it worked, I'd be a fugitive. Aside from an assault on a cop, nothing gets the law en-forcement community more enraged than an escape. It was tough enough to get a conviction, even tougher to get a prison sentence, and each guy who got incarcerated was a victory for truth, justice and the American way. An escape was a nose-thumb at those who'd labored to put the guy away, and the ultimate humiliation for prison authorities whose only function was to keep prisoners inside. They would hunt me down like a dog and, once they'd found me, wouldn't concern themselves with the niceties normally accorded an apprehended suspect. I wouldn't be a suspect, innocent until proven guilty and entitled to civil treatment until the state could prove otherwise. I'd be guilty as hell, with no further de-bate required.

I was also getting sicker. If there was something seriously wrong with me that required real medical attention, maybe even surgery, I'd have to go to Outer Mongolia to find a hospital that hadn't been notified to be on the lookout for me. There was also the possibility that I could be released legitimately before too long, and walk free again rather than spend the rest of my life running and looking over my shoulder. If I busted out, there would no longer be any chance of living a normal life; even if I was eventually exonerated of all the charges pending against me at the time, the escape itself was still a serious felony and there'd be no beating that. On the other hand, if I didn't escape and then all of my appeals failed, I would have blown the one real shot I had at getting away and would regret it forever.

By the time the day of my appointment rolled around, I still hadn't been able to come to a final decision. I'd been in for over eight months and my self-reliance had suffered to the point where I didn't trust myself to make important decisions. In my darker moments I had to admit that the ones I'd made before all of these troubles began weren't so hot to begin with, so why should I think I'd be any better at it now?

My shackles were chained to a steel bar inside the prison van. When we pulled up to the entrance of the medical building, a guard came in to unlock the chain and I shuffled to the door. I got out slowly—there's no way to move fast when your hands and feet are bound—and as I stepped awkwardly down to the pavement, I saw Bill Welling leaning against a low stone wall lining a garden near the entrance. He was lounging with feigned casualness and appeared to be somebody who had perhaps accompanied a patient and just sneaked out for a quick smoke, but he was watching me carefully. At that moment it occurred to me how hugely self-centered I'd been once again, so focused on what would happen to me under a dozen different scenarios that I'd never taken him into account. Here was a friend willing to lay his own freedom on the line, maybe even his life if things went really sour, and I hadn't considered the effect on him of what I was about to do.

Or Barbara. Or the kids.

I felt a mild push from the side, one of the guards letting me know it was time to go. Welling kicked off the wall at the same time, preparing to precede me inside and make sure we got into the same elevator. He gave one last glance in my direction, and when I was sure he was looking at me, I shook my head: *No go.*

After a moment's hesitancy, Welling whipped his head around and began patting his pockets, as though he'd lost or forgotten something, then turned back toward the stone wall and pretended to hunt around on the ground as I passed him by, the window of opportunity closing with an almost audible sigh behind me.

~

After two more visits to the doctor, and some telephone arguing between him and prison authorities that I couldn't quite make out from the next room, I was informed that I needed gallbladder surgery. This time they didn't tell me when, but one morning they came for me and took me to the hospital, where I was chained to a bed, even after pre-op sedation and as I was being wheeled into the O.R.

Afterward they had three shifts of guards watching me. They were a pretty aloof bunch, which was strange, because I knew a couple of them and they'd been pretty decent to me in the prison. Now there was only one who was being civil, spending time sitting by my bed, talking or playing cards, but he seemed to take a lot of care in not letting the others know we were on friendly terms.

He eventually let on that the Bureau of Prisons, or whatever they called it, was ticked about having to foot the bill for the surgery, the hospital stay, the extra guards and all the other expenses of my medical care. Everybody knew that I was not to be "coddled," and there were apparently a lot of heated arguments about what my medical care should consist of. Just a couple of days after the surgery I was taken back to the prison, where their idea of a recovery room was an isolation cell with a bare wooden bench instead of a bed or even a cot, and rat shit all over the floor. This was while I still had drain tubes hanging out of my side.

When Fred found out I'd been taken from the hospital, he went ballistic and came to the jail insisting on speaking to me. When the warden refused, on the basis of my being too sick to have visitors, Fred barreled his way into Judge Tyson's chambers and demanded to know what someone too ill to speak with his attorney was doing in the Broward County Jail. Tyson granted an emergency hearing, but even when I was brought into the courtroom looking like death warmed over, with Barbara standing nearby in tears, he refused to send me back to the hospital, but did order the warden to put me back in a regular cell that at least had a mattress, thin and dirty as it was.

Barb then went to the doctor's office and told him what was going on. At his insistence—by this time I think he had more animosity toward the authorities than I did—I was taken back to the hospital.

The doctor had made his point powerfully, and the prison authorities must not have thought they could easily get me back to the jail again. With hospital bills mounting, they didn't object when my lawyers requested another hearing in front of Tyson, which was set for November 3. The warden himself showed up and testified that they were unable to care for me properly. I would have liked to make the case that I wouldn't be needing medical attention anymore if I'd been treated better the first time, but we had a specific objective in mind and Ray and Fred didn't want to cloud matters by flinging accusations around. Besides, I was still in the hospital and not present at the hearing.

After everybody had his say, Ray stood to request that I be released on bond. Judge Tyson granted the request but imposed the condition that I stay at home except for visits to either my doctor or my lawyers.

Not wanting to exult in front of the judge, the warden and the prosecutor, Ray and Fred kept as solemn as they could as they left the courtroom. Once they were out of sight, they bolted for a pay phone and called Barbara, who raced them to the hospital, anxious to tell me the good news. They arrived together, all smiles and good spirits, and as soon as I saw them, I nearly started crying. It had been nine months since I'd been taken into custody, and even though I could be thrown back into jail anytime the judge felt like it and I'd be under house arrest even if he didn't, just the thought of being able to walk into my own home was overwhelming.

Ray and Fred were ready for some heavy-duty celebrating and practically dragged me out of bed, but I wasn't up for it. I guess they thought I'd been faking in order to try to get released, but the truth is, I really felt like shit and just wanted to go home.

The euphoria of being able to step outside without shackles and to smell something other than sweat, sewage and prison food was sweet but short-lived. I wasn't any closer to being out of the long-term woods, and within a day or two the desolation I'd been feeling, which I'd attributed solely to being in jail, began to reassert itself. Two impending hearings were still looming before me. One was on whether I'd actually violated my parole. The county hadn't been in any hurry to get the VOP hearing going, because they had me in jail, and all that would happen if they prevailed in the hearing was that I would stay in jail. They could lose, too, and then I'd be out again, so as far as they were concerned, they were happy to postpone it forever. At least that was the situation while I was still being held. Now that I was out, at least partially, they would probably be stepping up the process of trying to get me back once the doctor pronounced me fit.

The other impending hearing was about a new trial on the original charges stemming from the Ramada bust. Ray and Fred thought the most critical piece of strategy was to see to it that the trial took place before the VOP hearing. If it didn't, and I lost the hearing, I'd go back to jail and the county would stall forever. Since I had a constitutional right to a speedy trial, my lawyers would howl in protest, but the prosecutor could claim that none of my rights were being violated, because, regardless of the merits of the case, I did violate my parole. Even if I was eventually exonerated of the Ramada incident, and never should have been in a position to need parole in the first place, the violation could still stand. The situation is somewhat akin to a prisoner who breaks out of jail, and while he's on the lam, they discover he didn't do the crime for which he was convicted. That still doesn't excuse his breaking out. In my case, if we had the trial first and I was acquitted, Ray and Fred were fairly certain the parole violation matter would be dismissed. I'd already done ten months and had my health compromised, and the judge wasn't likely to put me back.

Now that I was out, the thought of going back was terrifying. I hung on Ray and Fred's every word, searching for hidden meanings that didn't exist, latching on to every casual phrase that might represent a glimmer of hope. I also started to suspect that I was being followed on my trips to the doctor, and I thought it a real possibility that someone might try to kill me. I was scared to go out alone, and to this day I'm not convinced it was just paranoia.

I couldn't sleep, had difficulty thinking straight and was getting angrier and angrier at nothing in particular. The only people close at hand to take it out on were Barbara and the kids, and they suffered more than when I was in jail. I think that, more than anything, I was completely exhausted and emptied of reserves. I was too mentally fatigued to fight my impulses, and it was easier to lash out than try to control myself. The worst part was that I knew exactly what was happening, could see my relationship with Barb deteriorating before my eyes, and I couldn't seem to stop it. I was mean, nasty-tempered and impossible to talk to.

I also began drinking heavily; it was the only way I could combat the enervating anxiety and fatigue and, if only for a few hours, get a break from the relentless tension that was the constant companion of every waking hour. Ray and Fred were the two worst possible friends to have in that situation, because neither of them saw heavy drinking as any kind of problem at all. In fact, it gave them a very creative idea.

I was under a court order not to go anyplace other than the doctor's or my lawyers' offices. Ray and Fred decided that their offices included every bar in greater Fort Lauderdale frequented by attorneys, cops and courthouse personnel. After all, they reasoned, some of their most productive settlement and pretrial discussions took place in those venues, and it was critically important for their client to be present. For some reason, none of the cops or bailiffs who saw me in those bars ever caused much of an official fuss, although I could almost see steam rising out of their ears. Maybe they didn't want to have to explain what they were doing there themselves so often. So the three of us drank ourselves into blithering idiots night after night, and I got even more belligerent, to preclude Barb from giving me any shit when I finally dragged myself home.

~

Ray and Fred were intent on getting the trial scheduled before the VOP hearing, and prosecutor Billy D, as everyone referred to Dimitrouleas, was just as determined not to have a trial at all. Eventually Ray figured out his game, which was so sinister and clever you really had to admire it. If Billy D won the VOP hearing and got me back in to serve out the rest of the twenty years, he'd simply drop the charges stemming from the Ramada bust. That way I could never be formally exonerated, and we couldn't go before a judge pleading that the original bust, and therefore the deal I'd accepted, was bogus. There would be no basis left on which to set aside my parole violation, and I would do the entire stretch.

On the other hand, if we got the right to a trial and we won, Billy D knew he'd never get the VOP to stand up, and I'd be off the hook forever. Doubtless he was working just as hard on his side of the case as my attorneys were working on mine. Since we never ran into him in a bar, maybe he was working harder. Every time Billy D got a VOP hearing scheduled, Ray and Fred would find a reason to get it postponed. Every time we got a hearing scheduled on whether we could have a new trial, Billy D would do the same thing to us. It kept leapfrogging like that, and we kept partying, getting more outrageous with each passing week.

Most days I would head down to their office, the one on their letterhead, where we'd have a few beers and talk about how their day in court had gone. It was one crazy story after another, and I didn't believe most of them (I would later), but they were fun to listen to, especially with a few brews under my belt. Then Fred would say, "Let's adjourn to the annex," and we'd head to a bar with some other attorneys or whoever else was around. Among the regulars were three of Fred's clients, Carl Coppola, Joey Cam and Tommy Harris. They were among the most notorious drug smugglers in the state and always had several cases under way. Seeing me with them made the cops even angrier, which is probably why Fred and Ray kept bringing them along: They enjoyed it when a tableful of Fort Lauderdale's finest would see us walking in. The cops would huddle closer, mumbling to one another, probably about what they'd like to do to us if they got us alone in a dark alley, but they were powerless to do anything at the moment.

It didn't stop there, though. There was more money in the drug trade than most people could even imagine, and the biggest problem wasn't how to make it, which was easy, but how to spend and store it, which was surprisingly difficult. Tracking huge money transactions was one of the feds' primary weapons in identifying and busting dealers, so it was a key goal of people in the trade to leave as few paper trails as possible. Cash was essentially untraceable and could be spent with no record, so staggering amounts of it tended to hover around smugglers like Carl and Joey, but not many of them were as fearless and contemptuous as they were.

One night around Christmas when we were all in a bar together, including a bunch of secretaries and support staff Ray and Fred had brought from the office, a guy walked in selling gold chains out of a portable display case. Joey Cam took a look and determined that the goods were real, then pulled out a sixteen-thousand-dollar roll of hundred-dollar bills and bought the whole thing from the guy, including the case. He started passing the stuff out to the women from the office, then moved on to all the other females in the bar and kept going until it was all gone. This was in front of half a dozen Fort Lauderdale cops, two detectives and two assistant D.A.s. It made me nervous as hell, but a few drinks fixed that up pretty quick. (Cam was later murdered in Fort Lauderdale after a money dispute during which he kidnapped Carl, who is now doing fifty-five years in federal prison. The cops even suspected me of killing Joey, but they suspected me in anything that had to do with anybody I'd ever been in the same ZIP code with.)

Tommy Harris was the wildest of the bunch, and the funniest. He was always telling hysterical jokes and crazy stories of his sexual escapades with his two girlfriends he called the Bookend Sisters. He always had cocaine on him and dispensed it freely to anybody he happened to be with. Fred was defending Tommy in a case stemming from his being busted driving past the Fort Lauderdale airport at two A.M. high on coke and with fifty thousand dollars and a derringer found in his car when he was stopped for a suspected DUI. Tommy would arrive for court each day in a car loaded with drugs and leave the keys with one of the secretaries. One of his buddies would come and drop off a clean car, exchange keys with the secretary and take the loaded car away. Right in the courthouse parking lot. Tommy would sit in court all day snorting cocaine out of a Vicks inhaler. Everybody thought he had a bad cold, and all his sniffling and nose-wiping seemed to cause everybody concerned to want to speed the proceedings up. I did a little paralegal research for Fred on the definition of a "derringer," and that charge got thrown out. Shortly afterward Fred won the rest of the case. I wasn't in court but heard he'd been brilliant.

Three weeks after the trial ended Fred called and asked me to go to a motel with him to see Tommy. He didn't say what it was about, only that it was very close to my house, but he sounded worried and I agreed. By the time we arrived, there were police and ambulances all over the place. Seems Tommy had sent one of his girlfriends into another room and then blown his brains out. Nobody could believe it about this guy who was always laughing and joking and seemed to be the most easygoing person you could imagine.

These are the kinds of guys I was hanging out with. If I didn't get to the law office by late afternoon, they would come by the house to get me, which didn't sit well with Barbara, so I usually made sure to leave before that happened. On weekends Ray and Fred would come to the house, but since it was only the two of them along with Ray's wife, Lollie, and Fred's (post-Cheryl) girlfriend of the moment, Barb was okay with it. The girlfriends would inevitably make a fuss over my son, Mark, who was nearly sixteen by then and already one of the coolest people I'd ever know. Superintelligent, athletic, artistic and witty, he would fall in love with each of Fred's squeezes one after the other.

We (adults) usually went out for dinner. The alcohol-fueled camaraderie was infectious and Barb did her best to join in the revelry, but I was pretty sure she was scared all the time. If Bill Welling was in town, he'd join us, too. He and Ray could trade jokes all night long if you didn't stop them, and the partying always went on until the wee hours. I think I was starting to get the idea I could keep this up forever.

No wonder my marriage was going to hell.

~

When Barb would loosen up on the weekends, I'd forget about how sullen and angry she was during the week and think that everything was okay, but it was those weekdays that were killing us. I came home drunk night after night, and if I wasn't thinking straight, I'd tell her stories that sounded funny at the time but that only scared her even more, and rightly so. Like about how Joey Cam kept sending hookers to my prosecutor, Billy Dimitrouleas, "compliments of your friend Bill Mason." When she'd ask me why I insisted on rubbing the cops' noses in everything, especially after all I'd been through and was likely to go through again, I had no answer, so I just got angry right back at her. How was I to explain that I'd fallen completely in the thrall of Ray and Fred, and their way of doing things, even though they weren't facing any charges and weren't running the same risks I was? I couldn't answer it myself, so how was I supposed to explain it to her? As if there was a rational explanation anyway.

My lawyers and I became closer all the time. We'd enter weekend fishing tournaments together, which Ray and I usually won, much to the chagrin of the highly competitive Fred. Ray trailered his boat over to my house and parked it in the driveway, and we spent a few weekends replacing all the teak woodwork and putting in a new diesel engine, Fred standing around critiquing our work and tending the bar.

I wasn't completely oblivious, though, and in between the endless bouts of partying I began to feel some niggling doubts about my attorneys. Those doubts increased after the third time I got called in the middle of the night to bail Fred out when he'd been arrested on a DUI charge, and after the fourth time I had to go pick him up from some drug smuggler's house where he'd gotten so blitzed, even his shady client was afraid to let him drive. I'd usually take Barb with me, because it wasn't safe for me to be out alone without my lawyers. She would freeze into near-catatonia for days after one of those little excursions, choosing to stay quiet rather than risk another blowup with me.

Other than at my hearings, I had never seen either of my attorneys in action and got curious about how they handled themselves in a trial. I wanted to see them blazing away at the enemy, my own personal cavalry warming up for the big show that would be my trial and their greatest triumph.

Ray was in the middle of a first-degree-murder trial. The defendant was the head of a local motorcycle gang, a huge guy appropriately named Big Jim Nolan. The judge and Ray hated each other, and on the very first day that I showed up to watch the trial, Ray was cited for contempt of court. Twice. The first time was for refusing to wear a tie, which was standard for Ray, but the second time was for calling the judge an asshole in open court.

Each day at court's end about twenty or so of Nolan's fellow motorcyclists would leave the spectator section of the court and stop at Ray's office across the street to talk and drink beer. I've never smelled such a group. After they left, we would have to open all the doors and run fans to try to get the body odor out, then the three of us would head out to a bar as usual.

I was becoming more and more insecure about Ray's abilities in court after watching all his antics, but my doubts were put to rest when Nolan was acquitted of every single charge.

13

Tickling the Dragon's Tail

ONE NIGHT I was driving Fred home because he was too drunk to do it himself. I didn't like this task, because after I dropped him off, I'd have to drive home by myself, and I wasn't supposed to be out. If I got stopped for some reason and the cop recognized me, it wouldn't be easy trying to convince him or the court that I'd been to a meeting with my attorneys until two in the morning. We were on Sunrise Boulevard just east of the interstate when Fred spotted a bar he liked and insisted on stopping in for one last drink. The place was a real dive and completely empty except for one guy slouching sideways at the bar—and who should it be but Judge Robert Tyson himself. Even from the door we could tell he was stone drunk.

Fred waved me to a bar stool to the right of the judge and out of his line of vision. Fred himself took up the seat on the other side. He looked at Tyson, waiting until the poor sot realized there was somebody sitting next to him. "Evening, Judge."

"Whoozat?" I heard Tyson mumble as his head jerked slightly.

"Fred Haddad. How're you doing?"

Tyson grunted something and let his head drop down. His hand was wrapped around a half-full glass of what looked like a scotch and soda.

The glass was tilted and appeared in imminent danger of falling over. I was tempted to straighten it up, but it was clear Fred didn't want the judge to realize I was there.

Fred managed to get some semblance of a conversation going, and, once roused, Tyson was a bit more lucid than I'd given him credit for. Eventually, Fred steered things around to current cases and said, "So what can we do to help Bill Mason out? Guy's been through a lot, so how do we give him a break?"

Tyson snorted and sat up a little straighter, then seemed to remember his drink and took a small sip. "Mason's too hot," he replied, shaking his head. "Forget it."

In the car a few minutes later, Fred said, "That sonofabitch." He went quiet for a few minutes, then said, "I got an idea."

"What?" I asked.

"Let you know tomorrow. Gonna call Ray first."

The idea was vintage Ray and Fred. They requested a hearing before a different judge, Joseph L. Price of the Broward circuit court, and gave as their reason that they needed to subpoena Tyson to testify as to the guilty plea I'd entered as part of the deal Dave Damore had offered. It was an entirely reasonable request, and as soon as it was granted, Fred ran right over to Tyson's courtroom and demanded that he disqualify himself from the case because he was now a witness. The judge nearly went crazy, but he had no real choice in the matter.

Several higher-ups from the Fort Lauderdale P.D. had been in attendance at the hearing, and they'd followed Fred to Tyson's court. They understood exactly what he was doing but were powerless to stop him. As soon as Tyson removed himself from the case, every restriction he'd placed on me was completely nullified, since he no longer exercised any control over the matter. For reasons I didn't fully grasp, even the fact that I'd been released primarily for medical reasons no longer applied. Unless somebody took specific procedural steps to try to take me back into custody, I was completely free, my only obligation being to appear in court when required to do so for either the VOP hearing or the Ramada matter.

The day was March 6, which I remember for more reasons than just having my restrictions lifted. Fred, Ray and I went out to celebrate, which didn't make it much different from any other weekday night except that now we had something to toast, rather than drinking for its own sake. After two hours of some pretty unbridled revelry, I decided to break the usual pattern, get home early and share the joy with Barb, something we'd done very little of in recent months.

I was feeling great and didn't want to be indoors or even in the car just yet, so I stopped at a little outdoor bar near the Jolly Roger Motel right on the beach, thinking I'd have a short one and just watch the waves break for a few minutes. It was only fifty feet from where I parked to the bar, but before I covered even that short bit of ground, half a dozen cops appeared out of absolutely nowhere and told me I was under arrest. As cynical as I'd become, I simply couldn't believe this was happening. "What the hell for!" I demanded as they yanked my hands behind my back and slapped cuffs on me.

"Prowling," one of them said.

"Prowling?" They began marching me back toward the street. "I haven't been here ten goddamned seconds, how the hell could I be prowling!" I knew better than to open my mouth under those circumstances, but it was so patently ridiculous, I couldn't help it.

Instead of answering, they stopped our little march and frisked me, whether to annoy me or because they'd realized they'd forgotten to do it before, I don't know, but one of them pulled a small knife from my jacket pocket.

"Well, what have we here?" one of them said.

"It's a knife," I shot back. "I always carry it." There was nothing illegal about it. Lots of people in South Florida carried knives for protection. This one happened to be an old piece of junk with a bent blade. It wasn't good for much, but it made me feel better to have it.

Down at the station they booked me for prowling and possession of a knife with a "specially curved blade." Now I'm getting good and steamed, and demanded to call my lawyer.

"Keep your shirt on," one of the arresting officers, a plainclothesman, told me. "You can be out of here in a couple minutes if you don't give us a hard time."

He was right. My bail was set at a puny fifty dollars, I paid it myself and walked out. I had to take a taxi to where the police had towed my car and bail it out, too, but nobody came after me when I went home. I called Fred and gave him the whole story. He told me he'd do some checking around and to meet him at his office before court.

~

I got to Fred's office before he did and read about my arrest in a newspaper in his waiting area. When he showed up, he looked worried. Understand: Fred *never* looked worried.

"There's an arrest warrant out for you," he said without preamble.

I asked him what for.

"Violation of parole," he answered, wincing.

I felt a sliver of fear deep in my chest. "I don't get it. How did I violate parole?"

"They say you were prowling and in possession of a weapon."

In other words, my arrest the previous evening *was* bullshit, a setup, an excuse for them to violate my parole. I'd managed to temporarily beat the original VOP, and now there was a new one, complete with a new judge. No wonder they'd let me out so easily: They weren't interested in prowling, they just wanted to have an official arrest on the record to document my misbehavior. "What the hell do I do now?" I asked.

"The first thing you do, don't go home."

I didn't. I went to Ray's, called Barbara and told her what was going on. That evening the cops showed up at my house to take me in. Barb was down the street at a neighbor's, and only my two daughters were home. Suzi, seventeen at the time, told the cops I wasn't there and that her mother was down the street, and that they should wait while she called her, but they shoved her aside and went in anyway. They looked around, satisfied themselves that I wasn't there and left. By that time Suzi and Laura were nearly hysterical, and that's how their mother found them about half an hour later.

I didn't turn myself in—I hadn't been officially notified of anything, the police hadn't left any papers and they hadn't indicated to Suzi that I was wanted. Their treatment of my daughters was written up in the papers the next day, Ray having informed reporters that he was preparing a one-hundred-thousand-dollar civil lawsuit against the police for their abominable and traumatizing behavior toward innocent minors. He also got a hearing scheduled for March 10, this time in front of a completely new judge whom Ray knew well and who had been at Ray's fifth, sixth and seventh weddings. Fred assured the judge I would appear and then told me it was safe to go home.

Everything was coming apart. I'd rather have died than gone back to jail for a serious stretch, and with that attitude I didn't see any reason to go quietly. I had three days to plan how to get out of it if things really went bad.

The first thing I had to do was speak to Barbara. Given all that had happened, it may seem difficult to believe, but I loved her very much and she felt the same about me. She may not have been sure if she could live with me, which I understood, but I'd never questioned the depth of her feelings for me.

I sat her down and sketched out how I planned to escape should it become necessary. For someone who'd barely had a sober breath in nearly six months, I thought I was doing a pretty good job, painting a perfectly reasonable picture of how the whole family could relocate and start a new life somewhere far away from South Florida. We'd talked before, many times, about buying a big boat and sailing around the world, maybe settling down in Australia, Brazil or Mexico. It had been some harmless fantasy-spinning then, but now I tried to treat it as though we'd been making serious plans.

She listened indulgently, but there was no mistaking the cloud descending behind her eyes. She'd heard me make too many empty promises in the past, watched me turn over new leaves with heartfelt intensity, only to see me revert to my old ways over and over. She'd watched me drink myself into a numb stupor night after night since I got out of jail and continue to thumb my nose at the police even though I knew they were hell-bent on putting me away again. She'd seen the kind of people I'd been hanging around with, and how I'd traded in a decent and respected lawyer like Dave Damore for two certifiable lunatics who were barely distinguishable from their clients. There was no sense in my pointing out to her that she'd had some pretty good times with them as well, because I didn't want to push her into saying out loud what we both knew to be true, that she'd only done it for me and would have been much happier sitting in front of the television with me and the kids.

Yet I still felt that I had a chance to convince her, if I could just be concrete enough about my plans and about the stability that would come into our lives once we got away. Oblivious to how absurd that must have sounded—stability while hiding from the police?—I told her that I'd pulled together a considerable amount of cash and stashed it in the van that we'd "inherited" from one of those smugglers who'd rented our house at Lighthouse Point. I didn't tell her about the guns that were also hidden in it (more stability there), but it made no difference, because she wasn't about to climb into it with me with our children in tow.

The next day I retrieved most of the money from the van and hid it in the house for Barbara. If I had to leave, I'd get in touch with her afterward and tell her where it was. I also grilled Ray and Fred on the details of the legal procedures we'd be going through but didn't tell them the reason I was asking, which was to identify opportunities to take off if it came to that.

On the morning of March 10, I showed up early at the law office. When the courthouse opened, Ray gathered every employee they had into a group with me in the middle, and we walked across the street like that to make sure no one would accidentally shoot or abduct me. The hearing was scheduled for eleven, but we were there at nine. The courthouse was unusually full of people, and it wasn't until we were inside that we realized it was because most of them were reporters. Some had it in for me, others had been glamorizing me as a modern-day folk hero and all were hoping to get a page-one photo of me in handcuffs standing before a judge. We were set upon by people popping flashbulbs and shoving microphones in our faces. Ray tried to move them out of the way while shouting "No comment!" over and over, and somehow we made it into the courtroom. Barb was already there, and some reporters as well, and two pretty serious-looking bailiffs were doing an excellent job of making sure everybody behaved. The sudden quiet of the place after the commotion in the hall was eerie but comforting.

Fred had gotten to the courtroom early, too. He and the judge were having a private conversation, and then Fred came over and sat down.

"A little problem," he said, "and I don't want you to panic, Bill."

I started to panic.

"What's up?" Ray asked him.

Fred jerked a thumb toward the rear doors, indicating the press in the hallway outside. "The judge doesn't like all this publicity. Doesn't want to be pressured by a bunch of ambitious reporters into doing something that'll satisfy them, and he's too rattled to listen to Billy D and me debate the merits."

Sounded reasonable, but it didn't speak to my most immediate concern. "Why'd you tell me not to panic?"

Fred leaned in close and spoke in a hoarse whisper. "He's going to put you back inside and let things cool down for a few days." When I jerked upright on hearing that, Fred put a restraining hand on my arm. "It's okay. Thing is, if he's got reporters watching, they'll crucify him unless he throws the book at you, on account of what the police have led them to believe."

Ray nodded his agreement. "But if we can do this quietly, there's a better chance of getting him to be reasonable."

"Exactly," Fred said.

But all I heard was that I was going back to jail, and I guess it must have showed.

"It's only to save face," Fred went on soothingly. "He can't let you just walk out of here when there's a warrant out for you. This way he looks tough, which means he doesn't have to be tough when we get down to the important stuff."

"When?"

"When what?"

"When do I go back in?"

Fred shifted around uncomfortably on the already uncomfortable wooden bench. "Now."

The only thing I could think about was Barbara. It had never occurred to me that I wouldn't be going home that evening. I hadn't said good-bye to her in any meaningful way when I'd left that morning, or to my kids, either, and I didn't want to do it with Barb now because of the reporters looking on. So far they hadn't really discovered her, but if I gave them anything to look at, they'd swarm her like maggots over a newly dead carcass. As for the kids, I may not have been the most attentive father for the last half year, but at least I was there. Now I wouldn't be coming home again, and they'd read about it in the papers.

But I didn't have a choice, so I thought I might as well be a man about it. We went before Judge Price, some important-sounding words were mumbled, then the bailiff came and handcuffed me. No photographs were allowed in court and so there were no popping flashbulbs or strobes, but some of the reporters shouted questions as I was led away, before the judge gaveled them into silence and threatened to ban them from his courtroom forever.

I can't bring myself to try to conjure up in words what it was like to hear a cell door slamming behind me yet again.

14

Been There . . .

THE FEW days Fred had spoken of turned into over three weeks. By this time I was too cynical to be surprised and didn't even bother to mention to my lawyers their gross misestimate when they came to see me.

It had been like homecoming when I went back into the Broward County Jail. A lot of the guards went out of their way to come by and say hello and offer me good luck. I suppose it could have been worse, and I tried to make the best of it.

Ray and Fred bombarded the court with motions, and we finally got another hearing scheduled for April 5, at five o'clock in the afternoon. The guards who came by to get me teased me about the late hour, pretending to ask for my autograph and offering to press my suit, since I must be some kind of celebrity. When we got down to the first-floor holding area, where I was to wait until called up to court, they left without putting me in a cell. I heard a lot of noise from behind a door leading to a hallway but didn't think much about it.

Ray was waiting for me, and I said hello.

"How you doing?" he asked back.

I told him I was okay. He nodded but didn't say anything more than that. This was pretty unusual, and then I noticed that he was inside one of the holding cells and the door was locked. "How come you're in there?" I asked him.

"I'm in jail," he replied.

"I know we're in jail, but what are you—?"

"No, no. I mean, I'm in jail."

When I figured out what he was talking about, I started laughing. It was probably cruel, but I just couldn't help it. My lawyer was in custody! "What the hell for?" I finally managed to ask him.

He began smiling himself. "Contempt. What the fuck else?"

It seemed Ray had gotten into some kind of heated argument with a judge over not wearing a tie, and Ray—big surprise—hadn't handled it well.

There was still a lot of noise coming from the outside hallway, and I asked Ray if he knew what was going on. "Reporters," he said.

This was after normal court hours, and since the court's daily schedule was posted on a preprinted form that didn't have any space for that time, our hearing hadn't appeared on it. Somehow, probably through their various informants inside the system, the press had found out about it anyway. This was bad news for me. Very bad. I'd just spent three weeks cooling my heels in jail because of the papers getting wind of my being scheduled for a hearing, and here it was happening again. "God-damnit . . ." I choked out.

"Take it easy," Ray warned me. "Just take it easy, okay?"

A different door opened. A big, burly cop walked in, nodded at Ray, then noticed me. "How the fuck did you get in here!" he demanded angrily. "Alla you are supposed to stay out in the hall!"

I started to explain, but he pulled out a set of keys and stuck one in a steel door I hadn't noticed before. He unlocked it and kicked it open. Bright sunlight streamed in, and as I blinked against it, I saw some steps leading right down to the parking lot behind the courthouse.

"Get your ass outta here!" the cop snarled, motioning toward the steps.

"Listen—" Ray started to say, but the cop shouted him down.

"You shut the fuck up!" He yanked his nightstick from his belt and pointed it at me. "Don't make me tell you twice!"

As my eyes got used to the outside light, I saw grass and cars just a few feet away and people walking casually on the other side of the street. Trees, too, and a kid on a bicycle. I thought about my van, just a short cab ride away.

"Don't do it," Ray warned, but was careful not to use my name.

"Don't do what!" the cop snapped.

My lawyer was right. "I'm waiting for a hearing," I finally said.

"Bullshit! It's five o'clock. Ain't no hearings at—"

"I'm in custody, you dumb fuck!" I was emboldened because this cop wasn't about to mess with me once he realized the awful, career-ending mistake he'd almost made. He needed me to stay quiet about it.

"Fuck's he talking about?" the cop asked Ray.

"He's my client," Ray answered, trying to stifle a laugh. "We got a hearing at five, like he said."

The cop looked back and forth from one of us to the other about a dozen times before deciding we were telling the truth. "Shit," he muttered as he quickly pulled the outside door closed and relocked it. By then Ray and I were cracking up and the cop left without another word.

"By the way," Ray said when he'd managed to get hold of himself, "Fred found out something interesting. All those motions we been filing?"

I sat down on the bench in the holding area. "What about them?"

Ray said that Fred had gone through the original police reports and come across one describing a potential witness, a woman from Connecticut who'd been registered in the room I was caught in at the Ramada.

"Jean Tierney," I said. Hard to forget a name like that.

"Fred wanted the judge to subpoena her for a deposition," Ray went on, "but he refused, because as far as he was concerned, there was no case pending. You'd already pleaded guilty."

"Then what's so interesting?"

"Fred went into his usual outrage dance. It's a good one; you should see it."

"I think I have. And . . . ?"

"He yells and screams about how this is all a conspiracy to keep you locked up, a violation of due process, and just about the time he gets to the very death of democracy itself, one of the detectives gets up and tells the judge there's no reason to subpoena the woman because she won't come down and testify anyway. The judge asks him why and the detective gives Fred this long look and says, 'Because *somebody* phoned her up and threatened her, that's why.' "

I couldn't believe this. "Are you telling me Fred—?"

"Hell, no. Are you kidding? We didn't even know who she was until that morning." Ray stopped and scratched at his chin. "On the other hand, what we were wondering . . ."

I knew exactly where he was going with this and headed it off. "Don't look at me. I never even knew what city she lived in. All I saw was the same report as you."

Ray knew I'd tell him if I'd done it, so he believed me, and it *was* true. "So who do you suppose . . . ?"

"Nobody, that's who," I answered. "You ask me, she never existed." But now the judge thought I was the type of creep who threatened potential witnesses. Wonderful.

Shortly after that two other cops came by to take us upstairs, but first they handcuffed us together. It took a few seconds for the reporters out in the hall to figure out what the hell was going on when they saw us, or maybe they didn't catch on at all, but either way they started snapping pictures like mad, all the way up to the courtroom. They even tried to get shots of us inside by holding up their cameras and shooting away every time the rear doors opened. It must have been quite a sight, the two of us cuffed together in front of the judge as Ray pleaded my case.

It was useless. Judge Price, a tall, slim, refined-looking patrician type, was constantly eyeing the rear doors, apparently reminding himself of the reporters who were behind them. He wasn't interested in the detailed arguments and refused to make any decision except revoking my bail. Barbara was there as usual and sat in shocked silence, watching Fred screaming bloody murder as Ray and I were taken off to the jail, me back to my cell, Ray to a holding area.

When the evening guard shift came on, I cajoled a couple of them into letting the trustees take all kinds of stuff to Ray, like doughnuts, fresh coffee, cigarettes and, for all I know, a beer or two. The next morning I asked one of the guards to take me down to see him. Along the way a couple of trustees stopped us to tell me how well they'd taken care of Ray and all the great stuff they'd brought him.

When we got to the holding area, Ray wasn't there. There was just one old man, smiling and seemingly quite content. "What's he so happy about?" my guard asked the one in charge of the holding pen.

"You kidding?" the other guard answered. "Guys have been bringing him all kinds of shit all night. Doughnuts, coffee, smokes . . ."

"Where's Ray Sandstrom?" I asked.

"Sandstrom . . . you mean that lawyer?"

"Yeah."

The guard checked his log sheets. "Somebody named Haddad got him out. Emergency appeal, I think."

I asked him when.

"Little before eight last night."

I looked inside the holding pen again. There were crumbs and cigarette butts on the floor and a couple of crushed paper coffee cups in the sink. I wondered if the old guy thought jail was going to be like this every night.

⁓

Four days later we finally got the "quiet hearing" the judge wanted. The highlight was when Ray called to the stand Judge Tyson, who'd sentenced me on the original charge.

"Nothing compelled Mr. Mason to admit the truth of the charges against him," the eminent jurist sniffed imperiously.

"Oh, yeah?" Ray shot back. "What about the fact that a prosecutor told him a witness was going to fabricate evidence against him?"

"So you say," the judge replied evenly.

After he left the witness box, Price said, "Anything else, counselor?"

"One thing," Ray answered. "We asked for the official record of the original sentencing."

"And I ordered it turned over," the judge said with a shrug.

"Well, we didn't get it."

Price frowned. "Why not?"

This time Ray shrugged. "Seems it's been lost."

"Lost." Price seemed to need a second or two to process that. "What do you mean, it's lost?"

"That's what the clerk of the court told us."

"But . . ." Price bit his lower lip. There was no sense interrogating Ray, who was under no obligation to account for missing court records.

Then the judge looked at me, but there was nothing on my face to read. I was as surprised as he was. He turned away and picked up a phone, and as he dialed, Ray came over to talk to me.

"What the hell—?" I started to say. I remembered the story about how Ray once pinched a gun right off a courtroom desk.

We stared at each other for a few seconds. Then I said, "Are you telling me you swiped the official court record?"

I thought Ray was going to fall over. "Me!" he nearly shouted. "I thought it was you!"

But it wasn't me. I wouldn't even know where to look for a document like that. Ray turned away and started to laugh and shake his head. "Jesus H. Christ!" he choked. "It's really gone!" He sobered up when we heard the sound of the judge hanging up the phone.

"Seems you're right, Mr. Sandstrom. It's lost." Price scratched the side of his head. "This has never happened before in my memory." He picked up his gavel and said, "Defendant is released on seventeen thousand dollars' bond."

In the news the next day, a veteran court observer echoed the judge's comment when he said, "It's never happened before. Something could be misplaced but never lost."

There was another hearing two weeks later, on some technical matters. I wasn't required to be present and didn't go. The question of my bail being continued didn't even come up, which got my lawyers debating when I met them later that evening about our next move. Given Judge Price's lack of concern about my not being in custody, Ray was confident that we could drag this out forever without worrying about me being remanded. "He's stayed put," Ray said to Fred, referring to me. "They set him up and busted him and still he didn't run. The judge won't bother him."

Fred didn't buy it. "Maybe not now, or next week, but when Joe Gerwens and his TAC boys see that we're stalling? They're convinced one of us swiped the court record, and they'll convince the judge as well. They'll rain hell down on Billy D and start pressuring him to get bail revoked, and the judge will agree."

"But what grounds will he have?" Ray argued. "What evidence? Nothing's changed; the case is moving ahead. . . . What kind of reason would the court have to revoke bail?"

This went on for a little while, and then they turned to me; it was really my decision after all, and it was an easy call. As far as Ray and Fred were concerned, every day that I was out was a gift, another excuse to party and taunt the police, and they saw no downside to delaying things as long as possible. To me, though, every day that passed without final resolution of everything I was facing was another day of unbearable tension and uncertainty. I couldn't work, I couldn't get to sleep without numbing myself with alcohol, my marriage was disintegrating and my kids could barely make it through a night without crying. Worse still, we were pressing ahead with the harassment suit against the police that had been filed in Barbara's name, and from what I was hearing, this was making the police completely nuts. Add to that the suspicion that I'd stolen a court record and I thought I was in very real danger of being set up for a bogus arrest again.

This was no way to live, and I knew I couldn't take much more of it. "We need to end it," I told my lawyers, "one way or the other." I knew I had a constitutional right to a speedy trial, a right that was routinely waived by defendants, especially those out on bail, because it gave their attorneys more time to get ready. But I wanted a trial on the prowling and weapon charges from the Jolly Roger to start not one day later than the statutes allowed, and earlier if the county was agreeable.

Ray and Fred understood without my having to elaborate any further and agreed to press forward as fast as the law allowed.

~

Ray went into court without me and informed the judge that we wanted a jury trial on the Jolly Roger matter. That afternoon he told Fred and me how it went. As the judge started leafing through his calendar, Ray threw in, "We want it in six weeks." The judge looked up, incredulous, and asked him what he was talking about. Ray repeated his request, and the judge started to get angry and called him up to the bench but waved Billy D back, a clear breach of procedure: Judges aren't supposed to have "ex parte" conversations, speaking to one side without the other present, but Dimitrouleas didn't object. And Ray was about to see another side of the normally patrician Judge Joseph L. Price.

As Ray told it, "The judge leans down over the bench and says to me, 'What the fuck is wrong with you, Sandstorm?' Sand-*storm*, he calls me! 'I let your guy out, so why are you busting balls on a trial that quick? You got any idea how full our calendar is?' And I told him, real polite, I said, 'My client wishes to invoke his right to a speedy trial, your honor,' and he says, 'Fuck you and your client!' I kept my cool, didn't raise my voice, didn't interrupt him. . . ."

"How come?" I asked. That wasn't Ray's style.

"I'll tell you why," Fred ventured. "Because it probably pissed him off worse than anything else Ray's ever pulled in his court, that's why."

Which may have been true, but after beating Ray around the head and shoulders and threatening him with everything he could think of, the judge had no choice but to start the trial in six weeks, as per the county's definition of "speedy."

"But what if you'd pissed him off so bad that he revoked my bail?" I asked, and the two of them fell all over themselves to be the first to explain how that would have been the best thing that could have happened.

"Clear-cut case of judicial bias," Fred said. "There would have been no reason in the world for him to do that—"

"Especially," Ray added, "when we were arguing to speed the trial up, not slow it down. We would have had a judicial misconduct charge leveled against him before the lunch break, accusing him of violating your rights because he thought we stole a court record."

Fred suddenly grew quiet. "Hey, Ray, you know what?"

"Yeah," Ray finished for him, "I bet he was thinking that was exactly what I was trying to do. And no way was he going to rise to the bait." Ray grinned and turned to me. "May have just done you a helluva favor, son. Made it impossible for him to revoke your bail without looking petty and vindictive." Ray must have had a scheming gene somewhere that could pull stuff like that without his even knowing it. He also hadn't bothered to inform the judge that it was Fred who would be handling the actual trial.

The court schedule really was full, and the judge in charge of the master calendar practically begged us to push things back a week, to which we graciously agreed. Because of scheduling conflicts, we had the trial in front of a new judge, a woman named Margaret Simmons. I was wearing a jacket and tie, and Fred wore what looked like a cowboy suit, including boots, a string tie and so much gold jewelry, it glinted off the walls every time the sun was at the right angle. During a break on the very first day following jury selection, one of the jurors approached the judge and asked her why the defendant was doing all the questioning of witnesses while the lawyer was sitting down. From the way we were dressed, the juror had simply assumed that I was the lawyer and Fred was the one on trial.

The prosecutor hadn't called the cop who'd actually arrested me to the stand, so Fred did and asked him to explain why he thought I was prowling. "How do you know he hadn't just stopped to take a pee?"

The cop said, "I didn't smell any urine."

"Are you an expert on urine?"

"No, but—"

"Did you get down on the ground and *try* to find the urine?"

"What urine?" the flustered cop asked. "There wasn't any—"

"How do you know there wasn't if you didn't try to find it! I'll tell you why: Because you didn't want to find it, that's why!"

The prosecutor jumped to his feet. "Objection, your honor! He's badgering my witness!"

"Your witness?" Fred hollered back. "He's *my* witness! I called him!"

It went on like that for two days. Despite Fred's transparent and theatrical antics, it became clear that the police had no case and no reason to have arrested me. After both sides rested, Fred got up and requested a directed verdict of acquittal without letting it go to the jury. "Your honor," he said, "if this absurd arrest stands, if the court really feels that sufficient evidence has been presented here upon which to ask this jury to seriously consider whether my client was prowling, then you might as well arrest every eighty-year-old in Fort Lauderdale who stops to catch her breath within a hundred feet of a police officer." He didn't even bother with the charge involving the knife, because if the prowling didn't hold up, it was inconceivable that the weapon charge would, and he didn't want to taint his argument by mentioning that I'd been carrying a knife.

The prosecutor, as his job required him to do, stood and argued against the directed verdict, but he knew his case was lame and his heart wasn't in it. After he finished, the judge took no time in deciding to acquit me without letting the jury have the case. She seemed a pretty good person with a sense of humor, so I asked her if I could have my knife back. She laughed and said, "Don't push it, Mr. Mason!" Then the smile vanished from her face as she looked toward the back of the courtroom. I turned around and saw three of Fort Lauderdale's finest standing shoulder to shoulder, looking back at the judge. Old clichés like "murder in their eyes" and "staring daggers" popped into my head; I'd never seen such raw fury on people's faces before. That they stood quietly only made those expressions more disturbing, as though they were perfectly willing to rein it in right now and release it in a more productive fashion sometime later.

Another celebration was in order for our team, but Fred split off from us and ran out of the courtroom, the cops following him with their smoldering eyes. He headed straight toward a bank of pay phones in the lobby. I told Barb to stay in the courtroom and ran after him. When I asked where he was going, he shouted back, "To call some of those goddamned reporters!"

I followed him to a phone and caught some scattered words as he spoke to one reporter who'd been particularly scathing in his remarks about the three of us. Toward the end of the conversation Fred jumped up angrily and opened the glass door. "That's why I never cooperate with you, you mangy fucking scumbag!" he was yelling into the phone. "You put the guy's arrest on the front page and now you're going to bury his acquittal next to the want ads? Yeah . . . yeah . . . well, *fuck you!*" He slammed the handset back onto its cradle so hard it shook phones three booths away.

Very little about me would appear in the papers for six months. Until October 23, to be exact. On that date I'd make page one again.

Back in the courtroom Barbara's reaction to my acquittal was muted.

Sure, she was happy, but she was also thinking straighter than I was. "All it really means," she said, "is that you're right back to square one." What she meant was that the pending VOP hearing and the Ramada matter were still hanging over my head. Nothing had changed, really, except for one thing.

"Now the police hate you worse than ever," she said.

⌣

What really scared me was that the open harassment by the police came to a dead halt. No more slow cruises down my street, no more dirty looks and whispered remarks in bars around town. I even got the feeling I wasn't being tailed anymore, but there was no way to know that for sure. I fretted over what they might be planning. Would Joe Gerwens and his men plant drugs in my car to set me up for a forty-five-year mandatory, or shoot me for resisting arrest? Had I finally pushed things that far? And if so, what had been the final straw . . . the missing court record everyone was still convinced I'd stolen?

But did we stop? Hell, no. We kept on hitting the bars and taunting the authorities simply by virtue of my very presence in any place other than prison. I became more circumspect about getting in their faces, but Ray and Fred, if anything, stepped it up. About a week after the acquittal Ray and I were trailering his boat from my house back to the water. We stopped for a cup of coffee and parked the whole rig in a restricted zone. When we got back, a squad car was pulling up, and two policemen got out.

"This thing yours?" one of them said in a nasty tone. I wasn't able to tell if he recognized Ray or if he was simply in a bad mood.

"What about it?" Ray said, just as gruffly.

"It's in a no-parking zone. Why don't you move it?"

Without a moment's hesitation Ray shot back, "Why don't you go fuck yourself!"

I cringed and tried to shrink into invisibility. The cop started for Ray, who stood his ground and didn't look away. I was certain the cop was going to shoot us both right on the spot, he was so mad, but his partner grabbed his arm and shook his head, which scared me more than anything. Here was a guy who'd hurled a belligerent epithet at a uniformed officer, and instead of confronting him or even writing a parking ticket, the cop just backed off. As far as I was concerned, the one who shook his head to tell his partner to stop might as well have said out loud, "No, not here. Later, like we planned. When nobody's looking."

Ray was oblivious to the nuance and smiled in triumph as the cops got back into their car and drove off.

Things got even worse at home, if that was possible. Since I'd been released on bond, Ray and Fred had started coming around the house again, which made Barbara tense and anxious. She was too polite to say anything to them directly and put up a pretty good front while they were there, but I heard about it afterward. Since I was usually drunk at those times, I didn't react well, and the downward spiral of our marriage continued. I still had everything in place to leave—the van, money, weapons—and kept trying to talk to Barbara about it, thinking maybe she'd get used to the idea if I kept bringing it up all the time, but she was too worn out to keep pretending it was a real possibility and I soon gave up.

The next few months passed in a haze. All the motions, the hearings, the drinking, the fights at home, the restrategizing after each new turn in the case . . . all of it ate away at me to the point where I sometimes felt like nothing but a bag of shot nerves and bad temper. I don't remember many of the specific legal details, only the thought beginning to take hold that all of it was just delaying the inevitable, that the system was determined to get me and wouldn't rest until it did, legally or otherwise. Once this hopelessness took a foothold in my brain, I could no longer avoid the reality that my life as I'd known it was over, and that in some way the cops were going to win after all. Part of this may have been a defense mechanism, something inside telling me that I had to get used to a few painful truths if I was to have any chance of saving myself. Still, I fought those truths to the last minute, avoiding them even when Fred, pain etched across his face, told me that we'd run out of legal options and the violation-of-parole hearing was going to take place before the matter of a retrial on the Ramada charges was considered. I kept on avoiding the truth right up until just before the hearing itself in October.

It was scheduled for nine in the morning, the first case to be heard when court opened that day. I'd been out until midnight the night before with Fred, Ray and Carl Coppola. Nobody had said much, and then we went home.

Those unavoidable truths swam up before me again as the sun rose the next morning. I was hungover, exhausted and fighting down the kind of anxiety to be expected when coming to a decision to chew off your own arm to escape a trap. At about six o'clock, I finally threw in the towel for good.

Barb stirred out of sleep as I nudged her and spoke her name, quietly, so as not to wake the kids. When I had her attention, I said, "I need to take off."

She glanced at the clock. "It's only six. We don't have to be there until—"

"No, I mean I'm taking off. I'm not going to the hearing."

There was simply no way I could face another judge, another venomous cop, another day in a jail cell, another hour of the particularly cruel brand of uncertainty that comes packaged with fighting your way through a horrendously complex and unpredictable legal system. I didn't need to explain all of this to Barbara, nor did she try to talk me out of it; she'd lived through the whole experience with me, and even though I'd caused her an incalculable amount of pain and worry, somehow she still loved me, and understood.

It was a very frightening moment, and I sought refuge in the minutiae of logistics. "You still have to go to the hearing," I told her as she began to cry. She shook her head, but I explained that she had to. "If you don't show up, they'll accuse you of aiding and abetting a fugitive. You have to go to court and look confused and upset when I don't show up. Tell them I left early to meet with Ray and Fred and you came to court by yourself."

Worrying about protecting herself while I was about to launch myself into such dangerous waters didn't sit well with Barbara, until I reminded her that her first obligation was to the kids. If she got into trouble, or if the court decided she was a bad mother and called in social services . . .

"Would they do that?"

I pointed out to her that we still had a lawsuit pending against the police, and that it was in her name. Once I hit the road, she'd probably have to drop it, but that didn't change the fact that there might be some enmity against her floating around.

As we lay there quietly, I spent about five minutes feeling sorry for myself and wishing with all my heart I could undo everything I'd done to put myself in this position, then called Barb's brother Augie and had him come pick me up and drive me over to Hollywood. I sent him on his way, then opened the door to Barb's aunt's garage and got into the van. A few minutes later I was northbound on I-95, trying to occupy my mind with detailed planning in order to avoid dealing with the enormity of what I was doing. I was going to need a new identity, and all that that implied: opening new bank accounts, getting a social security card and driver's license, retitling the van, finding a place to live . . . a thousand difficult and complex chores, each fraught with risk. I concentrated on them as I drove, because if I gave vent to how badly I already missed my family, if I conjured up for the hundredth time that morning Barb's confused, panic-stricken but still-loving face, I'd disintegrate.

By eight-thirty I was over fifty miles away, and it didn't take much of a calculation to know I'd already passed the point of no return: Within an hour after I failed to show up for the nine o'clock hearing, neither my lawyers nor my wife able to explain my absence, the judge would issue a bench warrant for my arrest. If caught, I'd have no defense whatsoever, because what could be more self-evident of violating parole than failing to appear for a VOP hearing?

I pressed the accelerator to the floor, a totally stupid thing to do when my entire existence at the moment should have been completely dedicated to not getting caught. As I began to pass other cars, though, I was surprised to discover that, despite my anger, bitterness and loneliness, I just plain didn't seem to give a shit about anything at all.

⁓

Two days later it was reported in South Florida's *Sun-Sentinel* that Shirley Thompson, who had been the court reporter at the time of my original sentencing and was now living in Chicago, had found her shorthand notes of the sentencing hearing tucked inside a book. She'd never transcribed her handwritten copy into an official record and had inadvertently taken it with her when she'd moved.

Part

III

15

~~~~

On the Run

I'D INTENDED to drive the 650 miles from Fort Lauderdale to Atlanta in one day and then put up for the night, stopping only for bathroom breaks and to grab some food that could be eaten while steering. But when I hit Atlanta, the thought of lying alone in bed in a motel was too much for me and I kept going, even though I felt like I was driving off a cliff and was so preoccupied and upset it's a wonder I didn't crack up the van somewhere along the way.

But at least driving was something to do, although I can't say I was being fully attentive to the road. Alone in a room it would be different. Hell, even in jail, people I loved and who loved me back were able to visit me. Despite the uncertainties of being imprisoned—and this will sound strange, I know—there really hadn't been a lot of things to *worry* about, except the big one: how and when I would get out. And people who cared about me and who were experts had helped me worry about it. Aside from that, there were few details to be attended to on a daily basis.

Now I would have nothing *but* details to worry about, hundreds of them, and it started to hit me what it would mean to be a fugitive. It wasn't about blithely outrunning the police and having a jolly old time outsmarting them. It was about never being able to relax and having the most innocent of daily activities—going out for a walk, getting a haircut, ordering a pizza—suddenly take on a dangerous edge. There was no way to know when you were just about to be spotted or had already been made, no way to know if "they" were closing in or even watching. I'd have nothing to go on but assumptions and would have no way of knowing if the precautions I'd be taking were overkill or dangerously insufficient. The best I could do was think about it rationally, come up with a plan and stick to it.

I hoped I'd be able to do that soon, because at the moment I was as far from rational thought as I'd ever been when sober. I had about two hundred dollars' worth of quarters for pay phones and was stopping every hour to call Barb, and occasionally Fred or Ray. I was concerned that I'd made my lawyers look bad when I hadn't shown up, but Ray just laughed it off. "My job isn't to make judges like me," he said. I wasn't worried about my home phone being tapped, because I wasn't important enough to warrant that kind of effort, but I made sure anyway not to let slip to anybody where I was or where I was heading. I was also careful in our conversations not to give the impression that Barb or my lawyers had known in advance that I'd be skipping.

I missed Barbara and the kids terribly, and every time I heard their voices and realized how much farther away from me they were getting with every call, it just got worse. Those were thoughts I didn't want to be alone in a room with, so I just kept driving until I finally hit Cleveland before dawn the next day. My aunt, who lived on the sixth floor of one of the buildings I managed, was out of town, so I let myself in, being careful not to let anyone see me. I was exhausted and slept for a few hours, but when I awoke I kept my eyes shut for a minute, unwilling to open them to greet the first light of an unwanted life.

My first order of business was to get some money. I stayed in the apartment all day and after the sun went down headed for my work locker where I'd stashed the jewels from the Blair House score. I spent time looking them over, deciding which could be sold as is and which had to be broken down to mask their origin. After I'd carefully taken apart the latter, which took the better part of two days to do right, I started a list of what I thought the individual items might be worth and how much I'd be willing to settle for from a fence.

I found out from Bill Welling that my name and photograph had been circulated to every police precinct in Cleveland, so there was no hope of unloading the Blair House goods with Blute Tomba. I was lucky enough that I hadn't been caught yet just going to twenty-four-hour grocery stores in the middle of the night. The second night I was in Cleveland, Welling picked up some pizza and a couple of six-packs and came by the apartment. I told him of my predicament and asked him to come with me to off-load the jewels.

"Where are you thinking?" he asked around a mouthful of pepperoni and cheese. I started ticking down some cities where I knew fences, and he stopped me when I hit Atlanta. "I got some business in Atlanta."

I told him that was good, because I'd probably get the best deal there. Neither of us saw any reason to mention that it was close to Florida and my family.

"You're probably not gonna get the same deal as you would from Blute," he said, "but . . ."

But it was a lot safer.

Later that night we went down to the garage and removed a few panels from the van and stashed all the jewels. The next day it was back on the road again and off to Georgia.

~

When we arrived in Atlanta, we checked in to a motel, then I called my contact and left a phone number for him to get back to me. He'd call back when it was safe, and that could be that same afternoon or not for a few days. With nothing to do for at least a few hours, Welling suggested we go to dinner.

"Did you know Carl Coppola had a restaurant here?" I asked him.

"The smuggler from Fort Lauderdale? I didn't know that!"

Carl had funneled much of his marijuana-smuggling profits into the She strip club and a string of Jilly's rib restaurants, and spent a lot of time in one fancy Jilly's northeast of the city on Roswell Road in Sandy Springs. We went out there and it was like old home week. You'd have thought we were all long-lost brothers or something, the way we carried on. A common affinity—we were all crooks—and a lot of alcohol will do that.

We were all crooks, yes, but some of us were much bigger crooks than others. It was probably just as well that at the time, I didn't know much about who Carl really was, or I might have picked another joint to hang out in. It would only be a few years later that he would become the subject of a federal trial that blew the lid off a vast empire rivaling anything that another Coppola—Francis Ford—had put up on the screen in his two *Godfather* movies, except for the fact that it was a good deal less lovable.

Joey Cam was one of the nicest guys you could ever meet and spent money lavishly on people he liked. Curly-headed and of medium weight and build, he was a gentle Italian whose only expression seemed to be a pleasant smile. Carl, on the other hand, was thin and wiry and mean as a snake, although he was always nice to Welling and me.

There were two others I hadn't met before. One was Alex Biscuiti, a henchman of Carl's, with a disposition that made Carl look like a choirboy. Biscuiti supposedly lived in St. Petersburg, Florida, but was always with Carl. The other was a guy named Gary Pierce.

I checked in with the motel periodically, but there were no calls, so we hung out with Carl and his friends. After a big dinner we gravitated toward the bar and started doing tequila shooters and bullshitting one another about what we'd been up to. Talk among this crowd inevitably turned to drug smuggling. Carl and Joey commanded a lot of respect in that circle; they'd been at it for years and had boatloads (almost literally) of money to show for it. Gary Pierce was an up-and-comer in the field. When he saw how affectionately Carl treated Welling and me, he must have thought it a good idea to be nice as well and invited us to his farm about twenty miles outside Atlanta. We went the next day. It was a huge spread and seemed an unnaturally bucolic place for a career criminal to be spending his time. He introduced us to his family, and the whole thing looked like something right out of *The Waltons*.

When we got back to the motel, there was a phone message waiting.

~

"You're pulling my leg," Welling said as he slowed the van at my direction and angled for the curb. A few feet away was one of the most prestigious jewelry stores in Atlanta. Welling had heard of the place even back in Ohio. "*This* is the fence?"

I don't know why he should have been surprised; after all, Blute Tomba's was a pretty upscale shop, too. But it was nothing like this. The store looked like one the queen of England would be comfortable in.

The jeweler greeted me warmly, although he called me by a different name. I introduced Welling, then the jeweler held out a hand toward an interior doorway and said, "Shall we?"

His eyes grew wide as I laid the stuff out on a felt-covered counter.

You'd think a guy would withhold his admiration prior to negotiating, but we were all professionals and there was no sense trying to downplay the quality of what I'd brought. The jeweler had obviously been through similar scenes countless times and knew the cardinal rule: Don't ask where anything came from.

"How come you didn't break this one down?" he said as he picked up a diamond-encrusted bracelet and checked it out with his loupe.

"Didn't look special," I answered.

"Well, it is," he said, then handed me another loupe. I examined the bracelet as he described what to look for.

"All those small diamonds," he said, "they're not just chips, the kind of stuff you sprinkle on for show." He used a miniature screwdriver to point some of them out. "Each one is beautifully cut, and they're all the same shape. Hell of a lot of labor went into this thing." He paused as I verified what he was telling me, then said, "Damned shame, too."

I knew right away what he meant. That kind of workmanship made this a dangerous piece to handle, because of its uniqueness. However, once those tiny diamonds were torn off the bracelet, their individual values wouldn't begin to approach what the unified piece would have been worth. The value was in the matched set of stones, and once that was broken up, all that was left was the worth of the separate diamonds. But nothing was worth getting caught.

I nodded and handed the bracelet back. "Would it help if I told you it came from over a thousand miles away?"

"Love to help you out, but no." He offered to let me hold it back from the rest of the stuff, but that would be more trouble than it was worth, and too risky. I told him to give me one price for the whole package. Apart from not having recognized the true value of that one piece—you never stop learning—my estimate was pretty close to the mark. The jeweler made an offer that was about 25 percent less than what I'd come up with, so I knew that after some bargaining I'd be very close. Since I hadn't known the true value of the bracelet and couldn't have gotten it anyway, I was pretty happy about that and was upbeat during the subsequent "hondling," which was generously soaked with shots of schnapps provided by the jeweler. When it was all over, we agreed that he'd bring the cash to our hotel room at eleven o'clock the next morning.

"You want me to hold these now?" he asked.

It wasn't as silly as it sounds. He was a well-established guy with a legitimate store of many years' standing, so I knew he couldn't easily run away. He was also a veteran fence with a thriving business and wasn't about to wreck all of that just to rip off one customer. In any event, a fence's cut is so big, there's not much incentive to steal from customers.

But I told him I'd take the stuff with me anyway. That was mostly to make sure he didn't get skittish and cause delays. It was also in case something happened on my end and I had to bolt before the meeting. He understood and took no offense.

Out in the car Welling said, "Just curious: What if he'd come in fifty G's less? Would you've walked?"

I thought about it for a few seconds. We both knew I needed the cash and wasn't in much of a negotiating position. "Yeah," I finally said, and he nodded approvingly. You can't show weakness or desperation to a fence. It takes years to build a reputation as someone who won't be trifled with, but only minutes to wreck it. Whatever straits I might have been in at the time, it wasn't bad enough to compromise any future dealings.

We went to Jilly's again that night. Buoyed by the thought that I'd soon be rid of the hot jewels I'd been carrying and would have liquid cash instead, I partied even harder than usual, and Welling followed suit. The next morning we awoke barely twenty minutes before the jeweler came by the hotel. There was so much stuff and so much cash and we were so bleary-eyed that it took us half an hour to go through it all and make sure we were squared away properly. As soon as the jeweler was gone, Welling blew out a long breath, leaned back on his chair and picked up the phone.

"Let's go," I said.

"Why don't we just order breakfast from room service?" he said, waving the phone around.

"We're checking out," I told him, and about fifteen minutes later we were out of that hotel and on our way to another one across town. No matter whom you were dealing with, you never knew where or when a double cross was coming.

~

That night we were back at Jilly's. Now that we'd visited with Gary Pierce and his family, it was like we'd known one another for ten years. Carl seemed pleased, and sometime during the postdinner festivities at the bar, he took Welling and me off to a quiet table in the back.

"Not sure what you guys are doing down here," he said, then put up his hands. "And I don't really give a shit. But if you got some time on your hands, you interested in a little work?"

Carl knew about my flight from Florida and probably assumed I could use some money. Even though I had plenty after fencing the Blair House goods, I had no idea how long it was going to last and whether more would be available. If I started running low and things got too hot for me to dip into my various caches of loot, I could find myself in a serious bind. "What'd you have in mind?" I asked.

However subtly, I'd just crossed some kind of a line. When you asked a guy like Carl what the deal was—and it was undoubtedly going to involve drugs—it was very difficult to turn it down once he'd laid it out. Welling knew all of that but stayed quiet and went along with me.

"Not much," Carl said. "I got a big load of weed coming into a little airport outside the city. I need help moving it to Birmingham. Got a buyer all ready."

Carl wanted Welling and me to help off-load the bales from the plane into a truck, then run lookout vehicles as Carl and Alex drove the truck to Alabama. Welling would be in a rental car about two miles behind, looking for any police that came onto the road behind the truck. I'd be in the lead in my van, about two miles up ahead, looking for cops as well as for open weigh stations. All three vehicles would be in constant radio communication.

"You'd also be backup," Carl threw in somewhat casually, "until I get my money from the buyer." He would supply the weaponry, machine guns known as Mac-10s. They were capable of firing sixteen hundred rounds per minute, and he was especially proud to tell us that not only did he have silencers for them, but they were a two-stage type that had been outlawed and were near impossible to get anymore. I had no idea what the hell he was talking about, but I knew the Mac-10 was a weapon that could take out a herd of elephants. These guys didn't kid around.

"For a night's work and a two-hundred-mile ride," Carl concluded, "you each get fifty grand."

The deal had every element I hated in a score: drugs, weapons, partners and somebody else calling the shots. "Sounds good to me," I said, and looked at Welling.

"When do we do it?" he asked.

As I said, I hadn't really been entirely aware of the extent of Carl Coppola's dealings when I was hanging around with him in both Fort Lauderdale and Atlanta. I knew he was a pretty heavy-hitting and successful drug smuggler, but I didn't know how heavy. Turned out he was one of the major distributors running cocaine from the southeast to New York. I learned that fact shortly after the Jilly's restaurants in Marietta and Sandy Springs were confiscated by the federal government in 1986, along with

$3.3 million of Carl's money, all as part of his arrest and indictment on a variety of charges that included racketeering and murder.

~

The next morning I gave Welling thirty thousand dollars for his help and backup with the fence, and drove him to the airport for his flight back to Cleveland. When I was alone again, I wanted nothing more than to head south to be with my wife and kids. But I was still a fugitive on the run, still driving the Ford van a smuggler had left in our rental house in Lighthouse Point, its panels stuffed with cash, and I couldn't go to Florida safely anymore. All that money didn't take away the pain one bit.

The deal with Carl was that I would stay in Atlanta and that Welling would be on the first flight from Cleveland as soon as I called him and reported that the load was on its way in. It sounded easy, but staying in Atlanta was awful for me. All I really had to occupy me was lying low, and that's not exactly the same as keeping busy. I moved into a motel after Welling left, spent half an hour getting familiar with the layout, then parked myself in front of the television. Everybody I knew was busy during the day. Whether what they were doing was important or not was beside the point, the point being that they were doing *something* and I wasn't. I found myself more and more looking forward to going to Jilly's at night, hanging with the boys and getting piss drunk, all the while ignoring the risk of that kind of exposure. New faces were constantly drifting in and out; one I'd have particular reason to recall was a fellow named Daniel Forgione, Joey Cam's father-in-law. Later on I'd also meet Tommy Papanier, one of Carl's bodyguards.

Meanwhile, after a few days Carl still had nothing definitive to say about the load coming in, and I was starting to get a little steamed. When you hang around all day with nothing to do, it's easy to work yourself into a lather. Gary Pierce seemed to sense this and started confiding to me about some things he was trying to get going. At first I listened politely, but the more days that passed without anything happening with Carl's deal, the more attention I paid. Pierce seemed to pick up on that and gradually shifted into trying to get me to take part. I was vulnerable to suggestion and he was very convincing.

After two weeks I'd had about enough of hanging around. I told Carl I was going back to Cleveland. "If it happens," I said, "we can be here in ten hours."

"Sure," he said, as though he'd expected it.

I didn't want to leave him any numbers, so I suggested an arrangement in which I'd call a pay phone in front of Jilly's every night at a certain hour.

He nodded, then said, "But talk to Pierce before you go."

"About what?"

"About he wants to talk to you. So do it."

It was about two A.M. at Jilly's. Pierce was three sheets to the wind but seemed to sober up a little when I asked him why Carl wanted me to speak to him. "I'm out of here in the morning," I told him.

"The deal I been telling you about," he said. "I need two hundred large to get it going. Carl and Joey are in for twenty-five each, and you and that other guy from Cleveland can come in for the same. Carl says it's okay. Your back end is two hundred and fifty grand, you and your buddy each."

Carl hadn't said a word to me about this, and I realized he was letting Welling and me in as some kind of compensation for the other deal, which apparently had fallen through. But I was too ticked off and drunk to make a decision on the spot, and told Pierce I'd let him know.

"I'm doing you a favor, Mason," he said. "Stuffing free money in your pockets. Let me know tomorrow."

I went back to the motel, got a few hours' sleep, then packed up and headed for Cleveland in the van. After I drove around there for a while to make sure I wasn't being followed, I went to Welling's place and told him about the deal.

"Never done a drug deal before," he said. "Except that thing with Carl that didn't happen."

I could tell he was trying to get me to make the decision for both of us. I think he wanted me to talk him into it, since it was pretty obvious that I wanted to go for it. If I didn't, I wouldn't have brought it up. That probably surprised him, but it shouldn't have. As much as I didn't like anything to do with drugs, the fact is that at that moment I was more of a hard-core criminal than I'd ever been. Before the troubles in Florida, I was just a neighborhood guy with a penchant for stealing jewelry once in a while. But now I was a fugitive from the law. My successful property business was a memory, as was my respectability. I was separated from my home and family, and I'd been hanging out with nothing but nasty crooks for weeks, listening to their endless bullshit and getting drawn deeper and deeper into the way they viewed the world. I was in no frame of mind to reject turning $25,000 into $250,000, nor was I about to help Welling see both sides of the proposition equally.

"Hardly anybody ever gets caught," I told him, and it was true. For every mule, peddler or middleman who got busted, thousands didn't. It wasn't just the absurd amounts of money that attracted people to the trade; it was the surprisingly small probability of getting arrested. You couldn't throw a rock in South Florida without hitting somebody who was somehow involved in drug trafficking.

If there was any single factor that triggered alarm bells in my head, it was that I would be working with partners, a violation of one of my most basic principles. But I was no longer operating from the cool distance of my former rationality. I was angry at the world, I was living in constant fear of discovery and I was bored. Offhand I can't think of a more lethal combination.

Welling, ready to gamble nearly everything I'd paid him for helping me fence the Blair House goods, gave me $25,000 in cash, and I drove back to Atlanta. I got in late at night, went straight to Jilly's and handed $50,000 to Pierce. After that, there really wasn't anything for me to do but wait and stay in touch. Welling and I had no major operational responsibilities; we were simply "investors" who'd put up some front-end money, and all we would really need to do is help if there were any last-minute snafus, so we had to stay in Atlanta until the deal was done.

Welling and his wife, Nancy, flew in from Cleveland, and Barb was going to come up from Fort Lauderdale in a few days. As soon as Welling and I got our money, the four of us would head down to New Orleans and see the sights for a few days.

The three of us had a good time in Atlanta. We, and that included Barb, had always gotten along really well and enjoyed one another's company. But after a few days, Welling and I started to get antsy.

"How come a guy like that needs a hundred grand to begin with?" he asked me one evening, referring to Pierce. "You saw his farm and all his other shit. What the hell did he need us for? He could have done the whole deal himself and netted nearly two million."

I tried to reassure him, but it was a damned good question. I could see where Carl might have strong-armed Pierce into throwing something my way, but Pierce had also taken money from Carl and Joey. We decided to call him.

"Some minor snags," he insisted. "Nothing serious. But call me at two tomorrow, case maybe I need you."

"For what?" I asked.

"How the hell should I know? If I knew, I'd tell you now." And he hung up.

The next day we went to a shopping mall in Atlanta. Nancy went off by herself for a while, and at exactly two Welling and I went to a pay phone and called Pierce.

"A little problem," Pierce said. "The plane's coming in from, uh, it started in Colombia, but . . . it had to gas up, you know? So it set down on the way."

"Where?" I asked, holding the receiver a little sideways so Welling could hear.

"Somewhere off Jacksonville," Pierce said. "I think."

"Isn't that in the ocean?"

"Yeah, well . . . it's a seaplane. Pontoons and shit."

"Okay, but where did it get fuel out in the ocean?"

"I don't . . . from a boat. There was a boat, waiting for it. The boat had fuel."

"So what's the problem?" I asked as Welling made a hurry-up motion with his hand.

"The problem," Pierce said. "Yeah, well, we need two guys to meet the plane and off-load the stuff."

Welling and I exchanged glances; had Pierce gone crazy? "What the hell are you talking about!" I shouted into the phone. "Didn't you arrange for that?"

"Sure, sure. Of course. Except, here's the thing: The guys who were supposed to . . . The plane was late, on account of the refueling. So the guys, the ones who were supposed to unload it . . ."

He went on like that for a while, and it sounded to me like he was making it up as he went along. I put my hand over the mouthpiece and asked Welling what he thought.

"I think you should hang up," he said.

I nodded, then took my hand away from the mouthpiece and cut in on Pierce as he was speaking. "We're gonna call you back," I said. "You better figure out—"

"No, no!" he said, nearly screaming. "Don't hang up! Listen, it's not a big deal. All we have to do, we have to—"

Welling grabbed the receiver out of my hand and dropped it into the cradle, then motioned for me to step out of the booth. I tried to make sense of the weird conversation with Pierce, but Welling nutshelled it for me right away.

"They got a goddamned refueling boat waiting in the middle of the ocean," he said. "So how the hell can it be a surprise that the plane needed to take on gas?"

I felt an actual shiver run down my spine and then saw Nancy coming toward us and waving. I grabbed Welling's arm and said, "Let's move away."

We walked to the other side of the broad central promenade and Nancy veered off to meet us. Just as we came to a halt in front of the mall's multiscreen movie theater, we heard a commotion and turned to see three guys bursting out of one of the mall entrances and running toward the phone booth. Welling tapped my shoulder and pointed to a different entrance. Another three guys were running out of that one and heading for the booth as well. All six of them wore blue jeans, running shoes, light windbreakers and sunglasses. As they converged on the booth and saw that it was empty, they started looking around in all directions.

"Hey, let's see a movie!" I said. Before Nancy could react, I had my wallet out and was buying tickets. I left it to Welling to explain to his wife as he hustled her inside why I was going to see a different film than they were. Both of us knew not only to separate but to stay put until the films were over.

When I came out some two hours later, the agents were nowhere to be seen. I waited for Welling and Nancy, then we went back to the motel to check out. I used the pay phone there to call Carl to warn him and Joey about what had happened.

We found a different motel and checked in there to stay overnight until Barb arrived. Welling and I stayed inside and didn't even use the phone. Nancy went out to get us some food, and the next day she and Welling went to the airport to pick up Barb and make sure she wasn't being followed. They swung by to get me and we headed for New Orleans. Barb, bless her, didn't ask why we hadn't just arranged to meet there in the first place.

Dealing with all of this stuff was a good deal easier than dealing with Barbara. She was not at all happy about my association with Carl, Joey and Pierce, and sneaking off to visit her fugitive husband while he was still hanging around with hoodlums made things pretty tough on her. I tried to relieve the stress on regular occasions by having us meet in other cities without that negative element. The trip we were starting on now, a long weekend in New Orleans with two people Barbara loved, was the best of them all.

We stopped in Montgomery and I called Carl. He told me he'd spoken to Pierce, who swore that his phone must have been tapped. Pierce also said that he was afraid to bring in the load.

"Bullshit," I said to Carl. "He gave us a whole song and dance about how the plane was late on account of it being refueled at sea. And he did everything he could to keep me from hanging up the phone." I was implying that Pierce had tried to buy time for a trace, which is the only way those federal agents could have gotten to us in that phone booth.

Carl agreed that Pierce might have been full of it, but Joey Cam didn't seem to think so. For the next few months he called Welling two or three times a week to get hold of me. Every time I called him back, Joey tried to convince me to come on board with Pierce's deal, as well as with a bunch of other ideas Joey had. But Welling and I were too leery at this point, although if it was just a question of going to Atlanta to pick up the money we were promised, we might have done that.

Sometime later I brought Pierce's name up to Carl again, and once again he voiced some reservations. "Something about him ain't right," he said, then added, "Only thing is, I don't know what his game is. Or if he has one."

Pierce's "game," as it turned out, was that he was an informer for the DEA. Frankly, I could understand why the DEA would want to go after big fish like Carl Coppola and Joey Cam, but what the hell was the point of sucking Welling and me into the deal? Until Pierce convinced us to take part, neither of us was dirty, at least as far as the feds were concerned. I was no lawyer, but it sounded to me like the very definition of entrapment. If not for an informer actively soliciting our participation in a criminal act and enticing us to accept, we wouldn't have been involved.

Thankfully, neither of us ever got into trouble for that episode, although we each lost twenty-five thousand dollars. I guess it was a moderately high price to pay for a lesson I should already have learned, but this time I learned it well. I was never to use a partner again.

I also resolved to stay the hell away from the drug business, and from Carl Coppola. But his name would pop up once more in my life and, not surprisingly, it would lead to trouble.

~

Carl's trial took place in 1987 and lasted fourteen weeks. DEA informant Gary Pierce was one of the main witnesses against him. Among the long list of allegations made by the government was one involving a misunderstanding between Carl and Joey Cam.

Carl had gone to New York to plead his case to the Gambino crime family, but Joey supposedly took a different route to enhancing his own negotiating position: He and his father-in-law, Daniel Forgione, kidnapped Carl and kept him tied up and drugged for two weeks. At some point Joey had a change of heart and let Carl go. In May of 1983, Joey and

Forgione were found dead in Fort Lauderdale, both having been shot in the head. The federal indictment charged Carl and his former employee and bodyguard Tommy Papanier with the murders. They denied it, and pointed the finger at Alex Biscuiti.

Assistant U.S. Attorney Jim Deichert was relentless in his prosecution of Carl. He told the jury that they should "consider Mr. Coppola as the Lee Iacocca of the drug business, and the murder business, too." He pressed the analogy of the CEO of a major corporation, saying that Carl filled the employee rank and file with contract killers and thugs whose tools of trade were Uzi submachine guns, pistols and sawed-off shotguns. Their method of ending someone's employment was to murder him, as they had murdered Joey Cam.

Fred Haddad did his damnedest on Carl's behalf, arguing that overzealous federal prosecutors were so obsessed about nailing Carl after spending three years investigating him that they cut deals with government witnesses to obtain damaging and questionable testimony. Ten of those witnesses were co-conspirators of Carl's who either got special consideration in their own cases or were granted out-and-out immunity.

Fred tried to convince the jury that it was Alex Biscuiti who'd killed both Joey Cam and Daniel Forgione. It was a vigorous and spirited defense, but Carl was found guilty anyway, and the sentencing didn't go much better than the trial: He got fifty-five years. Fred is still working on his appeal and, last I heard, Carl is currently the chaplain's assistant in a federal pen in Florida.

The reason all of this is relevant to me is that Barb followed the trial in the papers, as did pretty much everybody in the Sun Belt. Since it wasn't covered as extensively in the Midwest, she sent me a clipping about the sentencing. Years later, when I was arrested again, the FBI found this clipping among my papers and questioned me about Joey's murder. They thought for sure that I'd had a hand in it, or at least said they did, and used the possibility to bolster their case against me.

16

Crazy

I STAYED in constant touch with Welling. What an anchor he was in my life.

Bill is one of the only people I've ever known who rarely judged me but simply took me as I came. Certainly my parents loved me, as did Barbara and my aunt, but to say that I earned their continual disapproval would be an understatement. I'm not saying they were wrong; it's just that, somewhere in the back of my mind, every interaction seemed to come with a grade, depending on how clean I was at the time. My "okayness" with them was a variable thing.

With Welling I was always okay, no matter how badly I fucked up. That's just the way he was wired. Once he got around to determining that someone was a friend, judgment seemed to cease and you could do no wrong in his eyes. Unless, of course, the wrong was directed against him. Welling did not take betrayal kindly, maybe because he himself was so good to his friends that it was a shock when someone turned on him. Why anyone would want to cross someone with that intensity of personal loyalty was a mystery in the first place, but the world, and especially the circles I traveled in, were full of such mysteries.

Despite some mayhem in our younger, wilder days—I once saw him pick up a man and throw him through the window of a bar—Welling is basically a big teddy bear. Gregarious and fun-loving, the kind of person who takes big bites out of life, he adores being with people and is especially fond of family-style parties like weddings. He can dance, play with kids, tell jokes and sing for hours on end, and is one of the most contented men I know. He's also one of the most generous; it wasn't at all unusual for him to spend a month helping a friend rebuild a kitchen or do some other major project like that.

My kids were absolutely nuts about him when they were growing up, and still are. He's one of those rare types who make you feel like there's nothing else in the universe when they're talking to you. My mother and aunt and Barb's mother all loved to be with him; he would dance with them and make them feel special in many ways.

All in all, not bad for a bank robber. Grouch that I am, I've been lucky and privileged to have him for a friend.

Welling's brother, John, was a good buddy, too, and allowed me to "steal" his identity. I soon had a driver's license, credit cards, a passport, business cards and all kinds of other stuff identifying me as "John Welling," complete with photos. It's not as hard as it sounds, but it required that we both stay extra squeaky clean, because if one of us got into trouble and had his name circulated through law enforcement computers, it could make things awfully hot for the other one. I opened a bank account in Atlanta, too, and reregistered the van under my new name, still as the president of the "corporation" that owned it.

I rarely stayed in one place for more than a few days, and never more than a week. Mostly I stayed in and around the greater Atlanta area, but I also went back and forth to Cleveland, usually when my aunt was out of town so I could use her place. Sometimes I found myself mindlessly gravitating south, so I drew a line on a road map and promised myself I wouldn't go below it. All of that moving around was very hard on me. Surprising as it may sound, I've always been a real homebody at heart. I loved having a nice house, a comfortable, stable environment that I could always come back to no matter what else was going on.

When I told Welling I just had to see my kids, he understood, and didn't bother to lecture me on how dangerous it was. He just helped me work out the logistics.

"I have to go to them," I told him. "If Barb loads them into the car and takes off to come to me, they'll see that and might follow her. But if I can manage to sneak down there somehow, they may not know anything's happening."

Welling and his wife and another couple arranged to vacation in Florida. They rented an apartment about a mile north of my house, then visited with Barb and borrowed one of my cars. The next day I drove the van down to their apartment, which was on NE 48th Street and Federal Highway in Coral Ridge, and parked it behind the building. I had Welling move it daily so no one would think it had been abandoned, a fairly common occurrence in South Florida, where smugglers would buy a car to use for a few hours and then just leave it somewhere.

Welling drove me to my house in my car, with me sitting in the back. I scrunched down on the rear floor as we approached and waited until we were in the garage before getting out.

I was so happy to see Barb and the kids, I literally couldn't speak for the first minute or so. I stayed for several days, never leaving the house. Everybody kept to their normal routine so as not to arouse suspicion, and those glorious few days passed without incident. Suzi even canceled a date to be home with me, which is probably the biggest sacrifice you can make when you're nineteen.

Finally, on the fifth day, I poured drinks for Welling and me and said, "Time to go."

I hadn't originally given any thought to how long I could stay. I think I just subconsciously trusted myself to know when the time was right, and Welling didn't argue with me now. I took a long pull on the drink, though, and when Barb walked into the living room a few minutes later, she knew right away that I was leaving.

"What's going on?" she asked.

"Maybe nothing," I said. "One or two more police cars in the area than I saw the first two or three days."

"But maybe—" she started to say.

"Yeah, maybe," I said, more forcefully than I'd intended, but I didn't want to debate the issue. I'd vacated motels just because chambermaids looked at me funny. "We have no way to know, though."

"When?"

"Now. You need to drive me up to the apartment."

"The kids . . . ?"

"You'll have to say my good-byes."

Welling left first, and Barb and I followed a few minutes later. If anybody was following us, Welling would draw them off. He was safe because he had no outstanding wants or warrants and was therefore just another honest citizen. At least on paper.

The drive to his apartment was subdued and awkward for Barb and me. There wasn't much to say. I didn't know when I'd be back, and I wasn't even sure exactly where I was going. The kids were tough and would do their best to buck up, and that stoicism would only make Barb more sick at heart. It didn't make me feel any better to know that all that heartache was my fault.

We said good-bye in the car a few buildings away from Welling's, and then she drove off as soon as I got out. I went around back, where Welling was waiting for me in the parking lot. I don't remember how much time we spent standing there, or what we said, but soon I was behind the wheel of the van heading north on I-95. The plan was that Barb would go straight home and I'd call her as soon as I was out of Broward County. If I made it that far, I'd probably be okay.

I got off the interstate in Boca Raton and found a pay phone. There was no answer at the house, so I waited five minutes and called again. Still no answer. I didn't have the phone number to Welling's apartment; I hadn't used the phone in our house and so had never bothered to learn his number. There was no one else to call and I was starting to worry, because Barb was as reliable as the sunrise. Something had to be wrong.

What I should have done was just keep going and try again later, because even if something had happened, what could I possibly have done about it? As a compromise, though, I turned around and drove back toward Welling's place, thinking I'd get him to drive to my house and see what was up.

I got off the interstate at West Commercial Boulevard and headed east. Out of instinct I decided not to approach the apartment directly but instead went all the way to Route 1 and then south past Holy Cross Hospital, where I could get a good view of the building. I was still half a mile away when I spotted trouble: There were half a dozen cars clustered on NE 46th Street, about two blocks from the apartment building. They were all ordinary "your father's Oldsmobile" kinds of cars, and they were in the middle of the street pointing every which way. People were milling about, and as I got closer, I saw several of them talking into their hands. They might as well have had "POLICE" stenciled in yellow across their backs.

I noticed one car in the middle of the bunch that looked like it had been trapped there, and just as I went by, I saw that it was Barb's. Several of the police looked in my direction as a car horn sounded, and it took me a moment to realize that someone was honking at me because I'd drifted into the next lane.

Despite shaking from shock and rage, I forced my attention back to the road and soon got off Route 1. I was eventually able to get behind the apartment building without coming into the eye line of the police. I got up to Welling's place. He was alarmed to see me at the door but stepped back immediately and let me in.

"What the hell . . . ?" he began as he closed the door behind me.

I told him what I'd seen, which was all news to him. "You gotta go see what's happening," I said. He nodded, grabbed a pair of sunglasses and left me to go absolutely nuts with anxiety while he checked things out. He came back about twenty minutes later.

"Barb's sitting in the back of a police cruiser," he reported, then held up his hand to fend off the next obvious question. "Hasn't been an accident, I know that, but none of the cops would say anything else beyond that. They're all just standing around, some of 'em with guns out."

I sat down on the living room sofa. I'd been standing the whole time without realizing it. "Has to be about me." My instincts had been right after all; something had been up. If they'd arrested Barb, it must have been for harboring a fugitive. Had they been following me all day and then lost the trail somewhere?

Barely before I'd settled onto the sofa I stood up and headed for the door. Welling asked me where I was going.

"I've got to get the hell away from here."

That seemed to surprise him at first, my seeming abandonment of my wife in favor of my own skin, but he's a savvy guy and it only took him a few seconds to realize why I had to go. "Yeah," he said, and walked me to the door. "Without you they have nothing on Barb."

My mind seems to work best under pressure, and the situation was very clear to me. All I could do if I tried to "help" Barb was get her in even deeper trouble. If the cops saw the two of us together, it would strengthen their case against her for harboring a fugitive. And they'd certainly have me. Only one thing was for sure: There was no conceivable scenario under which I could get Barb out of that police car. Going down there now would make everything worse.

"What I'll do," Welling said, "I'll call Ray and let him know what's going on. Then I'll go hassle the cops, ask them why they're holding my friend."

I'd started to say something when there was a knock on the door.

Welling held up a finger for me to keep quiet and went to answer it. I listened from the kitchen as he asked who it was.

"Police," came the answer. "Can we talk to you for a second?"

Welling called back, "About what?"

"About a suspect," came the answer, and I froze.

Welling appeared at the kitchen doorway and motioned toward the ceiling, then pointed toward a hallway. I wasn't sure what he meant but went anyway, then saw a set of stairs leading upward. An old rule when you're being chased is never to run up, but Welling knew that one as well as I did, so he must have had a reason. I went up the stairs just as I heard him asking to see some I.D. and giving the cops a hard time.

Sure enough, there was a back entrance on the second floor. The service stairway was deserted, so I went down and walked through a narrow alley to where the van was parked. There didn't seem to be any activity and I was moving fast, so there was no way to stop myself without looking suspicious when I shot out into the parking lot just in time to see two policemen standing right next to my van. One of them was talking on his radio, and they were both looking right at me.

I didn't have a lot of choices here. To run would be foolish and dangerous. There were cops all over the place, and I would never get away and would probably get shot for my trouble. I might even get Welling and my wife into more trouble than they already were.

I knew that I'd already broken stride coming around the corner out of the alley, but that would not have been an unnatural reaction for an honest civilian unexpectedly coming upon two cops. So I simply resumed walking.

They did nothing but watch me as I walked past them, but one was still talking on the radio. It was possible he was calling for backup, because with all those other police in the area, why risk trying to take me with just two guys? They'd probably done their homework and would have heard from Fort Lauderdale P.D. that two guys trying to arrest me by themselves might not be such a good idea. (In reality, that was kind of an unfair rap; it was based on their surmise about my upper-body strength, but I'd never once resisted arrest.)

It was also possible they weren't sure who I was. These guys weren't from Broward County and might not have been familiar with my face except from a mug shot. They'd be calling somebody else to the scene and providing a description at the same time.

Whatever the reason, they were staying put. There was another garden apartment just a few yards away, and I walked into the back entrance, up to the second floor, and dumped my jacket. It was the most distinctive thing I was wearing and would be the first thing they'd look for. I left through the front entrance, then went in and out of two more buildings and into a third.

I was still on NE 48th, and from a stairwell window I could see cops all over the place, about thirty or forty of them, and no longer just standing around. They were on the move, although it didn't look very coordinated. I had no more buildings left and had to get the hell out in a hurry. If they came after me while I was inside, it was all over. Buildings like these were much too easy for the police to secure. They could surround one completely and there would be no way out.

I had to cross the street somehow, but from the entryway of the building I could see two detectives, guns out, standing smack in the middle of it. They were looking intently toward Welling's apartment building, which faced away from where I was. The only thing I could do was walk about twenty feet behind them and hope they didn't turn around. This was going to be worse than inching my way along Armand Hammer's slippery ledge, so I didn't want to spend a lot of time thinking about it, and just stepped into the street and started moving.

At first I kept my eyes nailed on the backs of their heads, then realized that made no sense. It would look unnatural to anybody else who might have been watching, and what good would it do me to know if they spotted me? So I turned my eyes ahead and just walked as normally as I could. That way, even if they did see me, there was a slim chance I might not get stopped. There was also plenty of traffic noise from Route 1, so they probably wouldn't hear me.

I made it to the other side and the two detectives never turned.

˜

There were still too many police around for me to try to leave the area, so I crossed Route 1 and walked into Holy Cross Hospital. I climbed up a few flights of stairs and found a large window with a commanding view of the parking lot, the back door to Welling's apartment and the clustered police cars. Turned out I'd walked into the maternity ward. I lit a cigarette and didn't have to fake looking nervous when a nurse came by to ask whom I was there for.

I'd had a few seconds to plan for this. "My wife," I said shakily, "my wife, she's . . . a friend called." I took a deep pull on the cigarette and blew a cloud of noxious smoke in the nurse's direction. "She's on her way here."

The nurse waved the smoke away in some irritation and walked away, which was just what I wanted her to do. That was about the time I realized that the television in the waiting lounge was tuned to a local station and they were reporting police activity in Coral Ridge.

"The police are searching for a suspect," I heard, "a white male about six feet tall, with a neatly trimmed mustache and beard, wearing brown trousers and a beige jacket."

Things were about to get hot. I couldn't stay in that hospital forever and didn't want to be trapped inside a building anyway, but I also didn't want to walk out just as the cops were deciding to shift to a different street to resume their search. So I stayed at the window for the time being.

To my amazement, less than two minutes later I saw Barb's car driving away. As she rounded a corner onto Route 1, I saw that she was at the wheel, and alone. What the hell was going on here? A few minutes after that, my other car appeared. Welling was driving, and he had what looked from a distance like his wife in the front seat and the couple they'd come to Florida with in the back. Three unmarked police cars I recognized from earlier pulled out after them.

Was the search being called off? What kind of sense did that make? They'd seen me only a few minutes ago.

I called Barb's brother Augie in Hollywood from a pay phone in the waiting area. He came and picked me up, and as we drove away he said there were still plenty of police around. I couldn't bring myself to leave the area just yet, not until I knew things were okay with Welling and my wife, so we went to a bar and I starting calling home every few minutes until Barb finally answered. By that time my nerves were so frazzled I could barely think straight, but there was no mistaking a lightness to her voice.

"You won't believe this," she said. "The cops were staking out a bank robber. They knew he was in one of those buildings, but not which one, and when they saw me drop you off, they thought you might have been his partner."

So it hadn't been me they were looking for after all. "Are you okay?"

"I'm fine. Where did you go?"

I told her that I'd been in Welling's apartment when the police had come knocking. "I walked right past two detectives in the parking lot."

Barb said that the police radios had gone crazy at about that same time. Everybody had been shouting that they weren't sure what the suspect looked like, and one guy was yelling that he had a description. When another cop asked him how he got it, he said that the suspect had just walked past him. By that time Barb had convinced them that neither of us had anything to do with a robbery, and that's when they let her drive away.

When I had my wits back, Augie and I drove back to the Coral Ridge area. He got out a few blocks from the apartment building and walked the rest of the way to retrieve the van from the parking lot. He then drove a very convoluted route back to Hollywood as I followed in his car to make sure the van wasn't being tailed. Then we switched and I headed north on I-95 again.

That evening I spoke to Welling from a pay phone at a truck stop. He'd refused to tell the cops anything, which made them suspicious as hell. After they left he'd rounded up his wife and the other couple and got into my car, then drove down to Parrot Jungle in Coral Gables with the three unmarked cars following them. It was a thirty-mile ride.

"They followed you all the way?" I asked.

"All the way?" Welling laughed. "They got out of their cars and followed us on foot all over Parrot Jungle for three hours!"

Later we found out that the police weren't actually trying to catch the robber, who'd hit three banks in the area. They had set up surveillance and were trying first to find out exactly what he looked like, and then they wanted to follow him, see if he had a partner and catch him with stolen money in his possession. But they'd blown the surveillance so badly—half of southern Florida knew they were there—they decided they had to arrest the guy immediately or he'd get away. They'd alerted the television and radio stations, giving them my description, then somehow found out what he really looked like, probably based on a tip. I think the public at large would be amazed at how many suspects are caught based on tips rather than brilliant detective work.

The guy was eventually acquitted.

17

~~~

The Loveman
Scandal

("Francine, we hardly knew you . . .")

I'D BEEN living as a fugitive from Fort Lauderdale authorities and the Florida-based FBI for nearly a year. Believe me, there's not a damned thing glamorous or enchanting about being on the run from very skilled people who get paid, promoted and emotionally rewarded for catching you. They get to call all the shots, because everything *you* do is purely defensive based on what *they* do, and the farthest you can ever get away from them is just one step from being caught.

I was still holing up in Atlanta motels, checking in under various assumed names and paying cash so as to leave no paper trail. I still traveled back and forth to Cleveland quite often, probably more than I should have, staying either at Bill Welling's house or with my aunt Nell. She lived on Shaker Square, in a building I used to manage that was still owned by one of her other nephews. Barb came to visit for New Year's, and it was an anxious, frantic and depressing weekend of furtive trips between Welling's place and two different motels. As wrenching as it was when she finally left, I think we were both relieved.

My mother lived right around the corner from Aunt Nell, and I knew I was still under active pursuit because the FBI had paid her a little visit. She invited them in for tea and stonewalled them completely, staunchly refusing to provide any details as to my whereabouts while insisting that I was a nice boy who couldn't possibly have done anything wrong. From what she told me, the conversation apparently went something like this:

"Mrs. Mason, when was the last time you saw your son?"

"Well, I remember that we were together at a cousin's birthday party about, let's see, would have been about a year ago. Yes, I saw him a year ago."

"But was that the *last* time you saw him?"

"Can't remember if it was the last time, but for sure I saw him then, because he brought along the cutest windup doll as a present. That's Bill, all right, very thoughtful."

"So have you seen him since?"

"Since what?"

"Since that birthday party."

"Would you like another cup of tea?"

"Sure. Have you seen him since that party?"

"Well, I really can't remember. There was this other time when I made him and Suzi a big lunch. He brought flowers, a big bouquet."

"Was that after the party?"

"No, after the party everybody went straight home."

"What I meant was, did he have lunch with you sometime after that party, or was it before?"

"I really don't know. Is it important?"

"Very important, Mrs. Mason."

"Then it's a shame I can't remember. More tea?"

And so on, for over an hour. It may sound funny in the telling now, but it was pretty nerve-racking to know that federal law enforcement officials were trying to get my mother to give me up. I kept a very low profile on my visits to Cleveland. The few people I unavoidably ran into who did know me had no idea I was on the run.

I also never flew, just drove. An airport is like a tiny sieve that gathers huge numbers of people into one small spot before disgorging them to their scattered destinations. As far as a fugitive is concerned, it's like being herded through Checkpoint Charlie, because it's relatively easy for cops to stake out an airport. All you need at the gate of an incoming or outgoing flight is a single officer watching faces, and there's no way to avoid being seen, because every passenger eventually has to go through the boarding area.

But there's no practical way to place every road leading into or out of a city under surveillance, and if you've got a clean (meaning "unsuspicious") car, driving is the best way to go. I still had the new but otherwise utterly nondescript Ford van that, while technically stolen, was completely clean on paper.

I also had the solid set of identification documents identifying me as John Welling. I never did get stopped by the police but was confident that my wallet full of legitimate-looking I.D. wouldn't raise an eyebrow if I had.

The most trying time of all was when my mother had to go in for a mastectomy. I left Atlanta to be with her in Cleveland, even though the FBI would surely be stepping up their surveillance in anticipation of my doing just that. Regardless, I visited her in Saint Luke's every day along with Aunt Nell, varying the hours I went to the hospital and using the service, basement and E.R. entrances whenever I could. Hospitals are not especially security conscious except for guarding their narcotic supplies, and it was easy to find alternative ways to get in.

After several unnerving days of such skulking around and refusing to cut the dangerous stay in Cleveland short, I was ordered by Welling to blow off a little steam before I imploded. Along with his wife, brother and a vanload of crazy Irishmen, he dragged me into downtown for the Saint Patrick's Day parade. They started drinking at around nine in the morning, and as soon as the parade was over, we began hitting bars one after the other, getting rowdier with each one. I stayed well behind them in terms of consumption, but "well behind" these guys still put me far in front of your journeyman boozer.

By the time I left them at around six, I was pretty well sloshed. Hospital visiting hours ended at seven and I rushed in with only thirty minutes left, smelling like a brewery and fairly disheveled as well. My mother was recovered enough to register her disapproval of my condition, and the visit wasn't very pleasant for either of us. When I left, I was in a foul mood and didn't want to go back to my aunt's. The last thing I needed was another drink, so naturally I decided to go out and get one.

Barbara and I owned the land lease under an east side restaurant and bar called the Ground Floor, a chic watering hole for the Shaker Heights crowd. The restaurant was upstairs, so I headed downstairs for the bar and knew I'd made a mistake the moment I opened the door. The place was so packed, it was an effort just to turn around, and someone in my condition would never be able to get anywhere near the bar for a drink. After several minutes of uncoordinated maneuvering that didn't get me anywhere, I did my best to aim for the door and found my way blocked by a drop-dead-gorgeous redhead.

I tried to focus my eyes and made out a mass of shiny curls, a mink coat and a huge diamond ring. Naturally drawn to the ring and totally focused on it, I almost didn't realize it was me she was addressing when she shouted above the din, "I know you!"

"No, you don't," I mumbled back, and tried once more to locate the door.

"Sure I do," she answered with a bright smile. "You're Bill Mason."

"Wrong guy," I insisted, and began deploying elbows in an effort to get away.

"I don't think so," she laughed, and held out her hand. "Francine. You were in my high school class and you managed the building where my in-laws live. I saw you in the garage all the time."

Francine? Couldn't be . . .

I took a closer look. If we'd been in the same high school class, she must have been my age, forty, but this was about the best-looking forty-year-old I'd ever laid eyes on. Her face was as beautiful as it had been in high school and she had the body of a model; not one of those stick figures who look like human clothes hangers, but curvaceously filled out. Come to think of it, I'd heard she'd done some modeling. I'd also heard she'd married well, some big-shot industrialist, which made sense, because Francine had been born into some pretty serious money.

Her father, Milton Kravitz, was a genuine rags-to-riches American success story. He and his brother Julie started with next to nothing and worked themselves hard, getting to a level where they and a friend could buy the Pick-N-Pay supermarket chain, the largest in Cleveland but struggling to stay afloat. They turned it around brilliantly, and eventually acquired Finast supermarkets as well. Despite his wealth, Milton remembered his roots, and it would have gone against his grain to send Francine to a private school. In 1956 he and his wife moved to Shaker Heights so their daughter could spend her last two high school years in a top-drawer public school. I remembered that she was an ace student, active in several clubs and the girlfriend of the star player on the football team. Years later the Cleveland *Plain Dealer* would call her "a glittering fixture of our city's social whirl."

As I explained earlier, Shaker Heights High was public, and the only thing that determined whether you went there or not was your address. But that didn't mean that students from different sides of the tracks did a lot of mingling. For all I associated with the likes of Francine, we might as well have been on different planets.

Fast-forward to some twenty years later in a crowded Cleveland bar. There was no way out of this now, so I stopped shoving and looked up. "Francine Kravitz?"

"It's Loveman now," she said as I finally took her hand. "Has been for about twenty years."

"Loveman," I repeated as we tried to move away from the crush, knowing damned well what her last name was now. But I pretended otherwise, still not sure if this was a safe situation for me. "Rich guy, right?"

It was a dumb thing to say. It only made sense that she'd married someone who was also to the manor born. Francine Loveman was a well-known figure in Cleveland society, generally referred to by the press as an "heiress" or a "socialite." I sometimes wondered what it must be like to have your entire life reduced to such insulting abbreviations, especially ones for which the male equivalents were rarely used.

Francine took no offense at my crude remark and laughed easily. By the time we finally made it to a wall, we'd already discovered we had something in common. Francine's eldest daughter was the same age as my daughter Suzi, and both of them had started college the previous fall. On this particular day, Francine had decided to step away from her life of charitable boards and other high-toned volunteer work and see what Saint Patty's Day was like at the Ground Floor.

"It's so *crazy* in here!" she marveled. To avoid the crowd she and her sister and brother-in-law had grabbed a table with a built-in Pac-Man machine and had stayed there until Fran spotted me.

Something occurred to me. "How come you never said hello when you saw me in your in-laws' garage?"

She smiled coyly. "My mother-in-law told me you were a bad man."

Great. "She was right," I said, smiling back and trying to give her the impression I was anything but.

Despite the usual warning sirens going off in my head concerning my safety, I found myself drawn to her. She seemed to need to talk, and I was happy to listen. That wasn't easy, though, and after a few more minutes we couldn't stand the noise anymore. Her sister and brother-in-law weren't ready to leave, so I offered to drive her home. Plowed though I was, she accepted. During the ride she mentioned that her father, in addition to owning a good chunk of Finast, also owned a bowling alley next to the Highlander. I tried to keep a straight face when she said this; what was it about that hotel that kept it popping up so often in my life?

As we drove, she told me that she'd gone to Ohio State after graduation but dropped out in her sophomore year to marry her high school sweetheart, a Dartmouth grad. Since then her life had been a whirlwind of civic and cultural activities, much of it with Jewish organizations that she and her husband avidly supported. I'd also heard correctly about her doing some modeling.

She gave me her number before she got out of the car, and I stuck it in my pocket, not thinking I'd ever actually call her. But two weeks later I was back in Cleveland and did, and we met for coffee. Fran brought along her sister Katie, a free-spirited type four years our junior who drove a fancy Jaguar.

Somehow we got around to talking about a terrible tragedy that had recently befallen the family. Fran and Katie's much-loved uncle Julie had been kidnapped, held for ransom and murdered by an employee, the son of the cantor of their synagogue. I'd already known about it, as it had been major news both in Cleveland and nationally, but had never really considered how it had affected the family. Hearing the details from Fran and her sister drove it home for me, and it was not lost on me that this was not the kind of conversation they'd have with just a casual acquaintance.

Some weeks later Fran invited me to an informal party around the pool at Katie's, another big Shaker Heights house. Fran and I had a few drinks and played backgammon, and I was introduced as "Bill," who lived in Atlanta and was in town visiting his mother. I was beginning to feel comfortable around these people and more and more attracted to Fran. The sirens in my head were getting louder, but even as I resolved not to let this go any further, I knew with a kind of helpless resignation that resistance was futile.

I wasn't able to get back to Cleveland for some months, but when I finally did, I phoned Fran and asked if she'd like to go to a party at my cousin Dan Renner's house. He was the prominent surgeon who'd put me back together after I'd been shot, but Fran didn't know anything about that. "One thing you ought to know, though," I added before she could answer. "My cousin and his second wife are skinny-dippers. There's usually a lot of naked people hanging around their pool, and some crazy stuff goes on." I figured it was now or never and tried to picture how the "heiress/socialite" at the other end of the line was reacting as I recounted some tales of prior frivolity. Even though that kind of thing was very much in vogue at that particular time, I had no way to know if she'd be insulted, intrigued, shocked, curious . . .

"Sounds like fun," came the answer.

~

When we got to Dan's big house in the upscale Gates Mills community, absolutely nothing was going on. Doctors and other of my cousin's hospital colleagues were sitting around, dressed and acting respectable, and it might as well have been morning coffee at an accountants' convention. I sensed some disappointment in Fran and was worried that she might think all my stories were just so much bullshit.

I pulled Dan aside during a lull—what the hell am I talking about; the whole damned party was a lull—and said, "What gives here? Where did you find these people?"

He shook his head, understanding perfectly. "We need some kind of spark to get this thing moving."

Absent any other candidates to take the plunge, so to speak, I stripped off every stitch of clothing and jumped into the pool with as big a splash as I could muster. It was as if a light switch had suddenly been flicked on, and in very short order nearly everyone was naked and in the pool, except Fran, who I doubted had ever seen a man other than her husband unclothed since getting married twenty years before. About ten minutes into it some guy with a neck brace and crutches rounded the corner. He took one look at all the nude bodies in the pool and seemed to undergo a miraculous recovery. Pausing only slightly to look around, as if to make sure no one from his insurance company was spying on him, he stripped off the collar, tossed away the crutches and dove in.

Later that night in a guest bedroom Fran and I made love for the first time. No doubt her inhibitions had finally come undone as a result of an afternoon of nude people cavorting in the pool, as well as frequent departures by various couples for some shenanigans. I couldn't tell then if it was me she was giving herself to, or the idea of me, someone far removed from her respectable world of volunteer work, cultural events and formal social engagements. If she noticed my gunshot and surgery scars, she didn't ask or say anything, and I wondered if she simply didn't know the proper etiquette in such situations.

And I had my own confusions to deal with. I have to admit that this wasn't the first time I'd been unfaithful to Barbara, but the other wanderings off the straight and narrow had been emotionally insignificant. With Fran it was different, though, and not just because Barb was a thousand miles away and I was on the run and lonely. There was hint of a real connection, and the last thing I wanted to do was encourage it, knowing as I did that this had to be a temporary thing.

Whatever wild stuff was going on at the party, Fran would have none of it, and we managed to keep to ourselves until we said our good-byes and left. We saw each other frequently after that, even though she knew I was married. What the hell . . . so was she. Interestingly, she didn't know much else about me, certainly nothing about my criminal activities, and that might have added somewhat to the intrigue. Maybe she was afraid to ask for fear of finding out I was a traveling shower-curtain salesman or something. After all, as far as she knew from her mother-in-law, I was just a building manager and onetime "bad boy."

About a month after Dan's party we were there again, and Fran left to go home while I was asleep. When I awoke, I saw that she had forgotten her jewelry, including a four-carat emerald-cut diamond ring she'd left sitting on the nightstand. Feeling like I was going soft, I called her to meet me later in the afternoon so I could return everything to her. We met for drinks, and as I handed over the ring, bracelet and two necklaces, she said, "Do you know anything about jewelry?"

I stifled a cough and said, "A little. Why?"

"I've got some stuff my mother-in-law gave me and want to find out something about it."

By this time it was obvious she was a bit smitten by me, and I cared about her as well, so I figured it was time to come just a little bit clean and break this thing off before it got out of hand. I told her I knew a good deal about jewelry, and then sugarcoated a highly abbreviated version of how I was framed by the police and hounded by a zealous prosecutor into my current predicament. I fully expected that bit of information to scare her into getting out as soon as possible, but it backfired. She only got more intrigued and soon after that even signed up for a Gemological Institute of America course in diamonds. I never took a course in jewelry, but my practical experience was the kind you can't get out of books, and I helped her whenever I was in town, which was becoming more and more often. Fran's social prominence still carried a lot of weight in the city, and one time she borrowed a full set of master reference diamonds from Marc Gluchov, a high-end Beachwood Place jeweler, when she was getting ready for her certification exam. I heard later that the poor guy almost had a heart attack when he found out who she'd been spending time with.

~

I finally left Atlanta for good and returned to Cleveland, despite serious misgivings that I might be getting complacent about my fugitive status. At first I took a room at a motel and rented it by the month. Fran was over three or four days a week but always went home at night. We couldn't really be seen in public and didn't go out, except to Welling's or my cousin Dan's, but we were so hungry for each other that staying in wasn't much of a burden.

After several months of this Fran told me a friend of hers had a very private two-bedroom condo for rent in the Georgetown Villas in Lyndhurst. I knew it was dicey, but by then I missed having an actual home so much, I thought it would be worth the risk. I took the place using my "John Welling" alias and set up housekeeping. First thing I did was indulge my legitimate paranoia and build an escape hatch in case the police came through the front door. I cut a hole in the ceiling of a closet that would let me climb up to an attic, then marked out where I could break back down into an adjoining condo and get away. This contingency arrangement made me feel a little better about the chance I was taking.

It was wonderful having a place like that, and having people come over to visit. By this time Dan was in the process of separating from his second wife, and he was a frequent visitor to the condo with various girlfriends in tow. The guy had a libido like a hamster and once had four different women in there at various times on the same day. I don't know where he found them or how he got them to do the things they did. On the outside these were prim and proper ladies of some substance and community standing, but once behind my closed front door it was like aliens took over their brains and insisted they copulate immediately and often. I don't know; maybe there really is something to being a doctor.

Meanwhile, I started pleading with Barbara to move away from Florida with the kids so we could be a family again. I figured that once she visited me and saw I was living like a normal human being in a nice apartment, she'd be tempted to forget all that had happened and give us another chance. While Cleveland would have been out of the question, I held out the promise of a place like Mexico or California, which I thought would be tempting for her.

That summer she agreed to come for a visit. My mother and aunt picked up her and our youngest, Laura, from the airport and drove them to my aunt's house. Despite my fervent wish to give the appearance of normalcy, I couldn't let them anywhere near me until I'd made sure they weren't being followed. Laura was just eleven, young enough to think all the intrigue was great fun, not old enough to know all the implications.

When she finally saw my condo later, Barbara really liked it. It was a far cry from that maddening and paranoid New Year's visit, and things went well for a few days, so I got a little bold and decided to prove I could walk around town like an ordinary citizen. Like the condo, it was part of my effort to demonstrate to her how much stability would be possible in our life together.

"What do you say we go out for a drink?"

Her eyebrows rose, but she didn't otherwise comment on the advisability of my being seen in public. "Okay."

"Any place in particular?" I offered her the choice so it wouldn't look like I was restricted in terms of my options.

"How about the Ground Floor?"

I winced inwardly but should have expected it, given Barbara's and my business interests in the place. I considered trying to let Fran know in advance but opted not to. The odds of her being there at the same time seemed remote.

Besides, despite her somewhat sheltered life, Fran was not naïve and could be surprisingly savvy about things. As much as we cared for each other and had great times together, she knew as well as I that it was simply an affair. I made no effort to hide how much I loved my wife, and Fran had no intention of divorcing her husband. She was aware that the reason I'd asked Barbara to come to Cleveland was to convince her to go along with my plans to reunite our family. Were it to work out, that would be the end of Fran's and my relationship, and neither of us tried to pretend differently.

Which didn't make me any less nervous when she showed up at the Ground Floor, her sister Katie in tow. As I'd assumed, though, both of them were exceptionally cool. They took to Barbara immediately, although Barbara wasn't too happy when several people wandered by our table and casually offered us coke from their specially manicured fingernails. But we had a few drinks, everybody got along, I was loose and relaxed, and when we were invited to continue the party at Katie's place I made no effort to try to get out of it. It may sound like an insanely risky thing to have done, but I'd lived with risk my whole life and it was like an old friend. I didn't realize it was another warning sign that I was starting to get complacent as a result of my having eluded capture thus far.

As the evening wore on, Barb must have sensed my easy familiarity with these people, and I think she suspected that I might have had something going on with one of the two sisters, but she couldn't tell which and never brought it up.

Sunday morning she said she wanted a divorce.

It absolutely floored me. We'd been married for twenty years, and up until that moment I had taken the solidity of our marriage for granted, never once entertaining the thought that all the pain and hardship I'd brought down on her would come to this. I assumed at first that the previous evening's casual drug use had thrown her into a tailspin, but an argument that lasted until Tuesday eventually disabused me of that notion.

What had brought Barbara to this point was so obvious in retrospect as to be a monument to the human ability to deny reality. Almost since the day we'd met, she'd been subjected to nearly unbearable stress. As if the ordinary strains of marriage, child-rearing and modern life in general weren't enough, she'd had the additional pressure of living with a professional criminal and never knowing if he'd be hauled off to prison. Even though she'd witnessed some of the miracles my extraordinarily tenacious lawyers had been able to pull off to keep me free, she'd also seen what getting shot was like. Bullets had little respect for due process, and no amount of courtroom wizardry could intervene if some quick-triggered cop or security guard or one of my bad-ass friends got off a lucky one. Still, she'd stuck by me.

It was only when I became a fugitive and the possibility loomed that life would never be the same that the last of her resolve began to wither. Living apart from me gave her more time to think and more perspective, and all that should have been surprising to me was how long it had taken her to realize that this was no life for her and our kids.

All of this was vague in my mind then, and I kept up my end of the argument about us starting a new life until she settled it by taking off back to Florida with our daughter. I realized at that point that asking for a divorce had been her reason for coming to Cleveland in the first place. If there had been even the slightest shred of doubt in her mind, the slimmest possibility of my convincing her that I'd turned things around, I'd blown it out the window by demonstrating my inability to avoid associating with a fast crowd that could easily land a hunted fugitive in serious trouble. It was over.

It was the saddest day of my life and still remains so, and all the blame fell squarely on my own shoulders.

~

I truly did understand where Barb was coming from, but it didn't make me any less hurt or angry. For the first few days after she left, I didn't want to see anybody, and didn't, but then I found myself badly wanting to talk to Fran. I don't think my feelings for her deepened, necessarily, because they'd been pretty strong for a while by that time, but there's no question that the nature of our relationship changed once I gave in to the reality that the future I'd envisioned for Barb and me was no longer a possibility. The baseline assumption Fran and I had been operating under, that what we had together eventually had to end in light of the practicalities of our respective home lives, had suddenly changed. Neither she nor I knew exactly what that meant, but we both felt the shift in atmosphere.

Being with Fran again eased the pain, but I still moped around for a couple of weeks. Then I did what I do best when I need a break from the stresses of everyday life.

18

"The Perfect Heist"

From the Cleveland Plain Dealer, *September 25, 1980:*

Thieves Grab Million in Jewels

by John P. Coyne

It was described as the perfect heist, the largest burglary in Lyndhurst history, and the $1 million caper.

On Tuesday evening, Joseph C. Mandel, an executive of Premier Industrial Corp., left his plush penthouse apartment in the Acacia-on-the-Green complex to take his wife to dinner. When the Mandels returned at 10 p.m., they found the deadbolt lock on the door locked from the inside. After a security guard helped him get inside his apartment, he discovered $1 million in jewelry, including family heirlooms, had been stolen.

Lyndhurst Police Sgt. Anthony J. Cecere said the burglars had evaded a sophisticated security system. Cecere said the complex has a guardhouse where all visitors are stopped unless they have permission to visit someone and security guards monitor closed-circuit TV pictures of the doors in each building 24 hours a day. "These thieves apparently knew exactly what they were doing," he said. "It was the perfect heist."

Mandel . . . has offered a $10,000 reward for the return of the jewelry, most of which was described as "one of a kind."

Four years later (December 8, 1984):

$500,000 Awarded in Lyndhurst Jewelry Heist

by W. C. Miller

Joseph and Florence Mandel moved to a plush condominium complex in Lyndhurst after 25 years of home ownership because they believed the larger building would afford more security. Their former home had been burglarized three times over the years, and they felt secure after moving to the complex in 1977.

But on September 23, 1980, while the Mandels were dining at a restaurant, burglars broke into their penthouse suite at Acacia-on-the-Green and made off with $1 million in jewels. The jewels—diamonds, rubies, emeralds, and other gems—were never found.

It was the largest heist in Lyndhurst history, a well-planned crime that still is unsolved.

The Mandels sued the then-managers of the complex, alleging the burglary was aided by lax security, and yesterday won some relief. A jury awarded them $400,000 plus about $100,000 in interest. The company's lawyers claimed security measures were adequate.

"We still really don't know who did it . . ." [Mandel's lawyer Donald] Traci added.

Following this one in the news made me almost as nervous as doing the job in the first place, although some amusing moments helped to relieve the tension.

First of all there was the old assumption that it was done by "thieves" rather than one man acting alone. Then there was the contention that there was no way the security systems could possibly have been working correctly, because nothing human would have been able to get past them.

I used to feel a little flattered by stuff like that. Upon further reflection, though, I decided that maybe admiring comments on my thieving skills were well-disguised criticisms of lapses in law enforcement's detecting skills.

Former astronaut and Eastern Airlines CEO Frank Borman coined an incredibly apt phrase in 1967. Testifying before a House committee investigating the deaths of three astronauts during a ground test, Borman attributed the disaster to a "failure of imagination." He said that the engineering team had been unable to envision such an occurrence in the first place, and therefore were completely unprepared to prevent it or deal with it when it actually happened.

Similarly, I eventually came to realize that when a detective or security expert used a flattering phrase like "superhuman" in connection with one of my scores, what he was really doing was covering up his own failure of imagination. If he couldn't figure out how I'd pulled off the heist, he retreated behind the excuse that the thief must have been a "human fly" or "the best there ever was." What other explanation could there possibly be, other than that the detective wasn't clever enough to figure it out, which is not something a law enforcement professional is anxious to admit.

You could clearly see a variation on this theme in the Mandel lawsuit. The condo managers, as the basis of their defense against Joseph Mandel's accusations of security lapses, contended that the security systems were more than adequate and were all up and running. Therefore, the wizards who pulled off this caper must have had nearly magical powers. How did they manage to float over the walls without tripping any alarms? How did they make themselves invisible as they walked past the security guards? How was it possible that none of their images ever appeared on any of the dozens of security cameras planted all over the complex? It was the only strategy available to the defendants, because the alternative would have been to admit that their security systems were inadequate.

The police added to the mystique, marveling as they did over the "perfect heist," maintaining that there was more than one perpetrator and confessing complete bafflement as to how the job was done. As part of their investigation they went beyond their own in-house people and queried experts from all over the country, including the FBI.

What they *didn't* do was ask a professional thief.

As it happened, they did come tantalizingly close to the truth but were left dangling for lack of any hard evidence. This occurred during the Mandel vs. condo management company lawsuit, in which the Mandels alleged that lax security made the theft possible. An astute attorney for the defense pointed out during the trial that two other people had joined the Mandels for dinner that night. They were the parents of none other than Francine Loveman, and wasn't Ms. Loveman known to be running around with a suspected jewel thief named Bill Mason? Isn't it possible that Francine arranged for the Mandels to be out with her parents so Mason could rob them?

And if that was the case, then the management company couldn't be held liable for lax security, because, according to the Fort Lauderdale police, Mason was the best cat burglar in the country, maybe the best there ever was, and how could anyone claim that security was inadequate just because Bill Mason got past it? That would be like saying a jail was inadequate because Houdini managed to escape from it. No building could be secured against Bill Mason!

I'm not bragging here. I'm just telling you what went on in the trial.

It was generally perceived to be a desperation move by the defense attorney. As it happens, though, he was the only guy involved who had it even half right. But by making me out to be superhuman, he missed the real point, which was that getting into that condo complex was so absurdly easy, I'm almost embarrassed to say how I did it for fear of disappointing anyone who actually thinks I really was some kind of a ghost.

I have a friend who does this absolutely mind-blowing card trick. All you have to do is *think* of a card and then tell him what it is. With you watching his every move, he'll slowly take a deck of cards out of a box and fan them open, and your card will be upside down in the deck. It's the damnedest thing I ever saw. There's no way it could be done unless he was psychic. I begged and cajoled him for months to tell me how it was done because it was killing me. When he finally broke down and showed me, it was such a letdown I was sorry I ever asked.

The Mandel case is a good example of why I don't believe in UFOs. When confronted with strange phenomena in the skies that have no immediate explanation, many people have a tendency to jump to the conclusion that we're being visited by extraterrestrials. But what they're really demonstrating is the failure of their imaginations to conceive of more ordinary explanations. You'll rarely find a professional stage magician who believes in UFOs or psychic phenomena, because he knows how incredibly easy it is to fool people. And for some reason I don't really understand but which every professional magician knows as gospel, the more intelligent your audience, the easier it is to pull the wool over their eyes.

My goal, though, wasn't to fool a boatload of very competent detectives. All I wanted to do was to rip off some jewels.

~

One afternoon in July of 1980 I was lying around Katie's backyard with some of her friends, playing backgammon with her then-husband, Tom, between cooling dips in the pool. They'd all been out to some fancy party the night before and were gossiping idly about all the swells they'd rubbed up against. Despite various degrees of morning-after sobriety, they were nevertheless recalling in impressive detail what everyone had been wearing.

The subject of Joseph and Florence Mandel came up. "You should have seen this diamond ring," somebody gushed. "Must've been the size of a golf ball!" I wondered if anybody could actually see my ears perk up at that, and I lost the next three backgammon games as I listened intently while pretending intently not to.

Joseph Mandel was always referred to in the press as an "industrialist," which I've come to understand is the same thing as a "businessman," only bigger and more important and generally involves making something other than just money. The Mandels were one of the most prominent families in Cleveland. Morton Mandel, Joseph's brother, was chairman and CEO of Premier Industrial Corporation, and Joseph himself was chairman of the executive committee and owner of 20 percent of the company's stock. (Premier has since merged with Farnell Electronics to form Premier Farnell PLC.) In 1982, Morton led a massive and hugely successful effort to completely revitalize the crumbling and decaying "MidTown Corridor" section of Cleveland, and this was only one of many of the more visible philanthropic endeavors in which they were engaged, operating through a handful of charitable foundations.

This was a serious-money family. They'd been robbed three times in their Shaker Heights home, and it wasn't much of a mystery why: Florence enjoyed bedecking herself with expensive baubles when she was in public. They'd moved to an upscale condo in Lyndhurst for the higher level of security, but as I listened to the people around the pool describing last night's party, it seemed to me that Mrs. Mandel still hadn't gotten it. What was the point of more guards and bars if you went around advertising the prize inside?

Acacia-on-the-Green (which I guess is what they tore up to build the place and then named it after) was so exclusive and secure, you couldn't even get into the lobby to look somebody up on the tenant reader board. It was time to muster up all of my magical skills and international intelligence connections . . . but I decided to go to the public library instead. There, I looked up the address and got the Mandels' phone number and unit number, then, after that grueling five minutes of work, walked over to the county building office and looked up the construction plans for the entire complex. The attendant behind the desk, a regular Pinkerton, offered to make copies if I needed them. I didn't take him up on it, because the numbering system for individual units hadn't yet been devised when the plans were drawn up, so I couldn't tell from the drawings alone which unit belonged to the Mandels. I had to know that in advance.

I can pinpoint the day I paid my first visit to Acacia-on-the-Green: July 29. The reason I remember is that on the day I'd originally intended to go, July 27, fifteen midwestern states and portions of southern Ontario in Canada were rocked by an earthquake centered in northern Kentucky. Alarms had gone off all over Cleveland and there were police cars and fire trucks everywhere. Although damage was minor, the whole city was jumpy and on edge, which meant that people were going to be more vigilant for anything unusual. Just two days later, though, I felt that things had calmed down considerably.

The two buildings of the condo were located on busy Cedar Road and were part of a complex of buildings backing up onto a golf course. I parked my van with blacked-out windows across the street and started watching.

I didn't have to watch for long. The first thing that surprised me was that although all vehicle traffic in and out was controlled through a single guard gate that I assumed was manned around the clock, the grounds themselves were wide open to pedestrians.

Several nights later I walked onto the property to have a look around. I noticed that all the exterior doors on the buildings, even the ones in sight of the guards, were monitored with television cameras, which undoubtedly were recording continually. It was a pretty good setup and I couldn't see how it could easily be defeated. And I still didn't know where the Mandels' unit was.

The next night I returned, but this time in my shifty robber's uniform, which consisted of a hand-tailored business suit of no particularly noticeable flair. Clean-shaven and with my hair neatly combed, I waited for a group of people to appear. Once they got past the guardhouse, I joined up with them as they neared the main door of the building. One of them opened it with a key card, and another one politely held it open for me. We shared an elevator. They got out about halfway up and I went all the way to the top.

Finding the Mandel suite was easy—they had their name on the door—and I got a good line on where their windows would be on the outside of the building. Most of their unit fronted on the golf course, and part of it faced the space between the two buildings. I counted off steps from each end to nail down the position.

Next stop was the roof, and I was already thinking about what I'd need to get out onto it once I found out how it was secured, but I can't say

I was terribly surprised to find the door unlocked. A failure of imagination again: If you can't picture somebody getting into the building, why would you worry about how to lock inner doors?

I found the approximate location of the Mandels' windows by pacing off the steps I'd memorized before, then began walking along the edge, looking over the side for patios. I didn't necessarily need *their* patio, just one that would afford me reasonable access to theirs. I was so intent on examining all the nooks and crannies that I hardly noticed the atrium until I almost fell into it.

Peering over the edge, I saw that the atrium opened right into the middle of an apartment. Having been startled into forgetting my step count, I went back to the far wall and started again, taking care to make my steps soft in case someone was home underneath, and could hardly believe it when I hit the right number at the very moment I reached the atrium: It led right into the middle of the Mandel unit, and there was nothing but a sliding glass door separating one of their rooms from the open-air area below me. This was their idea of security?

The only real question I had left was *when.* That was answered when Fran casually mentioned to me a few days later that Joseph Mandel had invited her parents to dinner the following Tuesday to celebrate his wife's birthday.

"Were you invited, too?" I asked her.

"I'm going to be in New York," she reminded me.

"Oh, right. So where's the party?" I asked, trying not to let her see me start to turn blue as I waited for the answer.

"The Ground Floor," she said.

Not Mandel's condo, I heard.

I let my breath out slowly. "Sounds like a great idea."

~

It was a Tuesday evening, and therefore perfect. Security people guarding private residences tend to relax on weekday nights, as those are the least likely times for people to be out.

This was the first time I'd ever used a police scanner. It was a portable unit, and I'd made a kind of shoulder holster that held it securely under my arm. The wire connecting an earpiece ran underneath my shirt. The point of the scanner was to buy me time to clear out if somehow the police got alerted to my presence. The unit continuously checked each of the individual frequencies used by the police, running through all of them about once per second. Whenever it detected that one was being used, it would lock in on it and play it through the earpiece. When that particular transmission paused, it would go back to scanning all the frequencies again until it found another one in use.

Mandel being who he was, it was a sure bet that the slightest suspicion of something amiss would bring half the force running amid a flurry of radio chatter. It was one of the risks of robbing rich people: If you think Joe Six-Pack gets the same response from the local constabulary as the heavy-hitters, you're living in a fantasy world. It's not that cops and firemen think the rich are any better than you or me. Quite the contrary, in fact, but what they do know is who is in a position to make the most trouble for them if they don't show up right away.

I was midway between two major suburbs, Lyndhurst and Beachwood, and had all the police frequencies for both places set up on the scanner. Getting them was another bit of brilliant spy work. When I went to buy the unit, I acted as a reluctant purchaser, unconvinced that this gadget would be any fun. The store owner, a former cop, said, "Come on, you can pick up all the police calls on this thing!" Baloney, I said. "I'm telling you," he replied. "Here, watch."

He pulled a slim book from beneath the counter, thumbed through it for a few seconds looking things up, then entered all the Lyndhurst police frequencies. Naturally I expressed amazement, and asked him if you could put in another town at the same time, like, say, uh, Beachwood? "Absolutely!" he said with delight, referring to the book again and entering all of those as well. "Hot damn," I cried with naked joy. But now I wanted that book, too.

I looked around, wondering how tough it would be to break into this place, grab the book and split. I'd be in and out so fast, I could probably risk tripping the alarm and get away in time. Problem was, once the owner realized the book was gone, it might cause problems. For all I knew, the police departments would change their frequencies immediately.

Maybe I could break in quietly, copy the pages I needed and slip away without anybody knowing what I'd taken, or even that I'd been there at all. The owner was a former cop, which is probably how he managed to get his hands on the book in the first place, so he wouldn't be stupid about security. Was it possible he even took it home every night to keep it safe?

No matter how I decided to go about this, I needed to see what the cover of the book looked like. I picked up the scanner and hefted it a few times. "Do you have any smaller ones? Not much room in my apartment."

"Let me have a look," he said, then turned away to a glass display case.

I leaned over the counter as if to follow his gaze, then flipped the book closed and turned it toward me to read the cover.

RadioShack. $1.95.

I stifled a laugh, then told the guy the scanner he'd pulled out would probably be okay, and did he happen to know where I could get one of these frequency books?

"Right here," he replied, pointing to a shelf I hadn't noticed before. There were about sixty or seventy copies. The one he was using covered the entire Midwest and had the frequencies for police, fire, the FBI and just about every other public service you could imagine.

For less than fifteen dollars I bought a set that covered the entire country.

∽

I have to admit that I was more on edge than usual as I drove up to a spot across the street from the condo. Armed security guards have a tendency toward hero complexes, especially when they've been on the job for a long time but haven't had an opportunity to do anything other than man a booth. They're aware that if they're efficient at their jobs, serious incidents will be few and far between and people will subconsciously come to take them for granted, or wonder if they're necessary at all, or perhaps even consider them to be nuisances.

Security guards, unlike cops, not only have a propensity to overreact when an incident occurs, they're also not as aware of the appropriate "rules of engagement." The guy who shot me in Pompano was a good example: No cop in his right mind would have put a bullet in somebody who was running away from him down a hall.

Now was no time for second-guessing myself. I found a good spot across the street but out of sight of the guard booth. My tools were in an elegant leather carryall, and I had a thin but very strong rope wrapped around my waist and out of sight under my expensive leather jacket. I didn't have to check the scanner, because I'd loaded it up with fresh batteries and had been listening to it for the past half hour just to make sure there was no special police presence in the area tonight.

At about six forty-five I saw Mandel's car pause briefly at the booth before driving off to dinner. I checked my watch and settled in for fifteen minutes, which was the time limit I assumed after which they wouldn't return for any forgotten items.

At seven o'clock I reached under my arm and turned the volume on the scanner down, then removed the earpiece and let it hang down inside my jacket. After setting a gray fedora on my head, I put the car key on the floor mat, picked up the carryall and got out, checked that the door wasn't locked and slammed it shut. The key I'd left on the floor wasn't attached to any other keys, so I wouldn't have to fumble around with it if I was in a hurry.

I walked toward the driveway leading to the guard booth, intending to stop about twenty yards before I reached it. That would give me a chance to wait, unseen, for a good candidate bunch of people to go in with as well as to take a few deep breaths and steel myself. I'd have time to enter the grounds a different way and join up with them at the door to the building.

But just as I started to slow down, a taxicab pulled up and a group of five people tumbled out, and they were perfect: young, boisterous but not obnoxiously so, smiling and joking with the cabbie and clearly headed for a fun evening.

It was too good to pass up. I pulled the fedora down lower on my forehead and smoothly blended in with them as they passed the booth and waved jauntily to the guard inside, who smiled back and waved them on through to the building.

I turned my head well away from the camera in the booth, and then away from the one over the main door to the building, flashing a bright smile to the young lady on my right to cover the moves. "Looks like you're all heading to a fun time tonight."

"Heading for a bore," she said with a laugh that was echoed by the others. "That's why we had a few first!"

A guy behind me jerked a thumb back toward the booth. "Sure got this place locked up tighter'n a drum," he said as he pushed a button to call up to whomever they were going to visit.

"Good thing," I said, declining to look where he was pointing. "You can't be too careful."

"Absolutely," another guy said as the door was buzzed open. Then he held it open for me. As I stepped through and thanked him, he said, "All kinds of lowlifes looking to rip people off." I nodded in sympathy with his trenchant observation.

"Where you headed?" the same guy asked as we all got into the elevator. I waited until he punched a number—it was 3—and said, "Top floor, thanks."

We exchanged some more thoughts on security until we stopped at 3. We all wished one another a good night and they got out.

This was going very well.

~

I'd been unable to see the condo window from the street and was relieved when I got to the atrium and found that the apartment was dark. That would not only make it easier to move around inside but also made it more likely that nobody had been left at home. I did nothing but watch the place for about ten minutes anyway, to see if any lights got flicked on or if there were other signs of life.

I'd put my earpiece back in after leaving the elevator, and the scanner continued to check the police frequencies, pausing every now and again for some routine bit of conversation between dispatch and a patrol unit. "I've left there, I'm here now, I'm going somewhere else, where are you, didn't see anything . . ."

It was annoying as hell. Each transmission started and ended with a burst of static, which sounded all the louder on that dead-quiet roof on which I was trying to make absolutely no noise. Trying to anticipate the next bit of scratchy dialogue was like the Chinese water torture, and it was making me jumpy. Worst of all, it was interfering with the most potent tool in the arsenal I carried, my own senses. I was used to relying on them, and while I didn't mind adding information to the mix, I very much minded compromising my eyes and ears. I was straining for any sounds coming from inside the condo, and every time the scanner latched on to a police transmission, it took me a few seconds to "reset" my hearing so I could start listening again.

Ten minutes passed and it was time to move. I had started to unzip my jacket when another gush of static shot through my head. I reached under my arm and turned the scanner volume all the way down. Better to crank it up and check every few minutes than go nuts waiting for the next blast of irksome noise.

I pulled on a pair of thin leather gloves and started unwinding the rope from my waist, turning my body with each loop so the rope wouldn't coil up and become difficult to handle. I wrapped one end around a nearby smokestack and secured it with the small climbing carabiner I'd attached to it that afternoon. Carryall slung firmly across my shoulder, I lowered myself over the lip of the atrium and began climbing down hand over hand.

I paused again once I was down, but there was no sign of movement in the apartment. It was time to get down to what I'd assumed was going to be the toughest part of the job, getting past the alarms protecting just this unit rather than the building in general. I couldn't count on the Mandels having left them unarmed, although I was hoping for that, and not unreasonably, since most people heading out for less than a few days rarely bothered to set them.

The sliding glass door leading from the interior of the apartment to the open-air area was locked. That meant that even if the alarm system was unarmed, I'd have no way to know and would have to assume everything had been switched on, so I needed to deal with that before anything else.

I couldn't find a magnetic trip. I couldn't find any wires leading away from the slider, which, I also noticed, didn't sport the kind of warning decal alarm companies liked to slap all over the place, more to advertise themselves than to scare away intruders. I didn't see any telltale blinking lights on a wall panel inside the unit. Either this was the most sophisticated system I'd ever seen or . . .

No way. I steeled myself against a loud and raucous alarm going off and jimmied the sliding door open. It was easy, which made perfect sense, because who'd bother to put a good lock on a door that was assumed to be impossible to get to in the first place?

Regardless, I went still to listen for any signs that I might have tripped something completely hidden, and took the time to look around.

The apartment was incredible: huge and filled with expensive furnishings, art all over the place and that unmistakable look and feel of having been professionally decorated so that it seemed more like a museum than a place in which real human beings actually lived.

My target was the dressing room, but first I turned up the scanner to check for unusual radio traffic, then turned it off, walked to the front door and slid the heavy dead bolt home. In case of trouble that would buy me some time.

The place was unbelievably quiet. The good news, which was minor, was that it would allow me to easily hear signs of trouble. The bad news, which was major, was that there was no noise to mask any sounds I might make. You might think that an absence of people in the vicinity is a benefit to a thief, and it usually is, but there's nothing like a lot of hustle and bustle to mask that a robbery is taking place.

The dressing room was also enormous, and there were drawers, cupboards and cabinets everywhere. I wasn't worried about having to search through all of them, though, because it was a sure bet that these people had hung out the standard sign saying, "It's all here": one cabinet that was locked.

I found it right away and picked it easily (why put a sophisticated lock on a cabinet whose sides could be cracked open with one good sneeze?) and nearly fainted at the sight of the treasures within. Diamonds, emeralds and rubies glittered like Christmas decorations, and the drawer seemed to groan under the weight of all the gold. I remember thinking, *With all this beautiful stuff still in the cabinet, what the hell must she be wearing to dinner!* One diamond ring alone was easily in excess of fifteen carats, even though the stone itself didn't appear to be of top quality.

I scooped everything into the carryall, then slid the drawer back and relocked the cabinet. It may seem like a useless thing to have done, but my feeling has always been that there is no sense red-flagging that a robbery occurred. The more time it takes for it to be discovered, the more time you put between the score and the onset of any investigation. The passage of time makes it more difficult for witnesses to recall details or at least to assign specific times to things they saw and, if you're very lucky, might make it hard for anybody even to know on what *day* the job was done. That makes the matter of an alibi for a detained suspect a whole lot easier, because "Where were you last night between seven and ten?" is a much different question from "Where have you been for the past three days?" Florence Mandel might come home and go right to that cabinet to stow her evening's baubles and discover what had happened, but then again, she might not get around to it tonight, or even tomorrow.

I took a quick look around the rest of the apartment but didn't find anything of great value I could fit in the bag. One more check of the scanner and then it was back out to the atrium and up the rope. It took me a second to realize why it was a tough climb, but I smiled when it hit me: It was the extra weight of all the goods in my bag that hadn't been there on the way down. (The Cleveland *Plain Dealer* reported that the "burglars" had shoveled all the jewels into two of the Mandels' suitcases, but where they got that idea is beyond me.)

Just as I eased myself over the lip of the atrium and onto the roof, I realized I'd forgotten to slide back the dead bolt on the front door. The Mandels wouldn't be able to get back in without help, and that meant they'd know something had happened. So much for trying to delay discovery of the heist.

But there was no way in hell I was going back down. I pulled the rope up and rewrapped it around my waist, hefted the bag once again and went down the stairs rather than the elevator. I waited until I heard some people in the lobby before coming out of the stairwell. I put the bag up on my shoulder, which shielded my face from all the video cameras, then walked out the main doors, past the guardhouse and onto the street to my car.

It couldn't have gone smoother. There had been no surprises, no especially tense moments, and it looked to be a monster haul. The newspapers reported a value of one million dollars. Based on what they knew, that was fairly accurate, but "what they knew" wasn't, as I'd find out within hours.

I dropped the carryall off at Welling's shop, which I had the keys to, and went home. Fran came back from New York two days later. I never mentioned it to her, and acted surprised when she read it in the papers and told me all about it.

⌣

The next day I retrieved the carryall and got ready for a close look at the haul in good light, which is when I got my first surprise of the caper: The enormous diamond ring, which turned out to be a whopping nineteen carats, also turned out to be fake. It was a damned good fake, but two seconds under my jeweler's loupe and there was no question about it.

Fighting back some welling nausea, I scrabbled around inside the bag and then just removed the tools and upended the whole thing on a workbench. Once everything was laid out, I started going through it one item at a time. There were plenty of other phony pieces, including a ten-carat diamond pin, but to my great relief there were a lot of real ones as well, enough to have made the whole job still well worth the effort.

I have no way to know whether the Mandels were aware of the fakes, or knew that they had now been robbed twice: once by me and once by whoever had sold them the phony jewelry.

I do know that they claimed the full million in their lawsuit.

⌣

By all media accounts, Joe Mandel was enraged at having been robbed. It wasn't because of the monetary loss or because some of the pieces were irreplaceable, one-of-a-kind family heirlooms, or even because someone had the effrontery to invade his "space." It was because he'd uprooted his family and moved them into new digs specifically for security reasons, and now some "thieves" had hit him again anyway.

Mandel didn't get to be the successful businessman he was by taking things lying down. He filed a lawsuit against the managers of the condominium complex, and his claim was pretty straightforward: If the security system had been working the way it was supposed to, nobody could have robbed him. The fact that a robbery did occur was prima facie evidence that the system was either inadequate or not working at the time, and therefore the management company was liable.

Security was a big selling point in real estate, but most of it, like Acacia-on-the-Green's, was junk. If you want to know how well a piece of property is secured, don't ask a cop, ask a thief. Look at some sales literature for security systems and you'll come to realize that the major point of most of it is to protect you from your own human fallibilities, such as forgetfulness, laziness and an unwillingness to be inconvenienced. Everything is as automatic as possible, so you don't have to remember to lock a door or go through the awful inconvenience of pushing a button every once in a while. This is impossible to do perfectly, and thieves rely heavily on the complacency and carelessness of their victims. Most people who live in densely populated areas don't even look up when a car alarm goes off, assuming that the car owner screwed it up again. The police get angry at false alarms, and this intimidates a lot of people into not setting their alarms at all. (The Los Angeles Police Department recently announced it would no longer respond to unverified burglar alarms.) Worst and craziest of all, people who have gone a long time without being robbed somehow get the impression that they're therefore not likely to be robbed in the future, so why bother being diligent about security? All of this plays right into a thief's hands, and sitting around debating the details of "systems" misses the whole point.

I wasn't able to follow the Mandel trial closely. It was covered in detail in the newspapers, but, as I was in jail at the time on an unrelated matter (the trial took place four years after the robbery), I wasn't really keeping up and had to piece it together afterward. You can't imagine how shocked I was to discover I'd become a key component in a trial about a crime that, to the best of my knowledge, the police hadn't even suspected me of committing.

This is somewhat oversimplified, but the basic contention of Mandel's attorney, Donald Traci, was that security at Acacia-on-the-Green was so lax, just about anybody could have gotten in without being detected. He cited the unlocked roof door as an example.

The management company's attorney, John Martindale, countered that security was top-notch, and only somebody with extraordinary skill could possibly have gotten in. This, of course, was bullshit, as you now know, and not just because of the unlocked roof door. Frankly, that was a very minor lapse. Had it been locked, it might have kept out a teenage vandal, but for an experienced burglar of even moderate skill, all it would have done was add a few minutes to the job.

I'm not trying to downplay what I accomplished by pulling off this score undetected. It was a good job, one of my best, but just because it was me doesn't mean that nobody else could have done it. That the sliding glass door to the Mandels' unit was not alarmed was unforgivable, especially when there was a huge atrium completely open to the roof leading right down to it. That there were no interior sensors to detect motion was also a serious breach. The underlying assumption seemed to have been that there was no sense doing any of those things because it would be impossible for anybody to get onto the roof in the first place, which was nonsense. If I'd learned early on that the guards were a lot more attentive than they were, making a casual entrance into the building risky, I would have found a way to climb the outside walls, which I'd done many times, or gotten into the garage in a service vehicle.

It also occurred to me later that had I not forgotten to unbolt the door to the unit, the management company's lawyer might even have tried to pin the robbery on the Mandels themselves. After all, aside from the building superintendent's confirmation that the Mandels had returned home to find their apartment locked from the inside, there wasn't a single piece of evidence to prove that *anyone* besides Joseph and Florence had actually been inside the unit. No trace of my presence had ever been found.

I was never charged with the robbery. Nobody ever questioned me about it, and no evidence was ever presented that I was even in the state when the crime was committed. The same was true for Fran, who had been in New York and didn't even know what had happened until her return. But the trial was a civil proceeding, not a criminal one, and the defendants were not bound by the rules of criminal procedure in trying to make a case against me, however hypothetical. If their attorney could convince a jury that I *might* have done it, that could be sufficient to get the management company off the hook. After all, just because "the greatest cat burglar in the world" robbed the condo doesn't mean it had bad security.

You've got to love a legal system in which a defendant can base his case on the guilt of someone who wasn't even charged with the crime. It's like me being convicted of accepting a bribe you were acquitted of giving me.

It's also the only system in which a case like this could take four years to come to trial. That delay actually helped the defense. Fran and I were arrested in September of 1984 (we'll get to that later), and the investigation leading up to it disclosed hard evidence that we had known each other at the time the Mandels had been robbed. Martindale called to the stand Chagrin Falls police chief Lester LaGatta, who produced dated photos that had been seized in a raid and that showed Fran and me together as early as 1980.

Far and away my favorite part was when Martindale flew in my old nemesis, Fort Lauderdale deputy police chief Joseph Gerwens, who told exciting tales of my skill and derring-do and called me "a master burglar who makes Jack Murphy look like an amateur." (He was referring to the notorious "Murph the Surf," who stole the Star of India sapphire from a museum in New York, and I hated the comparison because Murphy was a vicious degenerate and, despite his very real intelligence, often behaved like a complete idiot. I was to meet him a few years later and I liked him in person even less than I did from a distance.) Gerwens said I was the only person who could have done the job, and I would have found that flattering except that it was complete bullshit, another failure of imagination. Gerwens also probably wasn't nuts about the fact that I'd slipped out of his clutches and, even worse, that I might have been back in action pulling scores. Looking back on it now, I don't think he ever really hated me personally; he just hated criminals, especially those who went out of their way to thumb their noses at the law and its enforcers. When he gave his testimony in the Mandel trial, he apparently smiled through a lot of it, and observers told me he never expressed an ounce of animosity toward me.

The defense tactic didn't work completely—the jury refused to believe that anybody could have broken in if the system had been working properly—but it probably saved the management company some money. Mandel still won his case, but instead of the $1 million he sued for, the jury awarded him $500,000. My guess is that, given the fake stuff, a half mil would just about have covered the real loss, although maybe not what he'd actually paid had he not known about the fakes.

Like I said in an earlier chapter, nearly everyone I robbed made money on the deal. The Mandels would have, too, if they'd had the jewels insured. Instead, they just broke even, and they were lucky to do that, because there's one especially ironic twist to this whole affair that the participants were totally unaware of.

The trial was presided over by Judge John J. McMonagle, who heard my name brought up but didn't see my face and apparently didn't look at Chief LaGatta's photos very carefully. He'd also been the judge in a lawsuit Fran had been involved in two years before, in which I'd testified.

Back then, he'd seen my face but thought my name was John Welling. The judge was the only person in the Mandel trial who might have put the whole thing together, but he had no idea that the man whose skills Gerwens praised so highly was the same man he'd met right in his own courtroom barely twenty-four months before.

Part

IV

19

Domestic Tranquility

BARB FINALLY began divorce proceedings. I was still a fugitive and couldn't show up at any of the hearings without being arrested, but I didn't need to be there anyway, because I wasn't contesting either the divorce itself or the division of property. She got everything we had, including two houses in Florida, all the bank accounts, several cars, the land in Ohio and so on. As far as I was concerned, she deserved it all, and that's the way I wanted it, even though it wiped me out.

By now I'd been living in the condo at Georgetown Villas for about a year and a half, and when I was in town, Fran was over almost daily. When I traveled, to places like Florida, California, Saratoga Springs, Atlanta and Toronto, she would usually go with me. As much I liked being with her, I didn't want to see the life she'd built for herself get ruined, and kept urging her to go home. How her husband tolerated her constant absences was beyond me.

Gradually, she came to know all about me, and still she wouldn't leave. At the same time, she became great cover for me, usually without even realizing it. Fran had lived among the swells her whole life and moved easily in moneyed circles. With her at my side there was no place I couldn't get into. She also had the uncanny ability to find out a woman's entire life story in a single elevator ride. People loved to talk to her, and they'd spill things they wouldn't tell their best friends.

I first discovered this knack because of a lawyer across the hall from me in the condo. Her name was Caroline Stracher and we were nodding acquaintances for the first few weeks after I moved in—a smile and a hello on the way in or out, that kind of thing. She seemed smart and nice and that was about it.

Then Fran ran into her. That evening at dinner she casually told me about Caroline's childhood, her first boyfriend, how she decided to go to law school, her first job, the ups and downs she'd gone through as a female lawyer . . . Fran filled nearly an hour with details and had been with the woman for only twenty minutes.

A few months later Fran showed up one day and told me about an uncomfortable conversation she'd had with her father. Someone had told him he'd seen Fran's Cadillac parked at Georgetown Villas every day for a month, and what was going on? I don't know who that was, but it was interesting that they'd gone to her father instead of to her. I guess that's how you do it in polite society.

Fran didn't try to duck the issue, but told her father she'd fallen in love with someone and was kind of in trouble. Her father didn't get into any of the standard judgmental rants you might have expected, just got right down to the practical side. "You've got to make a decision, and make it soon, because this is no way to live," he told her, and there was no arguing with that. We were both forty-two at the time.

As I listened to her relate the story my heart sank, because I was sure she was going to break it off with me, then go home and reconcile with her husband and never see me again. I knew it was the right thing for her to do, but it didn't make it any less painful.

"So I'm going to get a divorce," she finished up.

I tried to talk her out of it, even though I desperately wanted to continue being with her. Like her father, I was trying to be practical. "I'm not an executive or a doctor," I reminded her. "I'm a *thief,* for crying out loud!" I couldn't even continue calling myself a real estate investor, since I wasn't in that business at all anymore.

It didn't seem to trouble Fran, so I reminded her that I was also a fugitive living under an assumed name, and what the implications of that were. "What happens if you throw your life with your husband away," I asked rhetorically, "and a week later I get busted and sent up for twenty years?"

For someone who'd always lived in the lap of luxury, it must have been a daunting prospect to be left out in the cold like that, but Fran was adamant, and nothing I said could change her mind. I at least got her to sleep on it, figuring the cold light of a new day would instigate some clear thinking, but all it did was give her time to plan how to handle things as gracefully as possible. "I'm going to go talk to Caroline before she leaves," she said over morning coffee. She went across the hall and hired my neighbor as her attorney, then filed the papers a few days later.

Things seemed to go smoothly, and it was a fairly amicable split. The only hitch was the size of Caroline's fees for handling the case, which seemed to grow after she learned who Fran was and how much money her family had. Fran was pretty taken aback but didn't really feel like making a big issue of it. Until we found out that Caroline had socialized with Fran's husband during the divorce proceedings.

It wasn't so much that Fran's soon-to-be ex-husband was dating. After all, she was suing him for divorce and was carrying on an affair herself, so there were hardly any grounds for her to get huffy about it. But she thought that her own attorney being squired to the opera by the opposition in a lawsuit was an unforgivable breach of ethics, and she was damned if she was going to cough up inflated fees after that.

Caroline sued, and who gets called as a witness but yours truly. Swearing to tell the truth, the whole truth and so forth, I was sworn in as "John Welling" and testified before Judge John J. McMonagle on Fran's behalf. Aside from my name, I did tell the truth, and Fran won the case.

⁓

By that time I was no longer living at Georgetown Villas.

My daughter Suzi was at Kent State, just an hour away from Lyndhurst. She got along well with Fran and was a frequent visitor to the condo. Just after starting her third year in college, she came to tell me she wanted to quit school and travel. I tried hard to talk her out of it, but I lost that argument, too. I did get her to agree not to formally drop out, and she promised she'd eventually go back to finish her degree.

Suzanne, my firstborn, was a special child and is a special woman. Although generally high-strung, she gets almost eerily calm in stressful situations that demand clear thought. Fiercely devoted to family, she would do anything any of us asked with no questions. I didn't realize at the time that I'd be counting on this quality before too long.

We planned her trip together, and then the two of us went to New York. After a few days of sight-seeing, I put her on a plane to London.

Later that day while I was moping around bemoaning my eldest's departure, Fran called to tell me she'd found a perfect house to rent. It was on Mill Creek Lane in Moreland Hills, which was part of the city of Chagrin Falls, barely half an hour outside of Cleveland, and she was right; it was perfect. It was at the end of a long, private lane in a heavily wooded area and overlooked a deep ravine. The place was gorgeous, and Fran, her divorce proceedings now well under way, wasted no time snapping it up and moving in with her youngest daughter.

I helped them move in and happily dove into a few projects to fix the place up to their liking. Once they were comfortably settled, I was over there all the time, having dinner or just hanging out and basically soaking in the serenity of being in their company.

My only concern was Muchka, a cat who'd adopted me. He followed me everywhere, and I was very attached to him. The problem was that I'd bought Fran's daughter a cocker spaniel puppy for her birthday. We named the puppy Killer, which was pretty funny because she was so small and sweet. We didn't know how those two animals would coexist in the same house, but the first time we put them together, they curled up into a single ball of fur and went to sleep. They did the same thing every night thereafter, and two months after Fran rented the house, I gave up my condo and moved in with her and her daughter, once again finding myself in a warm home with a family I loved.

We lived almost like a normal family for about a year and a half, and the house was always full of visitors. Various boyfriends of Fran's daughter were around all the time, usually around her but always around the refrigerator. My son, Mark, and my younger daughter, Laura, spent a lot of time with us in the summer, and we also got a lot of visits from my cousin Dan. (Suzi by this time had traveled all across Europe and then gone to New Zealand to be a sheepshearer, which I thought was a hell of a thing after I'd paid for two years of college, but it seemed to make her happy.)

I got along well with Fran's kids and even her parents, who were over often. Even though I had no visible means of support, they didn't ask a lot of questions. Fran told them I owned some income property and they let it go at that. I especially got to like her father, a great guy and an astute businessman. He was interested in real estate and property management, and since I knew something about both, we spent endless hours talking and soon became good friends.

Fran knew about my burglary sideline, but I did very little work at this time. In the evenings I rarely went out, because I didn't want to be seen in and around Cleveland. Occasionally we'd go to Dan's or Bill Welling's or

When a photo of Francine and me ran in a society
newspaper, I was identified as "John Welling."

Katie's, but only once did we go to a big social event, a testimonial dinner
for the man who'd succeeded Fran's uncle Julie as Pick-N-Pay chairman.
We ended up with our pictures in the paper (the caption identified me as
John Welling) and it rattled me pretty good. We never did anything that
visible again, at least not purposely, but I was still so glad to have a home
that I was happy to mostly stay in.

Fran's younger sister Katie was one of my favorite people in the
Kravitz family. Just as Fran had at first, Katie was content to take to the life
their father had carved out for them. Even as she struggled through a second bad marriage, she was reluctant to confront head-on whether it was
the life she really wanted.

Early on in my relationship with Fran, she and Katie told me about a
major dope dealer named Richard Delisi they'd met in Las Vegas. Originally from Fort Lauderdale, he was then operating somewhere in New
York. He played blackjack for huge stakes and had his own planes fly him
in more money when he lost. Fran and Katie got along well with him, and

since the two of them had been talking for weeks about a visit to New York City anyway, they thought it might be fun for the four of us to meet there. Didn't sound like my kind of guy, and meeting with a drug dealer probably wasn't the smartest move for a fugitive, but I had another reason to go to New York, and it was far enough off the path of the authorities who were looking for me.

At the time, Fran was still married and living at home and I was spending a lot of time in St. Petersburg, Florida, but I was in Puerto Vallarta when we began making arrangements for this trip. The plan was for the three of us to stay at the Sherry-Netherland in New York City, and Delisi would meet us there.

My reason for wanting to go to New York, at least the state if not the city, involved a business opportunity, so let me step back about a week.

~

Saratoga was an interesting town. For most of the year it was a sleepy little burg, but for one month every summer it became one of the most glamorous places in the world. When the horse-racing season opened, so much old money came to town, you could practically smell the difference between thems-what's-got and the rest of us.

The center of it all was the Gideon Putnam Hotel, located off the beaten track in a state park a short way out of town. Named for the founder of Saratoga Springs, who settled there in 1795, it not only played host to short-term visitors but was also the favorite haunt of the old-guard horsey set—owners, breeders, buyers and wannabes—who rented houses in Saratoga and spent the whole month going to parties, balls and the fabled Saratoga Race Course. The hotel had a patio bar right near the front entrance that offered an absolutely ideal view of everybody coming in and out. You could sit there and nurse a drink for hours and just watch, without arousing the least bit of suspicion. With Fran at my side, that was what I had come to Saratoga to do.

Presiding over the entire social scene was Marylou Whitney, about the closest thing this country had to royalty. She wasn't born into money, though. In 1958 she became a member of *two* of the nation's wealthiest families when she married Cornelius Vanderbilt Whitney, direct descendant of Eli Whitney, who'd invented the cotton gin, and Cornelius Vanderbilt, who'd made a vast fortune in railroads. Marylou was in and out of the Gideon Putnam all the time, and on this particular Sunday afternoon she arrived in a horse-drawn carriage, dripping with so much jewelry it was all I could do not to drool all over our table. As tempting a target as I've ever had, she had a fabulous house just outside of town, but when I took a look, it was filled with servants, which pretty much ruled out the possibility of getting into it.

A week before we were to meet in New York with Katie, I flew up from Puerto Vallarta and met Fran in Saratoga. We checked in to the lowest-priced room at the Gideon Putnam, which still made it the most expensive hotel I'd ever stayed in. Neither of us knowing the first thing about horses, we'd spend our days at the racetrack anyway, with twenty-eight thousand of our closest friends, betting on names we thought were clever or on horses who acted up being led out of the paddocks or who were mentioned in the conversations going on around us. Needless to say, we lost consistently and would then go back to the hotel to watch the evening's comings and goings. Even if I didn't manage to pull off a score on this trip—and although our money was draining away at an alarming rate—I was still compiling an incredible mental list of future prospects from places like Palm Beach, Monte Carlo and the Middle East. I think Fran had a pretty good idea of what was going through my mind, but we never discussed it.

The Gideon Putnam had the least amount of security of any hotel I'd ever seen that catered to people of means. The place seemed to be managed and run by college students, who worked almost all the positions from front desk to kitchen help to chambermaids. Because the hotel was located inside the state park, the only police that ever seemed to come around were forest rangers. This made it all the more disappointing that by the time Fran and I ran out of money and finally had to leave, I hadn't been able to come up with a way to take off Marylou Whitney.

On the other hand, I did have a set of master keys to the entire hotel that I'd lifted off some college kid's room-cleaning cart.

Fran and I checked out and went back to Cleveland together. The following week I returned to Saratoga Springs by myself, without telling Fran where I was going. While heading to the patio bar at the Gideon Putnam my first day there, I saw an incredibly elegant lady leaving the hotel with an entourage, apparently heading out for the evening. She was wearing some exquisite jewelry, and since nobody around there wanted to be seen wearing the same stuff twice, and there were a lot of parties, I could only assume there was a whole load of goodies sitting back in her room. It was a rare, opportunistic moment. No planning, no preparation . . . I didn't even know what room she was staying in. But those master keys were starting to burn a hole in my pocket.

How laughable was the security at this hotel? Just inside the front en-

288 ~ CONFESSIONS OF A MASTER JEWEL THIEF

trance there was a large board studded with the kind of hooks you hang teacups from. When people arrived and left their cars with the valet service, the guy who parked the car would hang the keys on a hook along with a little tag listing the person's name, make of car and license plate number. If they were guests of the hotel, he'd also write down the room number and leave the tag up on the board for the duration of the stay. All of this was right out in plain view. When this lady got into a mile-long car with the rest of her crowd, I made note of the license plate number, waited until all the valet guys were off parking cars, then wandered by the board and had myself a look. I found the tag with the matching license plate number, and, sure enough, there was a suite number written in as well. There was also a name, and a genuine electric thrill raced up my spine as I read it: "Du Pont."

I used the house phone to call the suite. I let it ring more than a dozen times, but there was no answer. Then I went there and knocked on the door, then knocked again and again, louder each time. Still no answer. I entered using my master keys and immediately found a jewelry box in the bedroom just off the living room. It was filled with glorious stuff, but I hadn't brought anything to carry it in. I couldn't use a pillowcase, as I'd be making my way out through the main lobby, and I couldn't use any of Ms. Du Pont's luggage, because it was all custom-made and there was a chance someone might recognize it. So I just picked out some of the best stuff—two diamond bracelets, a bunch of gold items, a ruby ring and one of the biggest but ugliest sets of pearls I'd ever seen—and put them in my pockets.

I was back in my car and heading down to New York City twenty minutes later. To this day I don't know which Du Pont she was.

~

I'd brought along some goods I had to off-load (not from the Du Pont score, though; much too soon for that, although I had them with me), New York for a variety of reasons being one of the safest places for me to do that. First, there was no better place for someone on the run. The average New Yorker probably saw more faces in a day than someone from the Midwest saw in a month, but rarely noticed any of them. It used to be one of the few places where even a major celebrity could walk around and hardly ever get bothered, New Yorkers having seen it all and then some.

Another reason was the vast array of places to sell jewelry without a lot of potentially embarrassing questions. Walk into most stores with a single diamond to sell and it's no big deal, but walk in with a bagful of precious gems and you can elicit some suspicious stares. In New York, though, I could sell a hundred stones one or two at a time in different shops without ever leaving Forty-seventh Street. As for complete pieces of jewelry like elaborate necklaces and bracelets, Sotheby's and Christie's were my reliable standbys. I wonder how much other stolen stuff those prestigious old auction houses have sold over the years. (It would be several more years before the two of them would begin fixing commission fees, a scandalous collusion that cost art sellers some $450 million over seven years. The European Commission eventually fined Sotheby's $20 million, which was less than 10 percent of their illegal take, making for a mighty good return on investment. Christie's, having been the first to blow the whistle, never paid a dime in fines. And *I'm* a crook?)

When I pulled up to the Sherry-Netherland, I noticed a black Mercedes parked right in front, in a clearly marked no-parking zone, but nobody was bothering it. There was no driver in the car, just two nasty-looking rottweilers. There was something awfully familiar about that car, but I couldn't figure out what it was.

Fran and Katie had already checked in. When I got upstairs and met Richard Delisi, we both knew in an instant that we'd met before, and it took less than five minutes to figure out from where: He was the guy who'd beaten the crap out of his wife's car with a baseball bat down the block from my house in Coral Ridge, Florida.

Not only that, he told me that the cops used to sit in his front yard to watch my house when I was feuding with them. He had no idea who I was or why they were watching me, but he'd come charging out of the house and tell them to get the hell off his lawn. Sometimes they'd come back anyway, so he'd turn his sprinklers on. Naturally, he'd made top ten on the police department's shit list of uncooperative citizens, so we had something in common. That and the fact that we were both on the lam.

Years later Delisi was arrested on the charges he'd skipped out on and served five years in prison. After that he was much too hot to go back into the drug business, but having served his time, he could safely go back to Florida. By the time of my own arrest in 1984 he was running an auto body shop in Pompano with his father. While I was in the joint, he did a major restoration job on Fran's Mercedes (she'd gotten rid of the Cadillac by then). The day I was released he was there with the car and wanted to talk to me.

He hadn't been able to crank back his lifestyle enough to match his new, legitimate income. Dead broke, he had a plan to bring in one last load. He asked me to come in with him and his brother, and assured me

290 CONFESSIONS OF A MASTER JEWEL THIEF

we would each clear a million bucks. All we had to do was receive a shipment of weed, haul it up to New York and sell it in one shot. I needed money after prison and it was a tough one to resist, so I thought about it for a few days but finally said no. There were just too many people involved, and I'd gotten burned on a drug deal once before, when Gary Pierce took me for twenty-five thousand dollars and almost got me busted. Besides, I'd never gotten out of my head the image of Delisi going after that Mercedes with a baseball bat, and didn't really feel like being in business with that volatile a personality.

He found another guy to go in and went ahead with the deal. Sure enough, there was an informer, and the police were waiting when the plane landed. Delisi is now doing a mandatory sentence in Florida. I make it a point to call his mother and father once in a while to see how he is. Not too good, as it turns out, but still hopeful about his appeal. He's been in for twelve years now, and his anticipated release date is 2034. I hope with all my heart that this guy isn't going to die in prison for wholesaling marijuana when possession of small amounts isn't even a crime in some states anymore. Meanwhile, rapists, child molesters and murderers routinely draw far less time.

~

That was a close call for me—I did seriously consider his proposal—but ending up like Delisi would have been all my own doing and fault. There was another close one involving Katie, though, and this one was a pure accident I never saw coming.

Katie was breathless with excitement because Kris Kristofferson was coming into Cleveland to perform. She had a long-standing crush on the guy and was dying to meet him, but had never really considered the prospect of actually doing so. When she and Fran told me about this, giggling like schoolgirls, I said, "Just for laughs, why don't you find out where he's staying?"

They went to work and found out he and his entourage were staying at the Marriott in Beachwood. I went over there and spotted some of the band members at the pool, and within ten minutes had struck up a conversation. They were very friendly and we got along well, so after about an hour (and a few rounds of drinks, on me) I mentioned that I had a friend who would like to meet Kris.

"No problem," one of the guitarists said. "Come around to the stage door after the show."

When we did that, the security guard had my name and let us in. The guys greeted me like an old friend, then introduced us to Kris. Fran and Katie behaved like the ladies they were, and I guess that must have made an impression, because after about a dozen interruptions from fans, managers, groupies and various hangers-on, he said, "Listen, why don't you guys come on over to the hotel?"

Kris had a huge suite at the Marriott, which the hotel had stocked with enough food to start a small restaurant. After we got comfortable, Kris pulled out some killer weed, and it wasn't long before we were all carrying on as though we'd been best buddies since the cradle.

He and Katie hit it off really well and became good friends. The two of them would come over to our house in Moreland Hills whenever he was in town. Kris always brought some great smoke and we'd do up a storm together. He was so warm and easygoing, I kept forgetting what a big celebrity he was, and that was what almost got me into trouble.

It happened at one of his concerts in Cleveland. He'd given the three of us tickets in the middle of the front row, and for some reason I was late getting there. The performance had already started, but when Kris spotted me making my way up the aisle, he suddenly stopped the show and waved his arms at the guys working the lights. Before I knew what was going on, there was a spotlight shining right on me, then I heard Kris calling me up to the stage. Of course, he had no idea I was a fugitive trying to keep a low profile.

I climbed my way up and tried to stand with my back turned to the audience, but Kris spun me around and then introduced me as his buddy John Welling. Fighting down panic, I had no choice but to flash my face to several thousand of his fans and hope that none of my *un*fans were there and might recognize me. One bear hug later Kris finally let me get back to my seat, and I was so scared, I'm damned if I could remember anything else of the show at all. I didn't know until later that Fran's parents were also in the audience.

So aside from some pretty exciting moments here and there, life was fairly normal for me for about a year and a half.

Then I decided to nick Phyllis Diller a second time.

20

Striking Twice
(or Not at All)

PHYLLIS DILLER was performing at the Carousel Dinner Theatre, which had been built in a converted supermarket in Ravenna, Ohio, about thirty miles southeast of Cleveland. It later relocated to Akron, with much fancier facilities, and became the largest professional dinner theater in the country, but even back in Ravenna it was still a great place to see a show.

My problem in planning this job was that Ravenna wasn't exactly Times Square. Once the show ended at the Carousel and the cars cleared out, the place looked like a morgue, except with patrolling police cars. I couldn't park down the street and just wait for her limo to leave and follow it, because I'd be about the only car out there.

I found a phone booth about a quarter mile down the road. I could pull over and pretend to make a call without arousing suspicion, so long as I didn't stay there too long. I called the theater and said I was a limo driver with a cranky boss and I needed to know, as precisely as they could tell me, when the show let out so I could be there waiting for him. Luckily, I got someone way down on the food chain rather than some office big shot. A bureaucrat would know when the show was scheduled to let out, but it was the working-class stiffs punching the clock who'd know exactly when it really let out, and know it to the second.

I assumed Diller's limo would be up and out of the Carousel parking lot before the crowd got out there and jammed everything up, so I stationed myself in the phone booth a few minutes before that. As soon as I spotted the limo in the distance, I left the booth and got into my car, prepared to follow once it passed by. It never occurred to me that it would go anywhere but Cleveland, since there weren't any decent places to stay in Ravenna, and I was surprised when it made a left turn onto Bryn Mawr, a side street right across from the phone booth.

I waited about half a minute before following, and as soon as I turned, I saw the limo stopped at the side of the road a few hundred yards up. I could see Diller walking into a small four- or six-unit apartment building, and as soon as she was safely inside, the limo made a U-turn and headed back my way. I kept going, passing the apartment building without slowing down, until I was sure the limo was gone, then I turned around.

There was a larger apartment complex next door with a big parking lot. I left the car there and walked back to the smaller building. There were lights on in a unit just to the left of the front door and a few steps up. The curtains were drawn, so I couldn't see inside, but it had to be hers, because I walked around the building and there were no lights on in any other apartment. I looked around a little to get a feel for the place. There were buildings all along that side of the street, but across the way there was only open farm acreage, bare now because it was late November.

The next evening I came back at around five o'clock with binoculars and wearing dark clothes and headed into the field. I came early because I had no idea if she would go to dinner first or leave for the theater just before show time, and I froze my ass off waiting for that limo to come and pick her up. I walked around and jumped up and down a little trying to keep warm, and kept my mind occupied by taking notice of as many details as I could, like a telephone junction box sitting smack in the middle of this otherwise empty field.

The limo finally showed up at seven-thirty and picked Diller up. She'd left the lights on in her apartment, but the rest of the building was still dark. As frozen as I was, I waited another half hour in case she'd forgotten something and had to come back, then I crossed the street and spent ten minutes trying to get my stiff fingers to pick the lock on the front door. I walked up the six steps to her apartment and stood there, listening. There were two units on her floor. Music was coming out of hers, but nothing from the other one. I remembered how she'd left the radio on back at the Highlander when I'd robbed her the first time, and thought it a safe bet that there was no one in the apartment.

The door to the place looked like a cinch, but I liked to cover all my bases. Remembering the telephone junction box, I decided to go back out to the field and buy a little insurance. I didn't want to have to deal with the front lock again, so I left the door slightly ajar on my way out.

My intention was to cut the phone wires so no one could call the police if they spotted me. I had no trouble getting into the junction box, but I was blown away by how many wires were crammed into the damned thing. I guessed that the box had been installed when the area was a lot smaller, and rather than replace it as the population grew, they just stuffed more and more wires in there. I had no way to know which went where, so I cut them all.

On my way back into the building I stuck a small pin in the cylinder of the front-door lock and pulled the door closed behind me. I could still get out, but nobody would be able to get in while I was inside, which could buy me a few valuable seconds in case of trouble.

It took less than five seconds to jimmy open her door with a thin strip of celluloid. I stepped in and closed the door behind me, and had to smile as I looked around. The place was every bit as messy as her hotel room at the Highlander had been. Her jewelry was also in plain sight again, and I scooped it all up quickly, along with what looked like a personal address book about the size of a paperback novel. I was out in a few minutes.

Downstairs I couldn't get the pin out of the lock. It wasn't that I was being a nice guy in trying to get it out; it was that you never want to leave more red flags around than are necessary. The fewer clues you leave, the longer it takes for someone to realize that something happened while they were gone. This can buy some precious time if you come close to getting found out while you're still getting away.

But it didn't look too good for me to be standing around fiddling with a door lock, especially since I was now holding stolen goods, which would make it a tad more difficult to explain myself if some alert cop decided to come snooping around. So I left it alone and got the hell out of there.

~

I hadn't even gotten around to looking over the haul and making some preliminary estimate of its worth before the morning papers did it for me. It was about sixty-five thousand dollars, and if Diller was as honest in filing her insurance claim this time as she had been when I first robbed her (turned out she was), it would be a fairly accurate number. At least in retail terms. From a fence I figured to get maybe a third of that, so it was a disappointing haul.

I felt bad reading that she'd had to climb through that high window—the paper said it was because the door handle came off in her hand, which was nonsense—and I bet she gave the limo driver some grief for not waiting until she was inside this time. She also must have had a hell of a walk to find a phone and report the robbery, because it seems I'd knocked out telephone service to three-fourths of Ravenna.

The papers also made a big deal of the fact that this was the second time she'd been robbed while performing in the area. It was written off to coincidence, of course, and it didn't seem to occur to anybody that both scores might have been pulled off by the same thief. (Or thieves, the police and reporters predictably referring to me in the plural again.)

I showed the address book to Fran a few days later. It was a treasure trove of the private addresses and unlisted numbers of hundreds of the rich and famous—Anne Bancroft, Rock Hudson, Carol Burnett, George Burns, Bob Hope—and Fran was absolutely riveted as she went through it page by page and line by line.

The job had been a piece of cake, but not too long afterward, I would come to wish I'd never seen that damned phone book.

~

I may be giving the impression that everything I planned came off without a hitch and that I always walked away with bagsful of dazzling stones. This is probably a good place to put that notion to rest.

Surprisingly often, I spent time and money planning a score only to discover that there was hardly anything worth taking in the first place. Once when Barbara and I were still together, I took her to Key West for a weekend holiday. We stayed at the Pier House Resort, a magnificent place that likes to advertise its address as "the corner of Duval Street and the Gulf of Mexico." On Saturday evening we went into the legendary Chart Room Bar for cocktails before heading out to dinner. Sitting at the bar was Truman Capote and another guy we didn't recognize but who seemed to be his boyfriend. It was only around six o'clock, but Capote was already three sheets to the wind. Barb and I sat down at the bar and struck up a conversation. Capote barely seemed to know I was even there, but he was mesmerized by Barb and talked her ear off. His friend, on the other hand, seemed to like me. It was clear from the conversation that the Chart Room Bar was their main hangout.

Capote, sporting quite a bit of rather gaudy gold jewelry, kept on drinking and telling story after story. He looked at his watch once in a while and said he had to meet Tennessee Williams later for dinner. After about two hours he could hardly walk, but his friend managed to drag him away from the bar. Barb and I helped them out to the parking lot, where I took note of Capote's car.

I drove back down to Key West by myself two weeks later and saw both of them at the bar on Friday night. Rather than go in, though, I waited in the parking lot for about two hours, then followed them to dinner on the other side of the island. I waited in that parking lot and then followed them home, which was fairly close to the restaurant. I went there the next afternoon, waited for them to head out to the bar and was inside the house probably before they got their first drink down. Turned out that Capote either wore most of the gold he owned or had a hiding place too clever for me to find. I was barely able to cover my room and gas with what I took.

I didn't even manage that when I broke into Bob Hope's room at a ritzy spa off Dixie Highway in Pompano Beach. He was performing somewhere in the vicinity and had gotten a lot of publicity, along with his wife, Dolores, who wore an awful lot of jewelry in the pictures. I didn't know which room they were staying in but took a chance that it was the "Presidential Suite," which was easy to find because of the words "Presidential Suite" emblazoned on the door in huge gold letters (another "Come rob me" invitation). I picked the lock, and although I'd gotten the right room there wasn't a single thing worth taking.

On a different occasion Fran and Katie were staying at that same spa. After a day of doing whatever it is you do at spas, they would have dinner with all the other guests, then adjourn to the lounge. Richard Delisi and I joined them one evening for dinner. They were on special diets, but we as guests could have whatever we wanted. After a day of working out, Katie was ravenous and ready to kill Richard and me because of all the good stuff we were wolfing down while she was eating things like butterfly wings and grass soufflé. After dinner we all went to the lounge and were introduced to some people. One was Margaux Hemingway, and while one doesn't like to speak ill of the dead, she was as snooty a bitch as I've ever had the misfortune to meet.

On the other hand, we also met Yolanda Betbeze, the 1951 Miss America who'd refused to honor the tradition of the crown-wearer modeling bathing suits for Catalina, a major pageant sponsor. Thereafter considered a pioneering Miss America, Yolanda was also very active in the civil rights movement. She was so down-to-earth and warm that none of us wanted to break off the conversation as the evening wore on. She had an apartment on Park Avenue and houses in Georgetown and Palm Beach. Fran and I called her once when we were in the D.C. area, and she insisted we stay in one of her guesthouses. A really generous, top-flight lady it never occurred to me to rob. Well, okay, it occurred to me, but I never entertained it seriously.

Margaux wore quite a bit of jewelry in the evening and I assumed she would leave it in her room during the day. She stayed on after Fran and Katie checked out, and I went back to the spa by myself. Since there were a small number of guests and all of them knew my face by then, I had no trouble hanging around. During the daily pampering when Margaux was reliably trapped beneath mud or whatever, I picked the lock on her room. No gems of any kind, a couple of pieces of gold, none of them worth the risk of alerting the police to the presence of a burglar.

When the McGuire Sisters, probably the most popular female vocal group of the fifties and sixties, were performing in Canton, Ohio, I saw in the paper that they were scheduled to do a radio interview prior to one of their shows. I followed their limo from the theater to find out where they were staying, then hung around until the limo came back to take them to the radio station. They had three large rooms right next to one another, and I used a piece of celluloid to get past the cheap locks on all three. Not one had anything except costume jewelry, which I didn't bother to take. I doubt they had any idea anybody had even been in their rooms.

There was one time that I didn't follow through simply because I didn't have the heart. Carol Channing was performing at the MusiCarnival in Cleveland and staying at the Blue Grass. I did some casing and decided it would be a fairly easy and straightforward job, but then I saw her show and she was so sweet, it caught me way off guard. I figured maybe it was just part of her act, so I followed her around a bit, but damned if she wasn't every bit as friendly and lovable offstage as on. Just couldn't bring myself to do it.

There was one nonscore I regret to this day. Fran and I had taken a cruise from Acapulco to Los Angeles, then checked in to a hotel to spend a few days in and around Santa Monica. As was my habit, I picked up a paper to have a look at the society pages, which in Los Angeles is really coverage of the entertainment industry in the "Calendar" section of the *L.A. Times*. I read that there was to be some kind of party for Neil Diamond at the Beverly Hills Hotel, and one of the guests would be Marvin Davis, a billionaire oil tycoon who was breaking big-time into the entertainment business. In fine Hollywood style, his wife was pictured in the column wearing scads of jewels.

Fran and I checked out of the Santa Monica Hotel and in to the Beverly Hills Hotel. She fit right in, looking like one of those people who everybody thinks is a celebrity but can't place, which was great cover for me to wander freely about the hotel and learn the layout. The Davises arrived on Friday for the Saturday-night party, occupying one of those famous bungalows separate from the main building. We saw them go through the lobby twice, and two things caught my eye. One was that Mrs. Davis always wore a king's ransom in jewelry, even during the day, but never stopped at the hotel's safety-deposit boxes to put them away or pick them up. The other was that they'd brought some security with them. The bodyguards were very discreet and kept their distance, but they were unmistakable and there was no safe way for me to follow the couple out to see which bungalow they were in.

Saturday evening rolled around and Fran and I sat near the Polo Lounge to watch the parade of notables: Burt Bacharach, Gordon Lightfoot, Diana Ross, Robert Wagner . . . and enough jewelry to open a Harry Winston franchise. When Mrs. Davis finally came swooping through, her necklace alone could have fed a small country for a year.

The party had its own security people, so the Davis bodyguards fell back and eventually went outside. I followed, hoping they'd lead me to the bungalow, but it didn't happen. Finding it was going to be very dicey, I started to wonder if maybe Mrs. Davis was wearing everything she'd brought and the risk might not be worth the possibility that there was nothing left in their room. Safety had always been my highest priority, and there was a new wrinkle this time: Fran was with me, and I'd never pulled a score with her anywhere in the vicinity before. If I got pinched, there would be no way to avoid her becoming involved. I made the decision to back off.

Some time afterward thieves in the south of France hit the Davises' room while they were out at dinner and got away with twenty million dollars in jewels. Those should have been *my* jewels. Lord only knows what I might have found in their bungalow at the Beverly Hills Hotel that night.

At least that hadn't been a lot of work for me, and the stargazing was great fun. It wasn't always as easy to let one go, though.

~

I'd been interested in Elizabeth Taylor for a long time. Her collection of pricey baubles was legendary, and I knew she (or her various husbands and handlers) paid attention to security. The combination made for a tempting challenge. Over the years I'd read extensively about her. One of the things I took note of was that, while Burton was filming *Night of the Iguana,* he and Liz had fallen in love with Puerto Vallarta and bought a house there. In that relatively remote location, a heist might be easier than in one of the better-known and better-populated locations Liz tended to frequent.

I was on the move in and around St. Petersburg, Florida, hiding out under my "John Welling" identity. I bounced around among various motels and also stayed with Barb's brother Augie, who was still a close friend despite the divorce. He was bringing in the occasional load of grass, and I met some of the people he was working with but wasn't particularly taken with any of them. I kept telling him how suspicious I was of those guys and how little I'd trust them, but he was making piles of money and wasn't being as particular about his associates as he should have. In other words, he listened to me about as much as I'd have listened to him had the situations been reversed. (Sure enough, one of those guys turned informer when the police put pressure on him, and Augie spent a long time regretting that he'd ever become involved with the guy.)

I got into the habit of disappearing whenever Augie's pals were around, and it was during one of the times that Augie was planning to bring in a couple of boatloads that I decided to head down to Puerto Vallarta to check out Liz's digs. I still didn't like the idea of flying, but it was better than being trapped on a boat, so I flew out of Tampa with my new passport. Even before I'd gotten to my room in a small hotel, I'd already found out where Liz's house was. My little bit of broken Spanish was all I needed: Everybody in the town knew where the place was and was used to hearing the question from tourists. I realized that I could ask all the questions I wanted without arousing the slightest suspicion, which was a real luxury. Bartenders working near her house were a great source of information and for a few bucks were willing to talk all night. The toughest part was separating fact from fantasy; it seemed those guys liked to make the stories as dramatic as possible, but when accounts from different bartenders matched, I assumed they approximated the truth.

I don't remember if she and Burton were still married at the time, but arguments between the two of them were legendary in Puerto Vallarta, and screaming matches often spilled out of the house and into the street. There were plenty of alcohol- and drug-laden parties, too, and it was all

Incognito in Puerto Vallarta.

of this visibility that made it easy for everybody to know whether she was in town or not. Right now she wasn't, but the house was occupied by servants who lived in the basement somewhere toward the rear of the property.

The house was in a hilly area, and there was a street that wound around above and allowed a good view down onto the building and grounds. In Bermuda shorts and a flowery shirt, I looked like just another tourist as I took pictures from every angle. There was a large central courtyard in the rear with rooms on three sides. The main house connected to a smaller house across the street by a kind of skyway. Thinking like a property manager, I eventually decided that the main bedroom was at the front of the house, about thirty feet above the street, with a small porch that faced the ocean. What more could a cat burglar of my climbing ability ask for?

By starting on the upper roadway I could easily reach the roof of the house next door, work my way across to a wall, rappel down to Liz's roof and then drop onto the little oceanfront porch. Piece of cake. All that was left was not to alert the servants in either Liz's house or the one next door, not let any passersby or other neighbors see me, and then get Liz to tell me when her jewels would be in the bedroom and she wouldn't be. That was something I'd have to piece together by staying on top of the society pages and gossip columns, and I knew it could take months. So after several days of intense casing, I flew back to Tampa, then up to Saratoga to meet Fran.

A couple of months went by without anything to indicate Liz's travel schedule. Then my cousin Dan Renner called to say he was going to a medical convention in Puerto Vallarta. He'd just been divorced from his second wife and was taking Denise, his girlfriend of the moment, and he wanted Fran and me to go down with them. Dan rented a condo in a fashionable tower complex, and Fran and I took a quieter place a little more out of town. It didn't take very long to find out that Liz wasn't in residence—some people have no consideration for the workingman—but I figured I might as well get the plan down pat so I could be ready to get there at a moment's notice and pull off the heist without a lot of fussing around should the opportunity arise.

The four of us usually spent the evenings at the outdoor bar of Fran's and my hotel watching the incredible sunsets. One moonless evening I feigned a headache and sent the others off to dinner without me, then took a taxi into town and walked the mile or so to Liz's. There was nobody home in either house. I got up onto the neighbor's roof and worked my way across, eventually dropping onto the porch, where I faced two locked French doors. I peered into the room using my penlight and saw light blue walls, a canopied bed and a gigantic painting or photo of Liz herself on the wall. A minute later I climbed down the thirty feet to the lower street and walked away. I was ready; now, if only Liz would get with the program and cooperate.

I could have gotten into that bedroom and checked around anyway, but I seriously doubted if she would leave anything of value during her long absences, and because of the way the doors were constructed there was no way of not leaving evidence that there'd been a break-in. Once that was discovered, they'd either alarm the place or make the doors more secure, ruining my chances of any future entry.

I went to Puerto Vallarta three more times when I thought there was a possibility she'd be in town, but she never was.

21

Another Close Call

MY AUNT Nell used to come over to the Mill Creek house all the time, but my mother refused. Even though we still got along and spoke all the time, as far as she was concerned, I was still married to Barbara and that was all there was to it. No way would she step foot in my house of sin.

Shortly after my divorce Mom called to say hello, and about ten minutes into the conversation she casually said, "Oh, I almost forgot. The FBI called me yesterday."

"The FBI?" I croaked, fear beginning to make itself known somewhere in my belly. But if they'd called her yesterday and she hadn't gotten around to telling me until now, how bad could it be? "What'd they want?"

"They want to come see me again," she said brightly. "To talk about you, just like the last time."

That's how bad. "You told them no, right?" I asked hopefully, trying to keep my voice as calm as possible so as not to alarm her.

"I most certainly did not!" she said defiantly. "I have a chance to tell them what a good person you really are."

There's such a thing as carrying sweetness and naïveté too far. My mother was a dear, kind woman, but how was it possible in this day and age for her to honestly believe that one conversation with her and the FBI would see the error of its ways and leave me alone? And where would I begin to explain how dangerous it was for her to meet with them at all, when the last time they'd come to see her, she'd served tea and found them all charming and well behaved?

"Don't do it," I told her. "It's your right not to tell them anything."

"Don't you think I know that?" she said.

"Then don't do it! Tell them you don't want to set up an appointment and—"

"But I already did," she said.

"For when?"

"Why, this afternoon. Two o'clock."

Less than three hours from now. I practically begged her to call it off, but it was no use. She saw the meeting as both an obligation and an opportunity and she'd already given her word.

"Where are you going to meet them?" I asked, resigned and thoroughly defeated.

"Nowhere," she answered, happy that I was no longer fighting her. "They're coming here. I'm going to make tea."

Beautiful.

My mother was of the generation that was brought up listening to *Gangbusters* on the radio and held J. Edgar's name in reverence rather than suspicion or outright contempt. She believed that the FBI never failed to get their man, and that I was therefore doomed to a hunted life until either I was caught or they decided they didn't really want me. She honestly believed that my only chance was for her to straighten them out regarding what a good citizen I was, despite the one or two "mistakes" I'd made along the way.

At about one forty-five Fran and I parked her Mercedes half a block away from my mother's apartment and I watched through binoculars as the agents pulled up to the building and got out. At least I'd get to see who was after me. I had a pretty good memory for faces and would be able to recognize any of the guys meeting with my mother should they ever just happen to appear somewhere in my vicinity.

As before, there appeared to be no fallout from that meeting. Two months later Mom had to go to the hospital for surgery. She'd had a bout with cancer before, but this was much worse. Aunt Nell and I took her in and stayed there during the operation. When it was all over, a doctor came out and I knew before he said a word that it was going to be bad news.

"It's spread too much for us to do anything significant," he said. "Best we can do is try to make her as comfortable as possible." *While she dies,* he didn't have to finish for us.

She was still under heavy sedation when we went in to see her, and by the time we came back the next day, she'd fallen into a coma. They'd moved her into the ICU and had her on a respirator.

Fran and I were supposed to go to Wimbledon, but we canceled the trip. I visited and sat with my mother every day, staying as long as I could stand it. Some days I'd bring my aunt with me, but when I didn't, I would talk to my mother and tried to believe that she could hear me. I told her how much I loved her and how sorry I was for all the pain I'd caused her. I didn't tell her about the gun I carried on every visit.

I rarely went anyplace armed, but there was no way I was not going to see my mother in her last days and I was extremely nervous about the feds. I couldn't exercise most of the usual precautions I'd come to rely on, and that sudden helplessness in the face of imminent danger was disorienting and acutely frightening. I'd park blocks away from the hospital and try to find walking routes that would keep me away from the streets and from looking suspicious to people whose property I had to cross. I discovered a large number of back ways into the hospital itself, some of which required jimmying locks without breaking them or leaving any other sign that they'd been tampered with. Once inside I had to study each face for signs of recognition or danger, staying alert for the little warning signals that would tell me when someone was on to me but trying not to show it, and I had to do that without staring. After sitting with my mother and trying to talk to her without betraying my intense anxiety and paranoia, I had to turn around and do it all over again to get out of there and back to my car. As for the gun, I had no idea what I would do if confronted, and thank God I never had to find out. To this day I still don't know why the FBI didn't stake out the hospital based on the high probability of my coming to visit my mother.

It went on like that for ten days and was one of the most traumatic times in my life. I'd come home sweating and trembling uncontrollably, and for someone who was used to crawling around on high ledges and hanging from ropes, it was new and terrifying. I drank heavily to try to keep my nerves in check.

I couldn't give the hospital my phone number, so they had just my aunt's, and she was the one who called to tell me Mom had passed away. I went to the hospital at four in the morning, but when they asked me if I wanted to see her, I declined. I wanted my last memory of her to be when she was alive, no matter how unresponsive she'd been.

When I finally got home, I couldn't find my little cat, Muchka.

~

I called Suzi in New Zealand and Barb in Florida and asked them to come and help with all the arrangements. (Calling Barb was not as strange as it sounds; after the divorce was finalized, we remained good friends and spoke frequently.) Suzi arrived first. As sad as the occasion for her visit was, we were happy to see each other and didn't try to hide it.

As she unpacked, I noticed her passport and something occurred to me, but I didn't mention anything right away. We spent the next two days at Mom's apartment sorting out her belongings and deciding what to do about them, and it was there I brought it up.

"We may have a problem," I said.

"What?" Suzi asked, but kept on working.

"I have a feeling the feds have your passport number on a tickler file. When you landed in the U.S., you may have triggered an alarm."

She stopped what she was doing and turned to me. "You think they followed me to you?"

I shook my head. "Couldn't have gotten organized that fast. By the time they were ready to mount a tail, you would've been long gone."

Suzi thought it over, then decided I was being too paranoid. "They knew Grandma was sick and didn't stake out the hospital, right?" She laughed and punched me lightly on the shoulder. "Come on, old man . . . you're not that important!"

She was right about that but also wrong. "That's why there might have been a delay," I explained. "I may not be important enough for them to have put a tail on Grandma or staked out an airport full-time, but putting a trigger on your passport is a no-brainer. They've got thousands of those in effect at any time."

I had no way of knowing any of that for sure, but I knew for a fact that setting triggers like that was very easy. The feds could do it with credit cards, too. If someone they wanted to catch used a credit card, it would set off alarms at the authentication center, and a phone call to the appropriate agency—FBI, CIA, NSA, DIA, DEA—would go out immediately, giving the exact location where the card had been used.

Suzi wasn't buying it completely but saw the wisdom of assuming the worst case. "So what do you think they'd do?"

I wasn't sure, really, and thought about it out loud. "They went to see Grandma a couple of months ago . . ." I began.

"Grandma!" she exclaimed. "What on earth for?"

"They were looking for me."

"And they thought she'd tell them?"

"Who knows what they thought? But she was a brick. Made them tea and told them what a good boy I was until they got tired of it and left."

Suzi smiled as she conjured up the image of her grandmother frustrating the FBI. Then the smile faded. "They'll know she just died."

"Yeah. Then you show up. So they know family is coming in." I let her think about that for a few seconds, then said, "We're supposed to pick your mother and sister up at the airport tomorrow."

Suzi saw it right away. "You think they might set a trap." When I nodded, she shrugged and said, "So I'll pick them up myself. Not too hard to shake a tail around here."

"You watch too many cop shows on television," I replied, but she was right. It's easy to tail someone in a big city, where the stalker can hide himself in crowds. In less populated areas, it's much tougher, unless you have whole squads of men and a helicopter or two, and Suzi had been right about something else: I wasn't important enough to warrant that kind of effort.

But if they'd wanted me badly enough to hassle my mother, they could surely stake out an airport. I had to get a better handle on just how important I was, and I wouldn't learn anything if Suzi went to pick up Barbara and Laura by herself. I also needed to make sure she didn't lead the feds back to me if they really were watching the airport.

"Here's what we'll do . . ." I told her.

~

We drove to Cleveland Hopkins International in two separate cars. Since I knew where Suzi was heading, I could follow at a safe distance without worrying about losing her and get a good view of whoever might be tailing her. I didn't really expect to see anyone doing that, because they would have had no way of knowing where she was coming from, or when she'd be leaving, or if it would even be her. If there was going to be any kind of trap, it would be confined to the airport. Anything else would be much too manpower-intensive. Just to make sure, though, we both carried walkie-talkies.

When we got to the airport, Suzi drove to a parking lot. I stayed well behind and out of the immediate vicinity but had a good view of where she was parking as well as the gate to the lot. She went into the terminal building, but I wasn't able to see anything unusual among the people milling around or the vehicles waiting at the curb or driving slowly past. Either these guys were very good or they weren't there.

I got my answer about twenty minutes later, when Suzi, Barb and Laura came walking out of the terminal. I counted six men on foot tailing them, signaling openly to one another, since the women had their backs to them. Two of the men were also speaking into handheld radios.

The two guys with radios followed my family into the parking lot as the others hustled off somewhere, and a minute later four unmarked cars suddenly materialized at the gate and blocked it completely. They must have assumed I was waiting in the car and were cutting off my escape. I could practically feel their blood racing as they anticipated their imminent triumph, and I must confess to a bit of malicious glee as I watched to see what would happen when they discovered that I wasn't in the car.

The two agents hung back as the girls headed for the car. One agent pulled a small pair of binoculars out of his pocket and stood still as he watched for a few seconds. Then he suddenly put down the binocs and reached for his radio. Obviously I couldn't hear what he was saying, but I could guess that he was reporting the nonpresence of their target: me.

I heard some tires squealing and glanced over at the gate to the parking lot. Sure enough, the drivers of the four cars blocking the entrance were scrambling to get them out of the way. In their haste two of them collided with a sickening crunch, which was followed by the involved drivers yelling at each other as passersby stopped to try to figure out what was going on. The driver of one of the other cars got out and motioned forcefully for them to pipe down and get the hell out of there, which they did just as Suzi's car pulled into the center aisle and headed for the gate. By the time she got there, all four cars were speeding away, one of them dragging its rear bumper along the pavement and raising a shower of sparks and a terrible racket.

Nerve-racking as it was, it was also funny as hell, in a Keystone Kops kind of way. But I'd had enough experience with embarrassed law enforcement personnel to know that they'd take all of this out on me if they ever caught me.

There was a caravan following Suzi that she had no way of knowing about, but we'd provided for that in our planning. I waited until she was clear of the airport and keyed my walkie-talkie, then said, "They're there," and nothing else. Suzi keyed her radio for a second without saying anything, but the burst of static I got back let me know she had heard and understood and would drive straight to my mother's apartment without going to the Mill Creek house first.

～

A friend of Fran's had helped us keep a death notice out of the papers, but, as we discovered, the feds found out about it anyway. There was no doubt that they were looking forward to the funeral, knowing I couldn't stay away from that, but Mom had decided some years before to be cremated without a service. (Wonder what she would have thought had she known I'd be arranging for it in a Jewish funeral home.) We shipped her ashes back to West Virginia to be buried next to those of my father, and thereby gave the cops one less avenue of pursuit.

I didn't spend much time congratulating myself on my cleverness, though; the more elusive I became, the madder those feds were probably getting. It didn't make them look good, and it sure as hell wasn't going to persuade them to give up and go home. My guess was that they were operating on behalf of several local law enforcement organizations who'd agreed to lie back and let them capture me. If they came back empty-handed . . . well, in reality there was no "if" about it. They'd keep at it until they got me or I was dead, because the alternative would be too humiliating for them to consider.

Because of all the work Suzi and I had done at Mom's apartment for two days, I figured there wasn't very much for Barb to do, now that she was here with us, except go through everything herself and make sure there was nothing in the giveaway pile that shouldn't be given away. I thought I'd go crazy trying to get her to finish up so I could get the hell out of there.

She and Suzi stayed in Mom's apartment, but Laura wanted to stay with Fran and me in Moreland Hills. In case somebody was keeping an eye on her, I mapped out a convoluted route to get her there. Suzi put her on a train, part of greater Cleveland's regional transportation system known as "the Rapid." From there Laura transferred to a bus that was also part of the system, then a second Rapid bus, and I finally picked her up on Van Aken Boulevard and took her to the house.

Beautiful and athletic, headstrong and moody, Laura is also ferociously loyal and committed to family, the one quality all my children share and maybe the one good thing they learned from me. She's the most complex of my children, and I think we both realize that this is because she's the one who spent the least amount of time with a father; I was gone for much of her childhood.

Laura is nuts about animals, too, and wanted to play with Killer and Muchka, but I still hadn't seen my cat since the day my mother died. When we got to the house, Laura and I spent hours searching the surrounding woods and the ravine and never found her. Killer missed her playmate and moped around the house the whole time Laura was there, and something about that poor little dog's sadness seemed to intensify our own feelings of emptiness at the loss of my mother.

It was a very tense and trying two weeks, but eventually we pulled ourselves together and got everything sorted out. We hadn't seen another fed since the airport and I figured it was all right to finally relax a little.

Bad assumption.

22

Sooner or Later

Slowly, things returned to normal.

Barb and Laura were back in Florida. Suzi decided she wanted to tour the United States by car instead of going back to New Zealand and was out on the road, and Mark was in college at Florida State in Tallahassee. I'd distributed Mom's money to Barb and the kids, which was the last thing that had to be handled in connection with her death, and I was back to living the suburban life and trying to grow a tomato garden.

About a year after Mom died, I had to go to the hardware store. I took Fran's Mercedes, the only car we had at the time, and as soon as I walked into the store, I saw a guy standing over in the lumber section toward the back of the shop. I recognized him as someone I knew from years ago named Rod Smith. As on a number of other occasions when I'd spotted people I used to know, I wanted to avoid recognition if at all possible. I didn't think Rod had seen me, and I had a beard that would have made me difficult to recognize from a distance, so I wasn't too worried. I made sure to keep my back to him as I picked up what I needed, paid and then left.

Once outside, I saw him sitting in a car two away from mine, reading something. Just as I got to my car, I saw that what he was reading was some sandpaper. Obviously, something was way wrong here, but I was already standing by the driver's door of my car and didn't want to abruptly walk away, because it would make me look suspicious. I probably should have done it anyway.

Smith had recognized me, all right, and he also knew I was on the run. He jotted down Fran's license number, then called a friend of his named Arthur Krinski, an FBI agent. Krinski scoffed at first, then made a few phone calls. Less than two hours after that he'd ordered twenty-four-hour surveillance on the Moreland Hills house and began organizing a meeting with several other law enforcement agencies.

That meeting took place two days later. Krinski reported that his surveillance team, which included bogus telephone-company personnel up on the poles around Mill Creek Lane, had yet to spot me and couldn't be sure I was actually in the house. For one thing, Fran's Mercedes had heavily tinted windows and the field agents were unable to tell who was in the car as it came and went. Somebody else, and I don't know who, suggested that even if they could confirm I was there, the house was a bad place to try to capture me, because I'd probably already planned a way to escape using the ravine. They eventually decided I had to be taken elsewhere, even if it took a lot more time and expense waiting for me to move. (Of course, I didn't know any of this was going on at the time. We pieced it all together from various sources later on.)

Suzi and I had made plans to meet in Atlanta and then drive to Tallahassee to visit Mark at school. Fran was going to fly to New York the same day to spend the weekend with her older daughter, who was teaching at the prestigious Dalton School. At the airport Fran and I separated to check in for our flights after agreeing to meet and say good-bye before boarding. I went to Delta and Fran went to Continental. As I was standing in line, I suddenly felt hands come all over me from behind. I started to react but got hold of myself quickly. It couldn't be a mugging, not in the middle of a crowded airport, and there was nothing casual about the way these guys grabbed me. There were also at least four of them, because I counted three hands on each arm, one on my neck and one at the small of my back. Even if I managed to inflict a little damage, I wasn't going to get away.

"William Mason?" a voice from behind me asked. I still hadn't seen any faces.

"No," I answered. "You made a mistake."

I knew that life as I had known it was over, and my mind was racing as they turned me around and slapped cuffs on me, never letting go of me as they did so. These guys were the size of refrigerators, and I was glad I hadn't tried to do anything. From the fact that there were four of them, I guessed that they'd spoken with the Fort Lauderdale Police Department and knew about their standing policy regarding arresting me. I also guessed that they weren't part of some local-yokel police department, but they were in plain clothes so I couldn't tell where they were from.

As they hustled me outside, I counted about thirty other plain-clothesmen, some of whom were now pulling on blue jackets with "FBI" stenciled across the back in yellow. I learned later that I wasn't far off—there were actually twenty-five—and that Fran had been trying to find me to say good-bye and had to get on her plane having no idea what had happened. Because it was utterly unlike me not to be where I said I'd be, she'd gotten a little frantic. I was glad that she hadn't found me and seen what was happening. The agents knew exactly where she was, of course, but had let her board her flight anyway.

"You have the right to remain silent," one of the guys still holding me recited, and I exercised it to the max. I didn't say a word, not even my name. I didn't even answer when they asked me if I understood my rights—kind of a dumb question anyway, just after you tell somebody he doesn't have to answer any questions—and this really made them mad, but what the hell did they expect? That I was going to break down on the spot and confess everything so they could get some gold stars on their J. Edgar scorecards? To their credit, though, they didn't handle me roughly even when nobody was looking.

They took me to some federal building in downtown Cleveland and put me in a holding cell with a phone. I didn't know how long I'd have access to that phone, so the first call I made was to Katie. I told her to call Fran in New York and tell her what was going on, and then Bill Welling, and then to have Suzi paged at the Atlanta airport and ask her to come here. Once that was done, I was able to relax just a little and start making calls of my own to get a few things going.

By late that afternoon Suzi and Mark had already arrived and Fran was on her way back, and something dawned on me. There I was, absolutely helpless, a guy who'd spent his life taking from people, especially women, and in a few short minutes I was able to mobilize an intensely loyal army of people eager to help me out. No way did I deserve any of that, yet there it was, and it made those extremely stressful hours a bit more bearable.

I had a lot of time to think about my situation. The feds had pretty much given up on trying to question me, since I wouldn't cooperate or even say a word to them, and Arthur Krinski was one pissed-off little agent. I also didn't really have anything to do once I'd gotten my friends and family into motion. All I could do was issue instructions and then sit back. Mostly what I did when I sat back was worry, especially since I'd had to talk to them by phone instead of during a visit. Had the feds been listening in, they'd have had a hundred ways to use the information against me without ever letting on that they'd eavesdropped.

Fran and everybody else involved on my side were nervous enough to begin with, but the next morning my arrest was front-page news in every newspaper in the Midwest. There was no doubt in my mind that the authorities were in the process of obtaining a search warrant for the house. Our lawyer told us that there wasn't any basis for a search—the house was in Fran's name only and there was no probable cause that could be established—but I was way past believing that everybody followed the rules. I didn't know how long we'd have, so I didn't waste time getting started on a little housecleaning.

Earlier in the day, Suzi had gotten a large amount of cash out of a bank box that was in her and John Welling's names. Now I needed to get it out of the house. I had Fran put it in a brown grocery bag, then she, Suzi and Mark drove to Private Safe Place, an outfit that rented out safety-deposit boxes. They signed up for one, using assumed names, and stuck the bag in it. Some magazine feature writers later reported that there was other potentially incriminating stuff in that paper bag, but there wasn't.

Unbeknownst to any of us, though, Fran had left a hundred thousand dollars of the cash back at the house, which she thought she might need to bail me out. She didn't want there to be any delay in getting the cash together once bail was set, and I appreciated that, but I wished she'd talked it over with me first. She could always have gotten it from the private safety-deposit box, and waiting an extra hour or two wouldn't have bothered me. The one place it shouldn't have been kept was at the house.

Keeping the cash on hand was deliberate on Fran's part, but there were some other things that had simply been forgotten, among them the clipping about Joey Cam's murder that Barb had sent me from Florida, a newspaper article about the million-dollar robbery of the Mandels that was headlined "The Perfect Heist" in inch-high type, and bunches of other clippings that, while certainly not illegal to possess, sure as hell didn't look good.

According to the *Sun-Sentinel,* there were also checkbooks that "showed that Mason routinely shuffled huge amounts of cash from bank to bank." There were no such checkbooks, but you try arguing with some-one who buys his ink by the gallon. Then try doing it from jail.

They did get one item right, though, and it was the worst one of all: Phyllis Diller's address book, which Fran had been keeping under the bed.

~

It was a daytime-only search warrant; I have no idea why.

I was on the phone with Fran Saturday morning when two dozen of-ficial vehicles arrived at the house carrying agents from the FBI, the DEA, U.S. Customs, the IRS and the Chagrin Falls Police Deparment. Fran stayed on the phone and read to me the search warrant they presented her with, which said I was suspected of a home-invasion robbery that hap-pened in Chagrin Falls. Never mind the fact that I'd never robbed an oc-cupied house in my life, at least if you didn't count that sleeping drunk woman at Blair House. Anticipating the search, I'd arranged for our lawyer to be at the house. He checked over the warrant and told Fran it was all proper and she had to let the cops in. The search took all day, and I called her periodically and almost shit myself as she reported to me what they were coming up with.

They found the newspaper clippings, Diller's address book, the hun-dred thousand dollars in cash, a box of .38 ammo and a photo album with some risqué photos that were meant to be funny rather than lewd. One picture that caused a bit of a ruckus was a shot of my cousin Dan Renner with a woman the local cops recognized instantly. She used to arrive in one of her two Rolls-Royces, looking like the prim and proper lady Cleve-land society assumed she was. Well, she wasn't, but there was no damned reason the cops could have for wanting that picture other than to use it to exert pressure. I spoke to my lawyer and insisted that he demand all the photos back. Surprisingly, he was eventually successful, probably because the police were absolutely determined not to compromise their case by doing anything that wouldn't look completely on the up-and-up in court. By that time, though, the press had made it out to look like we'd been shooting porn movies.

They also found a lot of jewelry. Fran told them it was hers and that she could prove it, but they took it all anyway. They tried to get her to talk, telling her there would be no charges against her if she told all she knew about me. She refused, as did Mark and Suzi, although Fran was pretty shaken by the thought that charges might be leveled against her.

Fran also told me they had seen the receipt for the rented safety-deposit box. I told Mark to go over there, empty out the box and mail the contents to Barb in Florida. He did that, and on his own also left a little smiley face in the box for the FBI searchers. Chip off the old block, at least in some ways. I think he inherited some of my deviousness but has enough brains not to act on it.

By the time the authorities left late in the afternoon, Mill Creek Lane was crowded with neighbors and reporters. Interestingly, none of those neighbors was ever on television or quoted in the papers. I guess the reporters were looking for the usual "I always knew there was something fishy about those people" comments but didn't get a single one.

What I remember most about those couple of days were my kids. I thought I already knew them well, but the way they handled themselves blew me away. I know I'm inviting some sarcasm here—after all, they were trying to help a criminal evade prosecution—but you have to remember that, as far as they were concerned, they were just doing whatever they could to help their dad. What kids wouldn't do that for a father they loved?

Suzi had been paged at the Atlanta airport, where she was waiting to pick me up. She called Mark and then scrambled to find herself a flight. Both of them were in Cleveland that same day. No second-guessing, no hesitation . . . Dad was in trouble and they simply came. I didn't even know at the time, because phones in the jail were cut off at eight o'clock.

Early the next morning they came to the Cuyahoga County Jail and finessed their way into an off-hours visit, which is extremely difficult to do. When I was brought to the visitors' room and saw them, I was so stunned, I didn't know whether to laugh or cry, so I took a minute or two to do both.

Mark looked around and said quietly, "I don't know how much time we have. I'm not even sure why they let us in this early."

"What do you want us to do?" Suzi asked.

That's when I had her take the money out of the box. "They've probably got every bank record we have," I told her. "They'll know about the box."

My kids did everything I asked, and did it flawlessly, without wavering or questioning me. I tried to make sure I didn't have them do anything that would get them in trouble—I relied on my lawyer and attorney-client privilege for the touchier stuff—but I also didn't kid myself that sufficiently motivated police and prosecutors could make anything look like aiding and abetting. The kids were at the house with Fran when it was searched, and were a great source of strength for her.

You have a lot of time to think in jail. I decided to use that time to beat myself half to death thinking about what kind of heartless bastard puts his loyal and utterly innocent kids through that kind of hell.

~

The newspapers did a pretty good job of parroting how the authorities wanted the search portrayed.

It was reported that jewelry was found hidden in boxes, plastic bags and a motor-oil can, and that the police thought the pieces matched up with items that had been reported as stolen in the area. In fact, it really was all Fran's.

The police connected Diller's address book to the robbery two years before and gave that to the papers, accompanied by a lot of self-congratulatory preening about the brilliance of the FBI in tracking me down after a "five-year nationwide manhunt" and about the excellent teamwork between the FBI and the Chagrin Falls P.D. in capturing me. They didn't mention that their brilliance included the tip special agent Arthur Krinski had gotten from Rod Smith, and I had to laugh when they reported the cash they'd found as $98,500 instead of $100,000. False precision was an old trick to make suspiciously round numbers not look like they'd been made up.

They were also pretty smooth about explaining the grounds for the search warrant. The problem they faced was that I was wanted only on a fugitive charge. The only way they could legally search anything was if they had "probable cause" to believe it would help them find me. Once they had me, there was no longer any justification for conducting a search. Although I was suspected of being a jewel thief, there were no warrants and no one had formally charged me in connection with any thefts. As a matter of fact, I'd *never* been charged with stealing. So there was no probable cause that would justify a search for stolen goods.

They did, however, have the right to search the immediate person of someone freshly arrested. "Unnamed investigators" told the Cleveland *Plain Dealer* that they'd searched my luggage when I was arrested at the airport and found "notebooks with detailed descriptions of homes and property stolen from victims in Shaker Heights, Lyndhurst and Chagrin Falls." The newspaper then got hold of the court affidavit filed by Chagrin Falls police chief Lester LaGatta in support of the search warrant for the house. In it he referred to those notebooks and said I was one of two men who'd committed a string of burglaries. He said we showed up in a truck, tied up the victims and "proceeded to then burglarize the homes, taking valuable items consisting mainly of jewelry, furs and cash."

By now you already know that if I'd done any of those things I'd admit it, so believe me when I tell you that the foundation for that search warrant was pure bullshit. I didn't use partners, I didn't use trucks, I've never tied anybody up in my whole life and I wouldn't know what to do with a fur if one fell on my head. As for the notebooks they'd supposedly found in my luggage, that was a total fabrication. I never felt compelled to tell anybody about the scores I pulled, and I was so careful a thief that I wouldn't even wear aftershave on a job for fear of leaving a telltale scent, so why on earth would someone like that write down the scores he pulled and carry them around with him? Once the magazine feature articles about me started appearing and the gist of my M.O. began to emerge, I imagine that whoever had spread the disinformation about notebooks felt like a jackass. Nothing about notebooks was ever brought up in any subsequent legal proceeding.

We found out much later that the FBI had contacted Chief LaGatta and asked if he had any unsolved cases on the books that might possibly fit my known M.O. LaGatta came up with a robbery in which two men had tied up an elderly couple, machine-gunned their Doberman to death and escaped with two hundred thousand dollars in jewels and coins. Despite the fact that the elderly couple had stated positively that both assailants were black, and that the FBI knew I never used a gun—or a partner—they declared me a suspect anyway and that was how they got their warrant.

⌣

The judge at the Cuyahoga County Common Pleas Court originally set a two-hundred-thousand-dollar cash bond, which seemed to satisfy everybody. But when the county prosecutor found out the next day that I had the money and was prepared to post it, he ran back into court and requested that it be raised to a million. Then, after the house was searched, he wanted it bumped to *two* million. The judge asked him if he was kidding, and the prosecutor launched into a speech about how I'd already demonstrated I was a flight risk. "As a matter of fact," he finished up, "the first charge we're filing in this case is unlawful flight from prosecution." The judge didn't ask where the flight was from—it was Fort Lauderdale, where he didn't have jurisdiction—but our lawyer, Jack Levin, stayed quiet, and for good reason: FBI representatives were in the room, and any hiccup in the proceeding would have prompted them to file a federal charge against me, which we were trying to avoid. The judge granted the prosecutor's bail request, and a court spokesman rushed out to the front steps to announce it to the press and make sure they knew that it was a record, the highest bail ever set in the county's history. Levin followed him to make sure he got his own statement in. "The two-million-dollar bond is unconscionable," he said angrily. "They're punishing him before he is convicted of anything."

As it happened, the FBI had the U.S. attorney file federal charges anyway, including falsifying my identity on the passport I'd had with me at the airport. On it my name was listed as John Welling.

The story was quickly picked up in Florida. Fort Lauderdale papers reported that several other federal agencies were investigating me for possible interstate offenses, and also said nine Ohio police departments were checking their unsolved crime logs to see if there might be links to me. I expected that; police hate having open cases on the files, and here was a chance to wipe a whole load of them off the books just by blaming them all on me. The best part for them was that they wouldn't even have to prove any of those links. They figured I was being competently prosecuted in other jurisdictions and would get what was coming to me there, so why should they spend time and money duplicating those efforts?

Reporters kept trotting out that quote from the Fort Lauderdale police comparing me to Murph the Surf and also discovered that I'd been referred to by the cops as "the Beachfront Burglar." (Not one of those investigative whizzes managed to find out that I was the one who told the police all those jobs had been pulled by the same guy, and it was only after I did so that they came up with "Beachfront Burglar.") The more the Florida police went on and on about what a terrific thief I was, the easier it was for all those other jurisdictions to blame me for every crime they couldn't solve.

The feds had a lot of pull at the jail and made things as bad as possible for me, probably because they'd been in touch with the Fort Lauderdale police, who still hated my guts. Although races were segregated, as they are in all jails and prisons (the joint is one place where reality, rather than romanticized politics, reigns supreme), I was placed in a max pod with thirty black guys even though the white pod was right across the hall. The jailers probably assumed I'd be beaten to death or something but hadn't counted on the fact that a handful of those black inmates had read about me. From their many and varied experiences in the system, they'd learned that Cuban prisoners in Florida had referred to me as "El Gato," the cat, and they thought I was way cool. They peppered me with more questions than the FBI had. I knew that there was probably at least one informant in there who had been planted by the feds, so I was careful to stick to stuff the cops already knew. To say I was treated respectfully by those guys would be an understatement. I was in that pod when Fran was arrested, and they were great about staying off the phone so I could call the house over and over until she finally answered and told me she'd been released.

My folder had big red block letters across the front saying "Organized Crime" and "Escape Risk." That might not sound so terrible, but it was. Jailers are just civil servants, guided by rules and regulations and fearful of making mistakes. Their major preoccupation isn't the welfare of the prisoners in their care, it's keeping their jobs and preserving their pensions. When an inmate is branded as "O.C." or an escape risk, all it means to jailers is more-than-normally-severe consequences for them if he breaks out or takes a hostage or secures special privileges or gets caught dealing drugs inside. When you have those big red letters on your folder, jailers take special pains to make sure you don't do any of those things. They don't give a shit how tough that makes your life, and they also know that their supervisors won't give a shit, either.

I didn't help matters much, I have to admit. As I've said, I wasn't very cooperative when I was arrested, and it wasn't just by keeping quiet. They took me downstairs to get fingerprinted, which was normal, but then they told me they were going to use some special procedure that included the sides and tops of my fingers, my palms from all different angles . . .

"Forget it," I said.

"What do you mean, forget it?" one of them asked. "You gotta get fingerprinted!"

"Then fingerprint me, but forget about inking up my whole damned hand."

"Listen—"

I took my hands off the table. "Get a court order."

I didn't really much care how they were going to print me, but I was angry and didn't feel like rolling over for something I'd never heard of just because they said so.

Dumb mistake. They threw me in solitary and kept me there until the court order came through. After that I was real easy to get along with, but a couple of days later they put me in isolation—no visitors, no phones, twenty-four-hour lockdown—and kept it up for four days. Never gave me a reason and never told me how long it would last. It fucked me up, just as they knew it would, because I had no way of knowing whether anybody outside knew what was happening to me (they didn't), and I couldn't tell what was going on out there. I conjured up all sorts of insane fantasies of my house being seized, friends and family being taken in for questioning, bargains being struck without my knowledge and even that I'd been reported as escaped and presumed dead so that prison authorities could do anything they wanted to me.

Sure it was nuts, but when all you've got for company is your imagination and your anxiety, they can team up to produce the worst enemy you'll ever have.

~

Meanwhile, the feds went to work on Fran. First, the head of the FBI's Cleveland field office came to the Moreland Hills house to offer her a deal.

"Your boyfriend's never getting out of prison," he told her. "You might as well save yourself and tell us what we need to know."

"If he's never getting out," Fran shot back, "what do you need me for?" And that was pretty much the end of that conversation.

So they went to see her parents and told them what a badass I was. They even said I was suspected of four murders, which they backed up by showing them copies of newspaper clippings they'd found in the house, the ones Barb had sent me every time one of the old Atlanta gang got whacked. They tried to get Fran's father in particular to influence her to rat me out in exchange for a free ride for herself and pointed out that the Moreland Hills house where the incriminating evidence was found was in Fran's name, not mine. If their goal was to scare the hell out of her parents, they succeeded, but they couldn't shake Fran.

About ten days later, on the eve of Yom Kippur, the holiest day in Judaism, Fran was home alone with the dog at the Mill Creek house. I happened to be on the phone with her from jail, when she suddenly gasped and told me that a string of police cars was pulling up in front of the house.

"They're going to arrest you," I told her.

"What do I do!" she whispered hoarsely.

"Don't give them any trouble whatsoever," I told her. "And don't say a word."

"They're surrounding the house!"

What the hell did they think she was going to do . . . shoot it out with them? I hung up and called Jack Levin to tell him what was happening and get him over to the courthouse to meet Fran.

"Friday night," the lawyer mused out loud. "They figure they can keep her in jail all weekend and scare the shit out of her."

"Hell or high water, I want her bailed out."

Levin was at the courthouse when the police arrived with Fran. They booked her on charges of harboring a fugitive, receiving stolen property, possession of a blank prescription pad and drug possession. There was one especially peculiar charge that demonstrated how much they were willing to stretch to put the screws to her: theft of trade secrets. The "trade secrets" were the contents of Phyllis Diller's address book. That was also the stolen property she was supposed to have received. I asked Levin how she could be charged with both receiving something and stealing it herself.

"They don't have to worry about that now," he explained. "Later they'll figure out which is the easier case to make and drop the other one."

The newspapers reported all of this the next day but left out a few things. One was that the drug possession charge was based on three one-hundredths of a gram of cocaine dusting the inside of a tiny glass vial found during the search of Fran's house. Another was that the prescription pad belonged to Dr. Daniel Renner, my cousin, whose name was printed clearly on every page. Dan was at our place all the time and he must have dropped the thing. Neither Fran nor I even knew it was in the house.

Levin told the Common Pleas judge that Fran had a spotless record, had been active in Cleveland's Jewish community, had run a day-care center and sponsored art shows and a whole slew of philanthropic events. Any other judge in the country would have recognized that her arrest was a police pressure tactic and that she wasn't any kind of flight risk and set her free on her own recognizance. This judge, however, not only set her bail at fifteen thousand dollars but imposed on it the condition that she have no contact with me whatsoever. On Levin's advice she agreed, and they let her go the same night. If I hadn't been on the phone with her when she'd gotten arrested, she might have spent the night in jail. As it was, a few hours just being booked was traumatic enough for a Jewish princess.

When Fran was released, she spoke with the reporters gathered in front of the courthouse. "Every jewel taken from that house was mine from my first marriage of twenty-one years," she told them, further explaining that many pieces were family heirlooms. "In fact, a diamond watch they took has my grandmother's initials on the back." She told them about how she'd tried to give the police a copy of a list of all her jewelry she'd drawn up for her insurance company years before, which would have gone a long way in proving it all belonged to her, but they wouldn't take it.

She also insisted she knew nothing of any crimes I'd committed. "We made grapevine wreaths, grew tomatoes and stayed home a lot," she assured them, and also said we liked to go into the countryside to watch birds. "I know it sounds corny, but it's true." She was convincing, but someone kept leaking stuff to the newspapers, like the contents of private letters from Fran to me in which she referred to me as her "desperado," as though that were some kind of smoking gun. I'm surprised that they didn't print that her daughter's adorable little cocker spaniel was named Killer.

It got worse. I had my own hearing before the same judge to try to get my bond reduced from the ridiculous two million dollars. It was reduced all right: to zero. He revoked it altogether and ordered me held without bond, and sure enough, right after that, it was reported that I "was believed to be responsible for the . . . breaking and entering of the C. S. Harris home on South Franklin Street where both occupants were bound and gagged and the family dog was shot." Now, I have to admit that using that incident to get a search warrant for our house was pretty clever. Even though it was blatantly absurd and unconstitutional and not much different from the kinds of malicious crap that got criminals thrown into jail, you had to admire the creativity.

But why feed the papers that kind of bullshit? That was just spite and an attempt to mount public opinion against me. The cops and FBI were probably really steamed that I was being portrayed as a "gentleman bandit" and wanted to put a stop to it. They went to work on Fran again, who still was not allowed to see me, and got her to agree to a meeting. Taking her parents and lawyer with her, she sat across a table from some agents and federal prosecutors who offered her complete immunity if, while hooked up to a lie detector, she'd tell them all about my criminal activities. To motivate her, they ran down everything of my criminal past they knew about or suspected or could make up. Her parents made sure she understood the implications, but they stopped short of trying to pressure her the way the feds wanted them to. Fran, in terms more appropriate to her pedigree than "stuff it," told the authorities to stuff it.

Afterward she directed Jack Levin to try to do something about the court order forbidding her from seeing me. Levin wrote a flowery plea about "star-crossed lovers" that was so sugary you could get cavities just reading it, but it worked. Fran went to the beauty parlor, got dressed in her Saturday best, then stood in line at the jail for two hours of suspicious looks and whispering from deputies and more "hardened" female visitors as she waited to see me. As awful as it made her feel, she did it week after week without complaint.

The pressure on my friends and family never let up. One night when Bill Welling and Suzi came to see me, some cops stopped them as they were leaving and started asking Suzi questions. They ordered Welling to get lost, and made some pretty serious threats, including arrest, but he wouldn't leave Suzi's side and she wouldn't say a word, so they let them both go. As it turned out, the police were only buying some time: They'd broken into Suzi's car and searched it while they were hassling her and Welling.

Only one thing surprised me in a positive way. Cleveland *Plain Dealer* reporter James Neff had an interview with my old nemesis, Deputy Chief Joe Gerwens of the Fort Lauderdale police department. Gerwens regaled Neff with stories of how I used to pull scores in his jurisdiction. "He was going up and down the sides of high-rise condominiums," Neff quoted him. "They had extremely good security systems and guards," and I'd never tripped a single one of them. Neff wrote that Gerwens at one point laughed and said, "Funny thing. Neighbors used to see him going up and down a rope tied to a tree, hand over hand, like in the service. They thought that was just the way he worked out." He also described how I'd cooperated with the police and cleared up "some 40 burglaries," but understandably never mentioned how I'd tricked them into letting me get away with all of them.

In the last paragraph of the interview, Neff quoted Gerwens again: "A nice guy, well-spoken and very good looking, very charming to talk to. It was fun working a case with him." You would have thought we were old drinking buddies or something, the way he went on about me, rather than a cop and a criminal who'd been at each other's throats for two years.

Less than two months later Gerwens would come up from Florida to tell the jury in Joseph Mandel's lawsuit that I could have robbed their condo no matter how well the security system was working. His testimony was supposed to bolster the condo management's contention that the best security system in the world couldn't be expected to keep a master thief out. When Mandel's attorney pointed out that there was no proof Fran and I had known each other at the time, Chagrin Falls police chief LaGatta was called to testify and produced photos found by police in the search of the Moreland Hills house showing that Fran and I had indeed known each other when the burglary was committed. Mandel's attorney countered that nobody could even prove I'd been in Cleveland at the time, to which the management company responded that it wasn't their aim to show I'd actually done it—they really didn't know—just that I *could* have, and therefore the security system wasn't necessarily deficient.

With fans like that . . .

～

What came to be known as "the Loveman Scandal" broke out following the search of the house, then really swung into gear when Fran was arrested. The "good girl gone bad" angle was simply too delicious for the media not to exploit to the hilt, and it rocked the normally unrockable Cleveland high society.

She was on the cover of the *Star* every day for a week, and every time she went to her local grocery store, she had to cope not only with federal agents tailing her (men in business suits reading cereal boxes for half an hour were pretty easy to spot) but with headlines blaring out of the racks near the checkout stands. "Blue-Blooded Heiress and the International Jewel Thief" screamed one, along with a picture of Fran that nearly filled the page. She'd done some modeling and the tabloids had no trouble getting their hands on dozens of professionally shot portraits. Accuracy wasn't one of their especially high priorities, either. They kept giving me "international" status, even though I'd never pulled a job outside the country. Come to think of it, up to that point the only other countries I'd even *been* to were Canada and Mexico, and those were as "John Welling."

What made it worse for Fran was that everybody in the grocery store knew her, but she could hardly shop somewhere else, because her father owned the place.

The *Plain Dealer*'s James Neff took a particular interest in Fran's case and wrote a series of articles with clever titles such as "Tarnished Gem?" He was really into implying things by posing tantalizing questions like "How could Francine, once a glittering fixture of our city's social whirl, be involved with an international jewel thief on the lam?" and "What, if anything, did Francine Loveman know about her lover's activities?" But at least he could write, and he wasn't stupid, and I'll admit those weren't exactly idle questions he'd asked. Neff was the reporter who broke the story that the Mandel score had taken place while the Mandels were at dinner with Francine's parents.

Others weren't so thoughtful or fair. One of the more memorable headlines from the *Star* was "Charming Jewel Thief Stole a Fortune—and Heart of Heiress Who Sacrificed All for His Love." The reporter, who was not named, made me out to be an overpowering Casanova and painted Fran as some kind of demure, submissive debutante who'd fallen under my spell rather than a fiercely independent and self-possessed woman who'd made a bold and risky decision to walk away from her comfortable life. Of all the things Fran had accomplished in her life, "heiress" was the adjective most journalists chose to describe her. That same month the cover article in *Cleveland Magazine* was titled "Why the Lady Loved the Outlaw: The Tale of a Shaker Heights Divorcée and Her Dangerous Romance with America's Top Jewel Thief." In that subtly nuanced style magazines are noted for, the story was presented as that of a thrill-seeking socialite sheltering a criminal who'd been the focus of a five-year nation-wide manhunt. They said she was obsessed with me, and implied that she'd gone crazy. Anything, it seemed, was fair game other than the notion that Fran had a mind and will of her own.

And I was hardly the object of a "nationwide manhunt," at least not in the traditional sense. That was the same phrase the FBI would use when they tried to pressure Fran into giving me up. Sure, they were looking for me and were ready to pounce on well-qualified tips, but it wasn't like they had a thousand guys fanning out all over the country desperate to catch me. For one thing, I wasn't violent, which automatically reduced my priority. My M.O. was well known to law enforcement people at various levels, and they'd later tell reporters that working my case was a plum assignment, and why not? Instead of hiding in putrid dumpsters or staking out squalid crack houses, the guys tailing me went to fancy parties, tooled around on boats for days at a time, brushed shoulders with the president of the United States and never had to worry about getting shot, at least not by me.

All of this slanted coverage had a devastating effect on Fran, but she held her head up and wouldn't let it show. To my amazement, her old friends from the circles of money and power rallied round and, with rare exception, stuck gamely by her. Her parents did, too, despite being very hurt at first by the intimations that Fran had helped set up the Mandel score. Joseph Mandel's lawsuit against the condo's managers was taking place at the same time that Fran's case was proceeding through the courts. Deputy Chief Gerwens from Florida was in town to testify for the management company, and the newspapers were covering the trial like it was the Rosenberg atomic spy case. Even though I hadn't been charged with the heist or even accused of it by the police, the papers just couldn't let go of the defense's contention that I *could* have done it. I didn't blame the attorneys; it was the only defense they had, so they ran with it. It wasn't their fault that the tabloids were hell-bent on keeping alive the titillating possibility that I really had done the job.

But Fran's parents quickly got over their initial hurt and believed her when she said she knew absolutely nothing about that score. On her side was the fact that there was not a shred of evidence to connect me with it and I'd never been charged with it. There was just a ton of speculation and a newspaper clipping about the burglary found during the search of the Moreland Hills house. What's more, Fran truly didn't know anything about it, and her sincerity must have come across to her folks.

That spring, Fran got herself an incredible sweetheart deal, but it came about in a weird way.

~

It hadn't been a promising start. Her case was being heard in front of Judge Terrence O'Donnell, who was known for handing out harsh sentences. In exchange for her pleading guilty to obstructing justice and receiving stolen property, prosecutors dropped all the charges involving assisting and protecting me. The deal also involved a reduced sentence, to be determined after O'Donnell received a pre-sentencing report from the probation department. As part of his review of her case, he decided to watch a videotape that the police had made of their search of the Moreland Hills house. The taping wasn't unusual; cops often taped themselves during searches not only to show where evidence was found but to prove that they'd acted properly.

While watching the tape, O'Donnell thought he recognized something being lifted out of a box as belonging to someone he knew. He phoned up the police and told them about it, reporting it as a possible theft and insisting they investigate. Fran's lawyer immediately leaped on this as a way to get rid of O'Donnell and, hopefully, draw a more lenient judge as a replacement. They used O'Donnell's report to the police as hard evidence that he knew someone who might have been one of my victims, which would prejudice him unfairly against Fran. O'Donnell said that was nonsense, but the very fact that he'd reported it to the police as a possible theft was enough to back him into a corner he couldn't get out of. That his wife had watched the tape along with him didn't bolster his defense of his judicial integrity.

It was a long shot, but O'Donnell soon announced that he would bow out, even though he insisted he didn't personally know the people he thought were the rightful owners. He said that "to avoid the appearance of impropriety and to promote the integrity of the judiciary," he was going to let Fran vacate the guilty plea she'd entered as part of the deal. He flatly refused to discuss that decision with anybody, but it was a sure bet around the courthouse that he'd intended to send Fran to prison, despite the pre-sentencing report he'd gotten that recommended probation.

The new judge was Francis Sweeney, who never took probation department recommendations. By that time Fran had a new lawyer, Gordon Friedman, who wrote a mini-bio of her that made her sound more like a candidate for sainthood than for a reduced sentence. He pointed out that she'd been division chairman of a cancer fund drive, had done volunteer work at Mount Sinai Hospital, sponsored the Cleveland Ballet and worked with retarded children. He saved the best for last: Fran had organized a Jewish women's group at Brandeis University with the wife of Senator Howard Metzenbaum of Ohio.

What it was in particular that moved Judge Sweeney, no one knows, but moved he was. He gave her two years' probation and two hundred hours of community service. Despite Fran's refusal to cooperate with authorities, there was no jail time and no fine. Involved law enforcement people were pretty incensed, and while they hadn't pressed for her to go away for a long stretch, they'd insisted back when the case was in front of Judge O'Donnell that she do at least a few months. The police had told him that they suspected me in a large number of jewel thefts of fashionable homes and estates, and that many of the victims were friends of Fran or her parents, implying that Fran had helped me gain access to those places. The police had also told O'Donnell that they'd seen her carrying bags of "potential evidence" from the Moreland Hills house to a private safety-deposit center. Fran's lawyer had pointed out sarcastically that they were also bags of "potential" groceries—and how much potential was the judge going to base his sentence on?—but O'Donnell had sure looked like he was buying the prosecution's arguments.

Judge Sweeney, however, was having none of that. He was one of those tough but fair types who wasn't about to be intimidated into doing something based on allegations for which not a shred of proof had been offered. Much as it might have pained him, he waved aside all the speculative bullshit they were throwing at him and instead cited Fran's complete lack of a criminal record and former good deeds in the community. "Justice was served," he said. "There was no good reason to put her in jail." I should note, however, that this judge who couldn't be intimidated had pronounced the sentencing early in the morning before law enforcement authorities had been able to get there and watch him do it.

It happened that he'd made the right call. Fran certainly knew I was a fugitive and had participated in my evasion of authorities, but she hadn't helped me commit any burglaries, at least not knowingly.

The cops had a point as well. I did do a few—not all—of the jobs they suspected me of. But in America you're not supposed to be punished for being suspected of something. Hell, if that were allowed, everybody would be in jail. Besides, this particular hearing didn't have anything to do with me, it was about Fran. Even though the cops were convinced I'd pulled a lot of those jobs, they didn't have any reason to suspect she'd known about them.

There was another aspect of all that publicity that struck me the wrong way. It seemed that anybody in the Cleveland area who'd lost a few pieces of dining room silver anytime over the previous few years, or had his golf clubs pinched from his car or a television set stolen from his living room, now assumed that I was the perp. Nobody seemed to pay attention to the fact that nearly all of my scores were high-value, high-risk and a lot more involved than a simple crash-and-dash for pocket change. The common thread connecting my jobs was the challenge of solving puzzles and overcoming formidable obstacles, and I didn't enjoy being mistaken for a kleptomaniacal shoplifter.

Nobody seemed to pay much attention to one additional condition that had been imposed on Fran, as though it was no big deal and nowhere near severe enough to substitute for the fact that she'd be serving no time in prison: She was forbidden from having any contact with me at all for the entire two years of her probation.

~

The newspapers seemed to get wind of everything the authorities were planning even before my attorneys or I found out. A few days after Fran's deal was arranged, we read that in addition to pursuing the old charges from Florida, the feds wanted to press their own case for the fictitious passport. Shortly after that we were informed—at the same time the press was—that I was also being investigated for the murder of Joey Cam, because of the clipping Barbara had sent me that was found during the search. I admit they had a point about the passport, but the murder rap was just something they cooked up as negotiating leverage for whatever deal they had in mind to strike with me in order to avoid a protracted trial.

I spent about three months in the Cuyahoga County Jail while all of this was going on, then my wild and crazy lawyers in Florida, Ray Sandstrom and Fred Haddad, had another of their wild and crazy ideas. They thought that if they brought me back to Florida I might be able to get bail, and they also thought it possible for me to fight and beat the original case. I resisted for a while, having no wish to walk back into a jurisdiction where I knew the police had a bad jones for me, but I eventually agreed. It was Fred who pointed out that I was actually safer inside the legal system, where there were some pretty strict rules, than I'd been when I was free and therefore at the mercy of whatever hogwash the police could concoct.

One Sunday, after the mountain of required paperwork had been completed, I was shackled and cuffed. Looking like Hannibal Lecter, I was escorted to Cleveland Hopkins International by two cops from Florida and two federal agents who were the size of NFL linebackers. The feds signed some handoff papers and the two Florida guys and I flew to Fort Lauderdale.

Ray had set up the bail hearing for the next morning. Barb showed up and offered as collateral the mortgage-free house she'd gotten from me in the divorce. Unfortunately, ten FBI officials from Cleveland also showed up, and their show of force worked: The judge denied bail and remanded me back to custody, and Ray and Fred went into a huddle with state, federal and county prosecutors.

The "huddle" lasted three months and then Fred came in to lay it out for me. He started by telling me that feelings were no longer running as high against me as we'd thought.

"The county prosecutor is the lead on the case," Fred said, "because the main warrant is for the fugitive charge and that's a county matter, and he doesn't seem to be a bad guy. The assistant U.S. attorney isn't out for blood, either."

I looked at Fred warily. "What about the cops?"

"The cops? Oh, they want your balls in a paper bag."

We both laughed, and he explained that the cops had no official say in how I was handled.

Then he sobered up. "On the other hand, all these guys have to work together, and when the cops kick and scream, the prosecutors listen. The problem you've got?"

I knew what the problem was. "I pissed them off."

"Worse than that," Fred said. "You made them look stupid. And there's no walking away from making them look stupid."

"So what were you guys talking about for three months?" I asked.

"We were talking about how to get out of this with the least pain for everybody."

Fred said that the prosecutors had openly admitted that their case against me wasn't as tight as they'd like it to be. I was definitely dead on the forged passport, but as far as skipping out on my trial five years ago, if Ray and Fred could get the original violation-of-parole hearing reopened, there was a chance I might walk on that one.

On the other hand, that strategy could fail. "And you might be looking at twenty years," Fred said.

It was easy to see how this was shaping up. No way were the prosecutors going to just drop the charges, but they'd as soon not take their chances on a trial, either. That meant there was some wiggle room to negotiate, and there was only one thing I had to offer. "So how much time do they want me to do?"

That was really the heart of the matter. What Fred had already told me could have been dispatched in the first five minutes of that huddle that had taken three months.

"A nickel," he said—five years—then held up his hand when I started to react. "They'll give you credit for the time you already spent—"

"Including the ninety days waiting for this offer?"

Fred nodded. "And once all of this has blown over and the papers aren't staring at it so hard, and assuming you behave in the joint, they'll listen to a parole plea."

"And everybody agrees?" Meaning everybody at the county, state and federal levels.

"Yep."

Fred didn't bother telling me what a good deal it was; it was obvious. They could give me five years each for the phony passport and driver's license alone. With the deal, I'd do less than two years, and when I came out my slate would be wiped completely clean. No more running, no more looking over my shoulder, no more false identities . . .

"One condition," I said, nevertheless.

Fred tensed up. He'd already gotten everything he could out of those guys and there wasn't any water left in the well. "What?"

"Gotta be a state prison, not federal."

State prison is harder time, because of tighter budgets, chronic overcrowding, fewer statutory protections and less stringent oversight. But overcrowding and tight budgets also means you usually do less time, especially if you're nonviolent, because they want to get you out of there as soon as possible. And I was willing to endure anything if it meant getting out sooner.

I had another reason to avoid a federal prison, and that was that the feds who seemed to have it in for me had less influence in state joints. It was a cinch that without their interference, someone with the time I already had in on the nickel would be in minimum security and then out on work release within a couple of months.

It would turn out to be another in a string of bad assumptions on my part. But I had no way of knowing that in advance, so Fred took my answer back to the prosecutors, and neither of us read anything into the fact that they agreed almost before Fred even finished speaking.

23

Back in the Saddle Again

In some ways, prison was preferable to jail.

Jail is a holding pattern, an agony of ongoing uncertainty of the kind familiar to any schoolkid who spends a whole day wondering what the hell his father is going to do to him when Mom spills what he did. Inevitably, the punishment and accompanying finality are almost a welcome relief after all the anguished speculation.

In jail there is no pretext of rehabilitation and very few quality-of-life considerations. Technically, you're still innocent and being held only to make sure you don't run away or cause more trouble prior to your next legal proceeding. There are no programs to help you become a better person because, officially, there isn't necessarily anything wrong with you. Even exercise isn't provided for, and the only time you get to see the sun is if you need to be transported for a proceeding. In Broward County, though, the jail and the court are in the same building. I never once went outside the whole time I was there. The only good thing was that a lot of the guys in the jail had already done state time, and I'd learned a good deal about what to expect.

Prisoners who were slated to be transferred weren't told about it until after eleven at night, when the phones were cut off. That way they couldn't make plans to have somebody waiting to hijack the bus. I got the word on January 13, a Sunday, two days after I'd cut my deal. At around eleven-thirty, twenty of us were rounded up and brought downstairs, strip-searched and placed in a holding cell, where we waited for the bus to arrive after picking up some prisoners from Dade County. Everything went along smoothly until they found a handcuff key on some guy. They hauled him back to jail to be arraigned on some new charges, then put the rest of us through a much more thorough strip search. It wasn't until two-thirty in the morning that I was shackled to another guy and placed on the bus.

Our first stop was the North Florida Reception Center in Lake Butler, a processing facility just outside of Orlando for new inmates prior to their assignment to other prisons. The "lake" was just a larger puddle of swamp water than the ones around it, and the "center" was a brick-and-concrete room full of wooden benches and harsh neon lighting, staffed by some of the meanest sons of bitches I'd ever seen standing outside the bars. It was like marine boot camp, except that these guys were allowed to beat you, which they were happy to do if you so much as blinked too fast. The first thing we did was line up to hand over our personal possessions, and among the things I turned in was the Seiko watch I'd stolen from Robert Goulet. The clerk who took it stared at it for a long time before dropping it into an envelope. Then we were taken away to be stripped, weighed and measured and get a ten-second haircut that left us all nearly bald. After that we stood at attention for about two hours while a group of guards took turns yelling at us before we were finally put in lockdown cells.

The next day saw a variety of productive activities. I was made to scrub the floor with a toothbrush but soon realized that it was one of the good jobs. Some guys were forced to stand at attention with their noses pressed against a wall. If they moved, they got a vicious slap to the head or worse. I saw two guys collapse and get carted away. One of the guards' favorite activities was spitting in a prisoner's face and reminding him that there was nobody there to protect him.

I was pretty damned scared. There were all kinds of stories running around, including one about how the guards had beaten a prisoner and then chained him to his bunk and let him bleed to death. From what I was witnessing firsthand, it wasn't much of a stretch to believe that it could be true. Some of the guards were the third generation in their families to work at Lake Butler, and it seemed to me that everyday brutality against people powerless to defend themselves was baked right into their culture.

I was one of the few nonviolent prisoners in the place. My bunk mate was an older guy and very quiet. I wasn't able to learn much about him, but several years later I saw his picture in the paper when the police began digging up female bodies on his farm in Alabama. Seems the state of Florida's idea of a good first step in getting me rehabilitated was to bunk me with a serial killer.

There were ten prisoner counts a day. Once a week you got a cold shower. The rest of the time you tried to avoid the guards who were doing their best to find excuses to beat the shit out of someone and usually finding them. There were lines for everything, even going inside to take a leak, and it was on one of those lines that I had my first serious confrontation.

We were waiting to go into the mess hall. Even with my head down I could see that the guy in front of me was massive, his back like an immense wall. All of a sudden he turned around and looked at me, a black guy with a head like a bowling ball. A very mean bowling ball.

"What the fuck?" he said.

I looked up.

"You coughed on me."

I'd done no such thing, but I didn't say a word.

His eyes narrowed, and movement around us ceased. "I said, you coughed on me."

I still refused to say a word.

"You heard what I said?" he demanded

There was no use arguing; he wasn't looking for a factual debate, and all I could do by talking was make things worse. If I stayed quiet, maybe he'd just insult me and then turn away and let it go. I couldn't believe that this guy would risk pissing off the guards, or that they wouldn't step in and break it up when they saw what was going on, but at that early stage in my Lake Butler experience I didn't realize that the guards loved it when two prisoners went at it. That's why a couple of them were standing off to the side smiling and making no move to intervene.

"Motherfucker!" the big guy mumbled, and began to draw back his fist as the men around us stepped away.

It was one of those defining moments in life that I knew in an instant would color my whole experience in prison, and not just the short time I'd be spending at Lake Butler: Whatever got linked to me in the next few seconds would stay with me and determine how I would be treated no matter where in the system I ended up. So even though this guy towering overhead outweighed me by over a hundred pounds and was no stranger to violence, I really had little choice in the matter.

I took a small step back and kicked him in the nuts.

I felt a hundred pairs of astonished eyes staring at me as he went down like a sack of flour. Keeping every trace of emotion off my face, I looked down at him as though coldly assessing whether I had hit him hard enough to keep him from getting back up or if I would need to hit him again. Then I stepped over him and resumed my place in line, as though nothing unusual had happened and I could give less of a shit than if a mosquito had gotten in my way. Throughout the whole episode I never said a single word, and I like to think I never showed any sign of fear.

The point wasn't to prove how tough I was. It was to demonstrate that I was volatile, unafraid and unpredictable, and that even though there might be plenty of guys who could take me in a fight, why start something with somebody who was guaranteed to give you trouble? I knew I'd be fine so long as I didn't get transferred to the same institution as this hulk moaning on the floor behind me was headed to.

It was that bad every damned day, but it lasted only two weeks and then they transferred me to a minimum-security facility down the road. All that surrounded it was a six-foot fence, and the guards were downright civil. I thought somebody must have finally figured out I didn't belong with the hard guys, but six days later I was moved again, to the maximum-security fortress in Raiford, about forty miles southwest of Jacksonville. Something was going on that I wasn't being clued in on.

Now, you might think that I didn't have a legitimate beef—after all, I was a convicted felon, and prison is prison, right? But prison is *not* prison, and there are some pretty strict protocols when it comes to incarcerating people. One of those protocols says that a nonviolent offender who is doing less than two years against a five-year sentence should be on work release or, at the very worst, in a minimum-security facility. So why was I being housed with rapists, serial killers and armed robbers?

The reason, as it turned out, was that the feds were systematically entering pending charges against me into the National Crime Information Center computers. There was nothing to stop them from doing that, since all it meant was that they were *thinking* about charging me with something, and who was to say that they weren't? But the effect it had, which was intended, was to signal to the prison authorities that I was a bad guy and should be treated as such. Since the manner of my treatment was not a matter of law but up to the discretion of the prison system, there wasn't anything my lawyers or I could do about it except argue to get the charges yanked out of NCIC. Out the charges would come, and then fresh ones would be lodged. The feds had no problem with this little game; so long as my status looked like it was up in the air, the prison authorities were justified in assuming the worst about me.

What I said about my previous stretch still held: The overriding feature of prison life is maddening, will-sapping tedium. Raiford was divided into two dormitories of about 250 inmates each. There was nothing to do all day except walk around a small track and wait in line for the phone. Other than the occasional fight, meals were the only thing that broke up the day. Fights were not a problem for me, though: Word of my little overreaction at Lake Butler had, as I'd intended, spread around the system, and nobody thought it in his interest to find out if I'd explode again if provoked.

I was lucky in that I could read (don't laugh . . . that put me ahead of quite a few guys in there) and Fran had managed to get a bunch of books to me. I spent a lot of time immersed in the bestsellers of the day, and also writing letters, and the more literate among the inmates were grateful to me for passing on the books when I was done.

Many of the letters I wrote were to Ray and Fred asking them to concentrate on getting me the hell out of maximum security. They went to

I took an awful lot of ribbing from fellow inmates when these two magazines hit the stands. For Fran's family and friends, the impact was a lot less amusing, and the parole board considering my case didn't laugh much either.

work with their usual zeal, and about four months after I entered Raiford, I was transferred to the Zephyrhills Correctional Institution, a medium-security facility about halfway between Orlando and St. Petersburg. It was surrounded by two ten-foot fences topped with razor wire, and armed guards in Jeeps were stationed at each corner. There were a lot of lifers locked up there, but the level of violence was much lower.

The last time I had seen Fran was when she visited me in jail back in Cleveland before she was given probation and forbidden to have any contact with me. I was so distraught when they made her leave, I couldn't eat for almost two days, and I can only imagine how much worse it would have been had I known that it would be the last time I'd see her for a very long time. Now, though, I was able to phone her twice a day. Legally, while Fran wasn't allowed to have contact with me, I was under no similar prohibition, so the Zephyrhills authorities didn't care if I spoke with her. Also, since she and her daughter had moved back into her parents' house, there was nothing to prove that it wasn't her mother or father I was speaking to unless the police tapped the phones, and nobody thought there was any reason for them to do that; Fran was small potatoes and had probably already been forgotten by everyone except the probation officer supervising her community service. The phone bills from all the collect calls were astronomical, but Fran's father paid them without ever mentioning them.

~

About a month before I arrived, another prisoner had been paroled out. His name was Jack Murphy, but he was better known to the world as "Murph the Surf," the most notorious American jewel thief ever and the guy Joe Gerwens of the Fort Lauderdale police had compared me to. Murph and two of his beach-bum cohorts broke into New York City's American Museum of Natural History in 1964 and stole the famed Star of India, at 563 carats the world's largest sapphire. He was caught less than forty-eight hours later (one of his partners gave him up; see what I mean?), did about two years in prison and in 1969 went back in for murdering two women. He became a born-again Christian and was let out of Zephyrhills on the condition that he come back to preach the Gospel to prisoners.

The prison officials had given me a job as a gardener, with my own little ten-by-ten-foot plot to tend. That lasted a month, because I heard you could get twenty days knocked off your sentence if you took GO LAB, a one-week course on how to write a résumé, get along with employers, start your own business and things like that. I did it, and when my business background made itself evident, they recruited me to teach it. A week or so into it, Murphy made one of his frequent visits to Zephyrhills.

I couldn't stand the guy from the first time he came up to me. I have to admit that I admired the Star of India job when it happened, at least the heist itself. A lot of people said Murphy was lucky, because building alarms had been turned off to save electricity and the battery powering the display-case alarm had died, but I knew that luck always played a part, and I didn't count it against him. It was the aftermath in which he got caught—a circus of amateurish errors and careless planning—that lessened him in my eyes. He was an egotistical showboater through and through, starting with the fact that stealing the Star of India was a useless thing to do, because there's no way to fence something that famous.

Then I heard about the murders of the two young women who'd been captivated by Murphy's smooth flamboyance, his brains and his gift of gab. All of a sudden this suave jewel thief, surfer and violinist wasn't a lovable rascal anymore; he was a despicable monster who'd gotten so high on his own publicity, he not only snuffed out two young lives but dumped their bodies in six feet of water just a few hundred yards from where people had seen them go out on his boat.

That was why I didn't like it when Gerwens compared me to Murphy during the Mandel trial. Gerwens was referring only to jewel-robbing skills, of course, but I didn't want my name anywhere near Murph the Surf's.

Now here he was, supposedly born-again and thereby so morally superior to us heathens that he would instruct us in the proper way to live our lives. He still looked like a degenerate to me and I wanted nothing to do with him, but for some reason he took an interest in me. The GO LAB classroom was in a small brick building in the middle of the yard and he kept coming around all the time, trying to strike up a conversation. All I ever said was "Hi," and then got on with what I was doing, but he'd stare at me and then go off and ask other prisoners questions about me. Normally those guys wouldn't respond to stuff like that, but Murphy was famous throughout the Florida prison system, which is how he got inmates to listen to his preaching: Most of them couldn't give a shit, but they wanted to be able to say they hung with Murph the Surf.

A couple of them told me that he had been asking about me, and I said to one guy who occasionally attended Murphy's lectures, "Why's he so interested in me?"

"Probably wants to get in your pants," he answered, then held his hands up in the air. "In the name of the Lord."

Murphy made me sick, and I tried to make sure I was in my cell whenever he visited the prison. It worked, and I never had to speak with him again.

~

One of the days I remember most vividly was January 28, 1986.

It may be a cliché to say they could lock up my body but not my mind, but it's a concept I took very much to heart. A lot of guys inside just kind of surrender and don't give a shit about anything, as though their stretch were some kind of purgatory so absolute and crushing there was no sense even trying to make the most of it. I'm not saying I made lemonade out of life's lemons or any goody-two-shoes bullshit like that—prison is hell no matter what kind of attitude you have—but I wasn't about to let myself just rot away.

I was one of only two inmates in the whole place who bought *The Tampa Tribune* every day. The prison charged us twice the newsstand price, which is pretty interesting when you stop to think about it—they should have given it to us free and had literate prisoners read it out loud to those who couldn't read for themselves—but I thought it was worth it anyway. Having some idea of what was going on outside the walls made me feel less isolated and disconnected.

I had read that a space shuttle was being launched on January 22, and got to wondering whether it would be possible to catch a glimpse of it. Cape Canaveral was a full hundred miles to the east, but those launch vehicles let off one hell of a lot of smoke and they did go several hundred miles into the sky, so I thought it might be possible. The paper called for the weather to be crystal clear all over central Florida, too, so if it was ever possible to see something, that would be the day.

The launch was scheduled for late afternoon, when I'd be on GO LAB duty. There were five of us teaching, but only one at a time, so the other four got to stand around and scratch their asses, which was actually one of the better jobs available in the Zephyrhills prison. I arranged to be one of the ones out of the classroom then, and ten minutes before launch time I positioned myself looking eastward. It says something that not one person in the yard at the time was even remotely curious why someone would be staring intently at absolutely nothing. Like I said, most of them just didn't give a shit.

Well, so much for that experiment. I couldn't see a damned thing and it was a bust. Except that the next day's *Tribune* carried an article about how the launch had been aborted due to some technical issues. It was rescheduled for the next day, and I didn't see anything then, either. Sure enough, it had been called off again, so I gave it another try on the twenty-fourth. This time, there was bad weather at one of the emergency landing sites somewhere in Africa, so it was pushed to the twenty-fifth, except then there was bad weather predicted at the launch site, and then there were other problems. But I didn't give up, although my fellow GO LAB instructors were starting to get annoyed at my constant juggling of the schedules.

On the twenty-eighth, right before lunchtime, there I was again, standing out in the yard by myself staring eastward. The guards must have thought I'd converted to Islam by then, but damned if I didn't suddenly see a thin plume of white vapor forming in the distance. It was much brighter and clearer than I'd expected, and I was transfixed. If I could see that thing from so far away, I wondered what it must be like to stand just a few miles from it. Then I got to thinking about the astronauts who were being flung free of the bonds of gravity while I couldn't even cross a street.

About a minute or so after I'd first spotted the vapor trail, there was another puff of smoke at the top of the plume. I assumed it was the booster rockets being dropped off, but then a very bright glow appeared, a fireball, followed by smoke trails forming in a downward direction. It was then I noticed that the original plume was no longer growing. Even though I'd never seen a launch before, I knew right away that something awful had happened. Soon there was nothing to see but dissipating smoke.

There was no sound at all. It was too far away. I looked around the yard and nobody but me seemed to have noticed. I turned eastward again and strained to find some indication that I'd been mistaken and all was okay but somehow knew it was hopeless.

I didn't know if there were emergency systems to get the crew away if something went wrong. Was it possible that those poor people on board were dead? All of a sudden my personal concerns seemed small and insignificant. Like millions of Americans, I desperately wanted to know the details of what had happened, if there was any possibility that it wasn't as bad as it looked.

There's not much that can change life in the joint. The television in the cell block was tuned, as it always was at that time of day, to an exercise program. The inmates watching didn't give a damn about fitness; they were watching the women in tight leotards, and looked ready to tear my head off when I asked if they'd change the channel for a second.

I had to wait until noon, when the pay phones were switched on, to call Fran. She was at her father's house and filled me in on the tragedy. All I could think about at first was that schoolteacher, then her family, then the kids who were her students and then my own kids. How fragile life was, and here I was pissing mine away. I felt that urge that others who had been jolted by the disaster were feeling, to be with people you cared about, but all I had surrounding me were cons so dense and oblivious, I couldn't even get them to switch a television channel. I don't know if it was just displaced self-pity or what, but the *Challenger* catastrophe hit me hard, much more so than I would have believed until it happened, and I had to deal with it alone.

~

GO LAB was a nice diversion, but it didn't make me forget how different, how dehumanizing, the culture inside could be. It seemed as though all the normal rules were left at the front gate, and I'm not just talking about the obvious kinds of things you have to have in place when people are being held against their will. I'm talking about the very nature of how human beings interact.

There was a mildly retarded inmate in my class named Bernie, who worked in the kitchen. At close to three hundred pounds and in for murder, he was a pretty scary guy until you got to know him. He was housed in my block and we somehow took a liking to each other. He was always coming around to my cell, and I'd help him with his schoolwork and with writing letters. He even had me come to the visitors' room to meet his mother a couple of times.

A side note here: *Everybody* in prison is in for murder or armed robbery or drug smuggling. Just ask them, they'll tell you. What they won't tell you is if they're in for wife-beating or child molestation. Hard-core prisoners tend to be aggressively and self-righteously moral about some things, largely because prison is so abasing and dehumanizing that feeling superior to someone is one of the only ways of convincing yourself you're not the complete piece of shit the system makes you out to be. Child molesters are among the most detested of all inmates and are terrified at the thought of the true nature of their offenses leaking into the yard. They tend to tell the most grotesque stories of murder and mayhem they never actually committed.

As a GO LAB instructor, I had access to prisoner personnel files, and I can tell you that Bernie really was in for murder.

Because I had to begin teaching early in the day, the guards would unlock the main cell-block door for me each morning and let me walk across the yard to eat breakfast before everybody else. I liked doing that because the mess hall was quiet and I could read. But one morning at about five-thirty it wasn't so quiet. When I got to the mess hall, half a dozen guards had Bernie cornered. He was wild-eyed and raving, and waved a large chunk of two-by-four at them menacingly every time one of them took a step forward. Just as I was taking all of this in, two of the guards were reaching for the Mace canisters on their belts, and I knew that Bernie was in serious trouble. An inviolable rule among the guards was that you never, *ever* let a prisoner get the best of you, and if one tries, you make it absolutely clear to the others what an awful mistake that was.

It's not my style to meddle, and especially not in the joint, but there was a good chance my friend Bernie was going to get killed in the next few minutes. I couldn't just stand there and watch it happen, or leave and pretend I hadn't known. Before I could give it a lot of thought and possibly change my mind, I sped up and headed for the guards. One of the ones reaching for Mace saw me from the corner of his eye and whirled on me. I quickly put up my hands and took a step back, realizing I should have yelled out or done something to let him know I was coming, rather than have it look like I was trying to sneak up on him.

"He's a friend," I said. "Let me talk to him."

The guard stared at me, and then another one nodded to him. As they stepped back, Bernie began whimpering, not quite understanding what was happening.

I called out to him and asked how he was doing. Breathing heavily, he didn't say anything back, but at least he stopped waving that piece of lumber around. I talked to him soothingly, and as I did so, the guards began backing away, and the farther back they got, the calmer Bernie became. Eventually I was able to walk him toward the door, and as we passed through into the yard, one of the guards whispered to me to get him to the infirmary.

Once there, I got Bernie to sit down on a cot. He no longer seemed threatening, just sad and lonely, and he soon lay down and threw his arm over his face. At that point two guards hustled me out, and as I went through the door, one of them said, "Next time, mind your own fuckin' business." It was a good lesson in never showing up a guard, even if it was in everybody's best interest to do so.

By morning, Bernie had been transferred to Chattahoochee. There are no second chances in the system, and I never did find out what had led

Bernie to pick up that two-by-four in the first place, or if it had even been his fault. All I knew was that as soon as he was seen to be a potential troublemaker, out he went to an even tougher pen, a place he clearly didn't belong, just so the guards wouldn't have to risk a blot on their records if he should act up again.

I taught GO LAB for a couple of months, then worked in a storeroom outside the front gate. If you're waiting for more exciting parts, there aren't any. The most exciting part of my day was brushing my teeth. I don't know how to convey to you how awful that kind of relentless boredom can be. Imagine yourself sitting in a bad traffic jam. For a year. Then try to imagine some higher-up testifying before a congressional committee about what a good job his department was doing moving the traffic along, which is how I felt about prison officials thumping their chests over how well they were preparing inmates for reentry into the real world.

Spend some time in prison and chronic recidivism is no longer a mystery.

~

A year after my transfer to Zephyrhills, I was released on one-year parole. It was a glorious day, obviously, but also a bit strange, because I had trouble getting used to the idea that I could walk around freely and use my own name without the constant fear that I might be captured and locked up again. I had an unshakable feeling that I was going to be greeted at the front gate by a bunch of federal agents with fresh charges to lodge against me, but it didn't happen.

The prison officials gave me a hundred bucks, with the understanding that I was going to get a bus ticket to Fort Lauderdale. Instead, I hired a car to take me to the Tampa airport, where Fran had arranged to have a prepaid ticket waiting for me. Tampa is on the west coast of Florida, the Gulf of Mexico side, about halfway up the length of the state, and it was about a two-hundred-mile flight to Fort Lauderdale, where I was met by my daughter Laura. It was a joyous reunion, and then we were off to do some chores.

First stop was the motor vehicle bureau to get a new driver's license, in my own name this time. When I went to the window, the lady on duty started pulling forms from a shelf and asked me if I was renewing.

"No," I said. "Mine expired."

She looked at me suspiciously over the tops of her reading glasses. "You ain't been drivin' all those years?"

"No."

This was getting awkward. When she kept looking at me, I said, "I was in prison."

"Oh," she said, with not a trace of surprise, and went back to gathering the necessary forms. "You gotta take all the tests again. You got I.D.?"

Laura had already picked up my birth certificate from Barbara, and the prison had given me a social security card with my correct number on it. I took the written test, then went out and took the driving test, and soon afterward walked out of there with my real identity intact for the first time in years. How strange it was going to be getting used to not having to think carefully before providing my name and other identifying information when asked.

Next stop was Richard Delisi's auto body shop in Pompano to pick up Fran's Mercedes. He'd completely restored it, and even though I wanted to head over to Barb's house and didn't want to be away from Laura yet, after all the effort Delisi had put into the job, I felt obligated to stay and talk with him for a while. I introduced Laura to him, then sent her home.

Delisi wouldn't accept any money for all the work he'd done. "But we gotta celebrate your release," he announced, and pulled out a bag of weed. Some of the guys gathered around and lit up, but I declined. I could just see myself getting busted for DUI on the same day I got out of prison. I didn't even want to be around the stuff, but didn't want to run out on a party in my honor, either, so I stuck around for a while. It was then that Delisi proposed to me that I go in on that score I told you about earlier, the one in which we were each supposed to clear a million bucks.

"One big score," he said. "Just one, and we're both on easy street forever."

I told him I'd think about it, and as quickly as I could after that, I made my exit. Six hours after walking out the gate at Zephyrhills, I was tooling down the interstate in a shiny Mercedes.

Barb's reaction upon seeing me again was less enthusiastic than I might have liked, but I shouldn't have been surprised. To start with, I'd shown up in another woman's car, which, while logistically sensible, probably wasn't the most sensitive thing I could have arranged. More important was that since I'd last disrupted her life for the umpteenth time, she'd become quite comfortable being on her own and was handling things well. The last thing she needed was this unpredictable troublemaker reappearing to screw everything up once again. She also didn't need me to be critical of how she'd kept the house up, and while I made a conscious effort not to overwhelm her, I suppose I couldn't always hide my disapproval of some things. As annoyed as she might have been, though, she didn't make a point of reminding me that we'd now been divorced for four years and it wasn't any of my damned business how she handled things. Marriage or no marriage, there was no denying that I still figured large in her life.

Parole isn't a simple free pass, but carries with it a number of conditions. Fran's, for example, stipulated that she couldn't see me. There'd be nothing they could do to me should we get caught together, but Fran could wind up in prison. Under other circumstances such restrictions might have seemed not only harsh but downright un-American, because there are few situations in this country under which people can interfere so obtrusively in the personal lives of others without some due process. But given the choice between those sometimes maddening limitations and being in the joint, it's an easy call.

Another condition was that I live in Barb's older brother's house in Hollywood. That one was kind of funny, though, because the overworked parole board apparently hadn't gotten around to discovering that Bob and I had been busted together years before for trying to knock over a gas station. Wonder if they'll read this and find out they'd ordered a parolee to live with a former partner in crime.

I hadn't even made it to the door of Bob's place before I knew that that wasn't going to work at all, parole conditions be damned. His two sons lived with him, and both were serious delinquents. Given all their other problems, housekeeping was down on the priority list somewhere below choir practice. There were junk cars strewn all over the driveway and yard, and the house itself looked as though someone had taken a bulldozer to the outside and then heaved a grenade through the doorway. Now admittedly, I'm a convicted criminal and not one to be tossing criticism of others around lightly, but I've always been personally neat and I've told you what a maintenance freak I am when it comes to dwellings. And even though I'd slept in some of the worst holes the state of Florida had to offer, this place just made me sick. Paint was peeling everywhere, and even the filthy floor tiles were buckling and curling. This was the utopia I'd dreamed of every night for well over a year? My solitary little cell had been a lot cleaner than this, and not much noisier.

It was a shitty end to a shitty day. In prison you spend most of your time visualizing what it's going to be like when you get out, and even though you're not stupid or naïve and know it won't be exactly like you remembered it, you still know it's going to be eight kinds of wonderful compared to the joint. Inside, people tell you when to get up, when to eat, when to go to bed and sometimes even when to take a shit. You ache for the freedom to make your own choices about little things, so much so that the thought of something as ridiculous as just being able to walk into a fast-food joint and order a burger is almost enough to make you dizzy. Then I actually get out and find that my ex-wife isn't happy to see me and I've been ordered to live in a smelly shit hole. I remember thinking, *What must this be like for guys who get released and have nobody and nothing to go back to?* No wonder the same people keep going back to prison; what do you expect when you send ex-cons right back to the same environments that got them into trouble in the first place?

I was supposed to report to my parole office within twenty-four hours of my release, and I lay awake all night dreading that meeting, which at least took my mind off what a pig sty I was holed up in. What would the P.O. be like? Would he be too overworked to pay attention to me, which would be a blessing, or would I get one of those insecure martinets who liked to lord it over people who couldn't fight back? From there my mind jumped to all the new problems I'd be facing, and I remember being so crazy with worry that at one point I started to consider how much easier life was back in the joint, where you traded a thousand little problems for one great big concern that you couldn't do anything about anyway, so why worry?

I had one good card in my hand, and that was that I already had a job lined up, as a salesman for the Broadway Prehung Door Company. It was owned by none other than Bill Welling, who would make all the right noises when the parole officer called him to check up on me. To a P.O., a parolee having a good job was the next best thing to his going into the priesthood. It was the ideal way to keep the P.O. off your case, and my only concern about that was, being out of practice for so long, would I be able to keep snookering the guy, since there really was no such job.

The next morning I cooled my heels for half an hour waiting for this meeting and trying not to let my annoyance show. I thought about telling the P.O. that I'd *had* a job but was going to get fired because he made me late, but this was no time to be a smart-ass. I knew the drill: You had to look straight and remorseful and respectful, even though everybody in the system knew it was all bullshit.

Finally, the little twerp comes out and calls me into his office. Right there in front of him he's got my folders with the words "Escape Risk" and "Organized Crime" screaming from the covers. I couldn't believe those damned things were still labeled like that, especially the organized-crime one. "Escape risk" I supposed I could see, even though I'd never escaped. I just hadn't shown up that one time.

With barely a question to find out anything about me, this guy launches into a dramatic reading of the riot act, warning me about how straight I had to be and how clean my nose needed to be and yadda yadda yadda. The more he talked, the better I felt, because as strange as it might seem, guys like this are easy to con. They're blowhards and know-it-alls, and what's important to them is feeling important. So I tried to look cowed and impressed, nodding over and over as I listened with rapt attention, hanging on to his every word. When he got forceful, I looked away, taking the opportunity to size him up a bit more. There were folders stacked up everywhere, which told me that this guy was probably ridiculously overworked and didn't have the time to delve into each client's particular situation. I was going to tell him about the job, and about how I needed to do a little traveling for it, but I got the sense that he didn't want one more scrap of work to handle or detail to think about than was absolutely necessary, and that my best course of action was to be as low-maintenance as possible, so I stayed quiet and just kept nodding.

Back out on the street I decided that there was no way in hell I was spending another night at Bob's, so I risked revocation of my parole by checking in to a motel on the waterfront. I thought it unlikely that my overworked P.O. would ever check up on me, but I called Bob and told him to say I was out should anyone ever come by. No one ever did.

Over the next few weeks I did a lot of work on Barb's house, mostly carpentry and painting. It was one of the only things I could think of to try to ease some of the guilt I felt, and it also allowed me to spend a lot of time with Laura. Mark was in college and Suzi was in South Africa, but Laura was in high school and still living at home.

Although Fran and I were not allowed to see each other, no such restriction applied to her parents, who were in Florida. I liked them both a great deal, and although I realized what an emotional risk I was taking, I decided to give them a call. To my surprise—although in retrospect, knowing what kind of people they were, I really shouldn't have been surprised—they were quite civil to me. Later on we got together and began meeting regularly for breakfast. Talking to Fran's father about real estate and business made me feel almost normal.

A month later it was time to report to the P.O. again, but it wasn't the same one as before. The new one was a heavy young lady who was obviously not used to dealing with guys who were cleaned up, soft-spoken and otherwise acceptable in polite society. After about twenty minutes of casual banter and a lot of warm smiles, I started to wonder if this might not be a good time to talk about traveling for my job, when suddenly she says, "So how's it going at work?"

"It's going great," I said, then I let my face fall and looked down at my shoes. "Only . . ."

"Only what?"

"Only, I got a little problem." I shrugged. "Don't worry about it."

But she insisted. "Maybe I could help. We've got some pull with local businesses."

"Thing is, I'm selling for them, and doing real good, but they want me to travel. They say a salesman who can't go to where the customers are isn't much use. And"—I waved around the room, taking in the whole parole system—"what with this and all . . ."

"Well, hell, that's no problem."

I looked up at her, all surprise and confusion. "It isn't? But I thought—I mean, I'm supposed to stay—"

"You got a good job and you're keeping clean?" She flapped a hand at me, then pulled open a drawer and began hunting around for something. "No way we want to get in the way of that."

I watched as she found what she was looking for, a handful of forms. She started writing on them and said, "I'll give you some permits that'll let you travel for your job. Eastern half of the country okay?"

I told her that would be just swell and walked out with permits that I could show to the police should I ever be stopped and have my name run through the National Crime Information Center.

The next day I was off to Cleveland to see Fran, and we soon established a pattern. Each month I'd drive to Ohio and stay with her for a week or two. She was still on probation, so even with my newfound freedom it continued to be dangerous and tricky for us to spend so much time together in Cleveland. In order for her not to be seen with me, I'd never leave the house, and the only visitors we'd have were Bill Welling and Katie. Then I'd head back to Florida to file my fictitious monthly reports, renew my travel permits and see Laura. Sometimes I'd stop in Tallahassee to visit Mark in college, or in Franklin, Tennessee, to see my aunt, who'd moved there while I was in prison.

After a few iterations of this pattern, I rented a small two-room apartment down on New River by the week, and continued to commute back and forth to Florida while we bided our time waiting for Fran to get off probation. Our thought was to then move to New York City and disappear into the teeming population.

A few months after my release Suzi called to say she was engaged and planning to get married in South Africa. She wanted Barb and me to come, but the parole people drew the line at my leaving the country. Laura was in school and couldn't go, so I offered to stay with her and let Barb go to the wedding alone. During those two weeks, Laura and I had a great time, and while she was in school during the day, I managed to completely repaint the interior of the house and take care of a lot of needed repairs—still trying to make amends any way I could.

If you play by the rules, the parole board will usually let you "off paper" early, but it seemed this bunch didn't want to get any law enforcement people mad at them, so they made me go the whole year. Then I was declared rehabilitated and given my permanent release. I was still living off my ill-gotten gains and was mighty happy I hadn't gotten into that deal with Richard Delisi, who was at the moment of my parole termination sitting in the Polk County Jail with no bond. That's not to say that the notion of "one more big score" wasn't swimming around somewhere in my head.

Old habits die hard. I started each day in Florida by going to a nearby bookstore and buying all the newspapers for Fort Lauderdale, Miami, Palm Beach and Naples. Over coffee I'd carefully scan the society pages, like old times but just for laughs now. I found quite a few things that seemed very interesting, but beyond reading, I didn't undertake any of the usual prospecting-type activities to see if any of them might fit the bill as The Last Big One. All other considerations aside, I was by now too well known to local authorities on the east coast of Florida.

Of course, Naples was on the west coast.

24

~~~~~~

Prey No More

Situated on the Gulf of Mexico, Naples is considered by many the crown jewel of southwestern Florida. The county seat of Collier County, it's a playground for the well-off that boasts the highest ratio of golf courses to golfers in the entire country. It has spectacular fishing, great shopping and pristine beaches, and is a convenient jumping-off point for a visit to the Everglades. The county was founded in 1923 by entrepreneur Barron Gift Collier, and the family name seemed to pop up everywhere I turned.

One place it popped up a lot was in the Naples society pages, in the form of one lady whose married name I can't recall but who was part of the Collier family. There was literally not one party, ball or charity gala I read about that she didn't attend, and most of the newspaper stories included at least one picture of her, always wearing a lot of jewelry. I could feel the old juices begin to flow but didn't take them seriously, because, after all, I was rehabilitated. I decided to take a ride down I-75, though, just to sniff around and see what it felt like to be assessing the potential again. Strictly for laughs, of course, and to see whether I might even have the balls if it was for real, because you never really know until you're right there.

When I got to Naples, my first stop was the public library to have a glance at my old friend the city directory. I found the lady, who was listed along with her husband as living in a condo that was actually on Marco Island, northernmost of the Ten Thousand Islands and even more of a subtropical paradise than Naples, twelve miles to the north. The handy little directory listed their suite number, and a bit of searching got me the names and suite numbers of all their neighbors as well. Then it was off to Marco Island.

Theirs was a spectacular high-rise, maybe sixteen stories, and from the suite number I gathered they were somewhere close to the top. It faced the Gulf of Mexico, and there was a large, fancy hotel just two buildings away, which was perfect, because there was a lot of foot traffic in and around the place. As was typical in posh Florida resort areas, the neighborhood was also dotted with low-cost motels. I checked in to one about a mile down the road, thinking maybe I'd wander back and see what the building looked like after dark.

Instinctively, I stayed in the room for the rest of the afternoon, a strange thing to be doing in such a beautiful place. But I didn't want to roam around and take the chance of somebody noticing my face. I felt a little dopey lying low like that, since this whole trip was such a silly idea in the first place, but, as I said, old habits die hard. One habit I did break, though, was carrying tools of the trade around with me. I used to not worry about it because I was in the property management business and could excuse a lot of tools, including lock-picking equipment, as necessary for my job. Now, though, I was supposedly in the "prehung door" business, and I was selling them, not making them, so it would be tough to explain away things like power saws and chisels. All I had with me was a screwdriver, a pair of old cloth work gloves and a penlight.

Nighttime arrived and it was moonless. I can't remember if I'd planned it that way or if it was just luck. I drove back and parked in the hotel lot, which was busy as hell and crowded, then walked to the beach and took a casual stroll down to the high-rise. Once there I turned inland, going past the pool and around to the front. To my surprise there was no doorman on duty, just an intercom with a buzz-in system. I slowed slightly as I tried to absorb all the details, but didn't stop walking. By the time I reached the glass lobby door, I had my screwdriver out. A little sideways pressure on the jamb popped the bolt free and the door swung open easily. A quick check of the lobby directory and then I'm in the elevator heading for the lady's floor, which is indeed at the very top.

There's another suite opposite theirs across the hall, but no others on the floor, so I'm guessing these units are huge. The locks on the door look formidable, especially since I don't have any tools, so it's up the stairs to the roof, which is (of course) unlocked, to have a bird's-eye look at their patio. When I emerge into the night air, I realize that it's been a long time since I was that high up in the sky without an airplane surrounding me. It's a dizzying but exhilarating feeling looking down from about 170 feet up, and the lights of Marco Island are breathtaking against the black of the sky and the even inkier darkness of the gulf.

The patio below me is about twenty feet long, and a concrete over-hang covers nearly the entire thing, leaving only the front railing exposed. The overhang is just four feet below where I'm standing, so this is no problem at all. Jump down onto it, then use a rope to lower myself to the patio. Piece of cake, really, except I don't have a rope. Which is a damned shame, and a challenge, and my mind suddenly starts to race. Go back down and buy a rope? Even if I could find a store with the right kind of rope at this time of night, buying one would look suspicious, and the odds were high the salesman or cashier would remember me if a high-rise robbery were reported the next day. I could always come back another time, but that would mean I was back in the well-planned burglary busi-ness, which I'm not ready to admit to myself. No, this may have been fun, but now it's over.

Stepping carefully so as not to alert anybody below me that someone is stomping around on the roof, I make my way back to the stairway door and can hardly believe it when I see a twelve-foot work ladder propped up against the side of the little structure that houses the top of the elevator. There's nothing at all on this roof except me and that ladder, and I'm feel-ing like this is a sign from God or something, without stopping to con-sider whether God is in the habit of giving encouraging signs to thieves.

Sign or no sign, I'm still a professional, so I head back to the stairs, down the elevator, out the lobby and onto the beach. Looking up, I can see that their entire unit is dark. Around the building to the street, an-other look up, and I see the unit across the hall is dark, too. So are the ones on the floor below on both sides of the building.

Back to the big hotel. I use a lobby pay phone to call their number, let-ting it ring ten times before hanging up and calling again, checking each digit carefully. No answer.

Now I start to get really stupid, and I can *feel* myself getting stupid,

Collier condo, Marco Island. The arrow shows where I tried to position the legs of the ladder.

but there's just no stopping it. I'm thinking, *It's only about nine o'clock so they'll probably be out for a couple more hours, or maybe they're not even in town at all tonight, and if I can get that ladder positioned somehow I may not need a rope and if the patio door is locked the screwdriver will open it and if they should come home I can get back up the ladder and pull it up behind me before they even know anyone is in there but if it all works it could be a great haul and then I'm back in the bucks and this will really be The Last Big One. . . .*

Nothing like a well-considered, carefully planned plan. The momentum of my thinking is making me nervous, because some part of me is still rational and knows exactly how irrational the other part is being, but it's still just a lark and I want to keep pushing myself just to see what happens. I can call it off anytime I want and come back again later with the right equipment.

Come back with the right equipment? What the hell am I thinking? I'm *rehabilitated,* for heaven's sake.

Right. Soon I'm back up on the roof. I carefully lower the ladder to the overhang above the patio, jump down after it and then walk to the edge and look down. The patio, which is much farther down than I expected, sticks out from the building about two feet more than the overhang I'm standing on. I can see that it's covered in slippery-looking tiles, but the ladder has rubber feet that might stop it from sliding around.

There is also the protective guardrail; jamming the ladder's feet up against it where it meets the tile floor should stop the ladder from moving.

I go back to get the ladder, swing it out over the edge of the overhang and then begin lowering it. I'm trying to ignore the cement walkway sixteen stories down, which is tough, because in order to prevent the ladder's weight from pulling me over, I've got to kneel awkwardly right on the edge of the overhang. I can't steady myself with one hand, either, because I need both hands to lower the ladder rung by rung, and suddenly I've got a real problem: Seems the overhang is a whole lot higher above the patio than I assumed. By the time I've got hold of just the top rung, the bottom of the ladder still hasn't touched down. There's no sense lowering it any further because there'd be nothing to prop the top of the ladder against once it went below the edge of the overhang. Some sign from God.

So I'm crouching there hanging on to this useless ladder, when one of the dumbest damned ideas I've ever had in my entire life pops into my head. The bottom of the ladder may not reach the patio floor, but it will reach the top of that guardrail. And since the guardrail sticks out about two more feet than the roof I'm standing on, the ladder will have some lean to stabilize it, but not so much that the bottom will be prone to slipping off the rail. Maybe my weight on it will help the feet grip the railing. Sure, that's a wonderful idea.

Holding the ladder over the edge with one hand, my other arm stretched back toward the building to balance myself, I lean out as far as I can without tipping over. It's just enough to position the bottom of the ladder above the guardrail. I lower it slowly until the feet touch down, then relax my arm to put some weight on the rail. When I'm no longer holding the ladder up but only balancing it, I jog it around a bit to make sure the feet are planted solidly, then push down and jog it some more to test how well it seems to be gripping. Then I let it lean against the edge of the overhang next to my knee and let go. So far so good.

I stand up. One hand on the overhang, one on the ladder, I swing a leg over and get one foot on the third rung from the top, and put a little weight on it. It seems to be holding pretty good, so I twist around a little more and now I'm standing with both feet on the rung. I've still got a hand on the edge of the overhang as I take one step down, then another, and then I grab the overhang with both hands. I don't plan to let go of that chunk of concrete until I absolutely have to.

Another step down, then another. My hands are above me now and I take one more step and finally let go of the overhang, and just like that and for no apparent reason the top of the ladder lurches sideways, and by the time I realize that one of the ladder's feet has slipped off the railing, I'm going sideways and down.

The ladder is falling, with me on it.

Instinctively, my hands let go of the ladder and shoot out for the only solid thing in reach, the edge of the overhang, which is high above me now. I barely get my fingers on it when the top of the ladder slams into my hands, the stinging pain almost making me lose my grip on the concrete. I'm swinging crazily back and forth as the ladder bounces off me and then suddenly vanishes. Hanging by my fingertips, I hear the sickening sound of crunching metal and look down over my shoulder, which is when I realize that I got thrown so far to the side I'm no longer above the patio. My feet are dangling above sixteen stories of empty space, and below me I see the ladder bouncing wildly off the patio two floors down, twisting in two directions at once and then smashing into yet another patio with an even louder sound, then another and another, and then it's in slow motion, growing smaller as it spins like a blade until it finally crashes into the cement walkway and flies apart, raising a racket that I'm sure can be heard in Miami.

One thought is ricocheting around in my head: *It could have been me.* The image is a paralyzing one, but this is no time to be paralyzed, so I fight against the panic and pull myself up until I can throw a leg over the edge of the overhang and scramble back up onto it.

I don't think I've ever been more traumatized. I couldn't even stand up, but just lay there, despite knowing that all that noise was going to bring a lot of people running. My limbs felt like limp ropes and my head reeled so badly I could hardly remember where I was. Struggling to think clearly, I eventually got up, climbed the four feet back onto the main roof and staggered to the stairway, but this time kept going rather than take the elevator. I didn't want to get trapped if somebody surmised that the noise had come from a malfunctioning elevator and decided to cut the power.

About five floors into my descent a young woman and an elderly man came through the doorway and into the stairwell.

"What was that?" the man said in alarm. "That sound, what was it?"

"No idea," I said. "Sounds like, uh, something fell off a balcony."

"I think it came from the gulf side," the lady said.

I nodded and ran down the stairs ahead of them. In the lobby about a dozen people were milling around, peering out the glass front and afraid to go outside.

"I think it came from the other side," I said as I marched toward the front door. "I'm going to go check it out."

"Be careful!" several voices rang out.

"I will," I replied bravely, and headed out the door, around the back and down the beach. I kept walking until I reached the hotel, found the bar and had two stiff shots of vodka even before I'd firmly settled on the stool.

Only after my nerves stopped screaming did it occur to me that maybe that ladder had been a sign from God after all.

~

Fran finally finished her probation and we moved to New York City to start a new life.

We went almost completely legit. We started buying large lots of costume jewelry and reselling it at antique shows around the tristate area of New York, New Jersey and Connecticut. Pretty ironic, when you stop to think about it: I used to just toss fake jewelry into a dumpster if I found some among the legitimate goods after a score, and here I was, old "El Gato" himself, hawking the stuff to tourists.

I also started restoring furniture, an enjoyable hobby and mildly lucrative when I wasn't giving the stuff away to the kids. Fran and I bought a place in Connecticut where I could work and store the finished goods, and soon I had a stream of steady customers coming by to see what I was working on. I sold almost every piece before it was even half completed. Mark was now married and getting a business started, and Laura was in college in Tallahassee. They visited us often, especially when we were in the city, but Suzi was in South Africa, which made dropping in a little difficult.

Mark had surprised us all when he decided that a normal job wasn't for him and announced that he wanted to go off on his own and become a sand sculptor. I can't say I was too pleased at this decision. Here was a superintelligent young man with four years of college under his belt, and I felt he was about to throw his life away. Just goes to show how wrong a parent can be. He started his own business and made it enormously successful. He and his "Team Sandtastic" travel the world creating sand and snow sculptures for conventions, fairs, festivals and theme parks on behalf of major international corporations. At it for over fourteen years, he's won a world championship title and holds three *Guinness* world records.

I said Fran and I were "almost" legit. Our businesses were enjoyable but didn't generate the income we would have liked. I still had a lot of stolen jewels secreted in Cleveland and Florida, and I'd periodically dip into the inventory and sell some pieces on Forty-seventh Street in New York, and some of the fancier stuff at Christie's and Sotheby's.

Barb's brother Augie was living on a houseboat on Biscayne Bay in Florida. We'd visited him several times and I loved the laid-back style of living right on the water. About two years after we'd moved to New York, he called to say that he and his girlfriend were buying a bigger houseboat and would Fran and I like to buy theirs. It took me about five minutes to decide, but Fran was a tougher sell. "Nice Jewish ladies don't live on houseboats," she sniffed.

"Nice Jewish ladies don't run away with jewel thieves, either," I pointed out. Eventually, I was able to convince her that we could move our business down there for the winters and come back north in the summers, so we packed up and moved. We were smack in the heart of one of the more upscale parts of Miami Beach, an area loaded with art galleries, fancy restaurants and impressive mansions, and friends and family were always visiting.

About two years after we got down there, another houseboat came on the market. It had been owned by the parents of the Bee Gees, and I thought that Mark, who'd recently moved to St. Thomas, might be interested. Mark loved the idea of living on a houseboat near us, so he came to Florida, bought the boat and lived with Fran and me while we completely remodeled. By that time Barb and Fran had gotten to know each other and hit it off well, so Barb was over often to see her brother, son and me.

Shortly after we finished, Hurricane Andrew decided to drop in on Florida, and we were ordered to evacuate. Mark was already away on a sculpting job, and I sent his wife, Fran and Barb to stay with Laura in Orlando, but I couldn't bring myself to abandon those boats. Then the police started coming around with loudspeakers ordering everybody to leave, and that sealed it for me: I wasn't going anywhere.

The storm moved slightly south and spared us its full fury. At daybreak, six of the seven boats tied to our dock had made it. The dock itself, though, was about 90 percent destroyed. Mark's boat, Augie's and mine came through with only minor damage, but boats had sunk all over the bay. The city got on our case to close down the dock, and even though we fixed it as best we could despite the fact we didn't own it, they still bitched. A year of legal wrangling went by and then Mark presented me with my first grandson, right on my own birthday, too. (As of this writing Fran and I are blessed with nine grandkids between us.) Mark decided it was now time to leave and I agreed, so we both put our boats on the market. Mine sold first, and we were terribly sad watching it being towed away.

~

Ray Sandstrom, beset by liability resulting from his numerous divorces, felt it necessary to leave southern Florida and went to Wyoming. He was killed there when his car was broadsided by a logging truck. Given Ray's penchant for hiding large sums of cash, there is no doubt in my mind that somewhere in that vast state, there are caches of money sitting just below ground inside well-protected safes. More than a few of his ex-wives paid good money to psychics trying to find out where.

Ray's partner, Fred Haddad, is not only still alive but has straightened out his life to such a degree that I sometimes wonder who took over his body and what they did with the real Fred. He has a phenomenally successful practice in Fort Lauderdale and is listed in the current edition of *The Best Lawyers in America*. I'm happy to say that the two of us remain close friends.

Fran and I moved back up to New York permanently, and life has been blessedly uneventful. We're still in the costume jewelry and antique businesses, and spend a good deal of time traveling, mostly to see family. It was the intense curiosity of our now fully grown kids and some close friends that led me to decide to lay all of this down in print.

One last story:

In 2002 the U.S. Olympic Committee hired Mark to build a giant maze made entirely of snow for the Winter Games in Salt Lake City, Utah. In addition to his usual team, he decided to bring in some new talent, namely Bill Welling and me. Mark did the design himself, then seven of us worked long hours setting up wooden forms, shoveling in snow and pouring water, then taking down the forms and hand-carving the finishing touches. It was the largest snow maze ever built, twelve thousand square feet in all, with over a thousand linear feet of seven-foot-high walls. While we were constructing it, we attracted the attention of only the local press, but once the Games were under way, the maze became about the single biggest attraction aside from the official ceremonies and the competitions themselves. Throngs of people swarmed all over the place ooh-ing and aah-ing, and about fifty thousand got to take a shot at navigating the walls of ice. NBC's *Today* show did a major feature, with Katie Couric, Al Roker and Matt Lauer having a ball running around inside trying to find their way out.

Wonder what they would have thought had they known that the phenomenally popular maze had been built by a bank robber and a jewel thief.

Epilogue

I GUESS the big question, when I look back on my life, is the same as it is for anybody who lived hard and takes a look back: Why did I do the things I did?

When friends began urging me to write a book ("Before you die," they politely declined to add), they of course had in mind a recounting of some of the more interesting scores I'd pulled, because aside from those I'm not much different from millions of ordinary guys. And right up until I started jotting down notes and reminiscences, it seemed that I myself thought this was what my life was all about. Now, having gone through some truly excruciating soul-searching, and having been forced to dredge up a lot of memories I always thought were best left buried, I realize that there was so much more I failed to appreciate at the time. To my everlasting regret, most of it seems to have Barbara at its center.

The scores were certainly exhilarating highlights, and writing about them in a book makes it seem that it was just one continuous string of whiz-bang burglaries. The reality is that, spread over some thirty-odd years, they were few and a lot of time passed between them. Most of the time our family not only looked pretty normal but actually was, and we were far

Fran and me, 2003.

from dysfunctional. A warm, close-knit bunch, we spent a great deal of time together and took a lot of family vacations, so it shouldn't be surprising that Barb was able to keep alive the hope that before too long I would see the light of day, appreciate what I had and avoid putting it in jeopardy.

To say Barb was a true lady and a wonderful mother to three great children doesn't even begin to scratch the surface of her character. I'm not nominating her for sainthood—she had her flaws, as all of us do—but she was a loving and loyal wife who deserved a husband much better than I ever was. She knew she could count on me for anything, but what must it have been like for her every time I walked out the door not to know whether I'd be coming back? I suspect it was much harder for her to sit at home and wait to see if I would come home or had been jailed or injured or killed than it was for me to be out doing the job. I, at least, had some control over the situation, whereas she had none at all. And since I never told her about scores, impending or completed, she never knew when I was leaving whether I was going out for a pack of smokes or was on my way to a major heist I'd been planning for months. Remarkably, we're still very close and see each other often (Barb and Fran are fast friends), which only intensifies the overwhelming guilt over how badly I served our marriage.

There were other late-life revelations as well. Shortly after I gave up the houseboat, Barb's younger brother, Augie, was enticed by a crook working for the DEA into buying some coke. It was a complete setup from start to finish and one of the most blatant cases of entrapment I have ever seen. Augie was no choirboy and has done a couple of bits in federal prison, but there was no way in hell he would have gone in on this deal and risked another collar had he not been coaxed and prodded into it. Now he faced a possible life term as a three-time felon.

The reason I mention this is that, almost from the time I first met him when I was dating Barbara, Augie has been like my younger brother and I've always tried to do everything—legal and not so legal—to help him. This was the first time I truly understood the torment and agonizing helplessness experienced by people trying desperately to get loved ones out of the clutches of "the system." The thought of a cheap hoodlum pressuring Augie into a deal at the behest of government authorities just to save his own neck threw me into a towering rage. Banging up against brick wall after brick wall as we went through the motions to try to do something to help him only made it worse, and when it was all over—Augie got five years—it finally sank into me what it must have been like for Barb, for Bill Welling, for my kids and for my mother when I was set up by the Fort Lauderdale police. Nights are the worst, when there's nothing to do but lie in a warm, comfortable bed and torture yourself with what the guy inside must be going through.

I'm so different now, it's hard to believe some of the crap that went through my mind when rationalizing away the risk to Barb and the kids of some upcoming score. I was selfish and loved the thrill and had plenty of ways to reassure myself. After a while it became easier and easier to leave the house, put the family out of my mind and concentrate exclusively on the job. Not just easier, but absolutely critical; mine was no business to be in if you were prone to letting your mind wander for even a moment at the wrong time.

Fran, too, has had ample opportunity and many reasons to walk out, but still continues to stick with me. And my second family has stood by and loved me like their own. I thank them for that, every day, and can only apologize for the pain I've caused them. I apologize to everybody I've hurt.

As long as I'm flogging myself here, I might as well point out something that may not be obvious. I'm thinking back to that immortal classic by Charles Dickens, *A Christmas Carol.* Despite all that Scrooge goes through when forced by the three ghosts to review his life, the one thing that finally turns him around is direct confrontation with his own mortality. Sure, he feels bad about all the sorrow he's caused other people and himself, but only when he sees his own gravestone does he at last fall to the ground and beg for a chance to change his ways. Only then does the magnitude of what an awful human being he was truly dawn on him.

It was much like that with me. I was aware of the chaos and heartbreak I was causing for people who loved me, but it wasn't until a ladder slipped out from under me at the top of a high-rise building that I finally swore off thieving. Now, of course, having thought about it a great deal and coming to understand the enormity of the anguish I caused, I would find it inconceivable to go back to pulling scores, but it took the immediate prospect of my own violent death to get me to stop in the first place.

I used to say that of all the things in my life I was sorry for, stealing jewelry from rich people wasn't one of them. That's no longer true, if it ever really was. It may have been a falling ladder that got me to stop stealing, but it was writing this book that got me to start thinking.

Putting it all down on paper was a wrenching experience, even sort of horrifying. In addition to the mental games I played all my life to avoid dealing with the effect I was having on my family, there was the fact of my not having had much consideration for the people I robbed, either. I talked myself into resenting that they had a lot of money but I didn't. In fact, I admired the well-to-do, at least those who had built their own fortunes. After all, wasn't I in some sense seeking to emulate them with my real estate businesses? But it was necessary not to allow myself to see them as good people, or else I wouldn't have been able to rob them.

Having now taken an acutely painful look back at my life, I find myself a lot less glib and dismissive about many of the things I did. That some of the items I took might have been of more than monetary value to their original owners was something I never gave much thought to, but it becomes harder and harder with the passing years to push that possibility aside, and that is part of the reason I'm donating a portion of my proceeds from this book to victim compensation organizations in Ohio and Florida.

The other part of the reason is that there's something else about a burglary that may not be apparent from sensational news accounts: a depressing and disturbing feeling of violation on the part of the victims.

If you've ever had your suitcase lifted from an airline luggage carousel, you know that even though it's a huge inconvenience and can entail considerable expense, it's not something you're likely to take personally or feel especially troubled about, regardless of how angry it makes you. In fact, you probably didn't think a lot about the thief but directed nearly all of your ire at the airline for failing to protect your luggage.

Having your house broken into is an entirely different matter. There's an unshakable uneasiness at the thought that some stranger walked around in your living room or bedroom and rummaged through your things. Interestingly, many victims are much more troubled to discover an empty bottle on the table and realize that the intruder opened the refrigerator, pulled out a beer, sat down at *our table* and poured himself a cold one than they are to find out jewelry and money have been taken. It's hard to explain, but it affects nearly everybody who's ever been burglarized, and isn't really about the fear that the perpetrator might return. It has more to do with some kind of a sacred barrier being breached, and having made people feel that way is the one thing about robbing them that I'm most remorseful over.

Still, it pales in comparison to the harm I caused those closest to me, whom I robbed in profoundly more important ways.

I realized other things as well. I would like to have given some hint in these pages as to what was going on in the minds of my family and friends, but found that I rarely could. I have enough trouble trying to figure myself out, and the more I go back, the more I realize how self-centered and spoiled I was. It was difficult for me to get into anyone else's head, since my main priority was self-gratification, except when I was in jail, and then the priority was getting out and having everyone work toward that end. I was too self-involved to think about what other people were thinking. Maybe that stemmed from the combination of being an only child and becoming the head of a family at a young age, but I don't really know and it's hard to figure out: As much time as I spend with the kids now, we don't talk much about that part of our past.

The question still remains: With a woman like Barb and three terrific kids in my life, why couldn't I stop myself from doing something I knew was self-destructive and selfish?

It certainly wasn't the money. I didn't need it, and I didn't spend a fraction of what I stole. It certainly wasn't a demanding, materialistic wife, either: Barb's idea of a big day was to go to a bunch of garage sales and never buy anything for more than two dollars, then go to dinner with me.

There is also no doubting that I was capable of intense self-discipline. I could be patient and lie completely immobile for hours when the job called for it. My exercise regimen was punishing, and I made myself so strong and fit that I could climb ropes without using my feet and hang by my fingertips for long periods of time.

I didn't spend a lifetime at the mercy of a variety of the standard urges, either. I smoked cigarettes and drank, and occasionally did some recreational pharmaceuticals, but at no point was I even close to being hooked on any of them. When I was in prison without alcohol or weed, I missed them, sure—in prison you miss *everything*—but it just wasn't that big a deal.

When it came to the thrill of the big score, though, that utterly indescribable euphoria that accompanies the perfect execution of a perfect and perfectly dangerous plan, I was as hooked as the hardest-core heroin addict. I was powerless before the lure of the adrenaline that soaked every high-risk burglary, completely undone by the challenge of doing the seemingly impossible. Walking casually out of a building with a bag full of sparkling stones after months of planning was a rush like no other. The one thing I dreaded the most, doing time in prison, was something I had complete control over—all I had to do was go straight—yet even that fear couldn't stop me from indulging the craving.

I think it fair to say that I'm far from being a sociopath. For one thing, I've formed several deep and lasting emotional relationships. You could accuse me of having seduced a perfectly respectable but very vulnerable Midwestern socialite into leaving her husband to join me in a dangerously illicit lifestyle—and you might have a legitimate point, even though I could make a pretty good case for her having seduced *me*—but our loving relationship still continues after nearly twenty-five years. I was also never in denial about what I was doing, and never tried to rationalize it using twisted logic. I was well aware that it was wrong, but simply lacked the will to stop myself, and over time just learned not to concern myself about it too much. Finally, unlike a sociopath, I have a conscience. My remorse over the pain I caused people close to me is genuine and profound, and I'm doing my best to make amends.

We're all familiar with drug, alcohol and gambling addicts who watch their home lives getting ruined but are powerless to stop it, so is it possible that there is a "crime addict" personality as well?

I'd like to be able to make the case that my outlaw life was born of a unique set of strengths, but those were only the enablers. At the root of it all was a very ordinary set of weaknesses. To be brutally frank, if I had those choices to make again knowing what I know now, I can't honestly say I'd take a different path, because I knew it then, too.

What I still haven't figured out is from what source that drive arose. I jokingly refer to my "bent Y" chromosome, as though my core personality was handed to me at birth, but it's equally likely that there were factors in my childhood that propelled me toward lawlessness. "Nature versus nurture" is, of course, an old controversy among scientists, philosophers and psychologists, and I'm not smart enough to make that call, but I suspect that there was a mix of both at work. Maybe if my father hadn't died so suddenly at a crucial stage of my youth, I might have turned out differently. Maybe if more enlightened counselors than the closet elitists in high school had gotten hold of me, or if I hadn't bought a car and begun to hang out in an auto shop with a whole cast of hardened career criminals, or if I'd gotten busted again right after that amateurish gas station break-in . . .

But who knows? All I know for certain is what happened, and nothing of what might have been.

PHOTO: SARA BARRETT

BILL MASON, by day an ordinary family man and real estate manager and investor, was by night the most successful jewel thief this country has ever known. He currently lives in New York City.

LEE GRUENFELD is the bestselling author of such celebrated novels as *The Halls of Justice* and *All Fall Down*. He has also written several novels under the pseudonym Troon McAllister, including the golf classic *The Green*. He lives in Southern California.